PAUL VALÉRY AND MUSIC

PAUL VALÉRY AND MUSIC

A STUDY OF
THE TECHNIQUES OF COMPOSITION IN
VALÉRY'S POETRY

BRIAN STIMPSON

Senior Lecturer in French, Froebel Institute,
Roehampton Institute of Higher Education

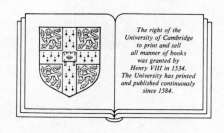

The right of the
University of Cambridge
to print and sell
all manner of books
was granted by
Henry VIII in 1534.
The University has printed
and published continuously
since 1584.

CAMBRIDGE UNIVERSITY PRESS

Cambridge
London   New York   New Rochelle
Melbourne   Sydney

Published by the Press Syndicate of the University of Cambridge
The Pitt Building, Trumpington Street, Cambridge CB2 1RP
32 East 57th Street, New York, NY 10022, USA
296 Beaconsfield Parade, Middle Park, Melbourne 3206, Australia

First published 1984

Printed in Great Britain at
the University Press, Cambridge

Library of Congress catalogue card number: 84-5891

British Library Cataloguing in Publication Data

Stimpson, Brian
Paul Valéry and music.
1. Valéry, Paul – Criticism and interpretation
I. Title
841'.912   PQ2643.A26Z/
ISBN 0 521 25608 9

BB

Concevoir en poète c'est concevoir musicalement.

(XI, 1926, p. 618)

Le problème *d'écrire* doit être assimilé à celui de *mettre en musique* (écrire pour la voix).

(IX, 1923, p. 190)

Poème de composition tout harmonique, très influencé par Wagner - sans effet de narration des états d'âme ou dêtre. Dans tout ce poème j'ai tout sacrifié impitoyablement à la musique des vers.

(In J. Robinson, 'Un nouveau visage de *La Jeune Parque*: le poème commenté par son auteur', *Bulletin d'Etudes Valéryennes*, 7, No. 25 (Oct. 1980), p. 50.)

. . . nous avons songé à remonter au plus près de la pensée et à saisir sur la table de l'écrivain le document du premier acte de son effort intellectuel, et comme le graphique de ses impulsions, de ses variations, de ses reprises, en même temps que l'enregistrement immédiat de ses rythmes personnels, qui sont la forme de son régime d'énergie vivante: *le manuscrit original*, le lieu de son regard et de sa main, où s'inscrit de ligne en ligne le duel de l'esprit avec le langage, de la syntaxe avec les deux, du délire avec la raison, l'alternance de l'attente et de la hâte, tout le drame de l'élaboration d'une œuvre et de la fixation de l'instable.

('Comment travaillent les écrivains', *Vues*, p. 317.)

CONTENTS

vii

Contents

ACKNOWLEDGEMENTS

This work is based upon an examination of material from two major sources: the *Cahiers* and the poetry manuscripts. The number of references to music which are to be found from a careful reading of the *Cahiers* is remarkable, significantly more than the writings published in the two-volume Pléiade edition of the *Œuvres* would lead one to suppose. Though perhaps reluctant to develop his thoughts in public, he covers in his own notes an astonishing range of issues related to music, from an attendance at a concert or a meeting with a musician to a detailed analysis of 'love' or 'the functioning of the mind' in terms of music, as well as a vast number of notes on 'Poésie-Musique', Mélodie', 'les Harmoniques' and so on. It has been necessary to select representative quotations among the many more that offered themselves, summarising others and omitting even more; the choice is not easy, as Valéry would seize upon an idea and rework it, rephrasing, adding further implications, trying to refine his categories, making connections with other topics, and these reformulations are the very substance of the *Cahiers*, the dialogue with the self that prompted him to scrutinise all that he had written and the process of thinking itself. But in order to allow the main drift of Valéry's argument to emerge, some areas of interest, such as the many attempts to explain the effect of music in terms of a chemical reaction on the muscular and nervous systems, may only be mentioned briefly, the reformulations not repeated unless adding an important qualification or development to his thoughts; above all, attention has centred upon those notes which seem to illumine most the questions about music and poetry.

Acknowledgements

The second main source has been the poetry manuscripts, the majority of which are to be found in the Department of Manuscripts of the Bibliothèque nationale. In attempting to focus upon the techniques of composition, the rough draft, with words scattered seemingly haphazardly over the page, is as important as the later ordering of stanzas or the variants from one edition to another; and therefore the dossiers of loose-leaf manuscripts have been of singular importance along with the early notebook *Cahier Charmes I*, entitled 'P. V. Petits Poèmes MCMXVII', and the small notebook *Cahier Charmes II* containing notes on poetry and composition as well as drafts of the poems. But Valéry did not work through these chronologically and the evidence of the poems shows that he would move from one to another adding and redrafting, so that it is only by a close examination of the internal development of each poem that it is possible to order the manuscripts with some uncertainty. A further notebook of importance is the *Cahier Voilier* which contains drafts of many poems, including essential stages of *La Pythie*; details from this notebook are to be found in J. R. Lawler, *Lecture de Valéry* (Paris, 1963).[1]

It is not possible to list here all the distinguished writers on Valéry to whom I am indebted, but I should wish to mention the following whose work has been particularly relevant to the subject: L. J. Austin, J. Duchesne-Guillemin, H. Laurenti, J. R. Lawler and O. Nadal.[2] W. N. Ince's work on *The Poetic Theory of Paul Valéry* has proved of enormous value in the preparation of this study: the influence of his authoritative analysis of inspiration and technique and his study of the theory of composition is evident in much of the discussion and is gratefully acknowledged.

The origins of the study lie in the seminar classes at King's College London given by Professor J. M. Cocking, for it was his teaching which excited my interest in Valéry. I am particularly grateful for the assistance and support of Dr Richard Smith who first supervised my research and read the drafts of the chapters: if this work has any clarity and cogency of argument it is in response to his penetrating questions. I owe

Acknowledgements

a special debt to Professor Norma Rinsler whose help has been so invaluable to me in the later stages of preparation: she read the manuscript of my thesis and I am deeply thankful for the judgements, the suggestions and the time so generously given. I should like to thank Madame Florence de Lussy, Conservateur du Fonds Valéry at the Bibliothèque nationale, who generously made available to me certain key sets of manuscripts and indicated important cross-references. My thanks are also due to the Ecole normale supérieure for the year I spent as a research student at rue d'Ulm, to the French Government and the University of London for the research grants they awarded me. I should like to express my grateful appreciation to the examiners of my Ph.D thesis, Professor Ince of Southampton University and Professor Rinsler of King's College London, for their invaluable comments and suggestions, to Dr Christine Crow who offered expert advice over the revision of the thesis for publication and to Michael Black and Iain White of Cambridge University Press for their editorial advice. Finally my thanks go to Madame Agathe Rouart-Valéry, to Éditions Gallimard and to the C.N.R.S. for permission to publish extracts from the poetry manuscripts and the published works of Valéry.

The following signs and abbreviations are used:

Dormeuse f. 22	:	Dossier of manuscripts for *La Dormeuse* feuillet 22
[Deux]	:	Deux written and subsequently deleted
[−]	:	illegible word
—	:	dash in Valéry's manuscript

Unless otherwise indicated the stanza numbers are those of the final version and are not in Valéry's manuscript.

INTRODUCTION

> Il n'y a que deux choses qui comptent, qui sonnent l'or sur le comptoir: l'une que je nomme *Analyse*, et qui a la 'pureté' pour objet, l'autre que je nomme *Musique*, et qui compose cette 'pureté'.
>
> XVII, 1934, p. 819.

At the age of sixty-one, at the height of his successful literary career, Valéry could wish that he had been a musician rather than a poet and reduce his most celebrated work to a gymnastic attempt to rival music: 'La musique m'aura manqué – et il me semble que j'auris fait qq. chose dans ce moyen – Mon 'système' trouvait là *son* moyen . . . Il a fallu faire des acrobaties comme la Parque.'[1] The references to music occur again and again throughout all that he wrote: music is the lodestone of all his efforts. In 1891 he wrote to Pierre Louÿs: 'L'idéal est de faire une symphonie';[2] in 1895 to his cousin: 'Amuse-toi de comparer la belle page de musique et la belle page de vers. Tu y apprendras presque tout';[3] and when approached by Gide to republish his early poetry Valéry wrote of his own reaction: 'ce père ennemi . . . se sentait je ne sais quelles envies de les renforcer, d'en refondre la substance musicale.'[4] The term is all-embracing: music means to Valéry in the Greek sense, the 'art of the muses'; modifying Pater's idea that all art aspires to the condition of music, Valéry states that music is the crucial feature of all the arts: 'La Musique est presque tout entière ce dont les autres arts font une de leurs parties, essentielles, mais parties.'[5] But even more than the ideal model for poetry and the arts, music becomes the perfect embodiment of all the principles, analyses and methods that he refers to, often not without irony, as

1

his 'system': he continually uses music to explain his ideas on the functioning of the mind, as a reflection of the processes of thought and the mind's power to construct and combine. In 1915 he wrote to Albert Coste: 'Mon idéal serait de construire la gamme et le système d'accords dont la pensée en général serait la Musique.'[6] Such an extension to the meaning of the term, however ambitious, is to be expected of one who writes, in challenge to Mallarmé, 'les autres font des livres, moi je fais mon esprit.'[7]

It was clear, when first approaching this topic, that there was a need to examine some of the basic questions: how much did Valéry know about music? was there any consistency in his use of the term? what did he mean by the music of poetry? My first task was to define the terms, to establish the essential reference points, to plot the constants and the variants – the 'Rhumbs' – of his attention: for what Valéry has to say about music is of great interest in itself as well as for the light shed upon a number of related matters. But as the work advanced, it became evident that the subject demanded more than a survey of all that Valéry had to say about music, that the questions had to be taken further to do justice to the restless, questioning nature of his thought. A more careful reading of his notes on music indicated an underlying problem which may be expressed as follows:

Valéry wrote a great deal about music and about the connections between music and poetry.
- Is this largely a reiteration of the symbolist desire to 'reprendre à la musique son bien', an interesting and fertile generalisation which neverthless defies precise analysis?
- Or can the confrontation of music and poetry illuminate particular features of Valéry's poetics?
- Furthermore, what is the relation between the theory and the practice? Can it be shown that his concern with music is reflected specifically in the composition of his poems?

In other words 'Valéry and music' is not a statement, it is a problem, masked by the ambiguity of the conjunction: what precisely is the relationship between the two terms, and what are the implications for the poetry?

The subject raises, first of all, problems of evidence,

demanding a careful scrutiny of the data provided by Valéry's writings to determine how he reacted to music, how he envisaged the effects of music in general, as well as specific features such as harmony, melody, rhythm. But it also raises important issues of critical method. It is not sufficient to say that because Valéry wrote about music (that he liked X and Y, but not Z), because he uses 'musical' terms, because sounds and rhythms are important in his poetry, therefore his poetry is musical. For unless each proposition is critically examined both in itself and in relation to the others, such a scheme of argument can only offer a spurious justification for some subjective musical similes added on to the finished work (such as the inaccurate comparisons of sounds to melody, or versification to rhythm). In order to demonstrate that there are specific links between Valéry's conception of music, his poetic theory and his poetic practice, a consistent critical approach must be adopted to assess and pursue the implications of the evidence. It is necessary to demonstrate first that Valéry's understanding and use of musical terms correspond to reasonably precise musical equivalents, not only to music in general, but even to some kinds and not others. Secondly it is necessary to show that the understanding of music and musical terms determines the very manner in which the music of poetry is envisaged. In other words it must be shown that he was aware of these things when writing his poems, which can only be done by close study of the drafts; and further that his awareness of these aspects and the reader's grasp of their significance can help to formulate a critically consistent approach to the finished poems, can help to make a more sensitive reading of them and organise a valid commentary.

This is not to imply that the writing of poetry can be deduced from music by a process of lucid analysis, as a kind of application of the theory of the universal mind. A more accurate model ought to show the constant interrelationship of theory, practice and inspiration. For what emerges most clearly from the poetry manuscripts is the sheer creative energy, the very personal force of inspiration which, in the first hurriedly hand-written version of now celebrated lines, is awe-inspiring. Indeed so central is music to Valéry's poetic work, that 'a study of the techniques of composition' leads to the very heart of the creative process: the techniques are not formal procedures applied with cold detachment, they are the form which his inspiration takes, the means by which he helps his inspiration to manifest itself.

One of the principal difficulties lies in determining what is implied by the term 'music' in each particular context, for, as can be seen already from the statements in the opening paragraph of this Introduction, the scope is extremely wide. But before proceeding to outline the different areas of meaning in Valéry's writing, it will be helpful to recall briefly the context of his interest in the association of music and poetry, the aesthetic ideal of Symbolism which is best summed up in his own celebrated formula:

Ce qui fut baptisé: le *Symbolisme*, se résume très simplement dans l'intention commune à plusieurs familles de poètes (d'ailleurs ennemies entre elles) de 'reprendre à la Musique leur bien'. Le secret de ce mouvement n'est pas autre . . . Nous étions nourris de musique, et nos têtes littéraires ne rêvaient que de tirer du langage presque les mêmes effets que les causes purement sonores produisaient sur nos êtres nerveux. Les uns, Wagner; les autres chérissaient Schumann. Je pourrais écrire qu'ils les haïssaient.[8]

Though interest in the relationship between music and poetry had become prominent among the poets of the 1880s and 1890s, the idea itself was not new and can be traced back through the history of poetry.[9] During the first half of the nineteenth century music remains essentially a term of comparison without for the moment direct influence over the structures and techniques of poetry; it forms part of the décor of the poem and is used to help evoke the appropriate mood.[10] It is less music itself than the attempts to recreate the forms of the medieval 'ballades' and 'chansons' which are most in evidence.[11] For Baudelaire music was an expression of the unity of experience: the soul of the listener is elevated and he is inspired to 'rêverie', meditation and the perception of beauty. In poetry the effects of harmony and rhythm are borrowed from music not simply to create musicality but to suggest a more absolute, more perfect harmony which is essentially spiritual. The words and sounds are not a description of 'la ténébreuse et profonde unité' but the essential means of prolonging that experience: 'C'est à la fois par la poésie et *à travers* la poésie, par et *à travers* la musique, que l'âme entrevoit les splendeurs situées derrière le tombeau'.[12] In 'Situation de Baudelaire' Valéry emphasises the connection between Baudelaire's interest in music and the redirection of poetry away from 'la tendance au prosaïsme' and back to its musical origins, while identifying in Verlaine the development of the emotional qualities of Baudelaire's music: 'le sens de l'intime, et le mélange puissant et trouble de l'émotion mystique et de l'ardeur sensuelle'.[13] Verlaine's 'de la musique avant toute chose' is a reaction against intellectualism in poetry and an attempt to achieve a singing quality by the suggestive flow of sounds: an impressionistic use of dream-like images, uneven metres and a fluid syntax combine to give an overall effect of fleeting appearances and delicate feelings. But this aspiration towards a suggestive, musical effect, which as Michaud points out was taken up by the Symbolists and implies a particular view of language,[14] carried with it a risk of reducing music to nothing other than a dreamy impression of complete vagueness: as Stuart Merrill remarked: 'La poésie, étant à la fois Verbe et Musique, est merveilleusement apte à cette suggestion d'un infini qui n'est souvent que de l'indéfini.'[15]

With Mallarmé the aspiration to the condition of music becomes both more precise and all-embracing. Music combines with metaphysics in an escape from matter towards the Absolute, the world of essences: 'faire de la musique' means for Mallarmé achieving 'un au-delà magiquement produit par certaines dispositions de la parole'.[16] In poetry he is concerned not with an accumulation of beautiful sounds for its own sake, as the Parnassiens for example, but with a synthesis of elements in which each depends upon its relation to others to create 'le mot total incantatoire.'[17] Thus the musical ambition and the interest in Wagner prompt Mallarmé to assert the supremacy of the word: 'la Poésie, proche l'idée, est Musique, par excellence – ne consent pas d'infériorité.'[18]

5

Music is supplanted by a poetry that is superior to ordinary language, different from ordinary poetry: it is effected by taking back from music techniques considered to be primarily and originally literary. Mallarmé seeks an architectural organisation of the poem, both complex and not dependent upon 'le hasard', to establish a set of non-representative relationships between the words, the lines, the motifs, the rhythms: the poem becomes a network of relations and the metaphor imposes a unity over disparate terms, fusing apparent opposites into a single intellectual image. The architectural complexity and the scope of Mallarmé's poetry prompt comparisons with the orchestra and the symphony especially with regard to *L'Après-midi d'un faune*.[19] Music there most certainly is in the very substance of the words, in the complex structures of sounds and rhythms, themes and images; but rather than any particular kind of music, it is above all the idea of music that is to be found in his poetry.[20]

It is evident therefore that the background to the notion of 'reprendre à la musique son bien' is rich in comparisons and theories, but less so in evidence of direct musical influences over poetry: music provides a confirmation of the poets' aims, an extremely important justification for the aesthetic doctrines after the poetry has been written. There are many instances of musical analogies and titles, there is envy of the rôle of the composer and of the power of music over the listener and there is above all a desire on the part of the poets to give their art an equivalent stature. But the attempts remain at a fairly general and theoretical level and apart from the rigorous intellectual approach of Mallarmé, 'music' is used as a term to cover the suggestibility, the atmosphere of yearning, the movements of the feelings. Apart from Wagner, and occasionally Beethoven or Schumann, the writings show little discussion of the precise musical models from which poetry may seek to 'reprendre son bien'; indeed, given the vast dimensions of Wagner's work – the scope of the subjects, the length of performances, the elaborate staging, the very size and volume of the cast and orchestra, and the continuous interweaving of music, chorus, aria and recitative – few models

6

could in fact have been less appropriate to the intimate suggestive effects of poetry. As Guichard aptly remarks, '"Reprendre à la musique son bien" fut un act de défense et non d'imitation.'[21]

The nature of Valéry's own contact with music and musicians and the extent to which precise musical models can be identified will be discussed in Parts I and II, but some preliminary remarks are called for in order to attempt to clarify the different semantic fields of the term 'music' in the work of Valéry. It is possible to identify three distinct though interrelated uses of the term: the first sense is of music as an art form based on the combination of vocal or instrumental sounds; the second sense is of music as a form of human experience which may occur in all sorts of ways deep within an individual and not simply while listening to music; the third sense is concerned with the analogical use of music in poetry and a consideration of the means by which – and the extent to which – it is possible to achieve music in language alone.[22]

There can be no doubt of Valéry's sensitivity to music and his own ambivalent attitude towards it is determined both by the strength of his reactions and his attempt to focus upon a more detached analysis of them. He saw music both as a language of the emotions and as a language of the mind: he considered it the artistic medium best fitted to the expression of man's compositional faculties and as such as 'l'écriture de l'homme complet'. His analysis though is not technical and stresses more the aesthetic, affective and intellectual responses which may be provoked. Thus phenomenologically:

une note vibre – alors choses possibles:
ou: c'est un signe? on cherche qui, quoi, où, pourquoi?
ou: un signe commencement – et on se souvient d'une mélodie qui chante intérieurement
ou: un simple dérangement et on se remet au travail
ou: d° et on se perd[23]

In the latter case the music may provoke a range of reactions including physical movement, it may suggest notions of space or balance, continuity or extreme contrasts, as well as particular emotional responses. The power of the music of Wagner, he notes, is to encompass 'des éléments psychologiques et physiques préparés à l'état pur':

Il y a en elle des effets de - souvenir, pressentiment, tension, oubli, attitudes et mouvements, surexcitations, le vague, le net, le détaché, le trouble - sont comme mis en formules éclatantes, toutes-puissantes, amplifiés par l'appareil mécanique de sa musique.[24]

Affectively music portrays 'toute cette tristesse, et cette torsion interne! ces rages rompues en elles-mêmes, et ces "regrets" et cette dissolution et ces regards et ces soupirs',[25] whilst intellectually if not the content of thought, the form and the manner of thinking: 'toutes les feintes et les démarches réelles du penser'.[26] Because its content is indeterminate, it is able to take over 'tout l'ancien empire des choses vagues': if philosophy is the metaphysics of being, music is 'une "métaphysique" des sensations de l'ouïe'.[27]

Although many of Valéry's remarks may be prompted by hearing a particular piece of music played, there are other notes which indicate that the music heard, if indeed any is heard at all, is only an aural pretext for a set of responses that are so to speak internally produced: the forms of experience that music provokes are forms of experience that arise from deep within the self and do not necessarily depend upon listening to a piece of music. This inner state, this music of experience, is an expression of the whole being as a living organism with thoughts, feelings and physiological reactions; often the case of music, as an art of heard sounds, is cited as an example of our general capacity to feel and produce such responses, the change of focus evident in the use of verbs such as 'représenter', 'illustrer', 'convenir à'.

La musique détermine 1° une excitation générale qui peut convenir à tout sujet de pensées. 2° plus écoutée - des états représentatifs d'énergie et des changements d'énergie/ régimes 3° des changements de systèmes fonctionnels.[28]

Valéry writes of fugue as 'une lumière pour l'étude et la représentation de l'esprit' because it illustrates 'cette question des indépendances dont l'extrême est la pluralité des personnalités'.[29] There is even a degree of interchangeability between the terms used, because the particular qualities of a comple-

Introduction

ted work may depend more upon the medium and the form
of that art than upon the experience or creative attitude that
is at its centre. Under the heading *'Poétique de l'Intellect'*
Valéry writes:

> Il n'y a pas de *frontières nettes* entre poésie et philosophie, entre
> poésie et musique, entre marche et danse. .
> et si l'on se retire dans l'intérieur, si l'on diminue la considération du
> matériel externe de l'oeuvre pour accroître la précision de l'idée du
> producteur – (symétriquement) celle de l'idée de l'impression du con-
> sommateur – on se trouve en présence d'un travail mental qui plus on
> le regarde, plus devient-il semblable dans les divers arts.[30]

Music and poetry in this sense are identical: 'Ce qu'il y a de
musical dans quelle chose que ce soit est poésie – Musical c.à d.
capable de combinaison avec les lois de la sensibilité *en tant
qu'exactes.*'[31] But Valéry is clearly not suggesting that the
terms always mean the same, nor that all of poetry is derived
from music: he will allow music as the essential part of all
the arts, but still only a part. What then does he mean when
he speaks of music in relation to poetry?

His reaction to the setting of poetry to music is both decisive and dismissive: the adding of music to a completed poem
in order to achieve some performed piece of words and music
is at best redundant, at worst subtracts from rather than adds
to the effect: 'Mettre de la musique sur de bon vers c'est
éclairer un tableau par un vitrail de couleurs.'[32]

> La musique x poésie = chant, mais pour des raisons matérielles, le chant
> n'est pas ce qu'il semblerait devoir être, c.à d. le plus complet des
> moyens possibles.
> Les paroles du chant doivent nécessairement être, trop simples, la
> musique trop retenue, et les deux facteurs se gênent. Le résultat tout
> beau qu'il soit est moindre que l'attente.[33]

As if to prove the point, there are no major settings of
Valéry's poems to music (see below p. 102); he did however
collaborate with musicians on a number of projects, which
have been studied by Huguette Laurenti in *Paul Valéry et le
théâtre* (Paris, 1973) and readers are referred to her authora-
tative study. Examination of the precise relationship between
the musical effects achieved in the text and the music itself
would be both premature and beyond the scope of this book,

9

for it demands not only analysis of what Valéry meant by the music of poetry and how it is achieved in a poem (which is my present purpose), but also, in the light of this, study of the texts of the 'mélodrames' alongside the musical scores.

Given the scope of his treatment of music in the first two senses, it is not surprising to find that there is no single definition to the third sense of the term – that of music as exclusively applied to poetry: it is both abstraction:

il faut pour se remettre aux vers y penser d'abord in abstracto – tout musicalement car l'abstraction en poésie est musique.[34]

and sensation:

Cette musique [de la parole] est notre suite de sensations – internes – viscérales et énergétiques – imaginantes.[35]

Though the poet does not want or need any notes of music added to his poetry, the quality of music is nevertheless a constant aspiration for Valéry, a defining ideal, a value that acts as both an absolute standard impossible to attain and a relative one that permits judgements and evaluations:

Ego Poeta. J'en vins, poète très intermittent à ne plus priser, tenter que l'exécution de périodes de vers en forme classique formant des phrases bien construites et aussi musicaux que possible – donnant l'impression de dessin mélodique suivi: syntaxe, règles du vers, sonorité continue.[36]

To speak of the music of poetry is therefore to make an analogy and establish common properties:[37] poetry is music in a way which links directly with the second sense of the term for it is an actualisation in the medium of language of that deep inner experience which is a music independent of the art of sounds:

La poésie, peut-être, c'est toute l'âme, – toute la parole, tout le dictionnaire possible de l'être, tout l'être en tant qu'appels, réponses, actes, émotions, considérés comme un instrument. Telle est le lyre, et non autre chose. . . . ce registre, clavier universel, aux cordes innombrables. . . .
L'univers, instrument de musique.[38]

But the means by which this may be achieved imply a close correlation between poetry and the specific techniques and stylistic features of music in the first sense of the art of combining sounds in time. The comparison may of course pro-

10

voke distinctions as well as similarities; nevertheless it is not only the idea of music, it is the particular effect of performed music that Valéry seeks:

Phrase. Art d'écrire. Je voudrais avoir la sensation du Virtuose qui l'oreille collée au bois du violon, écoute sa propre main et forme un anneau fermé de sens, avec la folle impression qu'il pourrait le parcourir dans les 2 sens. S'écouter, produire, unité.[39]

The instrument of the poet, however, is not the violin, nor the orchestra: it is, as Valéry recognised consistently, avoiding the temptation of vague comparisons with other instruments, the human voice. For Valéry this voice expresses itself musically as the voice of a living being struggling to achieve consciousness through activity, to assert aesthetic form as its most human achievement, to generate form and meaning in language.[40]

Poetry, for Valéry, is not a pale imitation of music, nor a diluted, derivative art form: it achieves a different kind of music which, precisely because of the constraints of language, is more difficult to attain, more precious in its realisation.[41] What has to be considered therefore is not only the general comparison between the music of poetry and music proper, but the specific parallels and differences that arise from the nature of language itself. As an intrinsically verbal art poetry must concern itself with the system of references which arise from the meanings of words; although not subject to the same rapid exhaustion of meaning as ordinary transactional or instrumental language, poetry does not on the other hand exclude referential content in the way that music does: in music 'la pensée-parlée' and 'la pensée par images visuelles' are restricted or absent altogether because of the strictly non-referential nature of sounds, and therefore 'en tant que la poésie est musicale, le rôle de la *parole-pensable* en est altéré'.[42] But, upon the example of all the other qualities of poetry, the referential quality is itself treated musically, brought into the 'univers esthétique', for the desire is not to exclude meaning but to achieve, against the arbitrary expendibility of everyday discourse, 'une sorte d'équilibre entre forme et fond' so that 'le sens' is treated as 'signe'.[43] The denotative and connotative values of language may thus be deliberately exploited by attempting to treat 'les choses' and 'les images des choses' in the way that a musician treats notes, that is using them as elements to be combined together to form complementary and contrasting patterns, and in so doing extend the register of their associations.

As in all other fields, Valéry is concerned to analyse the conditions of production, the physiological aspects which are determining factors in the language of poetry; he distinguishes between the language that occurs in the normal interchange of ideas and 'un langage qui s'associe . . . avec le fonctionnement phonique – auditivo – moteur – et qui est *corps*'.[44] Attention to the nature and form of the articulation of language varies from one situation to another; it is again a feature of poetry which does not strictly coincide with music, for 'la musique n'a pas de consonnes', but places it in a spectrum between ordinary language and song. Classifying the 'usages de la voix' according to their 'énergie et appareils moteurs' Valéry proposes:

discours ordinaire	– quasi automatique	
discours animé	– Ton. mouvement. Action du sens. but affectif	
discours poétique	– son = sens (valeur)	discret
discours versifié	– *prévision*	
chant sur paroles		
chant sans paroles[45]		

An art is therefore possible, he suggests, in which attention focuses upon 'le physique du langage' as act and as sensation, and his acute awareness of the conditions of production give special emphasis to the active rôle of the reader in creating the musical effect of poetry. In the performance of the poem the voice of the reader is the musical instrument which transforms the 'œuvre *virtuelle* en œuvre *réelle*'.[46] The poem depends upon a 'lecteur-exécutant' who through the act of reading contributes his own energy, brings to life the latent qualities of the work and thus Valéry notes with a full sense of the difficulties involved: 'J'écris des morceaux pour de rares exécutants'.[47] The poet will as far as possible write in the performance as a condition of the work but must depend ultimately upon the reader just as the composer upon the player:

Cette énergie humaine, ces forces intelligemment dirigées, que le constructeur avait prévues, cette vie, cet accent, ces sonorités que Racine ou Mozart avaient trouvés dans leur être, il appartient à l'exécutant de les retrouver en soi-même et de les appliquer au mécanisme que constitue une partition ou un texte. Et tout cela, toute cette part essentielle de l'œuvre n'est pas écrit. Cela ne peut pas s'écrire.[48]

Thus the voice of the reader articulating 'l'œuvre réelle' rejoins the inner voice of the writer creating 'l'œuvre virtuelle'; but the performer achieves at a single moment and with sustained expressive effort what the writer or composer created not only at a different time, but at a different pace and with a different sense of involvement, 'l'ensemble de son être ne participant à ce travail spécial que d'une manière inconstante et comme latérale'.[49]

Where the features of language previously discussed have tended to distinguish poetry from music proper, forcing poetry to invent its own music of meaning and conditions of production, the sound system is more easily comparable to music and immediately a different terminological difficulty arises from the wealth of terms available. There is no single term used consistently to refer to the patterns of sounds in language and confusingly those Valéry does use are of a different order to terms such as 'melody' or 'harmonics' where a degree of specificity is apparent. Expressions like 'la musique verbale', 'la musique de la parole', 'la musique des poètes', 'la musique des vers', 'la forme musicale', 'la continuité musicale' are problematic in that the degree of restriction to the term has to be deduced from the context of usage; although an awareness of 'ce qui sonne dans les propos', of 'la continuité du beau son' is involved in each case, the terms are seldom limited to the verbal sounds of poetry: they imply sonority in relation to rhythm, movement, voice and, ultimately, meaning. The ideal is a poetry in which words are music 'dans la sensation' and music 'par analogie, dans leur sens'.[50]

Music, in this third sense of the music of poetry, does not therefore encompass a single meaning: in some respects it

13

proposes more than an analogy, in others clearly much less. Valéry does not claim that everything in poetry is derived from music: poetry must have elements of referential denotation while music is never importantly referential; poetry demands for its delivery a more restricted range of voice than song, however much attention the poet has given to sonority; rhythmic repetition cannot be used in the same way as music; chordal harmony is not strictly possible. But though poetry is not derived from music, music constantly defines the ideal quality of poetic discourse. What Valéry does is to effect a transference of the terms from the sphere of music to that of poetry: the terms are redefined as a result of an analysis that identifies the underlying functional significance of the notion which is then generated in the act of poetic composition. It is not for example a matter of finding a simple parallel for musical melody in a poem, but rather of analysing the essential qualities of melody as a series of aural stimuli which effect certain psychological and physiological responses in the listener and demand certain capacities of meaning in order to identify it as such, as well as considering its relation to other mental and affective processes; if then it is possible to identify these melodic features in the composition of the poems the analogy may be said to be productive and meaningful, for it has enabled Valéry to achieve a poetry that is musical in its own inherently poetic sense:

l'analogie n'est précisément que la faculté de varier les images, de les combiner, de faire coexister la partie de l'une avec la partie de l'autre et d'apercevoir, volontairement ou non, la liaison de leurs structures.[51]

Music and poetry, in spite of the differences occasioned by the medium in which they are expressed, and in spite of 'la signification sentimentale' which is a tendency of both, are united above all in that 'la substance de ces arts [est] combinatoire'.[52] It is appropriate therefore to close this examination of the terminological problems with a definition of poetry which underlines its combinative quality and which, in identifying its different features, points forward to the detailed examination of the musical qualities and the means by which they are achieved in composition:

14

Introduction

Le vers est ce langage dans lequel la sonorité et l'enchaînement des mots, leur effet significatif et leurs résonnances psychologiques, les rythmes, les dispositifs syntaxiques sont liés si étroitement que la mémoire en est nécessairement saine, et que les paroles forment un objet comme *naturel*, comme issu de la vie, dans lequel la substance et la forme, l'élément et la figure, et toutes les 'qualités' sont indissoluble-ment liées en acte.[53]

PART I

Valéry's musical environment

Musique très belle tu élèves ma haine et mon envie.

IV, 1907–8, p. 354

Valéry's published works give little indication of the richness of his musical environment and tend rather to reveal a constant, almost obsessive avowal of his own ignorance. None of the other subjects of which Valéry speaks is treated in this way, so consistently, from his youth to his later years. The confidence which he found to deal with subjects such as philosophy, art, science or the contemporary world, was never in evidence where music was concerned. In a letter to Louÿs in November 1890 he expressed the pleasure of listening to Beethoven 'même aux épouvantables ignares qui ne savent pas les notes comme P. Val.'[1] Writing to him on 13 June 1917 he professes: 'J'aime la musique plus que je ne l'estime. Je l'estime un peu plus que je ne la connais.'[2]

And yet his publications leave little doubt as to the importance of music: there are unnumerable references in *Variété* and *Pièces sur l'Art*; music provides the main inspiration for such works as *L'Ame et la Danse* and the 'mélodrames'; and above all music is seen as the art to which poetry most aspires. What is absent from these works is specific reference to particular works of music and Valéry's own likes and dislikes. For it is not simply a question of reconstructing here Valéry's musical biography, but of attempting to discover what he felt about the music he heard, how much he understood of the composers' aims, and ultimately, to what extent it is possible to speak of musical influences on Valéry's work.

The complete picture emerges gradually, from an accumulation of detail from various sources. The *Cahiers* are the major source of information, though since they were not used as diaries, Valéry did not note down systematically every concert he attended, every musician he met, or every book he read. What references there are give a glimpse of an extraordinary variety of contacts, revealing a constant involvement in the musical life and a close acquaintance with many of the major musicians of the period: 'Je dis à Stravinsky . . . Dîner avec Rubinstein . . . Mme Rambert à Londres . . .' Apart from the *Cahiers* and some references in the correspondence, the biography written by his daughter Agathe Rouart-Valéry is an important source. Of the published works only 'Au Concert Lamoureux en 1893' and part of 'Avant-propos à la Connaissance de la Déesse' go into any detail, and both relate to the concerts avidly attended by Mallarmé and fellow poets between 1880 and 1900.

The first record of Valéry's interest in music refers to 1887 when he was nearly 16. He heard for the first time the prelude to *Lohengrin* while the family was staying at Genoa in August and it made a great impression upon him.[3] The revelation of Wagner's music continued through Valéry's friendship with Pierre Féline who lived in the same house in Montpellier.

Féline was a student of mathematics who from 1889 onwards discussed mathematical theories with Valéry and played Wagner and Beethoven to him, though somewhat clumsily it seems. Valéry in return spoke of literature, and in contrast to his later reluctance to commit himself to any interpretation, readily explained and commented upon the poems of Baudelaire and Mallarmé. They eventually formed weekly 'amicales', a kind of seminar for which each prepared a subject to elaborate upon, demanding the active participation of the other. They dealt with symbolist poetry, Mallarmé, Wagner and aesthetics, the leitmotif in music, Poe, and a number of mathematical subjects. But perhaps the enthusiasm for Wagner was the most significant aspect of the friendship with Féline. In his recollections of Valéry, Féline gives a picture of this musical initiation and reveals how much Valéry must have got from their talks. He is referring to 1890:

20

Chaque jour Paul venait s'asseoir à côté de mon piano. Je lui jouais Wagner. Tout Wagner y passa, de *Tannhäuser* à *Parsifal*. Malgré mon jeu fort défectueux, Paul se prit d'enthousiasme pour les formules wagnériennes.

Etait-ce bien la musique qu'il lui fallait? Certainement non. Une musique plus nuancée, moins emphatique aurait mieux convenu. Mme Valéry, par la suite, l'a bien compris. Elle essaya, et avec quel talent, de l'initier à Bach, à Schumann et à Debussy. Mais ce fut en vain. L'impression produite par Wagner sur l'adolescent avait été si forte, qu'il accordait peu d'attention aux spirituels dialogues de Bach, ou à l'émouvante mélodie de Schumann.[4]

Through this Wagnerianism in music and in literature Valéry found a youthful release of energy and sensuality, as is evident from the letter to Pierre Louÿs of 15 August 1890. He describes the intoxication of bathing at Palavas while shouting out the poem of Stuart Merrill, *La Chevauchée des Walkyries*.

Mon corps me semblait un peu affranchi de la pesanteur, et mon esprit, lui-même grisé de sel, semblait délivré de la raison, cette pesanteur de l'Esprit . . . Les lames scandaient le poème![5]

Féline also provides an amusing reflection on Valéry's progress at the piano. At the end of their meetings Valéry would try to pick out the main melodies by ear using one finger on the keyboard. Later in Paris, Valéry was able to read the leitmotifs from the music provided there were not too many sharps or flats involved.

Though there can clearly be no doubt that Wagner was the dominating musical interest in Valéry's life, it is important to realise that he was acquainted, from the time of his youth, with a wide variety of musical experience, and that this most significantly modified his attitude to Wagner. Evidence contradicts Féline's suggestion that Valéry did not become interested in other composers: he did, and he responded most keenly. In 1890 at Montpellier he heard *Hérodiade*, the opera by Massenet based on the story by Flaubert. This was a contemporary work, having only received its first performance in France in 1884. Though appreciating the music Valéry seems to have experienced a youthful rejection of its theatrical

quality, which is evident in this letter to Louÿs and is untypical of his later love of opera:

> Cette musique est par endroits vraiment suave et délicieuse. Ah! si
> l'opéra n'existait pas, si même on ne chantait pas, s'il n'y avait eu que
> les violons, combien j'en aurais joui davantage! Mais hélas! il faut se
> soumettre à l'horreur précise des décors et des costumes, dont la couleur
> locale imite, à la stupidité noble du livret, à l'habileté technique des
> interprètes![6]

He announced also to Louÿs that the concert the following
week was to consist of Berlioz' *Damnation de Faust* and a
Beethoven work 'ce qui fait toujours plaisir'.[7]

Around the time that Valéry was twenty, a vigorous
interest in music developed; he made contact with practising
musicians, his knowledge of the music of many periods
flourished, and he became acquainted with ideas on musical
aesthetics and their relation to literary aims. It was at this
time that Valéry met Mallarmé, through Louÿs and Gide, and
thus came into contact with his fellow poets and some of the
contemporary musicians. In the first volume of the *Cahiers*
he made a list of the main developments in his tastes and
ideas. Against the date 1891 'Musique' is written, and the
importance of this reference may be judged by the significance of the other preoccupations he lists: romanticism in
1887, *ornement* – i.e. Viollett-le-duc and Owen Jones – in
1888-9, poetry and Mallarmé from 1889 and 1890 onwards,
mathematical theories in 1890-1, and in 1891-2 'nombres
plus subtils', that is the idea of the hidden relationships and
laws of continuity existing between all things. After the
'reform' of 1892 only maths and the study of the mind
appear.[8] 1891 marks, then, the first real insight into the power
and expressive range of music, and with the help of his friends
he was introduced to some of the technical problems of
music.

With Louÿs and Gide, Valéry extended his enthusiasm for
music, and they formed together a trio with a common passion for poetry and Wagner, exchanging their reactions to
their own works and the concerts they attended. Louÿs visited Bayreuth during 1891, and Valéry wrote to Gide antici-

pating Louÿs' reaction and the vociferous pleasure he would relate after seeing a performance of *Parsifal*.[9]

As a boy Louÿs had wanted to be a composer and had undertaken a brief study of harmony. He was a pianist, though less competent than Gide, as well as a violinist. An indication of his performance at the piano may be gathered from a teasing reference in a letter from Debussy to Louÿs: 'Personne ne me joue plus du Bach, avec cette délicieuse fantaisie que seul tu sais mettre dans ces antiquités.'[10] In later life he claimed to know more music by heart than poetry; his knowledge of musical notation was sufficient to enable him and Debussy to exchange musical quotations and references in their letters, and Louÿs even 'composed' a 'Merci en sol majeur' – a cadence in the key of G – to thank Debussy for the three melodies on poems of Verlaine. In 1891 Louÿs was editor of *La Conque*, and Valéry noted, waiting for him one day in his office, 'Je suis entré dans son cabinet de poète ... Tout ce qu'il renferme disparaît devant l'énorme effigie de Wagner.'[11] Wagner was all-important, a touchstone of poetic loyalties; while on the same visit to Paris Valéry was recommended by Gide to meet Camille Mauclair, 'un confrère, un vrai, en Mallarmé et Wagner'.[12]

Valéry's appreciation of Wagner figures prominently in his letters to Gide at this time. In March 1891 he wrote:

Je vous suppose à Rouen pour *Lohengrin* et ne vous envie pas médiocrement. Un piano ami m'a seul révélé quelque peu cette musique et donc la Musique.[13]

And a few days later:

Mon cher André, je suis dans *Lohengrin* jusqu'aux yeux. J'ignore le premier mot de musique, mais j'écoute et j'imagine, quand un de mes amis au piano, le soir, me joue le Prélude ou le Duo, ou *La Marche mystique* du deuxième acte.

Cette musique m'amènera, cela se prépare, à ne plus écrire. Déjà trop de difficultés m'arrêtaient ...

Et puis, quelle page écrite arrive à la hauteur des quelques notes qui sont le motif du *Graal. Hérodiade* seule en poésie française peut se lire sans trop de dégoût et de gêne.[14]

In this same letter, however, Valéry indicates that his musical tastes were not restricted to the nineteenth century. He had heard on Palm Sunday a performance of Bach's *St Matthew Passion* and it evidently made a profound impact, reinforcing the young Valéry's Catholic mysticism. This religious idealism is manifest, for example, in Valéry's early poems, such as *Fleur mystique, Le Divin Adultère, Le Jeune Prêtre, La Messe Angélique.* In addition the mass reinforced his interest in the liturgical, ritual aspects of the service, features which through his reading of Helmholtz, he associated with Greek tragedy as a combination of poetry, ceremony and music. Though a long way from his later appreciation of the mathematical precision of Bach's composition and its effect as musical form, this early development of Valéry's musical taste towards classical purity and non-descriptive music is significant and can be seen the following year in his admiration for Mozart's *Jupiter Symphony* and the music of string quartets.[15]

He mentions in a letter to Gide in 1892 that he has been reading Hoffman's *Les Fantaisies à la manière de Callot* and *Le Vase d'or*; Hoffman conveys the effects of Beethoven string quartets performed in a warmly evocative décor, and Valéry mentions 'les timbres si *sapides* des beaux altos et violoncelles – voix commodes!', continuing: 'Moi, à tout appel de quatuor à cordes intimes, j'imagine vite l'intérieur qu'il faut . . . la magie du beau savant nom: Beethoven!'[16]

In 1893, having arrived in Paris, he was able to hear much more music. In May his brother Jules took him to the Opéra to hear the *Walkyrie.* And in this year he began attending the Sunday concerts at the Cirque d'Eté, the famous Lamoureux concerts where Beethoven and Wagner were the basis of the repertoire. These concerts, which also included Berlioz and Schumann, played an important part in the formation of the young poets with whom Valéry associated. The concert season lasted from late autumn until spring, and Mallarmé himself had been attending since 1885, with all the devotion of going to a religious service:

Chaque dimanche d'hiver il laissait – pour cela seul – une après-midi de travail afin d'aller au concert Lamoureux. 'Je vais aux Vêpres' nous disait-il en partant.[17]

Valéry left impressions of these concerts in the address he

gave on the occasion of the 50th anniversary of the Lamoureux concerts:

> Lamoureux paraissait; toujours digne; jamais souriant, même sous les bravos. Il montait au pupitre. On eût dit qu'il montait à l'autel qu'il prenait le pouvoir suprême; et en vérité, il le prenait, il allait promulguer les lois des dieux de la Musique.[18]

He went on to describe in particular the attitude of Mallarmé:

> [il] subissait avec ravissement, mais avec cette angélique douleur qui naît des rivalités supérieures, l'enchantement de Beethoven ou de Wagner. Il protestait dans ses pensées, il déchiffrait aussi en grand artiste du langage ce que les dieux du son pur énonçaient et proféraient à leur manière. Mallarmé sortait des concerts plein d'une sublime jalousie. Il cherchait désespérément à trouver les moyens de reprendre pour notre art ce que la trop puissante Musique lui avait dérobé de merveilles et d'importance.[19]

The envy arose from the rivalry between the two arts, and the feeling that music was doing more effectively everything that poetry sought. André Fontainas, who was by 1893 a regular visitor to Mallarmé's Tuesday meetings in the rue de Rome, gave an account of the reactions of the poets:

> Mallarmé nous donnait l'exemple, qui, assidu, s'absorbait en méditations approfondies et, de temps à autre, furtivement, formulait une suggestion précise de visionnaire prophétique sur un de ces petits carrés de papier dont ses poches étaient toujours bourrés. A la sortie, nous nous rejoignions, échangions nos impressions, en ayant soin de nous dérober aux commentaires oiseux. Qu'importe qu'un basson eût émis une note fausse ou eût manqué une reprise! l'œuvre seule importait et nous nous sentions peu disposés à lui faire supporter les agacements d'une interprétation parfoid médiocre.[20]

Though they were obviously intent on avoiding the pedantry of some music critics one cannot help wondering whether in their idealistic vision of the work, their avoidance of 'commentaires oiseux' was not determined by their inability always to recognise the wrong notes.

Not all the writers around Mallarmé were in agreement over music. Indeed Pierre Meylan provides an interesting insight into Valéry's reactions to these musical commentaries:

> Valéry a toujours été un membre zélé de ces réunions familières. Il s'est révélé le contradicteur le plus passionné de Mallarmé quand le maître s'avisait de disserter sur un sujet musical.[21]

25

And Gide too, in *Si le grain ne meurt*, gives an indication of the heated discussions which used to take place after the concerts:

Dans le cercle autour de Mallarmé, où je fus bientôt entraîné par Louis, chacun se piquait d'aimer la musique, Pierre Louis le premier; mais il me paraissait que Mallarmé lui-même et tous ceux qui le fréquentaient, recherchaient dans la musique encore la littérature. Wagner était leur dieu. Ils l'expliquaient, le commentaient. Louis avait une façon d'imposer à mon admiration tel cri, telle interjection, qui me faisait prendre la musique 'expressive' en horreur. Je me rejetais d'autant plus passionnément vers ce que j'appelais la musique 'pure', c'est-à-dire celle qui ne prétend rien signifier; et. par protestation contre la polyphonie wagnérienne, préférais (je le préfère encore) le quatuor à l'orchestre, la sonate à la symphonie.[22]

Gide was a pianist and undoubtedly far more proficient than either Féline or Louÿs. He might well have become a concert musician, such was his love for music and technical skill. He shows in *Si le grain ne meurt* the extent of his early training, and his repertoire later came to include some of the most difficult pieces of piano music: he played all of Chopin's works, the Beethoven sonatas, as well as Schumann and Bach. Gide regularly played for Valéry, who recalls for example in a letter to his brother a dinner at which Gide played until 2 a.m.[23]

Gide found in music a liberation from his personal anguish and moral doubts, while his interpretation tended to confirm Valéry's awareness of purely musical emotion divorced from description and emotional assault. For Gide refused the overwhelming musical effects of Wagner and later even of Schumann and Beethoven, disliking the use of repeats and the tendency towards rhetorical effect. But though there is a healthy reaction against the indulgent virtuoso techniques, his approach to nineteenth-century music seems almost to go too far in the opposite direction. His early insistence on the merits of Schumann, for example, was based upon the element of control in the music. He wrote to Valéry in August 1892:

N'écoute jamais les imbéciles qui te diront que Schumann est un médiocre, et dis-leur qu'ils n'y ont rien compris. J'y trouve toujours de nouvelles choses; c'est un éducateur prodigieux. C'est un volontaire; un *compositeur*; il a l'inspiration arithmétique et folle. Il est comme il faut être.[24]

Such formal ideas were bound to impress Valéry. Similarly Gide stressed in Chopin the formal, classical aspects of his composition, a feature which interested Valéry, but at the same time reinforced his feeling of poetic impotence in the face of music.

It was in 1893 that the circle of friends came to include Debussy. He was an irregular visitor to the rue de Rome and certainly did not meet Louÿs until that year. In February 1893 Debussy was present at a banquet at the home of Louÿs' brother Georges, along with Valéry, Gide, Régnier, Wilde and Heredia. Valéry recounts in *Le Tombeau de Pierre Louÿs* how Louÿs was a great support to Debussy, giving him guidance and opening up new literary visions, and helping him throughout his career.[25] In November 1893 the two young poets and Debussy planned to rent a house together in Neuilly, though nothing came of the idea. They maintained a close friendship over the next few years, meeting fairly often. On 27 July 1894 Debussy wrote, 'J'ai dîné avec André Gide et Valéry. On parla beaucoup de toi et ce ne fut pas les endroits les moins charmants de ce trio.'[26]

During 1894–5 Louÿs held his 'mercredis' at his home 1 rue Grétry; Valéry, F. Hérold, Vielé-Griffin, P. Quillard, A. Fontainas, J. de Tinan, J.-E. Blanche, H. de Régnier and A. Lebey were among the frequent guests and Debussy would often play his own works. Interest was shown especially in Debussy's *Pelléas et Mélisande* which he was in the process of composing at this time. Louÿs wrote to him on 31 May 1894:

J'invite les gens *pour entendre Pelléas*
Ne l'oublie pas.
Tu dînes avec les Natanson et Robert. Après le dîner viendront
cinq ou six amis, invités spécialement, je te le répète, pour
Pelléas.
 Sois donc assez gentil pour apporter:
 1° le premier acte,
 2° la scène de la fontaine,
 3° une troisième scène si elle est faite (la scène des cheveux même
 incomplète).[27]

J.-E. Blanche gives an account of these evenings in *Le Tombeau de Pierre Louÿs*, with Debussy playing a harmonium and murmuring the vocal line in his unsonorous voice. Valéry and Debussy continued to meet for many years, planning to collaborate on a work more than once. The earliest project discussed was for *Amphion* in 1894, though nothing more was said at this stage.[28] A note in the *Cahier* for 1895 reads:

Libretto for C.A.D. Tristan comme modèle.
effets naturels. réalisme abstrait. sommeil. lumière – vue
le fantastique réglé psych. sur les nécessités.[29]

though again the plans appear to have gone no further. The most detailed project was made in 1899–1900 when they considered collaborating on a ballet. Valéry made notes in the *Cahiers* for a 'quatuor à cordes' with four dancers and later wrote to Debussy suggesting 'le mythe d'Orphée' as a subject.[30] Valéry supported Debussy's music against hostile critics, attended the stormy première of *Pelléas* at the *Opéra Comique* on 28 April 1902; and there is also a letter from Debussy to Louÿs offering him a box for the dress rehearsal on the day of the performance and expressly asking Louÿs to invite Valéry.[31]

Valéry's association with Louÿs was particularly rich, for not only did it introduce him to Debussy, but gave him the opportunity to discuss musical problems at length. The *XV Lettres de Paul Valéry à Pierre Louÿs* (1915–17) contain an important section of Valéry's writings on music, and there is no reason to suppose that their earlier letters do not contain as much fruitful and spirited material, though only a few have been published. Probably, with Louÿs, Valéry felt less inhibited by his own limited knowledge of the technicalities of music than he did with his other friends and practising musicians. But the lack of inhibition is also a reflection of Louÿs' open friendship, which seems to have been generous to all concerned. Valéry's remarks are still hedged with the usual professions of ignorance, but this does not stop him from writing to Louÿs for several pages. Letters N and O are particularly interesting. In the former, after a bantering play on words on the musical form of the chaconne, he writes:

Revenez, Monsieur Ciboulet, revenons à ce J.-S. Bach, dont on nous a toujours dit le plus grand bien. N'oubliez pas que vous écrivez à Mr. P. L. qui sur les questions musicales, est positivement dangereux.[32]

Valéry's life in Paris in the years leading up to 1900 was however by no means restricted to the circle of Mallarmé, Gide, Louÿs, Debussy and the fellow poets around them. Gradually he built up a wide range of contacts with people distinguished in all artistic fields, so much so that one has the impression that far from cutting himself off from all artistic production – as has been suggested by the myth of 'le grand silence' – Valéry was writing, creating and thinking in an incredibly rich artistic field: and above all he was reading, discussing and assimilating. His contact with the world of painters led to his meeting with the Gobillard sisters, Paule and Jeannie, nieces of Berthe Morisot, and Julie Manet, her daughter. After meeting them in December 1898, he frequently visited their house, attending musical evenings. At the reception to celebrate the signing of the marriage contract between Valéry and Jeannie Gobillard and between Julie Manet and Ernest Rouart, which took place on 26 May 1900, the great cellist Pablo Casals and the violinist Jules Boucherit played.

Madame Valéry herself was a gifted pianist, and took lessons with Raoul Pugno, the famous concert pianist who was also professor of pianoforte at the Conservatoire from 1896 to 1901. There is an interesting account of Valéry's visit to Pugno with Mme Valéry, given in a letter to Gide in which he discusses the problem of assessing the artistic merit of the virtuoso performer.[33]

The musical evenings which she gave were continued in their new residence in the rue de Villejust. Valéry seldom notes the programme of these recitals, but the remarkable prose poem 'Piano et Chant' shows his great sensitivity to such music. Agathe Rouart-Valéry in her contribution to the *Entretiens sur Paul Valéry* gives an indication of this musical environment at home:

Une partition de Wagner restait toujours ouverte sur le piano. D'un seul doigt, et encore hésitant, mon père, qui aimait Wagner presque à l'exclusion de tout autre musicien, la parcourait tout en esquissant de la voix les grands airs de *Wotan* ou *Brunehilde*, ou bien demandait-il à ma mère de lui en donner, de ses deux mains expertes, une plus complète interprétation. Une amie parfois, la femme du peintre Charles Lacoste, venait chanter le troisième acte de la *Walkyrie*, préféré à maint autre passage de la *Tétralogie*, faisant de ses notes amples et belles trembler de peur les cristaux du lustre, au plafond du salon.

Le clavier de ce piano, qui a bien souffert ensuite de nos gammes et arpèges, était encore valide à ce moment-là, et un Ravel n'a pas dédaigné d'y jouer sa *Sonatine* et l'*Alborada del graciosa*. Darius Milhaud, dans le temps où il accommodait les mélodies que j'écrivais à cet âge avec le sérieux de sept ans, l'a sans doute effleuré aussi, et plus tard Arthur Honegger lorsqu'il venait soumettre à mon père l'un des thèmes des deux œuvres, *Amphion* et *Sémiramis*, qu'ils ont ensemble créées.[34]

The year after his marriage Valéry returned to Paris in the summer and experienced the revelation of Gluck's music which was to provide such a profound influence. Writing to his wife, he said:

Orphée m'a empoigné, surtout le 1er et le IVe actes. Cela a eu le don de toucher en moi une très ancienne roche abandonnée. Je me suis souvenu de l'*Orphée* que j'avais moi-même chanté jadis, et voulant l'être . . . quand j'attribuais à mon imagination et à ma volonté une puissance divine . . . Je suis rentré lyrique.[35]

He heard the work repeatedly, for example in February 1905 sung by Caron (as well as Monteverdi's *Orfeo*) and was also much impressed by *Alceste*, from which the recitatives were to act as an inspiration in the composition of *La Jeune Parque*. The appeal of Gluck seems to lie basically in the purity of the vocal line, the continual modulation of sound coming closest to his poetic ideal. The music is certainly less romantic and overpowering than Wagner or Beethoven, less complex than Bach and appears, as Duchesne-Guillemin puts it, 'une musique appropriée à sa frugalité intellectuelle'.[36]

During this period after the turn of the century, Valéry became more and more closely involved in contemporary musical events, both in the salons and in the concert halls. He notes a performance of Beethoven's 7th in 1904: 'Je pullule et me colore mais de mes impressions je ne remonterais certes au texte musical.'[37]

An important contact was with the salon of Cipa (Cyprien) Godebski, the brother-in-law of the editor of *La Revue Blanche* Thadée Natanson. Godebski used to entertain at his flat in the rue d'Athènes on a Sunday evening and among his visitors were Valéry, Gide, Fargue, Cocteau, Valéry-Larbaud, Arnold Bennett, La Fresnaye, Redon, Vuillard and a number of musicians, Roussel, Florent Schmitt, Milhaud, Auric, Roland-Manuel, Ricardo Viñes, Ravel, Casella, de Falla, Stravinsky, Satie and sometimes Diaghilev and Nijinsky. Clearly, though, Valéry did not meet all of these during the first decade of the century, as the meeting with Stravinsky, for example, did not take place until 1921–2.

He had the experience of hearing such virtuosi as Viñes, who used to interpret all the modern piano music; but the contact with Ravel is more significant. The first time they met was, as far as can be ascertained, in 1906 or 1907. Valéry, writing in the *Cahiers* some 25 years later, remembers a conversation with Ravel and dates it 1906 or thereabouts.[38] Ravel is supposed to have understood nothing about the 'system' which Valéry explained to him, calling specifically upon the example of music. But if Ravel did not understand, he was certainly not the first; Gide too was often overwhelmed by Valéry's conversation. In any case the importance of this remark of Valéry's should not be overestimated, for when Ravel visited Valéry on 26 March 1908, he told him that *La Soirée avec M. Teste* was 'une de ses plus profondes impressions.'[39] Valéry drew a sketch of Ravel from the rear, while Ravel played his *Sonatine* and the fourth piece of *Miroirs, Alborada del graciosa*, both of which were composed in 1906. His contact with Ravel was close during the following years, at the Ballets Russes given at the Théâtre du Châtelet, as well as at the Godebskis. In 1910 he wrote to Jeannie Valéry noting Ravel's absence from one of these soirées:

Autour d'un piano un tas de gens penchés, collés, une mosaïque de dos . . . Viñes qui ne veut pas encore jouer les dernières études de Debussy, *La Cathédrale engloutie* . . . dont on dit des miracles, Ravel pas là . . .[40]

Again in 1911: 'Ravel, rencontré chez les Godebski, dit à

Valéry qu'il rêve de mettre en musique des bruits de sirènes et de machines',[41] an intention which was to be supremely achieved by Valéry's future collaborator Honegger in *Pacific 231* and *Rugby*. On 18 May 1911 Valéry was invited to hear *L'Heure espagnole*. And in June 1912 *Daphnis et Chloé* was performed at the Ballets Russes. Valéry's contact with Ravel was clearly of long standing, for later in 1923 he was in London with Ravel staying at the home of the singer Mme Alvar in Holland Park.[42]

It would appear to be largely through the Godebskis that Valéry was drawn into the tumultuous musical developments of the early years of the century in Paris. In January 1908 Debussy conducted *La Mer* and Diaghilev gave his triumphant production of Moussorgski's *Boris Godounov*, sung by Chaliapin. Thereafter came the ballets with Nijinsky, Pavlova, Fokine; Stravinsky's *Firebird* at the Opéra in 1910; *Petrouchka* at the Châtelet in 1911; Nijinsky's ballet on *L'Après-midi d'un Faune* in 1912. And in 1913 the Théâtre des Champs-Elysées was completed, with Valéry attending the inaugural concert on 2 April conducted by Fauré, Debussy and Vincent d'Indy. Valéry attended all the premières of the works presented by Diaghilev, Nijinsky and Chaliapin and was present at the riotous première of Stravinsky's *Le Sacre du Printemps*, at which some parts of the audience, in outrage at the new music, 'laughed, spat, hissed, . . . began to whistle . . . and make cat-calls'.[43] Evidently some of the more superficially elegant members of society were among these people, for Florent Schmitt was provoked to stand up and shout 'Taisez-vous garces du seizième.'[44] In spite of all the storms of acclaim and disapproval which this work initially stirred, and of Stravinsky's triumph the following year when it was given as a concert performance, there is only a brief allusion in the *Cahiers* which might be taken as a reference to the work, a note headed 'Son et bruit':

> Audition attentive.
> Perspective intérieure de la sensation . . .[45]

Perhaps the most surprising omission among Valéry's contacts during this period was that with Stravinsky, in spite of

the number of friends they had in common. Stravinsky read
La Soirée avec M. Teste before 1914 and talked about it with
Gide. And both Ravel and C. F. Ramuz spoke to Stravinsky
of Valéry; yet it was not, according to Stravinsky, until 1921
or 1922 that they first met:

> But whatever had kept us apart, we made up for the lost time, and in
> the later nineteen-twenties and in the thirties up to my departure for
> America we saw each other so regularly we might be thought to have
> formed a 'circle'.[46]

This 'circle' was not so much built around one particular
salon, but on a mutual friendship in a number of groups.
Apart from the Godebskis, where in 1919 Valéry heard Satie's
Socrate narrated by Gide, there was the salon of the princesse
Edmond de Polignac, to whom there are several references in
the *Cahiers*. Her Paris residence was on the avenue Henri-
Martin where many musicians came to play, and where she
herself played the piano with Fauré; she was a patron of the
arts and helped Diaghilev with the productions of *Mavra* and
Renard at the Opéra and *Oedipus Rex* at the Théâtre Sarah-
Bernhardt. It was she who commissioned Stravinsky to write
Renard. Stravinsky says of her:

> Excellente musicienne, d'une vaste culture générale, peintre doué d'un
> talent incontestable, elle protégeait et encourageait les arts et les artis-
> tes. Je me souviendrai toujours avec reconnaissance des soirées où
> j'exécutai chez elle nombre de mes nouvelles créations, comme outre
> *Les Noces, l'Histoire du soldat*, mon *Concerto* et ma *Sonate* pour piano,
> qui lui est dédiée, *Oedipus Rex*, etc.[47]

These must have been occasions of outstanding artistic interest, for Stravinsky was of course a fine concert pianist, giving
regular performances at this time.

During the 1920s and until about 1935 Valéry was deeply
involved in the musical life of Paris. In addition to the salons
and Stravinsky the *Cahiers* reveal a wide experience of different works and a number of contacts with musicians, which
are sometimes commented upon in detail, but often merely
noted alongside a date.

In 1923 or '24 Valéry met the musician and writer Louis
Aguettant. He was greatly impressed by Aguettant's article

on 'Les Dialogues de Paul Valéry' and though they met infrequently, the occasions were, according to Valéry, 'insignes'. On hearing of Aguettant's death Valéry wrote to their common friend Henri Rambaud: 'La dernière fois que j'ai vu Aguettant ce fut ici, et même au piano de ma femme, où il se mit pour m'expliquer une certaine étude de Chopin dont la composition m'intriguait.'[48]

In 1927 after a performance of Mozart's Symphony in G minor he commented: 'Ne rien *dire* . . . Mais le dire si bien'[49] and the same year he read Wagner's autobiography: 'Lu *Ma Vie* par Wagner. Quelle "Vie"!'[50]

In 1928 he saw Strauss's *Rosenkavalier* at the Opéra, commenting 'Je retrouve mes impressions de jadis. Epoque Teste.'[51] In this year also began the series of discussions with Ida Rubinstein and Honegger on the plans for *Amphion* and subsequently *Sémiramis*. These meetings took place fairly regularly over the following years, with the notes in the *Cahiers* recording their conversations and details of Valéry's plans for the composition of the works.

1929 appears to have been full of musical activity. He attended a dress rehearsal at the Théâtre des Variétés of an opera by Offenbach with Madame l'Archiduc,[52] and saw on 16 May *Les 2 Vera*, 'grotesque op. buffe', at the Champs-Elysées.[53] The same evening, no doubt after the performance, he met Max Schneider, the German musicologist and specialist on Bach and his predecessors, as well as the mezzo-soprano Lucienne Bréval, famous for her Wagnerian rôles: 'Souvenirs de *Walküre*. Comment elle trouve le cri *Ho ja ha ha*.' He also records a conversation with Georges Auric and a performance of Wagner's *Walküre*,[54] *Götterdämmerung* and a work by Meyerbeer,[55] and a dinner with Anna de Noailles and Artur Rubinstein.[56]

At the beginning of 1931 he saw *Parsifal* at the Opéra.[57] In February he attended a concert recital by the virtuoso pianist Emil von Sauer, though without any pleasure and only confirming the general opinion of the virtuoso performance: 'Son affreux des pianos de concert. Etourdissement. La vitesse et autres qualités, le délire invraisemblable ne font penser qu'à une machine.'[58] Later in 1931 there was Mozart's *Don Giovanni*,[53] Bellini's *Norma* at San Carlo, and *Orontea*, an opera written in 1649 by Pietro Cesti,[60] as well as a performance by dancers from Bali which he saw with the Maurois.[61] Probably the most outstanding of all was a performance of Gluck's *Iphigénie en Tauride* on 28 June: 'Et voilà le *beau* à l'état pur . . . la musique place le tout hors du vrai et du faux, isole le drame de l'expérience. Pas d'*amour* dans cette pièce . . .'[62]

Also in June of this year *Amphion* was performed at the Opéra in Paris and at Covent Garden. All involved seem to have felt a certain disappointment with the result. Though generally well-received by the press, with praise for the conception, the libretto and the music, the imperfections of the performance itself were pointed out. In particular the staging and the delivery of some of the lines seem not to have been always well-suited to the intentions of Valéry. He saw the work, having just returned from Oxford where he had been awarded an Honorary D.Litt. and noted afterwards in the *Cahiers*:

nous allons à l'Opéra. Loge 17. Vais voir Ida. Cette scène et ces gens. Amphion. Aussi loin que possible de mon dessein. Il n'en reste rien. Il faut paraître sur la scène avec Ida. puis revenir 2 fois avec Honegger et elle. quelle belle chose que cette salle pleine et comme chauffée en rouge, vue de la scène. Assemblée des dieux – quand on pèse ces dieux . . . pour lesquels les individus s'épuisent! Avant hier matin, je figurais en rouge dans l'enceinte du Sheldonian dans une rite cocasse; – Hier soir en frac sur la scène de l'Opéra après un coup de vent d'Est! Poor Mr Teste![63]

Clearly, though, Valéry was attracted by this more public form of presenting his works and the possibilities of combining the effects of poetry, music and dance. In 1932 he met Prokofiev and outlined to him proposals for collaborating on a ballet entitled 'Figures'. One can only regret that such an interesting plan should fail to materialise, though no doubt the formalism of Valéry's proposals was likely to be unacceptable to the composer who returned three years later to Russia subscribing to the ideals of a music accessible to the general populace.

Conversation avec Prokofiev.

Nous comparons ce qu'Ida m'a demandé – (Temple de Salomon!) avec ce qu'il veut. (Il songe à la Russie – où ils ne veulent pas d'impressions *destructives*!!) Qui ne veut pas 'd'érotique'!

Bref je lui propose un ballet 'géométrique' *sans sujet.*

'Figures' serait le titre provisoire. Je lui parle d'ornements arches nombre de personnes essentiel.

Il s'agit de trouver une fonction cachée des êtres dansants. Si le danseur est telle chose, les figures successives s'en déduisent . . .[64]

Also in this year there .are references to a concert in Vienna with a Mozart quartet and works by Schubert and Schumann sung by the Austrian bass Richard Mayr,[65] a meeting with the Australian violinist Leirus in Brussels[66] and a reading of the study by G. de Pourtalès, *Wagner: histoire d'un artiste.*[67]

Valéry's response to the human voice is evident in two quite different musical experiences during 1933. While in Madrid in May he was entertained at the home of Professor Marañon with Spanish music:

Chanteurs – guitare – ces voix sont comme fluides en charge sur l'état desquels – des incidents engendrent des modulations, des discontinuités. On sent que l'essentiel ici est le fluide même. D'où signification principale est *Espace désert.* Parfois (dans les *Saetas*) la détresse à l'état pur, l'être perdu. Pas de *détails.* C'est le 'Silence éternel' rendu par l'effort extraordinaire de l'homme seul qui n'a que sa voix pour compagne, et que la *durée de sa voix* . . .[68]

The second occasion was during the summer after an evening of recorded music:

réveillé 3h 20 . . . Il faut noter que hier soir divins disques des Maîtres. Lotte Lehmann – Sachs – Schorr – avaient irrité mon Amour – Intellect – mes *lointains* et mes infinis *éveillés.*[69]

Around this period there are further details of the involvement with Stravinsky. On 10 January 1934 Valéry notes a 'charmant dîner à 6 chez Monaco' at which Nadia Boulanger, the princesse de Polignac, Thérèse Murat and Stravinsky were present.[70] Valéry showed consistent support for Stravinsky's music throughout their acquaintance as is clear from the incidents surrounding *Perséphone.* Stravinsky dwells at some length in his 'Memoir' on the composition of this work, which was based upon a text by Gide. Problems of musical adaptation were posed, and particularly the question of fidelity to the text. Valéry acted as arbitrator between the two, but seems to have favoured Stravinsky's position. As well as the moral support he provided, he attended the première on 30 April 1934 and all subsequent performances.

By this time Stravinsky's music had progressed from the Russian folk elements to a rigorously formal phase through his interest in eighteenth-century classical forms. In Stravinsky, Valéry found the perfect expression of the opposite musical approach to Wagner, the idea of a music that has no 'expression', that refers to nothing but itself. This point is made in a letter Valéry wrote to him (translated for publication in an English language work):

> I could not get to you Monday evening to tell you of the extraordinary impression the *Persephone* music made on me. I am only a 'profane' listener, but the divine *detachment* of your work touched me. It seems to me that what I have sometimes searched for in the ways of poetry you pursue and join in your art. The point is to attain purity through the will. You expressed it marvellously well in the article yesterday which I immensely enjoyed. LONG LIVE YOUR NOSE.[71]

And yet there seems to have been little possibility of collaboration between the two artists. Though they approached their work in a remarkably similar way, the underlying differences concerning its religious significance appear to have presented the major obstacle. As Valéry laconically remarks:

> 7 fév 33 Dîner avec Gide chez Ida. Il paraît que Stravinsky a dit à Gide qu'il ne pourrait travailler avec moi car je suis athée.[72]

The reservations were clearly mutual, for Valéry rejected Stravinsky's openly mystical attitude just as strongly. Again in February 1934 they discussed this subject, though Valéry only noted his own words:

> Conversation avec Stravinsky. son mysticisme. Icones un peu partout chez lui . . . J'ai dit sommairement que le dieu ne pouvait exiger que le développement de ce qui ns semble à nous l'indication de l'accroissement de notre *différence avec l'animal*.[73]

Their common friend, Nadia Boulanger, was also a great source of musical knowledge. This celebrated teacher who was to become one of the outstanding figures in French musical life, taught composition at the Ecole Normale de Musique and at the Conservatoire, as well as to many young American composers. later she became 'maître de chapelle' to the Prince of Monaco. She was largely responsible for furthering the understanding of early music.

Grâce à elle et à ses *cours de cantates*, qu'elle donne chez elle tous les mercredis, une pléiade de musiciens se sont familiarisés avec les œuvres des maîtres, notamment avec les cantates de J.-S. Bach, avec Monteverdi, avec Schütz etc.[74]

Valéry used to attend some of these classes and the discussions and musical examples were a great inspiration, as they were for Valéry's son François also. On 7 March 1934 for example Valéry was taken along by Monaco: 'Elle fait étudier 2 cantates de Bach. belle leçon. "Ce *la* bémol est presque un sol." '[75] An illuminating view of their contact is given in the article which Valéry wrote for the *Revue Internationale de Musique*; since the article has remained generally unnoticed, it will be of interest to reproduce it in full.

La Musique n'est pas mon affaire. Je la sens fortement dans certains ouvrages; mais à ma guise, qui n'est pas la bonne. Il ne m'est donc pas permis de parler des mérites techniques de Mademoiselle Boulanger. Mais je l'ai souvent observée à l'œuvre: debout; de longs plis noirs vêtue; le visage pâle et comme enchanté, illuminé des scintillements du cristal d'un lorgnon; une main frappant le clavier, l'autre menant d'un doigt le petit orchestre en éventail autour d'elle, Nadia conduit. On dirait qu'elle respire ce que l'on écoute, et qu'elle n'existe et ne peut exister que dans l'Univers des sons.

Même l'ignorant que je suis en retient une impression extraordinaire. Il voit de ses yeux produire par une créature vivante, l'enthousiasme et l'ordre, qui sont les deux puissances symétriques du grand art. Mais ces deux vertus maîtresses de l'exécution, comme elles le sont de toute création, ne s'accordent que par une contrainte et un exercice soutenus qui transforme leur antagonisme en équilibre. On ne fait rien de bon sans passion; rien d'excellent par elle seule. Nadia Boulanger me semble pénétrée de quelque principe analogue à celui-ci. La joie de comprendre, la volonté de faire comprendre se composent en elle avec une fermeté soucieuse de ne sacrifier jamais la structure d'une œuvre aux effets locaux, la précision aux avantages de l'*à peu près*, la pureté aux intentions particulières de l'interprète. Ingres, dans son langage énergique et bizarre, disait en parlant dessin: 'Il faut monter sur l'échafaud pour les *plans*'. Nadia Boulanger en dirait tout autant pour la mesure, je pense.

Je m'entretiens quelquefois avec elle. Je crois que nous nous entendons assez bien. Il y a une philosophie de l'exécution qui domine tous les arts, et nous permet d'échanger plus d'une idée née de la pratique, de celles que donne l'action, et non le projet; l'expérience, et non le propos. Au cours de ces conversations, Mademoiselle Boulanger me donne parfois l'illusion que je comprends quelque chose aux délicatesses et aux savantes combinaisons de la grande Musique . . . [76]

Also in 1934 Valéry notes a performance of Strauss's *Don Juan* at the Opéra,[77] his enjoyment on reading Nijinsky's Diary edited by his wife,[78] and a meeting with Madame Rambert in London.[79] And on 11 May 1934 the first performance of Valéry's *Sémiramis* with music by Honegger was given. The reception was somewhat mixed, the first two Acts generally considered quite impressive, but the third Act with its long and largely inaudible monologue seemed to break up the unity of the work and prompted unfavourable reactions. Valéry noted: 'Lifar me place au 1er rang de l'orchestre près de lui. Au III, monologue très long. Sifflets à la fin, jusque dans mon dos – peu de siffleurs, mais vifs et armés.'[80] There were some adjustments made to the work and it was repeated on 20 January the following year along with *Perséphone*.

In 1935 a special performance of Schütz's oratorio *Historia der fröhlichen und siegreichen Auferstehung unsers einigen Erlösers und Seligmachers Jesu Christi* took place at the Polignac's which Valéry attended.[81] Later in the same year he heard Weber's Overture to *Der Freischütz*, noting the 'charme magique, enchantement'.[82] Valéry's daughter has expressed the pleasure her father had from Weber's music:

il ne se lassait jamais d'entendre les opéras du maître, éprouvant chaque fois la même émotion; le souffle romantique et le dynamisme d'*Euryanthe* ou d'*Obéron* balayaient tout scrupule par trop intellectuel.[83]

And while in Nice to preside over the fifth session of the 'Comité des Arts et Lettres de la Société des Nations' he attended a performance of *Tristan* and an apparently excellent version of Gluck's *Orphée*.[84]

There are fewer indications of Valéry's musical interests in the remaining years of his life, consisting in the main of a few brief references. He contributed in 1936 to the special edition of the *Revue Musicale* after the death of Paul Dukas. Brussel's biographical sketch refers to the acquaintance between the two artists, though it was clearly not close:

je voudrais . . . signaler l'amitié intellectuelle – étroite, bien qu'elle ne se manifestât pas dans le plan de la vie quotidienne – qui liait entre eux Paul Dukas et M. Paul Valéry. Ils ont failli faire œuvre commune, et cependant se voyaient peu . . . Tous deux sont des constructifs. Tous deux, par instinct, se plaisent, dans l'œuvre de leur création, aux rigoureuses architectures.[85]

Valéry was in Rome during 1937 and he notes a performance of a work by Malipiero, a composer noted for his contemporary treatment of earlier operas like *Orphée* and *L'Incoronazione di Poppea*.[86] He mentions also in this year a meeting with the pianist Bock,[87] the 'Danse rituel' of the Yemeni dancers[88] and Beethoven's 9th Symphony conducted by Furtwängler.[89] He attended the première of Stravinsky's *Dumbarton Oaks* the following year, maintaining his contact with the composer and providing valuable assistance with his *Poetics of Music*.[90] And he read the *Petite Chronique de Magdalene Bach* which he says made a greater impression on him than anything he had read for a long time.[91]

Valéry had been working on his *Cantate du Narcisse* which was set to music by Germaine Tailleferre. The work was read on 23 February 1939 at the 'Société des Auteurs, Compositeurs et Editeurs de musique', though not performed with music until 1944, on 14 January at the Conservatoire, and on 8 December at the Studio des Champs-Elysées. With the advent of the Second World War Valéry's contacts with music came to an end, at least so far as public recitals were concerned. It is significant though that one of his last references to the subject should evoke the composer who had dominated his musical interests throughout his life:

20/6/43   Je trouve dans la correspondance Wagner–Liszt – p. 325 un passage auquel je suis très *sensible* – étant tout sensibilisé à l'idée émise puisque je l'ai souvent conçue. C'est que l'homme est une monstruosité du développement animal. Cf. *Mauvaises pensées*.[92]

And again in 1944:

En fait de 'mystique' rien ne me convient mieux que le Prélude de Lohengrin.
Là, *pas de mots*. (Baudelaire traducteur? . .)
Cela est donc 'pur', non mêlé de paroles.
Dans le Prélude, il n'y a que l'excitation du type 'émotion mystique'[93]

There emerges from this survey of Valéry's musical contacts, however incomplete it must necessarily be, a picture of a wide range of interests and experiences. Indeed, given that the *Cahiers* are a diary of his thoughts rather than of the events of his life, the absence of the names of certain other great composers cannot be interpreted as indicating lack of interest or approval on Valéry's part. His musical environment was clearly very rich: he was familiar with the major musical developments of the period in which he lived and knew well not only the music, but a number of the outstanding composers and performers.

He refers frequently to his lack of understanding of music. Yet this was basically of a technical nature: he could read the notes of a piano part only very slowly and knew little of the rudiments and theory of music. It was no doubt precisely because he was in constant association with musicians of the highest order that he should be so hesitant over his musical judgements, his uncharacteristic inhibition provoked both by their obviously superior knowledge as well as their practical ability as performers.

But the understanding which all these musicians gave to Valéry was a crucial feature of his attitude towards poetry and music and to his understanding of the process of composition. While it is not possible, or even desirable, to talk of a direct influence upon him, it is evident that in his contacts with the world of music Valéry found both an understanding of contemporary developments and confirmation of ideas that he had developed independently. He gained an insight into the working of music, into particular examples and into some of the different theoretical approaches. Above all this musical environment gave actuality to his own more abstract preoccupations.

The proliferation of references to music in the *Cahiers*, though not focusing on particular musical examples, reveals an unceasing attempt to understand the effects of music and how they are created. Though aware of his limited technical knowledge, he tackles directly general questions of musical aesthetics and the relation to poetry. As Stravinsky comments: 'Valéry knew little enough about music. But he knew that he knew little and therefore did not utter banalities of the type one so often hears from literary people.'[94] Far from being banal, the profusion of private notes on music which Valéry made reveal a searching analysis of individual composers and of aspects of musical aesthetics, as well as a determined attempt to make the practical connections between music and the art form in which his technical and theoretical ability were second to none: poetry.

PART II

Music and poetry

1

MUSIC AS A LANGUAGE OF THE EMOTIONS

La musique n'est autre chose que la déduction des émotions.
                                                XI, 1926, p. 468

There can be no doubt that Valéry was extremely sensitive to musical experiences: in his youth he was particularly impressed by the emotional impact of the great nineteenth-century works played at the Lamoureux concerts, 'à la fois excitation de vie intérieure intense, et communion'.[1] The music had an intoxicating effect on the young poet that was sometimes overwhelming: 'Que faire contre cette musique si puissante! Si facilement transcendantale? où sont possibles de vraies surprises, de vraies rapidités.'[2] But Valéry's taste was wide, and in the course of his life he became familiar with a variety of musical effects of different periods and styles. Though increasingly aware of the compositional techniques, of the forms and styles of different works, his reactions display a strong emotional response which was clearly a feature of his own temperament. As a poet he felt a rivalry with the expressive power of music; as an intellectual he found that music could pose a threat to the conscious control of his mind; and yet, next to poetry, music held a greater fascination for him than any other art form, due largely to the directness and immediacy of the emotional responses it provoked in him.

It is understandable therefore that the notes in the *Cahiers* should reveal different, and sometimes conflicting, attitudes to music, for his reactions might vary between admiration and envy. In order to expose these reactions this chapter will seek to answer three questions: what is the nature of Valéry's emotional responses? how does he seek to explain the effects of music? and how does he attempt to defend himself against the powerful emotions that music evokes?

Readers of Valéry's essays and even his poetry have often been tempted to emphasise the intellectualism of his approach and to interpret the poetic images as portrayals only of mental states: this is, particularly in the poetry, to overlook the importance of the natural world, of sensation and of emotional reactions. Nowhere is this side of his temperament more explicit than in the notes on the expressive power of music. He sees music as the pre-eminent language of the emotions and identifies the feelings which it conveys with a sense of admiration.

One emotion above all is expressed in music more effectively than in any other artistic medium: 'A-t-on jamais vraiment saisi l'amour autrement que par la musique?' he wrote after a performance of Gluck's *Orphée*.[3] And again some twenty years later: 'Le divin de l'amour est musique – n'a d'expression que musicale.'[4] Valéry was not just thinking of vocal music, for, 'la musique heureuse peut faire un "chant d'amour" sans paroles c.à.d. une imitation de l'état d'enchantement d'êtres aux yeux dans les yeux – et les mains pleines l'un de l'autre – ceci est muet.'[5]

It was often through the comparison with music that Valéry analysed the various facets of love that came to be a major preoccupation of the later part of his life. In one note in 1943 he examined the difficulties found in writing the parts of *Mon Faust* involving Lust. He had projected in the fourth act of *Lust* to express love in an ultimate form, as an acceptance of a new experience of tenderness. The special quality of love was, for Valéry, to include all aspects of the reactions of the sensibility, according them and the person an infinite value, in a state of 'imminence':

Il en résulte des effets intenses et extrêmes sous des causes imperceptibles. Et primairement, des effets *irrationnels* et impulsions dans le domaine organique sexuel. Contact, vue, idée, faveur des circonstances . . .

Les sensations émotionnelles arrivent à se produire *sans cause*, au moindre écart du présent . . .

Music as a language of the emotions

L'art littéraire, hélas! ne permet pas de jouer du temps – de faire attendre – ce qui appartient aux musiciens seuls. Or c'est cette attente qui représente et communique l'*imminence*, le potentiel caractéristique de l'amour.[6]

The ability of music to express a deep emotion yet dispense with words is a recurrent feature of the mixture of admiration and envy felt by poets from Baudelaire on. For along with feelings of love, music can well express religious feeling. Valéry found a sense of spiritual transcendence in the *St Matthew Passion*. And recalling Baudelaire's reaction to *Lohengrin*, he notes 'En fait de "mystique" rien ne me convient mieux que le Prélude de Lohengrin' and suggests that Baudelaire's article is a translation of the piece into words. 'Il serait intéressant de faire littérairement une tentative analogue sans termes autres que ceux que donnent l'observation de soi, et non des acquis . . . C'est bien le "mystique sans Dieu" – (cf. Teste).'[7]

What interests Valéry above all is the possibility of creating a mystical state without the connotations of belief in God, a state 'in itself' without exterior reference. His interest focuses upon the work of music itself as a spiritual experience. Music becomes a religion and the composer himself a god; the writer may be a 'voyant', a prophet, a 'Napoléon' or a 'statesman', but 'Quant au musicien, c'est Dieu – c'est la création, par l'orchestre, l'ordre et le chaos en *mib majeur*'[8] Music is able to communicate the religious sense of faith without demanding belief, a mystical sensation of beauty and complete emotional power. It is the shared experience of emotional liberation which is of particular interest to Valéry, an experience which can occur in the concert hall when one's deepest emotions are stirred and one feels alone with the music yet in communication with the experience of everyone else; it is 'la condition religieuse par excellence, l'unité sentimentale d'une pluralité vivante'.[9]

Music presents not only an intensification of human experience, but an exploration of the hidden recesses of feeling and a magnification of these until they take over the whole of one's being. Music in this sense tends to represent the irrational characteristics of man. Valéry mentions the irrational feelings which love may provoke, and in 'Piano et Chant' notes the feeling of 'une force inconnue'.[10] The dominance of irrational sensation is the denial of rational lucidity, 'comme si j'agissais et sentais nettement sans pensée'.[11] Music experienced to this intense degree is more than the possibility of pathos, sorrow, joy etc.; it has all the uncontrollable effect of a poisonous or intoxicating substance: it becomes a kind of addiction, stimulating at once a constant fascination and a certain horror.

La musique est un toxique. Ceci est clair. Pourquoi t'y prendre? D'abord parce que les toxiques se font aimer. Ensuite, parce que le fonctionnement dû aux toxiques est toujours une expérience importante. Tel poison dissèque un système, montre un groupement fonctionnel aggissant dans des conditions autres que les ordinaires. Les émotions musicales sont de la même nature que le vomissement ou le flux provoqués par l'art – du pharmacien.[12]

This mixture of fatal attraction and horrified rejection is seen in the brilliantly lively letter written to Pierre Louÿs on 10 June 1917, in which he proposes the hypothetical ancient civilisations deliberately suppressing music and its powers of unleashing the irrational, in favour of a balanced view of man at one with the world and whose controlled outlook on life was expressed in poetry. The composer and virtuosi were semi-devils, the Bachs, the Wagners ('à pieds de boucs') were subject to Apollo – the Apollo who stood for moderation, opposed to all excesses and who controlled music, poetry, philosophy, astronomy, mathematics, medicine and science. Music proposed a 'jouissance . . . *qui se passe d'idées nettes*': 'L'ivresse totale pour eux [les Anciens] *contredit* et *s'oppose* à – une excitation légère et contrôlée, une ébriété dominée . . .'[13] Though Valéry in part supports this control – he had written only four days previously to Louÿs: 'Ne pas oublier non plus que nous sommes *contre* la musique. Apollon *contre* Dionysus',[14] – he now speaks of this hypothetical ancient civilisation in order to assert '*Nous ne sommes plus ces gens-là.*'[15] Music has become the language of the instincts, of the inner drives, of a spontaneous liberation of the self, such as is found in the music of 'le nègre et le ballet russe'. And Valéry sees himself as one of the dangerous, subversive supporters:

Ces gens-là ne comptaient parmi les joussances avouables, nobles, dignes des meilleurs, le *fait de perdre pied.* Ils sentaient le danger de très loin. Ils pressentaient l'alcool, la mystique, l'aéro*, Pelléas, Apollinaire, P.L., P.V., etc.

*Avant-hier 288km. à l'heure sur Spad?[16]

Music is like a drug, releasing the 'vie intérieure' and the 'vie intense', childhood memories, dreams and emotional disruptions, all of which disturb the orderly working of 'les hommes qui possèdent la plénitude du *net* et de l'*actif* . . . Les Beethoven et Wagner sont parfaitement inutiles à l'homme intact.'[17] Beethoven is seen as the first of the modern musicians using notes to create immediate effects hitting at the root of emotional reactions.

But one recognises also in Valéry a more delicate ear, responsive to the more intimate and subtle music of recitals. His reactions are expressed in passages akin to prose poetry in their evocativeness. The most outstanding is the short piece 'Piano et Chant' describing a song recital in a salon, and perhaps inspired by one of the musical 'soirées' held in his home. It shows not only the sensitivity of his reactions, but the remarkable ability to convey the atmosphere which the music created in the room.

La voix vibrante se marie étrangement à la voix abstraite du piano. Le souffle de la rousse, les mains de la châtaine, excite le temps et la matière.

La chambre vibre. Les murs chantent. La substance de l'air attaquée par une fraîche et forte gorge, entièrement émue par ces milliers de chocs cristallins, et par ces ébranlements volumineux que les cordes d'acier frappées lui communiquent, devient le lieu de transformations admirables. Mon âme tendue reçoit successivement toutes les figures qu'une âme agitée par la vie est capable de former d'elle-même.

Je frémis. Je sens une force inconnue. Je subis la mélancolie et les déchirements de la tendresse dans la solitude. Ecoute encore. Reconnais les formules de l'attente, et considère comme l'angoisse est bien présentée maintenant!

Ce point d'orgue touche aux secrets mêmes de ton être. Ce mouvement est un sommeil dans la forêt. Cet accord surprenant prophétise toute une philosophie, qui jamais ne sera pensée.

Music and poetry

Un amour infini passe comme une feuille en tournoyant . . .
–Quelle voix, mon enfant! –Vous accompagnez à merveille, madamoi-
selle!
Toutes mes puissances se retrouvent sur la terre. Elles se sentent lourdes
et maladroites. Et la parole a honte.[18]

The text reveals a number of Valéry's crucial attitudes: the
human element brought to music by the voice, vibrant with
life, while instrumental music is more pure sound; the different appreciation of time in music which can portray the
transition of feelings in a much shorter time than in life.
This reduction of time is seen as he begins to note down personal impressions, but the music is going too fast for him and
one can imagine him trying to catch up, as he omits the personal pronouns for brevity and returns his attention, almost
breathlessly, to the music: 'Ecoute encore. Reconnais les formules . . .' The idea of the musical atmosphere permeating
the structure of the room itself leads to a transference of
cause and effect, and an attribution of living affective reactions to solid inanimate substances. It is an effect which
Valéry uses in *Eupalinos* where the temples 'sing' and which
is reversed in *L'Ame et la Danse* where the fluid movement of
music and dance seems to become solid, almost stationary. In
'Piano et Chant' the music seems to come from the walls
themselves, the air becomes a solid enveloping substance
involving the listener, as a prisoner of sound, in the shared
experience.

The music is highly suggestive and acts as an invitation to
the listener to respond emotionally, which Valéry, in a somewhat romantic vein, clearly does by providing his own interpretation. The music transports him to another world until
the spell is broken and he is back 'sur la terre' again. It conveys dreamlike impressions, the profound, inexplicit movements of the deepest self, a way of life that cannot be expressed in words, that can hardly be conceived of intellectually.

Such is the impressionistic nature of Valéry's description
that it is impossible to distinguish entirely between the effect
of the musical phrases and the content of the song. For having set the scene in the first two paragraphs, he proceeds to

describe his reactions and alludes only indirectly to what the song is about. One can pick out the element of melancholy, of agonising tenderness, of anguish, of dreaminess, of a sense of expectation which does not materialise, and of an intense experience of love which dies away. The music is equally evoked in impressionistic style: the 'chocs cristallins' of the voice and the 'cordes d'acier' of the piano; the melodic repetitions seem to imply an unresolved anguish which reaches a climax as the rhythmic movement of the song is temporarily suspended by a pause '[qui] touche aux secrets mêmes de ton être'; the rhythm picks up again imperceptibly like 'un sommeil dans la forêt'; this quiet movement is punctuated by an 'accord surprenant', supposing an unresolved chord such as is not found in classical harmony, a strange new sound left lingering prophetically; finally there are the gently swirling rhythms that the piece closes on.

Valéry's attitude is at once one of involvement and detachment; he experiences the music directly and observes the way it creates its effects. He recognises the 'formules de l'attente', the phrases that arouse one's expectation, the unresolved harmonies, the melodic snatches that lead elsewhere before they are completed, all the techniques that make the listener attentively involved. As an onlooker Valéry 'considère comme l'angoisse est bien *présentée* . . .' before then becoming completely involved in the music again.

Thus it can be seen that Valéry tends to see music as the supreme language of the emotions, achieving its effects through the inherent 'énergie esthétique démesurée'; his responses reveal a great sensitivity to the emotional effects and a temperament which reacts strongly to its suggestive power:

Elle joue des profondeurs de la vie, des extrêmes de la passion, invite les combinaisons de la pensée, semble remuer la nature; agite, apaise, parcourt tout le système des nerfs, – et ceci obtenu par action irrésistible, en quelques instants; parfois, par une seule note. La musique se joue de nous, nous faisant tristes, gais, ivres ou pensifs, nous rendant à son gré plus ardents, plus profonds, plus tendres ou plus forts que jamais hommes ne le furent.[19]

51

Not content to identify the different emotions which music is able to evoke, Valéry was concerned on a number of occasions to attempt an analysis of how such effects may be produced. The notes in the *Cahiers* reveal several approaches which vary from a concept of music's essential ambiguity, to a rather mechanistic view of psychological reactions. In either case, Valéry was not so much concerned with the problem of how certain combinations of notes can come to embody particular feelings, but more with the relationship between a piece of music and the listener.[20]

The impressionism which was discerned in 'Piano et Chant' is closely associated with the contemporary aesthetic doctrine of ambiguity: vagueness and the possibility of multiple interpretations were seen as part of the work's evocative effect. It is a characteristic of Valéry's thought particularly up to about 1910, when his main musical experience had been of Wagner and Debussy. According to this idea, the expression of the work, though suggested by the title or by certain recognisable effects, is principally contributed by the listener. Indeed an 'understanding' of music is based essentially upon the importation of extra-musical events or reactions.

Comprendre un morceau de musique c'est lui trouver ou lui donner un *sens*. Et cela consiste à produire *involontairement* des phénomènes internes (ou externes mais musculaires) qui ne sont *plus* musicaux – et qui sont déterminés à chaque instant par le morceau – on reçoit des *impulsions* et cette impulsion est la partie cinétique de chaque sensation – et donne <u>ailleurs</u>.[21]

The influence of Debussy on Valéry's thinking is crucial in this area, for Debussy gave little guidance as to the meaning of the thematic symbols in his work. He sought to create evocative effects, aural images with pictoral or literary associations, rather than the imitative effects of the sounds of nature found for example in Beethoven's *Pastoral Symphony* – a work which Debussy abhorred.[22] His ideas on harmonic ambiguity, as a means of extending the range of expression, were an attempt to build indefiniteness into the work. He sought to undermine the tradition of classical harmony, for the range of expression it had acquired as a pattern of tonal relationships was no longer relevant to him as a musical language.

As Valéry realised, the attempt to give a rational explanation of music is fundamentally opposed to the essence of music 'qui est la puissance de l'incomplet – l'extension illimitée de ce qui n'est pas viable'.[23] He felt that the deepest musical effect was one which 'n'a pas de nom qui n'est ni homme, ni signe, ni sensation nette – ni tel souvenir ou désir mais le vague tout-puissant d'un mélange indécomposable de tout cela'.[24] Such ideas were at the basis of symbolist thought, and Valéry repeatedly comes back to the concept of ambiguity. The interpretations of the listener will depend largely upon the person's own capacity to identify and experience particular emotions; and in Valéry's case there would appear to be a very strong reaction to music as immediate sensation. As with poetry, whatever the intentions of the composer, the reader or listener is free to interpret, to adapt, to use the experience as he sees fit, contributing part of himself, participating in the creative discovery himself. And thus the work itself is not laden with a message, it simply is; it exists as an object in its own right. The power of modern music is based upon the exploitation of 'le domaine des *effets sans cause*': music is 'mensonge', 'massage', 'sentiment artificiel'.[25]

Valéry contrasts the effects of music to those of our imagination and real life situations. The image, or the object of the imagination, which in most arts is the starting point for the reactions, is in music a complement to the reaction; it is something which the listener contributes himself, in order to explain his own reaction:

Musique. Le phénomène construit sa *cause*, sa machine productrice – et plus avant parfois les désirs, images, émotions qui construiraient sa machine . . .
La Musique, pouvoir des *opérations inverses*. Le problème de l'auditeur est de se trouver la cause des émotions qu'il éprouve et des motions qu'il tend à fournir. Le principe de la Musique est qu'il lui est impossible de ne pas subir ces émotions et impossible de ne pas les expliquer, justifer.[26]

Music thus effects a reversal of rôles between subject and

object and suggests, in the simultaneous ability of the listener to experience the most profound feelings whilst observing, as though from outside, the experience of those feelings, a duality that clearly appealed to Valéry's analysis of the divisions within consciousness.

On me fait danser, on me fait souffler, on me fait pleurer, penser, on me fait dormir, on me fait foudroyant – foudroyé, on me fait lumière, ténèbres; diminuer jusqu'au fil.

On me fait quasi tout cela, et je ne sais si je suis le suject ou l'objet, si je danse ou si j'assiste à la danse, si je possède ou suis possédé. Je suis à la fois au plus haut de la vague et au pied d'elle qui la regarde haute. *C'est cette indétermination* qui est la clef de ce prestige.[27]

Music represents in this way an analysis of the self, or rather of the multiple self able at once to act and not act, to submit and resist: 'Entre la chose qui est ce qu'elle est, et la chose dont la fonction est d'être autre que ce qu'elle est, il y a un intermédiaire. C'est cet intermédiaire, le moyen de la musique.'[28] The act of production becomes identified with the sensation of reception. He was no doubt thinking of the importance of technique, of hand position and posture required to achieve a particular sound quality or shape to a phrase when he wrote: 'Dans la musique, l'on perçoit nettement la *liaison de la sensation avec l'acte. L'acte* producteur de la note est ressentie comme elle, et il importe dans la perception le sentiment de sa durée d'acte.'[29]

This analysis of the effect of music determines equally his conception of the goal of poetry, which is to recreate in the reader the experience of listening to music through a participation that is not passively submissive, but engages the reader in actively recreating the emotional states suggested in the work: 'En toute chose il faut trouver la *musique des actes* et elle *recontrée* – tout chante et se fait merveilleusement.'[30] It may, he recognises be more readily achieved in music because of the nature of the material of the musician and the poet, but the rôle of the artist remains identical: to seek to generate responses from within the listener or reader: 'La musique (et parfois les lettres) fait des émotions "synthétiques" au sens des chimistes. Elle fait de la tendresse et de la fureur comme on fait de l'alcool *de toutes pièces.*'[31] The responses are artificial in the sense that they are fabricated artistically, but within the experience of the recipient may come to be indistinguishable from the state of creative potentiality that gave rise to the work:

> La poésie n'est que l'état chantant. L'état de l'être qui produit naturellement le chant et l'invention du chant, – 'l'émotion' 'créatrice'. Mais en tant qu'art – c.à d. quand il s'agit de re-produire, de reproduire en autrui cet état au moyen de ses produits mêmes,
>
> il s'agit de produire en autrui par les paroles a, b, c, l'état dont l'expression est précisément a, b, c – tellement que le souvenir brut et l'émanation de soi soient indissolubles – indiscernables.[32]

It is possible to see in the concept of the creative participation of the reader in the act of production a means by which the idea of total ambiguity or polyvalence of meaning may be limited or to some extent mediated between writer and reader and between one reader and another; and thereby the central paradox between expressive communication and formal purity may be partially resolved.[33] For the concept of ambiguity does not imply complete indeterminancy, or else communication would be impossible. The ambiguity is generated through the multiple responses possible and will certainly vary from one reader to another; but Valéry does not propose total randomness of response: the responses are controlled by Valéry's intellect through a verbal music that seeks to suppress the intellect of the reader. The reader must in a sense submit to the will of the artist and join in a discovery that leads ultimately to the self – 'car on ne peut connaître des choses sans se connaître'[34] – to the point at which, perhaps, if successful, the poetic voice and the self of the reader are at one.[35]

In 'Piano et Chant' the feelings which the music provokes in the listener are as real and as intense as those 'qu'une âme agitée par la vie est capable de former d'elle-même.' Valéry recognises that the justification is the listener's and that the music itself 'n'exprime rien mais nous place dans l'état où il faudrait exprimer. Crée le besoin d'exprimer ou d'agir.'[36] Valéry here seems to move towards the attitude of modern composers such as Stravinsky and Hindemith who, in denying all spurious feelings of sentimentality in music, have tended to deny that music expresses anything at all. Stravinsky categorically asserts that 'if, as is nearly always the case, music appears to express something, this is only an illusion and not a reality'.[37] While Hindemith says 'The reactions which music evokes are not feelings, but they are the images, memories of feelings.'[38] But Valéry is also careful to distinguish between music and poetry: 'La musique peut agir sur *le souvenir* et la poésie sur *les souvenirs*.'[39] The capacity of music to express the image or the memory of a feeling is almost formal, acting upon 'la forme de la mémoire, en tant que le *seul fait de se souvenir* est affectif'.[40] Language is both more specific and more variable: the material which the poet uses to prompt the creative participation of the reader is laden with representational images at once too direct and too uncontrollable.

L'art donne: ou bien une représentation de chose ou bien une production de l'état où la chose place un homme.
    Or en littérature cette *production* est contrainte de se servir des *mots*: c.à d. des moyens plus spécialement appropriés à donner des *représentations*. On usera donc de ce qui dans les mots et les effets de mots est actif, non tant représentatif, – leur son, figure. Mais ce sont des chances *rares*.[41]

In an attempt to extend his understanding of musical expression Valéry made a few tentative explorations into the realms of psychology and the functioning of the central nervous system. He recognised the importance of these aspects and pursued his investigations independently, although at the same time scientists were studying the unconscious processes of the mind, while certain musicians were intuitively exploring the same area.

The parallel between scientist and artist may be seen in the case of Freud and the non-tonal music of Schoenberg during the period of *Erwartung*, each of them separately uncovering the notion of the unconscious. Donald Mitchell makes the point that, having abandoned tonality and its subconsciously functioning sense of form 'Schoenberg had only his Unconscious to look to as a potential source of the means and principles of unity and organisation which could replace the lost paradise of tonality.'[42] In fact Valéry's notes in the *Cahiers* at the beginning of the century anticipate the direction that music was to take.

> Du moment que R W [Wagner] a organisé les moyens d'agir ad libitum sur le système nerveux général par sa musique sans inertie – c.à d. où les changements s'introduisent indépendamment les uns des autres (entrées de timbres, modes, etc.) comme dans un système vivant – il faut aller plus loin et faire de cette musique, le langage, un langage du syst. nerveux –
> Car il n'y a pas de raison a priori, pour que ce système soit mieux exprimé par les mots d'un traité de philosophie ou les équations d'un traité d'analyse que par l'ensemble de sons et des *opérations* de ce groupe.[43]

Wagner's ability to do this depended, according to Valéry, upon his exploration of the psychology of each of his characters, delving into the darker side of man's nature:

> Certains coins dans Wagner, traînements rauques, et profondeurs renfrognées où grognent d'informes mystères, des mystères pour le mystère . . . Engendrement sourd de menaces et d'enigmes et de doutes. Et il y a un mystérieux en soi – un menaçant, inférieur, incommensurable état de l'être.[44]

He attributes to Wagner a method which is similar to his own theory of 'le moi pur': by searching deep within his own self Wagner reached a point of generality from which all kinds of psychological developments were possible:

> Wagner a . . . occupé le point stratégique de l'être. Il place toujours sa composition sur le Moi, sur un point tel que tous les possibles et probables sont disponibles, et avec leur perspective toujours actuelle. Il est le seul.
> De là, il ouvre et ferme à volonté toutes émotions, passé, futur, entrailles, lueurs –
> Quant aux choses, lieux, il les peint par leurs effets.[45]

In addition to the theory of ambiguity and the exploration of the unconscious, Valéry also seeks to explain the effects of music by a more mechanistic psychology. He attempts to establish a model for the functioning of a system in terms similar to electrical or chemical charges, with forces of energy translated into 'mimiques auditivo-motrices' and thence into musical phrases.[46] Music, he says, stimulates internal reflexes through the ear, which are identical to those stimulated by other means:

Chaque excitation partielle ayant été isolée et représentée, et à chacune correspondant un moyen défini de la produire, et à ce moyen un symbole, on a substitué à l'ensemble confus des bruits, un ensemble énuméré, ordonné et rendu maniable. Ce qui a permis de former des combinaisons. Alors l'acte du musicien est devenu comparable à la pratique du Duchenne de Boulogne d'exciter électriquement et directement les muscles de la face, tantôt reproduisant des physionomies *réelles*, sur le visage du malade, tantôt formant des combinaisons non réalisables par le jeu ordinaire des émotions.[47]

While such ideas have been studied scientifically both in terms of clinical research and behaviourist psychology, the ideas remain at a fairly general level in the *Cahiers* without any attempt to link the 'excitation partielle' or the 'mimique auditivo-motrice' to particular musical phrases or effects. As such it remains one of the possible applications of Valéry's theory of functions, rather than throwing any particular light on the creation of musical responses. On the other hand, Valéry's understanding of music's essential ambiguity and his exploration of the unconscious does show considerable insight into the way that musical effects are achieved and reflects a contemporary attitude that links his aesthetics firmly to those of twentieth-century composers.

While Valéry envied the emotional power of music, he felt a constant need to refuse its effect upon him. Although showing an extremely sensitive reaction, he tends, as in 'Piano et Chant', to stand outside the music and observe the effects upon himself and others. This emerges even more clearly in *La Soirée avec Monsieur Teste*: there is no account at all of the music played at the opera, but the narrator describes the audience and looks at the way they react. He associates with Teste's scornful comments on their lack of self-consciousness: ' "Qu'ils jouissent et obéissent!''. . . . La stupidité de tous les autres nous révélait qu'il se passait n'importe quoi de sublime.'[48]

The very power of music is reason enough for him to reject it:

la musique m'ennuie au bout d'un peu de temps, et d'autant plus court qu'elle a plus d'action sur moi.[49]

The vexation to which he often refers is explained to a certain extent by the rapidity of the different suggestions, the mood of the music changing before he has fully exhausted the possibilities of the previous passage, as these suggestions tend to lead his mind away from the music:

il est impossible d'écouter en entier un morceau de musique car si le dixième note (ajoutée aux 9 autres) – me dit quelque chose, je perds le onzième.[50]

But there is more to Valéry's objection than the 'ennui' of not being able to keep up; it is rather because he cannot under any circumstances make any retort and take up a dialogue with the music: he is forced to submit to the experience, to give himself over to an 'alien' force. 'Je ne puis supporter de prévoir, de subir sans répondre – de ne pas prendre l'initiative', a reaction which he feels towards both music and poetry: 'Je ne les aime que par fragments précieux – modèles.'[51] It is the sheer intensity of the experience which he comes to reject:

Mon 'injustice' à l'égard de la Musique vient peut-être du sentiment que de telles puissances sont capables de faire vivre jusqu'à l'absurde.[52]

When Valéry is listening to music he is aware of the different reactions that are stimulated and thereby confirms ultimately his own self-awareness: he sees his own consciousness distinct from the varying sensations. Describing one such experience he says:

Je me suis détaché de ma forme assise ... Je me suis laissé, les mains sur les genoux et la tête penchée; quitté; divisé; me suis senti voisin de moi ... Ce n'est plus là de la *pensée*; mais une expérience et aussi un *exercice incomparable* de *présence* et *absence*.[53]

In his view it is this heightened sensation of consciousness which is the only sure guarantee of his individual self and must be jealously protected:

Temps – considère un morceau de musique. Il y a des sons filés, des sons détachés, des silences, des trilles – du côté *Moi*, il y a des attentions, des rythmes, des attentes, des surprises – et il y a une certaine *conservation qu'il faut que j'attribue* à quelque chose. Ce peut être le sentiment de la possibilité de pousser à autre chose; – ou bien quelque sensation de mon dos appuyé; – ou bien une fatigue – Mais quoique

ce soit, cet élément de présence sensible et d'écart (étranger au sentiment de développement 'en moi' de valeurs excitées par la musique
entendue) a la propriété de conduire à la possession de tout mon possible – de *Moi*.[54]

The rejection of music is formulated then in a number of
ways: an assertion of moderation over excess, of reason over
instinct and irrationality; he heaps unfavourable comments
upon music – 'vomissement, flux, grincement d'un canif sur
une vitre' – and associates it with 'ce trompeur: le sentiment'.[55]
He attempts to reduce music to a mechanistic psychology
and constantly attempts to detach himself from the experience. But the variety and intensity of his attacks are in themselves testimony to his regard for and fear of music. He realises that reason alone cannot dominate the powerful influences
nor master what could be called his fatal attraction towards it.

Nous n'avons plus la force de nous maintenir *toujours* et *toujours* dans
le domaine de l'Articulé. Cette faiblesse = la puissance de la musique.[56]

The attraction towards music, springing from within himself,
is too overpowering in itself and will not be driven out by
conscious control:

Musique très belle tu élèves ma haine et mon envie. Je sais que tu mens
et pourtant je te suis. Tu fais semblant de savoir, de tenir – tu recrées,
tu formes et reformes – et je sais que tu ignores et tu émeus comme si
tu conduisais au secret.[57]

As Monsieur Teste realises, the power of music is like that
of physical pain, intense and threatening to consciousness, an
expression of what E. Sewell has called 'the deeps of the
body'.[58] If pain could be isolated from consciousness then it
might be studied in order to reveal '[une] connaissance de
l'ordre de celle que nous trouvons dans la musique':

La douleur est chose très musicale, on peut presque en parler en termes
de musique. Il y a des douleurs graves et d'aiguës, des andante et des
furioso, des notes prolongées, points d'orgue, et des arpèges, des progressions – de brusques silences, etc. . . .[59]

Sewell has perceptively demonstrated the importance of the
very personal and physical qualities that underlie even
Amphion's construction of a temple by the power of music.
Beneath 'Olympian control and beauty in the world of things

made perfect by the operation of music and architecture in the constructive mind . . . there is an undertone to [the] classical harmony, a different and deep-sea current'.[60] This force is there at the end of the melodrama as a female figure barring Amphion's entry to the temple just as he is about to enjoy the full triumph of his creation; the important movement is conveyed in Valéry's final stage direction:

> Amphion recule. La forme voilée le saisit et l'enveloppe avec tendresse, lui prend doucement la Lyre sur laquelle elle fait entendre quelques notes profondes, et qu'elle jette ensuite dans la fontaine.
> Amphion cache son visage dans le sein de cette figure qui est l'Amour ou la Mort, et se laisse entraîner par elle, cependant que l'orchestre se réduit à un chant très suave, sombre et comme intime.[61]

Amphion is unable, because of his own mortal and sensual nature, to become his own creation: divinity is denied man because of his very humanity.

Essentially the struggle is located within one person, as can be seen from the versions of the myth of Orphée and Eurydice planned in the *Cahiers*.[62] Though the tension between 'esprit' and 'amour' is given dramatic form, the real conflict is in Orphée himself; Eurydice dies and the image of her which he has created himself has a stronger power than the real woman. Indeed he willingly sacrifices her, since the human, bodily love she represents is an obstacle to the struggle for knowledge. In Gidian fashion he rejects the easier path of a wordly happiness that is all too readily within his grasp: 'Recherche du "bonheur" – preuve de médiocrité.'[63] Instead he calls the infernal gods down on Eurydice, causing her death, choosing 'esprit' before 'amour' and leaving himself free to confront 'Les Enfers (qui sont spirituels)', 'Les Enfers qui sont en nous'. Orphée descends into his own Hades, struggling between the 'connaissance' and 'volupté' that are within him; but as a musician he transforms this experience and the song which emerges is a tragic moving expression of the whole being:

l'opération qui consiste à tirer de ma douleur un chant magnifique – Cette douleur stupide a conduit mon sens à des extrêmes de détresse, et de ténèbres et de furie impuissante.
Mais depuis que je n'y suis pas demeuré, puisque je suis remonté

des enfers pour pouvoir y redescendre, j'ai appris du moins la continuité de cette chaîne de tourments, d'espoirs et de catastrophes, et donc comment le plus haut au plus bas se relie, toute la modulation de l'être, et la conservation de la vie entre les bornes qu'elle ne peut franchir. – C'est là *le chant*, le registre. Et la mesure de cet intervalle qui est vivre a plusieurs unités qui sont rythmes.[64]

2

MUSIC AS A LANGUAGE OF THE MIND

La grandiose musique est l'écriture de l'homme complet.

IV, 1910, p. 406.

Traiter musicalement les choses de l'intelligence – mais au fond n'est-ce pas faire *travailler* et comme *sonner* toutes les parties du discours.

IX, 1924, p. 742.

The idea of music as the most complete of all arts, as that which is capable of encompassing within it the effects of all the others, was taken up initially by Valéry from Wagner's concept of total art. For Wagner, the 'art work of the future' was to be achieved by the combination of art-forms within opera; each element would fulfil a different rôle so that, for example, words would convey intellectual understanding and hint at the deep meaning through poetic suggestion, while music would give clear expression to all the areas of feeling which words could not convey.[1]

The particular interpretation given by Valéry went much further: instead of ascribing separate rôles to each of the components, his approach was to look at music, as a whole, as a reflection of man's mental and affective states. And thus all forms of music, including purely instrumental music, may represent the process and form of thought:

[la musique] va parfois jusqu'à l'insinuation, sinon de l'intelligence même, du moins de ses actes.[2]

Comment décrire ce fond si variable et sans référence – qui a les rapports les plus importants, mais les plus instables, avec 'la pensée'. La musique seule en est capable.[3]

As such music becomes the most powerful medium, able to convey, in a way that words are unable to, the forms and structures of consciousness.

The idea of the completeness of music is to be found in Valéry's increasing interest in the works of seventeenth- and eighteenth-century composers and in the analogies he draws between the formal structures of these works and the formal processes of thought. It is therefore with these two issues that this chapter will be concerned, in order to identify firstly Valéry's interpretation of the principle of classicism, and secondly the connection he establishes with the structures and patterns of thought.

Probably the greatest influence bringing Valéry to an appreciation of earlier classical music was the work of Gluck. Valéry saw the operas performed many times and found not only the portrayal of love and of his favourite Orpheus theme, but also a marriage of realism and mythology. The nature of the subject and the more noticeable formal structure serve to place the work at one remove from everyday life and 'accidental' occurrences, and thereby intensify the effect in Valéry's eyes. In a note on a performance of *Iphigénie en Tauride* in June 1931 one finds some of the key words which explain Valéry's conception of classicism.

Et voilà le 'beau' à l'état pur (du moins les deux premiers actes) . . .
Amitié 'classique'
Ainsi la simplicité – atteinte, sublime du *faut*, je veux dire du voulu.
'De l'action volontaire dans les arts'
La musique place le tout hors du vrai et du faux, isole le drame, de l'expérience.[4]

By the simplicity and the clarity of the plot and musical style Gluck was seeking to create a greater generality than might be achieved by anecdotal plots or diverting operettas. Indeed the further music is able to move from direct representation and the greater the element of ceremony and abstract development involved, the greater the attraction which Valéry finds.

Valéry's reaction to Rameau's Mass, which he heard at the funeral of Forain,[5] is a clear example of this understanding of classicism. He identifies the lack of realistic presentation and proceeds to equate the abstract qualities of the work with a symbolic effect:

Music as a language of the mind

C'est décidément ce type *messe* qu'il serait intéressant de reprendre. Invention progressive remarquable, et en somme le théâtre le plus digne – le moins naïf le moins réaliste, le moins embarrassé de *ficelles* et d'*individus*, où il n'y a point d'ambiguïté sur le vrai et le faux, où le sérieux est possible.

Ceci soupçonné par Wagner et totalement manqué dans Parsifal – qui est une singerie et une mixture (Avec sublime musique) –
Messe de Rameau. Modèle admirable. 3 voix. Mais sans musique, que faire?
– L'action symbolique – c.à d. à chaque instant plus générale que l'incident.
répondant à chaque phase autant à l'état qu'au sujet ou thème.[6]

It is evident too that the symbolic effect lies in the internal structure of the work, in the effects created by the parts upon each other. As Valéry says in enigmatic form of Mozart's Symphony in G, the intention is less to signify, than to demonstrate the responses provoked within the work in terms of subject, counter-subject, repetition, variation etc: 'Ne rien *dire* . . . Mais le dire si bien – ou plutôt, dire seulement tout ce qui est autour du dire même. Les temps subtils, les reprises, coups d'œil. Les fonds et les directions. Les commencements de . . . Parfois des ombres de phrases.'[7]

Along with Mozart, Bach comes to epitomize for Valéry a purity which is defined in terms of the abstraction of the work:

| Bach | Brahms | plus on sera musicien, plus on |
| Mozart | Wagner | préférera les premiers.[8] |

Though apparently making no allowance for differences in musical temperament, this comment, made in 1920, does reflect both Valéry's emphasis upon the formal construction of works and his acquaintance with practising musicians. While the friends of his youth were Wagnerians and mainly literary people, the musicians he met and from whom he gained a more technical knowledge did tend on the whole to prefer the earlier classical music. His subsequent friendship with Stravinsky and Nadia Boulanger strengthened this idea. Boulanger's classes on Bach confirmed the notion of music as the resolution in act of a series of problems. Bach's music is called 'intrinsic' by Valéry, a word which he uses synonymously for the more ambiguous 'pure'. Music is the actual working out of the problem it creates itself, and is thus a representation of consciousness itself, of 'le Moi le plus général'.[9] 'Pas d'ombres. Pas de sentiment, pas de mystère, autre que celui (qui est le suprême) de l'existence par soi.'[10]

One work which Valéry singles out is Bach's Orchestral Suite in D major, the 'miraculeuse Suite en Ré majeur' referring no doubt to no. 3.

Exemple *adorable*, où je n'entends ni melos, ni pathos, ni rien qui soit . . . *réel*, qui ne se développe qu'en soi-même . . . Intensité de pureté. Nul emprunt au cœur, ni au hasard heureux, ni à moi, ni au passé – Quel présent! Exemple adorable. Action en soi, qui semble à l'infini de tout objet, pure de tout dessein, volonté isolée, acte pur.[11]

Suite en ré majeur. Chose sans prix. Donnant l'idée de l'exploitation totale formelle fermée d'un possible tout commensurable.
La basse représente l'attention.[12]

Valéry here points to the harmonic function of the bass which indicates movement and expectation in relation to the tonic key. The impact of the Suite and the Cantatas lies in the exploration of developments and contrasts to the theme, some of which are merely hinted at, and the way in which all these possibilities are worked together.

Un pas de plus *dans le possible*, et la figure est fermée, avec certitude, nécessité, élégance, signification à la fois 'universelle' et intime.
Si au sentiment particulier qui se propose (par un thème ou amorce de thème) on adjoint le groupe (ou le pressentiment ou soupçon ou *dessous* du groupe) de possibles du même domaine, on généralise, par cette symétrie suggérée, le dessin prononcé, et on fait ainsi participer tout l'être à l'*attention de l'ouvrage*.[13]

Bach's work, with its capacity to 'émouvoir par des formes' represented for Valéry an ideal towards which literature can only aspire.

Une œuvre de musique absolument pure, une composition de Sébastien Bach, par exemple, qui n'emprunte rien au sentiment, mais qui construit *un sentiment sans modèle*, et dont la beauté consiste dans ses combinaisons, dans l'édification d'un ordre intuitif séparé, est une acquisition inestimable, une immense valeur tirée du néant.[14]

Valéry recognised also that similar principles could be found in much modern music, and particularly in the way that it creates a self-contained world with its own logic.

Dans cette musique 'moderne' rien n'est banal, et tout est insignifiant.[15]

It is clear that Valéry was aware of these preoccupations not only in someone as evidently neo-classical as Stravinsky, but also in composers such as Debussy and Ravel. In fact Valéry first met Debussy at a time when he was engaged in composing his first String Quartet and planning the second and a Violin Sonata (1893–4). As Lockspeiser comments:

We see that he was . . . drawn to the idea of pure music at the very time when he was engaged on his most important works issuing from the symbolist aesthetic, *L'Après-midi d'un faune*, the *Proses Lyriques*, and an early form of the *Nocturnes*.[16]

In 1915 Debussy told Stravinsky that he considered his own recently finished *Etudes* and sonatas to be illustrations of pure music; and certain aspects of his later style can be seen to contribute to the neo-classical movement of the 1920s which claimed to be anti-Debussian in essence. The point is not only a warning against the too rigid division of art into opposing schools, but more specifically demonstrates that the concept of purity is entirely compatible with a refined view of the suggestive power of the symbol.

The comparison with Ravel is perhaps even more striking. In 1932 Valéry qualified not only Bach but Ravel as a 'musicien pur'.[17] The purity which Valéry developed out of symbolism is paralleled by the rigour which Ravel sought to introduce into his musical explorations of the sensibility. His music gives the impression of a man writing down his dreams in a fully awakened state, as Roland-Manuel has observed, quoting from *L'Ame et la Danse*: 'Une rêve de vigilance et de tension que ferait la Raison elle-même! . . . Rêve, rêve, mais rêve tout pénétré de symétries, tout ordre, tout actes et séquences!'[18] He describes a feature of Ravel which is immediately relevant to Valéry:

Il veut avant tout produire un effet sans laisser deviner son industrie. Il s'abstiendra donc de paraître dans son œuvre, de s'interposer entre elle et nous.

Roland-Manuel argues that Ravel and Stravinsky see no distinction between the aesthetic and the functional aspects of music, and illustrates his point with a passage from *Eupalinos*:

Ravel et Stravinsky se plaisent l'un et l'autre à confondre le *beau* et l'*utile*. Sensibles avant tout à cette espèce de volupté qui naît de 'la conformité presque miraculeuse d'un object avec la fonction qu'il doit remplir . . . Rien, dans ces heureuses fabrications, rien ne figure que d'utile: elles ne retiennent plus rien qui ne soit uniquement déduit des exigences de l'effet à obtenir.'[19]

The similarities between Ravel and Valéry are great in terms of their temperament and intellectual rigour and their approach towards composition. Though their contact was not extensive, it is possible to see that each, within a common cultural background, arrived independently at a fairly similar position. Both placed great emphasis on the formal structures as part of the process of composition, and saw it as a matter of organising blocks or balancing sections one against another. Valéry remarks that if he needed a green to balance the composition of colours in a painting, he would put in a tree, for example, or a hill if he needed a curve;[20] Ansermet says similarly of Ravel, 'on voit qu'il cherche des effets de couleur, ou de comique, ou de pittoresque, alors qu'il évalue des volumes, des poids ou des densités'.[21] Such an approach demands a subtle mixture of freedom and constraint. The search for freedom led to the exploration of new orchestral timbres and a liberation from strict classical harmonic progressions with the use of the 9th, 11th and 13th intervals in chords. But the freedom was not total and at this stage of musical history could not have been.[22]

While Valéry and Ravel were concerned to explore through poetic imagery or through timbre and harmony a subtle albeit wide range of feelings, they recognised above all the need to control and order these sensations. In music the pure sounds must be classified to provide a set of reference points, beginning with the scale and leading on to the conventions of musical forms: 'On construit un *réseau* conventionnel permettant de définir un son quelconque de l'ensemble: c'est la gamme.'[23]

The classical principle acquires therefore for Valéry a significance which is not restricted to a particular moment in history, but which is expressed rather by an attitude or an approach such as he identifies in Greek art:

le grec cherchant à rejoindre *la beauté*, c'est-à-dire à donner une forme aux choses qui fît songer à l'ordre universel, à la sagesse divine, à la domination par l'intellect, toutes choses qui n'existent pas dans la nature proche, tangible, donnée, toute faite *d'accidents*.[24]

Music that is constructed according to this principle is all the more complete according to Valéry because it reflects all aspects of man's mental and affective states: 'la musique excitant général par l'ouïe d'un clavier nerveux presque complet – suscitant l'attente et la hâte ad lib. pressant, retardant, suspendant . . .'[25]

For Valéry music is particularly suited to convey an image of the mind because it presents not the content of thought but the pattern or form of thinking.

La Musique peint les changements de la connaissance, et non la connaissance même, et elle les peint mêlés aux changements de l'être et sans distinguer les uns des autres.[26]

As such it has a more generalised significance of the kind he sought to express in his own notes.

la musique telle qu'elle est constituée maintenant dans sa puissance et sa liberté – sera peut-être aux mains de quelque grand individu – le moyen par excellence d'expression pure, 'elle' qui permet de simuler et imposer tout ce que la littérature ne peut que désigner – toutes les feintes et démarches réelles du penser, retours, symétries, tendances vers – durées nulles, absences, spontanéité, attentes, surprises, niaiserie, éclairs.[27]

The idea of purity is particularly important for it is because 'la musique est le plus puissant engin à exciter le possible pur',[28] that its structure can demonstrate intellectual processes.

Valéry recognises that the most perfect works, like those of Bach, may appear inhuman if thought of as 'un enchaînement de théorèmes'.[29] But he does not identify intellectuality with inhumanity; for, on the contrary, by animating the formulae of thought, music is able to bring to life the patterns of feeling and thinking:

la musique donne *valeurs* c.à d. existence à des formations qui seraient vaines sans elle et tout arbitraires. Elle fait vivre des schémas.
Elle joue le rôle de la forme et des forces – ou plutôt de la liaison ou identité des choses.
Et cela se voit bien dans la musique des vers.[30]

The relationship between music and the mind may be further qualified in particular areas. Repetition, for example, which is an important feature of music satisfying certain demands of the sensibility, may in certain cases be 'contre-pensée': strict regular repetition can hold no interest to the inquiring mind constantly reducing what has been grasped and searching for the new.

Répétition
Mathématiques et Musique – qu'on rapproche souvent – dans le vague – sont en opposition en ceci que la mathématique est pour une grande partie de son affaire un art d'*économiser*, et comme de *résorber la répétition*, de substituer un *petit nombre* d'opérations à un grand ou à une infinité. Tandis que la Musique vit, en grande partie, de répétitions plus ou moins variées, mais reconnaissables.[31]

But if exact repetition is contrary to the working of the mind, varied repetition is not:

la répét. irrégulière *est au contraire la pensée même*, qui consiste dans son état supérieur, dans un ensemble de transformations intérieures conservant indépendance.[32]

The mind is an instrument which, when presented with something familiar, will pass quickly to the underlying structure, reducing it to a formula and thereby fulfilling its instinctive tendency to 'épuiser'. But while the content of thought will be reduced, as a static element, the mental processes themselves form 'un ensemble de transformations intérieures' undergoing constant modification:

ce qu'il y a d'excitant dans les idées n'est pas idées
c'est ce qui n'est pas. . pensée, ce qui est naissant et non né, qui excite.

and thus for poetry:

Il faut des mots avec lesquels on n'en puisse jamais finir – qui ne sont jamais identiquement annulés par une représentation quelconque, des mots musique.[33]

The mind, therefore, exists as an energy system perceived through the relationships and transformations from one state to another. The problem for Valéry was to find a way of expressing 'la suite et la *connexité dans le successif* des phénomènes conscients, leurs liaisons dans l'instant'.[34] He attempted to relate it to non-euclidian geometry, to the theory of groups and to Gibbs' theory of phases,[35] but the example of music was constantly present as a demonstration of the relationships in action.

Accomodation. Attention. Gibbs.

. . . la tentation de faire une théorie des *phases* – c.à d. des transformations sensitivo-mentales dans lesquelles le système vivant-sentant-
pensant peut se ragarder comme un syst. isolable. . . . Je voyais alors
[19101] le rêve, l'attention, l'action comme des *phases* entre lesquelles
des passages brusques ou modulés.

Ici, *rôle de la musique de Wagner.*

Prodigieux enregistreur des modifications, qui me semblait avoir travaillé pr moi et avoir eu la 'génie' de percevoir nettement en lui ces
variations des valeurs et fonctions cardinales, et de *produire* les moyens,
les excitants de l'ouïe qui reconstituent les états en question par une
sorte de *mimétisme* ou de mimique irrésistible.

Wagner me faisait *entendre* (*qui est vivre*) ce que je voyais ou
modelais de mes quasi sensations motrices, cette suite de modifications
– le long d'une durée – en équilibre réversible avec???[36]

Valéry refers also to the example of fugue, a formal construction in which the important feature is not so much the fugue
subject, often quite inexpressive, as the way in which it is
built into a larger construction with counter-subject, inter-
woven lines, balance of sections and large-scale symmetry.
The balance and tension between the various lines gives the
effect of movement and expectation:

Une notion comme celle de la fugue, est une lumière pour l'étude et la
représentation d'un esprit.
C'est, en somme, la musique qui a découvert le problème ignoré encore
des 'psychologies' des croisements de mouvements de l'esprit, des correspondances croisées, – de la pluralité des thèmes.[37]

Though particularly evident in fugue, the concept of 'la
suite' is present to a greater or lesser degree in all music. In
fact, comments Valéry, 'le moderne ne perçoit plus les suites
que dans la musique.'[38] Each element in music is part of
larger sections which are simultaneously implied; a single
note which is part of a melodic phrase suggests to the listener
how that phrase may develop in the immediate future:

Celui qui perçoit 'tout ce qu'il y a' dans une note ou un accord – peut
en déduire une *nécessité actuelle* – cette fois – unique – une suite
comme rigoureuse – comme suite par *complémentaires.*[39]

The development of the phrase will then either confirm or
deny the listener's prediction. The importance of the notion

of 'la suite' is that it places the possible developments firmly within the context of the material – notes, phrases, time values, rhythms, harmonies – present so far. 'La suite' is therefore closely associated with 'l'attente', the expectation provoked by the internal organisation of the material: 'la modif.[-ication] de cette attente est le commencement de la suite'.[40]

Chaque phase a sa gamme.
Je veux dire que chaque instant se trouve nécessairement pourvu d'un système d'*attentes*, – avec des *tons* et des contrastes – des harmoniques.[41]

'La gamme' implies the organisation of each of the possible 'éléments purs' into a system of reference points which forms the 'réseau conventionnel' of classical music. It is this idea that explains Valéry's remark in a letter to Albert Coste in 1915 and which he develops at the same time in the *Cahiers* as:

Essayer de construire la gamme et le système d'accords dont la pensée sera la musique. Ceci est gladiator même.
Comme l'ensemble des sons est dérivé de l'ensemble des bruits, les idées nettes le sont du *rêve*.[42]

The idea is expressed again with specific reference to a work of literature:

Sonorité   Mots
la sonorité – qualité de certains musiciens – a pour analogue dans le style le mode d'écrire qui fait sentir que chaque mot *travaille*.
   Ce qui conduit à penser que le bon écrivain a conscience de chaque mot et de ses harmoniques, et donc possède une classification ou gamme cachée, – il ne saurait la construire. Et cette gamme des mots, gamme d'éléments à plusieurs caractères ou variables est le guide, et aussi le but caché de son ouvrage.[43]

Thus it is evident that Valéry's formalism represents an attempt at the ordering and structuring of essentially non-specific material – 'dénué de toute référence et de toute fonction de signe' – in order precisely to extend the range of expression. In the same way, Valéry writes to Coste, the organisation of sounds into scales did not impose finite limits upon musical ideas, but presented the opportunity 'de les multiplier, de les enrichir, d'ajouter toute la richesse formelle à ces heureux hasards isolés du début [de l'histoire musicale]'.[44] In these formalist terms a work will present its own logic and time patterns rather than following a strictly chronological development, which is in fact a procedure adopted in *La Jeune Parque*:

Ainsi réduite à elle-même, la suite de nos sensations n'a plus d'ordre chronologique, mais une sorte d'ordre intrinsèque et instantané qui se déclare de proche en proche . . . il suffit de songer aux productions que l'on groupe sous le nom général d'*Ornement*, ou bien à la *musique pure*, pour m'entendre . . . Par là, *il n'y a jamais confusion possible de l'effet de l'œuvre avec les apparences d'une vie étrangère; mais bien communion possible avec les ressorts profonds de toute vie.*[45]

Music is able to create a state in the listener and capture his attention as it proceeds to effect transformations in his mental and affective substance. In order to perceive the succession of phrases and their internal organisation the listener depends upon his memory and sense of form, develops in fact a second level of awareness separate from his immediate reactions. By a 'division de soi-même' similar to that required in the analysis of one's own thought-processes, the listener is able to identify the various developments and transformations of a piece of music, so that the continual movement acquires in retrospect a solid form.

Using another analogy, Valéry identifies the organisation of form in music as an essentially architectural activity.

Même dans les pièces les plus légères, il faut songer à la durée – c'est-à-dire à la *mémoire*, c'est-à-dire à la *forme*, comme les constructeurs de flèches et de tours songent à la structure.[46]

In music and architecture the accommodation between form and content is achieved all the more exactly because 'il n'y a pas réalité à singer'.[47] A great architectural work can be simultaneously decorative and functional; architecture becomes 'une peinture des propriétés dynamiques et statistiques de l'espace'.[48] Similarly, Valéry argues, music should neither follow an empty formal arrangement nor be dominated by a 'programme' (whether of drama, ballet, narrative or description). The form of the work *is* its argument, and those with no technical knowledge of music can nevertheless appreciate something of this because, as Deryck Cooke says, 'the form is apprehended as an emotional shape'.[49]

The links between the two arts are developed especially in 'Histoire d'Amphion'. What Valéry finds particularly compelling is their ability to impose intelligible forms on the medium of stone or sound-waves by the application of almost algebraic calculations and create effects that may be physically overwhelming: man is enveloped in a work built by man that is all the more complete because it satisfies his intellect, his emotions and his senses.

Musique et architecture sont les deux arts qui enveloppent notre personnage; leur accord donne ce qu'on peut faire de plus complet et de plus physiquement majestueux – Celle-ci paraissant la voix de celle-là.[50]

Transposed into the area of poetry, this approach demands from the poet an architectural skill of combination in placing the words and phrases so as to build a whole structure with shape and internal rhythm. As Socrate explains, 'il faut donc ajuster ces paroles complexes comme des blocs irréguliers, spéculer sur la chance et les surprises que les arrangements de cette sorte nous réservent'.[51] It is ultimately the idea of a sufficiently pure language which gives hope for the development of a language of the intellect and even for a poetry of comparable status.

L'esprit et le verbe sont presque synonymes dans bien des emplois. Le terme qui se traduit par *verbe* dans la Vulgate, c'est le grec 'logos' qui veut dire à la fois *calcul, raisonnement, parole, discours, connaissance,* en même temps qu'expression.[52]

The development of a more complete view of music as an art form and as an exercise of composition is characterised therefore by Valéry's increasing interest in music based upon classical ideals, epitomised essentially by an extention of interest from Wagner to Bach. In Wagner's music everything is spelt out more obviously, at greater length, and the suggestions of the music are made more explicit through the dramatic settings. In Bach, Valéry found a completeness less overwhelming and more in tune with his own sensibility. Bach's music communicates in concise, formal statements full of suggestion and possibility 'à l'état implexe'; and it is in this classical concept of completeness, of unity of form and meaning, of concision and suggestiveness that one finds the closest identity to Valéry's poetic ideals and practice. It is however noticeable that his developing appreciation of Bach was never to the detriment of Wagner, and he sought to unite them where others sought to oppose them:

Comme on opposait, selon l'usage, Bach / Wagner je dis comment on pouvait considérer un passage de l'un à l'autre. W. faisant une représentation de l'homme organico ou neuro psychique complet, Bach développant *insolitement* des systèmes de possibilités complets – à l'état implexe dans l'h. [homme] complet.[53]

The links between Valéry's poetry and music of classical conception is most clearly expressed by the notion of 'sensibilité intellectuelle'. The poetry and the music both reveal an emotional vibrancy which is thoroughly integrated into the structural conception of the work: the formal preoccupations allow the emotional release while the abstract patterns themselves take on emotional significance. Thus his own poems are not allegories of states of mind, they are a direct portrayal of the working of the mind and its affective states; they are concerned with

ce qu'il y a d'amour, de jalousie, de piété, de désir, de jouissance, de courage, d'amertume, d'avarice, de luxure dans les choses de l'intelligence.[54]

When he longs to recreate in poetry the effects of music, it is to evoke 'le mouvement de l'âme . . . dans une infinité de combinaisons':

Oh! faire une phrase longue en vers avec le modelé de la musique à inflexions suivant à la trace les changements de l'être voilé, sans arrêts du mouvement jusqu'à la fin, comprenant surprises éveils, retours, reprises, – tableau de la pensée même quel que soit l'objet.[55]

The poetic quality to which he aspires is analogous to 'ce que les chanteurs entendent par *placer la voix*' ('to sing using the natural tonal qualities of the voice'): 'Cela seul permet d'obtenir cette possession qui suppose le développement complet d'un esprit – et passe de l'abstrait pur au sensible, garde ce qu'il faut de liberté.'[56]

Valéry expresses the idea of music as 'l'écriture de l'homme complet' in a note which portrays the 'versant affectif' and the 'versant combinatoire' as two inter-related sides of a triangle:

Les 2 versants de la musique
La musique ns ramène à nous
L'art le plus organique – le plus corporel – plus que la danse!
L'ouïe – et les grands syst. affectifs. viscéraux.
Pathos.
Mais d'autre part l'art le plus structural – Art d'opérations –
Intuition de transformations
Paradoxe apparent d'un Art *abstrait* – fondé sur la *sensibilité générale* . . . à partir de la *sensibilité particulière auditive.*[57]

Music thus came to epitomise for Valéry the most complete expression of human aspirations and achievement; he found embodied in music all his ideals both of abstract analysis and of human love so that it could accommodate without contradiction the opposing tendencies of his own character: the tension between Eros and Noûs, and between the artist and the thinker.

3

THE THEORY OF COMPOSITION: WAGNER AND THE UNIVERSAL MIND

L'homme que j'ai envié, c'est Wagner – et non pour autre chose que pour le plaisir que j'imagine qu'il a dû avoir à construire, combiner, composer ses grandes *machines* musicales.

XVII, 1934, p. 12

The admiration for Wagner is a feature of the *Cahiers* which cannot fail to impress the reader. The music, the man and the theory of composition are aspects to which Valéry continually refers as enthusiastically in his youth as in his later years. He wrote in 1941, 'Il y a 50 ans que je ne puis me lasser de cette extraordinaire magnificence génératrice' which he found in the combinations of themes in the third act of *Die Walküre*.[1] Often his attempts to analyse the effects of music are made with reference to Wagner rather than any other musician. In the course of his collaboration with Honegger over *Sémiramis* and *Amphion* Valéry explained what he had in mind by examples from Wagner. In letters to Franz Rauhut and Gustave Samazeuil he attests to the profound influence of Wagner over his conception of art. He took issue with 'les gens qui blaguent W. et font la petite bouche'[2] and with 'ce nigaud de Ravel [qui] me dit – il y a 15 our 20 ans – que W. ne savait pas écrire pour le chant!'[3] In 1933 as in 1899 he remains enthusiastic for Wagner's achievement, as great music and as the musical equivalent of Poe and Mallarmé, demonstrating the importance of 'la méditation théorique'.[4]

And yet it has to be recognised that Wagner presents something of a problem when attempting to evaluate Valéry's own approach to artistic creation. Not only does it appear, as Duchesne-Guillemin has pointed out, that a more modern sparsely evocative music might seem more compatible with his 'frugalité intellectuelle'.[5] More seriously, Valéry ascribes to Wagner a theory of composition which is intimately connected with his own theory of the universal mind, and which is put forward as a model for his own practice. What is at issue therefore is not Valéry's musical taste, for a variety of interest can after all only add richness to artistic experience; and perhaps it is a common occurrence that the music which makes a profound impact during one's youth remains a deeply personal part of one's make-up whatever the direction of later intellectual development. It is rather certain aspects of Valéry's theory of composition, linked to Wagner and his music, which demand careful scrutiny. What does this theory of composition consist of, then, and how useful is it in an approach to Valéry's own poetic technique?

Valéry's attraction to the music of Wagner and his association with the Wagnerian friends grouped around Mallarmé in Paris led him to see the composer as the greatest musical idol, more important even than Beethoven to the romantics. No one felt they could achieve anything worthwhile which did not fall under the reflected light of the master. The extent of this admiration can be judged from the words of Camille Mauclair:

Jamais les hommes d'aujourd'hui ne pourront absolument comprendre ce que Wagner, vers 1892, a été pour nous, l'immense zone de lumière que sa magie nous ouvrit, la lame de fond qu'il souleva dans nos âmes, le terrible dégoût qu'il nous imposa pour tout ce qui n'était pas lui.[6]

Coupled with this admiration was despair, for there arose inevitably the feeling that Wagner had outstripped them, as an ideal which they could not live up to. Mallarmé's admiration for the music provoked a contrary 'défi à Wagner', an assertion of literature over music.[7] Although Mallarmé found in Wagner a confirmation of his metaphysical conception of art, a shared ambition for the work of cosmic importance fusing all the arts, there are important reservations to be made. Mallarmé undoubtedly knew Baudelaire's article on *Tannhäuser* and had been introduced to the theoretical writings of Wagner by friends such as Catulle Mendès and

Villiers de l'Isle Adam, but it was not until 1885 that the *Revue Wagnérienne* appeared and Dujardin took Mallarmé to the Lamoureux concerts where he first heard orchestral performances of Wagner; it is questionable whether he ever heard a complete operatic performance and Wagner's *Beethoven*, translated by T. de Wyzewa, though his bedside book for close on fifteen years, remained on his own admission unopened. In 'Richard Wagner, rêverie d'un poète français' (1885) Mallarmé criticises Wagner for compromising in his operas the ideal which he had expressed in his theoretical writings: the linking of 'le drame *personnel* et la musique *idéale*' is a violation of the purity of 'l'acte scénique . . . strictement allégorique . . . vide et abstrait en soi, impersonnel'.[8] The works of Wagner and the musical ambition prompt Mallarmé to assert the supremacy of the word:

ce n'est pas sonorités élémentaires par les cuivres, les cordes, les bois, indéniablement mais de l'intellectuelle parole à son apogée que doit avec plénitude et évidence, résulter, en tant que l'ensemble des rapports existant dans tout, la Musique.[9]

For the young Valéry the effect was still more overwhelming as he wrote to Gide:

Cette musique m'amènera, cela se prépare, à ne plus écrire. Déjà trop de difficultés m'arrêtaient. Narcisse a parlé dans le désert . . .
Et puis, quelle page écrite arrive à la hauteur des quelques notes qui sont le motif du *Graal*? *Hérodiade* seule en poésie française peut se lire sans trop de dégoût et de gêne.[10]

The prediction was fulfilled the following year, 1892, although it was rather an abandonment of publication than a total break with writing. Undoubtedly the impossibility of surpassing Mallarmé must have been the paramount reason. But notes written much later indicate the part played both by Wagner and by Valéry's general approach to composition at that time:

Rien ne m'a plus désespéré que la musique de Wagner. (Et je suis loin d'être le seul)
N'est-ce pas le but suprême de l'artiste – *Désespérer*!
Et celui-ci m'a donc appris quantité de choses. Il m'a désespéré autrement que Mallarmé – le dernier plus directement car son métier était plus intelligible.
Mais M. lui-même était désespéré par W.[11]

J'ai abandonné Poésie en 92 - à cause de l'impuissance où je me sentais de faire de la *composition*. Rien de plus difficile - et je n'en vois guère d'exemple. J'avais conçu un poème à organisation très composé. Mais je me suis convaincu de mon incapacité à l'exécuter ... Du point de vue que je me suis donné alors, et qui demeure le mieux - presque toute la littérature en est encore à l'état élémentaire.[12]

For Valéry had himself set the stakes very high indeed. Wagner was not only the predominant musical model, he was a nineteenth-century equivalent of da Vinci, a total vindication of his theory of the universal mind.

Wagner - donne l'impression - fantastique du 'plus grand homme possible' - c.à d. du pouvoir et savoir le plus étendu - simule secrets de la vie et de la nature - les exerce, combine
Illusionniste sans pareil - Il a le génie de l'application des forces et a fait tout ce qu'un art qui joue des connexions les plus étendues et possède intensités - redites contrastes brusques pouvait produire.[13]

Wagner was thus a proof in Valéry's eyes that the method, which had its origins in Poe and da Vinci, might after all be possible.

In many ways like any other subject that Valéry studied, music was partly a means of finding out about himself, about the way in which his reactions were provoked and about the relationship of the self to the outside world. Valéry sought to refine the analysis of the self to such an extent that he would find in his deepest self, not an understanding of the purely subjective aspects, but of the universal principles he believed to lie at the basis of every activity. In the *Introduction à la méthode de Léonard de Vinci* he puts forward the view of the universe as composed of apparently unintelligible components; among these components it is possible, given sufficient intellectual reflection, to discover the 'relations ... entre des choses dont nous échappe la loi de continuité'.[14] The mind will perceive relations that the eye at first cannot. At this point of total insight the potential of the mind is all-embracing. The most succint definition of what he envisaged by the universal mind is provided in 'Note et digression' written in 1919 as a commentary upon the earlier essay on da Vinci.

Je sentais que ce maître de ses moyens, ce possesseur du dessin, des images, du calcul, avait trouvé l'attitude centrale à partir de laquelle les entreprises de la connaissance et les opérations de l'art sont également possibles; les échanges heureux entre l'analyse et les actes singulière-ment probables.[15]

This passion was inspired in part by Edgar Allan Poe, who in his 'Philosophy of Composition' seemed to offer the possibility of an entirely calculated work of art, in which the effects would be certain and the realisation would depend solely upon the intellectual rigour of the artist during the stages of composition. Mallarmé seemed to be taking this element of intellectuality to its supreme point in a form of language of metaphysical import. But even this, formidable enough in its conception, was not enough for the young Valéry with the precocious sensation of having seen and done everything. A letter to Gide in 1891, full of vigorous expression, reveals the origins of the method and acts as a useful counterpart to the complexities with which he was to enshroud his method in later years.

J'ai galopé sur toutes les routes, crié l'appel sur toutes les horizons! Un coin de ma vie passée – inconnue à jamais à tous m'a éclairé sur le battement de la petite bête. Sensualité exaspérée! La Science m'ennuie, la forêt mystique ne m'a conduit à rien, j'ai visité le navire et la cathédrale, j'ai lu les plus merveilleux Poe, Rimbaud, Mallarmé, analysé, hélas, leurs moyens, et toujours j'ai rencontré les plus belles *illusions*, à leur point de genèse et d'enfantement. Où trouverai-je une magie plus neuve? Un secret d'être et de créer qui me surprenne?[16]

Artistic creation, seen by Valéry as an application of the analytical method, becomes a question of applying the right formulae. Theoretically at least, once the method has been elaborated, the composer/artist can apply the techniques of illusion required to create the desired effects. Wagner's supreme accomplishment for Valéry was to have formulated a theory of composition based upon a calculation of the effects upon the listener: it was a conception in direct line of descent from Poe. In his first article, 'Sur la technique littéraire', written in 1889, Valéry announced that 'la littérature est l'art de se jouer de l'âme des autres'. Poe's technique of composition is 'entièrement *a posteriori*, établie sur la psychologie de *l'auditeur*, sur la connaissance des diverses notes qu'il s'agit de faire résonner dans l'âme d'autrui'.[17] This element of consciousness in the composer was taken up when Valéry wrote to Samazeuilh and is fully equated with the Wagnerian heritage in music:

J'ai toujours médité sur la musique, à laquelle je n'entends rien, sachant à peine mes notes et ne concevant pas même les éléments de sa technique. C'est vous dire que je suis un wagnérien endurci. Rien ne m'a plus 'influencé' que l'œuvre de Richard Wagner, ou du moins certains caractères de cette œuvre. Telle que je la vois, elle m'apparaît la seule entreprise dans l'art moderne qui conserve l'équilibre des facultés diverses à exciter dans l'homme, et qui en exige la connaissance ou l'instinct dans l'auteur.[18]

One can imagine Valéry's enthusiasm when he read in Wagner's autobiography that *Tristan* was a kind of 'cocktail' of his love for Mme Wesendonck and his 'méditation théorique'.

Wagner devine ici un auditeur qui résiste à sa musique, il sait trouver l'endroit sensible de cet homme, et il lui envoie un accord savamment composé qui perce cet endroit.[19]

Valéry's early approach to artistic creation led him to assert the image of the universal man as an intellectual giant forming vast compositional structures and achieving a kind of vicarious emotional satisfaction by manipulating the emotions of other people, his potential audience. This approach separates the mind of the creator from his own emotional responses: 'Je pratique depuis 1892 le système . . . que j'ai créé pour me défendre d'une douleur insupportable.'[20]

Mon rêve littéraire fut de déterminer tout un ouvrage a priori par la pluralité simultanée des conditions indépendantes que sont les relations à exprimer, les états probables du lecteur, ses actes à exciter, ses demandes à provoquer et à satisfaire, les temps correspondants, la prévision de ses défenses, l'anticipation de ses désirs, l'étendue ordonnée du sujet choisi, le langage etc.
C'est l'idée de l'acte à accomplir et à faire accomplir qui doit donner le ton.[21]

But in assimilating Wagner as a support to this theory, Valéry tended to overlook the fact that Wagner's theoretical statements were essentially accounts of what he had already achieved. Wagner's theories are formulations of his own practical experience of composition rather than a 'recipe' conceived in advance. For, as Wagner himself explains in the 'Lettre sur la Musique', the plan for the series of operas based on the Nibelungenlied was already present in his mind when he formulated the theory, which was a development of his experience of composing the *Flying Dutchman, Tannhäuser*, and *Lohengrin*.

Ma théorie n'était guère autre chose qu'une expression abstraite de ce qui s'était développé en moi comme production spontanée.[22]

Equally Valéry's own approach to composition is substantially modified as a result of his own poetic practice. The volumes of analysis which the *Cahiers* present may be seen as a kind of wager on the eventuality of arriving at a universally valid method. But Valéry came to realise that he had lost the wager, and indeed the doubts set in early, even before its intended scope was fully outlined. The glimpses of possible failure have been charted by Duchesne-Guillemin, and they date from well before the turn of the century.[23]

It is significant that 'Note et digression', the most clear and detailed account of his ideals published after *Vinci* and *Teste*, contains its own critique. Written in 1919 while deeply involved in working on *Charmes*, it confirms that the universal techniques do not come into contact with the practical problems of composition:

Tous mes préceptes, trop présents et trop définis, étaient aussi trop universels pour me servir dans aucune circonstance.[24]

He realised that the ideal was impossible; he saw the extent of discontinuity in the universe as opposed to his earlier search for continuity; he saw that the work of the composer, the builder or the engineer could not be based upon an all-embracing theory. The number of factors which have to be taken into account in the construction of any work are so great that, as he wrote in 1920,

Il n'y a pas de formules pour des cas si particuliers, pas d'équation entre des données si hétérogènes; rien ne se fait à coup sûr.[25]

And the marginal note added to 'Note et digression' in 1929–30 offers a further qualification:

Le nom de Méthode était bien fort, en effet. Méthode fait songer à quelque ordre assez bien défini d'opérations; et je n'envisageais qu'une habitude singulière de transformer toutes les questions de mon esprit.[26]

Valéry came to realise that even if the method had been fully elaborated, its application to poetry, for example, would have been pointless, for it was not concerned with practical achievements. If the universal principles were fully worked out the whole concrete world would become irrelevant: man would remain in a state of permanent immanence, and 'pouvoir' would completely replace 'faire'.

Le monde continue; et la vie, et l'esprit, à cause de la résistance que nous opposent les choses difficiles à connaître. A peine tout serait déchiffré que tout s'évanouirait, et l'univers percé à jour ne serait pas plus possible qu'une escroquerie dévoilée ou un tour de prestidigitation dont on connaîtrait le secret.[27]

The method could only lead to the repetition of the same effects and would offer in art none of the necessary fascination of the mind and senses, none of the air of mystery which Valéry held to be so important both for the composer and for the audience. Why spend time applying the same formulae? As he says in comment upon Mallarmé's algebraic conception of art:

du moment qu'un principe a été reconnu et saisi par quelqu'un, il est inutile de perdre son temps dans ses applications.[28]

Or, as he had written in 1914:

La théorie dont la littérature est une application, si elle existait, l'application n'en vaudrait plus la peine.[29]

The notion of a 'recipe' for writing poetry is clearly rejected:

S'il y eût une recette p. *faire de beaux vers* on en ferait tant qu'il faudrait bien choisir – C.à d. définir une catégorie de *beaux vers* – *au carré* – C.à d. trouver une *deuxième recette.*[30]

It is evident therefore that Valéry came to recognise the relationship between an oversimplified concept of composition, and the oversimplified effects produced. Gide had however perceptively commented upon this very aspect in 1899 in reply to a letter from Valéry outlining his theory. Gide pointed to the discord between such a theory with its gross effects, and Valéry's actual sensibility as he knew it and as it is revealed in the poetry

J'ajoute, à propos des recettes, etc., procédés, que je crois qu'on ne les acquiert qu'aux dépens d'une sorte de finesse artistique, finesse sensuelle; la musique de Wagner m'apparaît d'un art terriblement grossier. A vouloir préjuger la volupté ses sens s'étaient désaffinés. Il y a toujours en art quelque chose d'imprécisable que ne pourra saisir l'instrument, etc. Art des fausses fleurs.

Beaucoup à dire; nous causerons, mais tu triompheras parce que je bafouillerai. Toi, tu seras net et tu réussiras ton calcul, mais ce sera *parce que* tes chiffres seront faux.[31]

When, later, he was approached by Gide to republish his earlier poems, Valéry initially 'resigned' himself to what he considered the rather inglorious practice of poetry. After all, having considered that 'les autres font des livres. Moi, je fais mon esprit',[32] to revise a few poems, some of which were twenty years old, must have seemed meagre indeed. But the return made him realise the importance of practice and application, and of the created work over the theory. Out of this transformation there developed a view of composition which, while retaining many features of the early one, is essentially pragmatic, which is concerned more with the posing and solving of particular problems than with an all-embracing theory. It is not so much a method as a series of techniques that are employed according to the demands of the situation. Valéry still emphasises the element of construction, but as an expression of the composer's own attitudes and feelings, and no longer as a calculated manipulation of the emotions of others. Personal feelings and technical considerations are combined, just as Eupalinos' temples are created from the interaction of his own intellect and emotions:

Ce temple délicat, nul ne le sait, est l'image mathématique d'une fille de Corinthe, que j'ai heureusement aimée. Il en reproduit fidèlement les proportions particulières. Il vit pour moi![33]

Thus it would appear that, apart from revealing Valéry's personal taste in music, Wagner and in particular the theory of composition occupy a less significant rôle in Valéry's artistic theory than at first seems the case. As long as Valéry saw composition in terms derived from Poe and Wagner, associated with an ideal but unattainable universal method, there could be little connection with the practical composition of poetry. And thus *Charmes* presents not an application of the universal method, but a severe compromise with that ideal.

Valéry's reaction to Wagner, a mixture of uncritical enthusiasm and partial interpretation, is in fact firmly rooted within the context of symbolism, and subject indeed to the same reservations. The indivisible coupling of admiration and despair is well put by Julien Gracq:

C'est par ses admirations surtout que le symbolisme a été grand. Il a mis presque tout son génie à choisir ses patronages, Wagner, Baudelaire, Poe: nulle école n'a été plus exemplairement, plus impitoyablement renseignée dès le début sur ses plus intimes exigences – seulement, ce qu'il voulait, *c'était déjà fait*: elle ne s'en est jamais remise ni consolée.[34]

Léon Guichard, in his extensive study of the influence of Wagner over the literature of the latter half of the nineteenth century, concludes that though there is a widespread reference to Wagner, the influence was not at all profound; Wagner remains a presence rather than a deep influence in French literature.[33]

This is certainly the case for Valéry. Though he refers to Wagner more than to any other musician, it is not this music which is the most illuminating so far as Valéry's poetry is concerned. Wagner embodied an ideal for Valéry, and as such takes on an all-pervasive presence in the *Cahiers*, the presence of a giant. But the direct influence and practical connections are far less in evidence, and a far more revealing influence is to be found in the music of other periods and of a different conception.[35]

4

VALÉRY AND STRAVINSKY

En toute matière, rechercher l'élément complexe de combinaisons
– les règles de combinaison.

IX, 1924, p. 693

Of all Valéry's contacts with musicians of his time, undoubtedly the relationship with Stravinsky was the most significant. They formed a circle of their own in the 1920s and '30s, supporting each other's achievement and sharing their ideas on artistic creation. Stravinsky noted that Valéry made a point of attending the performances of his works, and he was touched by this.[1] Valéry for his part found in Stravinsky a musician who shared his approach to composition and his aesthetic judgements. Though they did not meet until the poems of *Charmes* were virtually completed, it was precisely during this period that Valéry was formulating the more complete analysis of his poetic theory. Indeed, such was the common ground between them that Stravinsky's *Poetics of Music* may be read as a useful introduction to Valéry's mature poetic theory.

It is not intended to propose Stravinsky's music as the 'equivalent' of Valéry's poetry, for Stravinsky was clearly far more adventurous and aggressive in his work. But there are a number of analogies which indicate a similar approach to the problems of artistic creation in the early part of the twentieth century. Not least of these is the element of control which appears in Stravinsky's work especially around the 1920s. And even the violent effects of *Le Sacre du Printemps*, though appearing uncontrolled to Debussy, are meant to be strictly regulated by the conductor. Stravinsky moved away from the fluid, unaccentuated style of impressionism towards

a more vital, rhythmic expression. The same movement towards rhythmic vigour, tighter composition and a more asser-
tive frame of mind is shown in the contrast between Valéry's
earlier poetry and the taut poetic style of *Charmes.*

The ideas of both artists developed out of their own creative activity, so that when they met, they found a considerable
area of agreement over both practical and theoretical issues.
The convergence of their views is evident on two particularly
important occasions when Valéry was, in Stravinsky's words,
'a deep source of intellectual and moral support.'[2]

The first of these arose from the collaboration between
Stravinsky and Gide over the composition of *Perséphone.*
Gide wrote the text first and then seems to have disagreed
with Stravinsky over the adaptation of the text to music.
After discussing the relationship between words and music
Stravinsky, in his account of the incident, points to Valéry's
part in the dispute:

[Gide] had expected the *Persephone* text to be sung with exactly the
same stresses he would use in a recitation of it. He believed my musical
purpose should be to imitate or underline the verbal pattern: I would
simply have to find pitches for the syllables, since he considered he had
already composed the rhythm. The tradition of *poesia per musica*
meant nothing to him. And, not understanding that a poet and musician
collaborate to produce *one* music, he was only horrified by the dis-
crepancies between my music and his.

I turned to Valéry for support, and no arbiter could have given me
more. I do not know what he said to Gide. But to me he affirmed the
musician's prerogative to treat loose and formless prosodies (such as
Gide's) according to his musical ideas, even if the latter led to 'distor-
tion' of phrasing or to breaking up, for purposes of syllabification, the
words themselves.[3]

The mutual support of Stravinsky and Valéry and their constant discussions are evident again in 1939 when Stravinsky
was preparing a series of lectures, called the *Poetics of Music,*
to be given at Harvard University. Both were staying at Le
Mesnil during the summer:

Nadia [Boulanger] habite à trois cents pas d'ici et hébergeait jusqu'à ce
jeudi Stravinsky, en partance pour l'Amérique (si partance possible).
Nous nous sommes beaucoup vus.[4]

A note in the *Cahiers* at this time indicates Valéry's involvement in discussing the content of these lectures.

Stravinsky – conversation dans la presque nuit sur le rythme. Il va chercher les textes des conférences qu'il vient d'écrire et ira faire à Harvard. Il appelle cela *Poétique* et les idées premières ont plus d'une analogie avec celles de mon cours du Collège. 1re leçon.[5]

Stravinsky's account in *Memories and Commentaries* stresses the help which Valéry provided with the language and style, about which Stravinsky was unsure, having written the lectures directly in French.

I had asked him to read and criticize my manuscript . . . I was not quite confident about some of the writing. Accordingly I read the manuscript to him in a country house near Paris sometime in late summer 1939. He suggested various changes in phrasing and word order, but to my great relief endorsed the style of the lectures without reservation.[6]

Valéry later commented upon this reading in a letter to Gide and makes a final remark which perhaps contains as much irony as genuine surprise:

S. nous a lu son futur *Cours de Poétique* (lui aussi) *musicale* qui a des analogies avec le mien (chose assez curieuse).[7]

In this chapter I point to the common features of their approach, particularly as revealed in the *Poetics of Music*, and then propose that Stravinsky's *Le Sacre du Printemps* was a major influence on Valéry's *L'Ame et la Danse*.

In his lectures Stravinsky analyses the process of composition, and, emphasising its creative nature, defines 'Poetics' as the study of the work to be done: its derivation is the verb *poiein* meaning 'to do' or 'to make'. 'La poétique musicale' therefore means '[le] *faire* dans l'ordre de la musique'.[8] The technique which is employed is not separate from the meaning, but is an integral part elaborated as part of the meaning during the stages of composition. For classical philosophers *techné* embraced the fine arts and the useful arts and was applied to the knowledge and study of the certain and inevitable rules of the craft. In the first lesson of his *Cours de Poétique* at the Collège de France on 10 December 1937, Valéry expressed the idea thus:

Poétique . . . c'est la notion tout simple de *faire* que je voulais exprimer. Le faire, le *poïein*, dont je veux m'occuper, est celui qui s'achève en quelque œuvre et que je viendrai à restreindre bientôt à ce genre d'œuvres qu'on est convenu d'appeler *œuvres de l'esprit*.[9]

The artist then is like an artisan, 'homo faber', acting in accordance with his material, and with the self-imposed restrictions of the convention chosen for a particular work. As Paul Collaer says of Stravinsky:

L'œuvre musicale n'est pas, pour lui, un moyen d'exprimer ses sentiments, ou pour mieux dire, d'exprimer le 'moi'. L'œuvre est un objet à faire, une certaine matière à manier, et à laquelle il faut donner une forme appropriée. Il se place en face de la matière comme un orfèvre en face du métal dont il devra faire un bijou, comme un architecte dans l'espace qu'il doit organiser en tenant compte des matériaux qui sont mis à sa disposition.[10]

The result is a work which is a-personal rather than impersonal, though the composer is so deeply involved in the formal elaboration of his work that his personality is nevertheless stamped upon the product, and each work, however different in style, is unmistakably his.[11]

Stravinsky maintained that inspiration is 'une manifestation secondaire dans l'ordre du temps' which follows on from 'le principe de volonté spéculative qui est à l'origine de toute création'.[12] He quotes John 3.8: 'L'Esprit souffle où Il veut' and proceeds to define this feature, which Valéry tends to refer to as the 'état poétique':

Toute création suppose à l'origine une sorte d'appétit que fait naître l'avant-goût de la découverte. Cet avant-goût de l'acte créateur accompagne l'intuition d'une inconnue déja possédée mais non encore intelligible et qui ne sera définie que par l'effort d'une technique vigilante.[13]

In some cases, as in the composition of the 'Danse sacrale' episode of *Le Sacre du Printemps*, inspiration provides the material which passes through the medium of the composer: he could, he says, play it, but did not know how to write it:

I was guided by no system in *Le Sacre du Printemps* . . . I had only my ear to help me. I heard and wrote what I heard. I am the vessel through which *Le Sacre* passed.[14]

In other cases the composer may develop certain formal aspects arising from the nature of the material already written and find the excitement and emotional response as a result of this work:

Je ne songe pas à refuser à l'inspiration le rôle éminent qui lui est dévolu dans la genèse que nous étudions; je prétends seulement qu'elle n'est aucunement la condition préalable de l'acte créateur, mais une manifestation secondaire dans l'ordre du temps . . . C'est ensuite, mais ensuite seulement, que naîtra ce trouble émotif qui est à la base de l'inspiration.[15]

Invention and technique thereby take on a particular purpose: they are the means of bringing a work from conception to realisation. The 'état poétique' does not of itself guarantee a poem, or as Valéry says, 'Quand la mélodie naît dans le compositeur elle est antérieure à la musique – (au *faire*).'[16] The melody may indicate rhythm, time signature, notes and accents, but it is still not yet the work of music: the theme in music represents the possibility, the 'produit brut', but without the exercise of 'le faire' and the 'élaboration organisatrice', it will not become music. There is a constant interaction between the creative appetite and the vigilant technique, between 'le faire' and 'le produit brut'. Their rôles are not therefore in opposition but are a mutual incitement to activity. The organisation of sounds into music is an assertion of human consciousness; composition is thus at once a means of attaining consciousness and a means of preventing loss of personal control:

ce qui compte pour la claire ordonnance de l'œuvre – pour sa cristallisation, c'est que tous les éléments dyonisiaques qui ébranlent l'imagination du créateur et font monter la sève nourricière soient domptés à propos, avant de nous donner la fièvre et finalement soumis à la loi: c'est Apollon qui l'ordonne.[17]

This interaction of Apollo and Dionysus is best expressed in Stravinsky's reference to his dialectic conception of form; it is based upon the idea of dialects as an art of logical discussion, and thus 'musical form is the result of the "logical development" of musical materials'.[18] These ideas are closely paralleled by Valéry when he speaks of language as 'un moyen de conscience'[19] and of the initial line of poetry which 'exigeait une suite musicale et logique'.[20]

Valéry and Stravinsky do not therefore seek to deny the rôle of inspiration, but to assign it a special place in the creation of a work. Inspiration is unbiased: it serves the creative will just as readily as the imaginative musings. But they believed that it acts all the more effectively by struggling against constraint; it is paradoxically through control and order that the artist finds his greatest freedom. The restrictions stimulate the imagination and at the same time provide a basis for evaluating all that is thrown up by the inspiration. 'Ma liberté sera d'autant plus grande et plus profonde que je limiterai plus étroitement mon champ d'action et que je m'entourerai d'obstacles', says Stravinsky.[21] And in praise of the fugue and the totally pure form it represents, he quotes Leonardo da Vinci: 'La force naît par la contrainte et meurt par liberté.'[22] In 'Fontaine de mémoire', the introduction written to the collection of poems by Yvonne Ferran-Weher, Valéry praises the use of the complex 'chant royal' verse form, and makes the same comparison with fugue as Stravinsky:

Je me suis étonné quelquefois . . . que l'on n'ait, depuis Bach, cherché d'autre formule que la fugue; mais on me dit qu'elle suffit à proposer ce qu'il faut de difficulté sytématique pour instruire le liberté naïve à poursuivre une liberté d'ordre supérieur.[23]

The constraints are imposed either deliberately by a conscious choice on the part of the composer, or by the nature of the materials being used. One example is Stravinsky's *Piano-Rag-Music*: the piece was composed at the piano, the inspiration seeming to come from his fingers.

ce qui me passionnait surtout là-dedans, c'était que les différentes épisodes rythmiques de cette pièce m'étaient dictées par les doigts mêmes. Ceux-ci prenaient un tel plaisir que je me mis à travailler la pièce. Il ne faut pas mépriser les doigts; ils sont de grands inspirateurs et, en contact avec la matière sonore, éveillent souvent en nous des idées subconscientes qui, autrement, ne se seraient peut-être pas révélées.[24]

In the *Cahiers* Valéry comments on the results which may arise from physical restraints such as the muscular dexterity of the composer, or even the key signature deliberately adopted for an Étude:

Parfois la souplesse même de la main fait trouver des effets sur piano et engendre une composition, quoique faite en principe pour la seule exécution.
L'oreille s'étonne d'un effet trouvé par la main, le ressaisit, le confie à

l'esprit qui le réfléchit et le développe, lui donne un sens, des causes, une profondeur etc.
C'est un échange merveilleux.[25]

Perhaps even more significant were the self-imposed stylistic conventions of Stravinsky's neo-classical works. For he does not use the eighteenth-century styles simply as an application of out-dated principles, but he incorporates for example the dotted rhythms that are characteristic of the period as 'conscious stylistic references' in order 'to build a new music on eighteenth-century classicism using the constructive principles of that classicism'.[26]

As far as the actual procedures of composition are concerned, studies of Stravinsky's works and manuscripts have shown that he tended to compose in fragments: he would develop each section, not according to any imposed plan, but from the inside, exploring the possibilities from within. The work opens out like a fan as the fragments are composed, and his attention is then concentrated on the transitions, using the end of one fragment to introduce the beginning of the next, sometimes with considerable overlap of themes. It is therefore less a matter of establishing a linear development from one subject to another, than of creating a complex pattern of cross-references. 'Les thèmes', says Collaer of Stravinsky, 'ne tirent pas leur importance de leur aspect premier, mais de l'infinité de combinaisons dans lesquelles ils sont engagés.'[27] This is a procedure which, as will be shown, Valéry had also employed in the composition of *La Jeune Parque*.

Furthermore Stravinsky's use of polyharmony may be compared to Valéry's use of metaphor.[28] Polyharmony refers to the use of two chords superimposed to form a unity, when the function or meaning is not polarised towards either one or the other, but is multiple. A chord or even a note may have many functions, often serving as the only common point of contact between otherwise unrelated melodic lines; these notes were called 'notes polaires' by Stravinsky. The comparison with the multiple effect of Valéry's imagery and the semantic depth of his language is striking. As a 'note polaire' one is reminded of the unifying force achieved by the central image of a poem like *L'Abeille*; there are really three separate fields of meaning and imagery in the poem: the natural world of fruit and bees; the human physiology; and the world of human emotions. The shifting associations of 'the bee' serve to link these three areas of meaning: the bee is attracted to the fruit which is also the female breast, the sting which draws blood becoming the sting of pain in love which at least assures its vitality and continued presence – a positive sensation and reaction which prevents the love from dying of torpor. The idea of the 'note polaire' is thus important for the effect of modulation which Valéry sought to establish between the parts of his poems, for musically modulation involves the passing from one key to another by means of a common note linking two harmonies.

The intellectualism of Stravinsky's approach is evident when in *The Poetics of Music* he goes on to consider aspects of the performance of music and the reactions of the listener. Both Stravinsky and Valéry aspire to a higher, more exclusive, form of communication in which the listener, given sufficient education and ability, becomes part of the creative process itself, 'le partenaire du jeu institué par le créateur'.[29] Or as Valéry puts it: 'Il ne faut pas tenter de communiquer la vibration au public – mais faire qu'elle naisse en lui.'[30] Stravinsky continues:

Cette participation exceptionnelle apporte au partenaire une jouissance si vive qu'elle l'unit dans une certaine mesure à l'esprit qui a conçu et réalisé l'œuvre qu'il écoute et lui donne l'illusion qu'il s'identifie au créateur. Tel est le sens du fameux adage de Raphaël: comprendre c'est égaler.[31]

It is possible, then, to identify a number of common features in Stravinsky and Valéry, particularly with regard to their ideas on art and composition; sufficient indeed to speak of a mutual influence. It would seem certain that Valéry's aid to Stravinsky with *The Poetics of Music* was, extended over the years of their acquaintance, much greater than the immediate help with language and style that Stravinsky refers to. And similarly, Valéry's understanding of music, including its techniques and aesthetics, gained appreciably from his long friendship with Stravinsky. But the latter always remained a much more spontaneous and adventurous artist than Valéry. His interest in techniques, constraints and the conscious application of styles was always with a creative work in mind. He sought constantly to innovate, and his concern with the particular work 'à faire' allowed no room for applying a 'universal method'. Collaer says:

On ne peut attendre d'un tel homme qu'il crée à son usage un langage invariable, utilisable pour la solution de tous les problèmes qui se posent.[32]

For Valéry on the other hand the exercise, the 'gymnastique de l'esprit', the analysis of the process came almost to acquire more importance than the final work: the daily notes in the *Cahiers* were a kind of training, repeating the exercises to the point of perfection in preparation for performance or publication. This explains the repetitious nature of some of the material, which Valéry himself realised: 'J'écris ces notes un peu comme on fait des gammes, et elles se répètent sur les mêmes notes depuis cinquante ans.'[33] And it is useful therefore in this context to note the essential difference between them, in a judgement of Stravinsky's which seems eminently sound:

Valéry is not one of the great innovators of our age, as Joyce was for example, or Webern, or Klee. He had been altogether too fascinated by the process of creation. And, he worshipped intellect too much – indeed, to the point of valuing himself more as an intellectual than as a poet. The result of this Teste-ism was his contentment with *epistamenos*, with 'knowing how', at which point he would stop.[34]

And thus the mind becomes the 'performer', regulating the creation and appreciating the product: 'Ecrire pour "le cerveau" dans son meilleur état comme on écrit la musique pour les mains qui exécutent.'[35]

The relationship between Stravinsky and Valéry has been discussed so far largely in terms of their ideas on composition. In one particular case however it seems likely that Stravinsky played a decisive rôle. Although none of the critical works on the dialogue makes any reference to it, there is sufficient evidence both in the background to the composition and particularly in the work itself to suggest the *Le Sacre du Printemps* was a major influence on Valéry's *L'Ame et la Danse*.

The dialogue first appeared in December 1921 in a special edition of the *Revue musicale* devoted to 'Le Ballet au XIXe siècle'. When Valéry was originally approached for a contribution he refused, for reasons which he later explained to Louis Séchan:

> Je n'aurais jamais projeté d'écrire sur la danse, à laquelle je n'avais jamais sérieusement pensé. D'ailleurs, j'estimais, – et je l'estime encore, – que Mallarmé avait épuisé le sujet en tant qu'il appartient à la littérature. Cette convinction m'a fait d'abord refuser la commande de la *Revue musicale*. D'autres raisons m'ont déterminé à l'accepter.[36]

On this evidence the difficulty of rivalling Mallarmé and the feeling of having no particularly original approach must be seen as the main factors which discouraged him. What could have been the 'other reasons' which caused him to change his mind?

Some of the clues are to be found within the letter to Séchan. The necessity of making a living as a writer no doubt played its part. And also, having struck upon the dialogue form it was possible to include Mallarmé, since he could not be ignored, as one of the possible interpretations:

> J'ai pris le parti de faire figurer, parmi les interprétations diverses que donnent de la danse les 3 personnages celle dont l'énoncé et l'incomparable démonstration par le style se trouve dans les *Divagations*.[37]

And yet the idea of a dialogue form cannot be seen as the main reason, for he had after all already written *Eupalinos* a few months earlier in 1921, and the adoption of this form did not in itself solve his main difficulty, which was to write something different from Mallarmé.

To a certain extent the influence of sources from antiquity must be considered, given the names of the characters, Socrate, Eryximaque and Phèdre. This area has been most closely researched by critics, but nevertheless the evidence suggests that this had only a fairly general significance, providing a framework and a few references. Valéry disclaimed knowledge of any of the more erudite sources and said that he only consulted the work of Emmanuel in the library and the book by Marey which he had possessed for 30 years: 'ces épures du saut et de la marche, quelques souvenirs de ballets furent mes ressources essentielles'.[38]

Perhaps this rather allusive reference to 'quelques souvenirs de ballets' provides the most significant clue. For it seems likely that the recollection of Stravinsky's *Le Sacre du Printemps* may have been just the sufficient inspiration to make him change his mind about the article: it provided a general outline, a dramatic setting, interesting and original in itself, which, combined with his ideas on the related function of the mind and the body, would be clearly striking and authentically different from Mallarmé.

Valéry had seen the work peformed in 1913 with the original choreography by Nijinsky. Though the ballet version was not a success and the work quickly established as an orchestral piece, Diaghilev in fact revived it as a ballet at precisely the time that Valéry was considering writing on dance. With a new choreographic version prepared by Léonide Massine it was first performed at the Théâtre des Champs-Elysées on 15 December 1920 conducted by Ansermet. It is not known whether Valéry saw it, but the performance could not have passed unnoticed.

There is furthermore a close parallel between Valéry's statement of his intentions in what he calls 'mon Ballet', and Stravinsky's achievement in uniting the argument of the ballet and the musical form: it was a concept of ballet which gave music an organic rôle rather than a purely accompanying, decorative rôle.

Quant à la forme d'ensemble, j'ai tenté de faire du *Dialogue* lui-même une manière de ballet dont l'Image et l'Idée sont tour à tour les Coryphées. L'abstrait et le sensible mènent tour à tour et s'unissent enfin dans le vertige.[39]

The most convincing argument lies however in the unfolding of the work itself, for *L'Ame et la Danse* shows a remarkable similarity to the structure of the second part of *Le Sacre* which is called 'Le Sacrifice'. Stravinsky described his work as

le spectacle d'un grand rite sacral païen: les vieux sages, assis en cercle
et observant la danse à la mort d'une jeune fille, qu'ils sacrifient pour
leur rendre propice le dieu du printemps.[40]

The sections of the second part are entitled 'Introduction –
Cercles mystérieux des adolescentes – Glorification de l'élue –
Evocation des ancêtres – Action rituelle des ancêtres – Danse
sacrale – L'élue.' With the dance of the young girls, the
appearance of the main dancer and her solo performance
building up to a total collapse, Valéry adopts the same overall setting which is presented by Stravinsky especially in the
sections 'Cercles mystérieux, Glorification de l'élue, Danse
sacrale, l'élue.'

In Valéry's work the dance is seen through the eyes of the
'vieux sages', Socrate, Phèdre and Eryximaque. It is night,
and they are seated deep in discussion as they finish eating
until the entrance 'on stage' of the dancers. In *Le Sacre* the
wise men have already made their solemn entrance half-way
through the first part; 'Le Sacrifice' opens with a nocturnal
introduction (originally titled 'Pagan night' by Stravinsky).

The dance of the novices takes place first, making in *L'Ame
et la Danse* a solemn and delicate entry: 'Voyez-moi cette
troupe mi-légère, mi-solennelle! – Elles entrent comme des
âmes.'[41] The dance of the 'parfaites pensées' seems at once
light and swirling, the actual speed and emphasis of the music
lightly suggesting the dream state. 'Je rêve à la douceur, multiplié indéfiniment par elle-même, de ces rencontres, et de ces
échanges de formes de vierges' says Phèdre while hearing 'les
accents de cette sourde symphonie sur laquelle toutes choses
semblent peintes et portées.'[42] It is however 'un rêve de vigilance et de tension que ferait la Raison elle-même'. The
dancers continue, changing patterns, coming together, sweep-
ing away, intertwining, encircling each other:

La divine pensée . . . engendre les redites de ces manœuvres délicieuses,
ces tourbillons voluptueux qui se forment de deux ou trois corps et qui
ne peuvent plus se rompre.[43]

The dance of the novices follows closely the second
sequence of 'Le Sacrifice', the 'Cercles mystérieux des
adolescentes', which builds up to a fortissimo chord and leads

immediately into the 'Glorification de l'élue' as the main dancer appears, generating excitement and disarray. The same dramatic effect is created by Valéry:

SOCRATE

Mais que font-elles tout à coup? . . . Elles s'emmêlent, elles s'enfuient! . . .

PHEDRE

Elles volent aux portes. Elles s'inclinent pour accueillir.

ERYXIMAQUE

Athikté! Athikté! . . . O dieux! . . . l'Athikté la palpitante![44]

Athikté's dance follows the same pattern as that of 'l'élue'; from a controlled beginning it builds up to a climax until she finally collapses. Stravinsky's music in the 'Danse sacrale' has regular chords at a steady controlled tempo before the rhythm is broken up, becomes unevenly accented, and the explosive climax occurs. Athikté first shows her skill as a dancer by walking in regular controlled steps; the rhythm is so equal as to give the impression of no movement at all. 'Je ne m'attache qu'à l'égalité de ces mesures', says Socrate.[45] Then there is a momentary silence before the music changes and gradually incites her to faster rhythmic movement:

PHEDRE

La musique doucement semble la ressaisir d'une autre manière, la soulève . . .

ERYXIMAQUE

La musique lui change son âme.[46]

The dancer moves faster and faster, while the music shows a gradual crescendo and increasing intensity, cymbals crashing and jagged rhythms striking across a regular pulse: 'ne vous sentez-vous pas enivrés par saccades, et comme par des coups répétés de plus en plus fort . . .?'[47] And then comes the most intense moment of the dance in the ecstatic gyrating movement as she turns round and round: 'Elle tourne sur elle-même, – voici que les choses éternellement liées commencent de se séparer. Elle tourne, elle tourne . . .'[48] The expression is repeated several times by Valéry to give some measure of the duration; the rhythm continues relentlessly without any respite seeming possible: 'On croirait que ceci peut durer éternellement.'[49] The steady advance of time has ceased and a single moment becomes lasting. Athikté's flurry of movement seems to become transparent, while at the centre of this movement there is a solid, apparently unmoving shape.

The same effect is created in *Le Sacre*: the climax is achieved by the repeated ascending phrase; it occurs again and again, and it seems that it will not, cannot, stop and time becomes suspended. The end of the piece comes not as a conclusion, but with the sudden finality of collapse; the ascending phrase goes one note further up the scale, stops, balanced precariously, totters and falls. Like Athikté:

SOCRATE

Elle reposerait immobile au centre même de son mouvement. Isolée, isolée, pareille à l'axe du monde . . .

PHEDRE

Elle tourne, elle tourne . . . Elle tombe!

SOCRATE

Elle est tombée!

PHEDRE

Elle est morte . . .[50]

Athikté is not however dead: 'Je ne suis pas morte. Et pourtant, je ne suis pas vivante!'[51] The notion of sacrifice to the gods of spring is not present in Valéry, although in both works the dance is a symbolic affirmation of life, and the erotic element of *L'Ame et la Danse* closely related to the theme of rebirth in spring. Valéry presents a preoccupation with life and death such as one finds in Stravinsky's treatment of sacrificial rites. For Valéry there is no solution to 'l'ennui de vivre': 'Cet ennui absolu n'est en soi que la vie toute nue'.[52] Life stripped of all its masks and trappings, pierced by the lucid gaze of the self, is empty; the opposite response is a form of intoxication, whether artificial or provoked by action and emotional involvement: 'l'ivresse due à des actes' is the opposite to the 'ennui'.[53] Dance offers the greatest example of this: action is an escape from the destiny of man, an assertion of life not through the work of the mind but through the work of the body. Freedom and lightness of movement are substituted for freedom and clarity of thought.

The vibrant movement of Athikté becomes like the nourishing flames for a phoenix; she lives within the flames and the dance becomes an all-consuming fire. Athikté represents 'cette exaltation et cette vibration de la vie, . . . cette suprématie de la tension, et ce ravissement dans le plus agile que l'on puisse obtenir de soi-même'.[54] This extremity of dynamism, of tension and of rhythmic impulse is, as one finds in *Le Sacre*, the supreme assertion of a life-force.

However direct or indirect the influence, the similarities between the works of Stravinsky and Valéry are so strong that one cannot but feel that the dialogue is a commentary upon the music, a drawing out of the implications with the sounds of Stravinsky's music in the background. Both the overall shape of the work as well as a number of particular details seem to provide convincing evidence that Stravinsky's ballet must be counted among the major sources of *L'Ame et la Danse*.

There exists clearly a similarity of approach between Stravinsky and Valéry which is based upon their parallel views on artistic composition. But the impact of their works was clearly different and it will be useful therefore, in conclusion, to assess briefly Valéry's position in relation to the new music of the twentieth century. Certainly Stravinsky was a much greater innovator than Valéry. Stravinsky's own points of reference were of a much more modern nature and he created new ones while Valéry tended always to refer back to those he knew from his youth. There is no evidence of Valéry's reaction to the works of composers such as Schoenberg and Webern, although Stravinsky himself does comment:

Robert Craft: Valéry said: 'We can construct in orderly fashion only by means of conventions.' How do we recognize these conventions in, say, Webern's songs with clarinet and guitar?
I. Stravinsky: We don't. An entirely new principle of order is found in the Webern songs which in time will be recognized and conventionalized. But Valéry's essentially classical *dicta* do not foresee that new conventions can be created.[55]

This may well be true; it is almost certain in any case that he never heard the songs; furthermore Valéry never claimed to be a prophet of future developments in art. And yet in spite of this, and in spite of the fact that Valéry considered himself the final expression of a dying civilisation, there are a number of quite striking parallels between the ideas of both Mallarmé and Valéry and the musical developments of the twentieth century. Similar artistic ideals of rigour, concision and intellectual tension were pursued by the musicians of the next generation, with Schoenberg and Webern for example elaborating advanced musical ideas and forging a new musical language for a small group of associates, just as Mallarmé had done for poetry in the 1880s and 1890s.

Indeed the comparison with these younger musicians has not escaped some of the music critics. Beaufils compares Schoenberg's *Erwartung* to Mallarmé's work, pointing to the dual effect upon the listener.

Deux délibérations intellectuelles se conjuguent, celle du formel-pur et celle du verbal-pur. Il ne fait aucun doute qu'un certain atonalisme peut aussi bien, comme dans l'*Erwartung* de Schoenberg, nous prendre par tous les sens à la fois, nous baigner dans une atmosphère de pur frisson, qu'à l'inverse nous transporter sur quelque haute cime où le sentir se désincarne jusqu'au penser; et cette sorte de sensibilité à l'idée pure, qu'en poésie a su élaborer Mallarmé, semble bien l'une des acquisitions les plus élevées de la musique contemporaine.[56]

And Collaer has compared the concision of language and thought in Webern to the perfection and dense use of poetic language in Valéry.[57]

There have of course been a number of works of Mallarmé set to music, including Ravel's *Trois poèmes de Stéphane Mallarmé* and Boulez' *Pli selon pli*. While a number of musicians have used texts of Valéry, none perhaps are outstanding. The best-known is Arthur Honegger who collaborated with Valéry on *Amphion* and *Sémiramis*; but two others of the group known as 'les Six' also set works of Valéry to music. Louis Durey composed *Trois poèmes de Paul Valéry*, opus 31 (1921–3) settings of *L'Insinuant, Intérieur* and *La Fausse morte*; the second of his *Trois quatuors vocaux à capella*, opus 37 (1926–7) uses *La Dormeuse*. In 1938 Valéry worked with Germaine Tailleferre on the *Cantate du Narcisse*; she had turned more towards Ravel and classicism than the other members of 'les Six' and this is brought out in her account of the composition:

Mes complexes, le peu de confiance dans mes possibilités musicales tout cela me paralysait. Toutefois, l'idée d'adopter un style classique me rassurait. Je n'avais plus l'angoisse de la page blanche, concevoir une œuvre dans un style donné représentait déjà un support. Dans mes œuvres précédentes, j'avais fait preuve d'un certain retour au classicisme; aussi me sentais-je moins perdue. C'est ainsi que nous avons écrit la *Cantate du Narcisse*.[58]

Clearly, though, it is not yet possible to indicate any major works of music inspired by Valéry which are performed regularly in concerts or recitals. In Valéry's case the connections with music lie rather more in a similar approach to the question of artistic composition. His work corresponds not so much to the adventurous experiments in atonal and twelve-tone music, as to the reworking of classical forms in Stravinsky or to Ravel's closely argued yet evocative music which strives to maintain a formal control over his own powerful sensibility. Both composers would seem to exemplify Valéry's image of the man writing down his innermost dream in a fully awakened state, observing himself and somehow detached from his own inner reactions. It is the image of the work of art which Socrate defines when the young girls are dancing in *L'Ame et la Danse*:

Ame voluptueuse, vois donc ici le contraire d'un rêve, et le hasard absent . . . Mais le contraire d'un rêve, qu'est-ce Phèdre, sinon quelque autre rêve? . . . Un rêve de vigilance et de tension que ferait la Raison elle-même! – Et que rêverait une Raison? – Que si une Raison rêvait, dure, debout, l'œil armé, et la bouche fermée, comme maîtresse de ses lèvres, – le songe qu'elle ferait, ne serait-ce point ce que nous voyons maintenant, – ce monde de forces exactes et d'illusions étudiées? – Rêve, rêve, mais rêve tout pénétré de symétries, tout ordre, tout actes et séquences![59]

PART III

Musical techniques in Valéry's poetry

5

COMPOSITION

Je ne puis plus penser 'Poésie' – concevoir la poésie, en juger que que sous la clef de la composition.

XVII, 1935, p. 789

La composition d'une œuvre est toute comparable à un de ces jeux mêlés de hasard et de calcul. Le hasard et la *prudence* du joueur . . . Au fond, une combinatoire générale des *mots*. J'ai passé dix ans à chercher une langue 'absolue'.

IX, 1922, p. 23

However ready he was to discuss the process of composition, Valéry remained reticent about the details of his own work, perhaps sharing occasional confidences with fellow writers, but most often turning to other examples or taking a general view: seldom did he offer a specific example from his own writing. Even in the *Cahiers*, where Valéry constantly returns to different aspects of composition, the analysis is very rarely linked to a particular poetic example. There are in fact remarkably few accounts of the poet at work with which to preface this study of composition; the experience of Jean Ballard was clearly typical:

Si on le questionnait sur sa ou ses techniques, il éludait le plus souvent le sujet, évitant de se mettre en scène. Et alors défilaient les beaux vers d'Hugo – qui n'étaient jamais ceux qu'on attendait –, les accents peu connus de tel poète d'une époque déserte, et de temps à autre une réflexion sur un contemporain . . .

'Voyez-vous, un poème se juge d'après trois critères. D'abord, j'écoute sa musique, sans plus, comme une suite de notes – puis je goûte ses mots, sa langue (et il promenait la sienne contre le palais, comme on savoure une crème), enfin je passe aux idées, s'il en reste!'[1]

Maurice Goudeket provides a glimpse of Colette and Valéry sharing their fascination with the process of writing; both were prodigiously attentive to the redrafting of material, but again the details are lacking:

> Elle n'avait pas souvent l'occasion de rencontrer Paul Valéry, mais leur accord était alors intime. Penché l'un vers l'autre, ils chuchotaient longuement, l'air absorbé. D'après ce que Colette m'en a dit, ce n'est pas, bien sûr, de littérature qu'il était question entre eux, mais de leur métier et de son alchimie, de ses tabous. Si différents par l'origine et l'inspiration, ces deux artisans supérieurs se rencontraient sur des secrets de façonnage, sur des tours de main, des nombres.[2]

An article by André Fontainas provides a unique account of Valéry's creative powers in the act of composition; Fontainas relates that he was visited by Valéry one morning in 1896 seeking urgent assistance to complete the poem *Eté*. But every suggestion that Fontainas made was greeted with ' "Non! C'est trop loin de ce que je veux exprimer; ce serait plutôt ceci, cela, mille autres choses", et des adjectifs lui jaillissaient aux lèvres, expressifs, convenables.'[3] This glimpse of the sheer inventiveness of Valéry's writing offers an important perspective on his attempts to understand the act of composition and pinpoints the essential interrelationship between conscious control and inspirational force.

Composition represented for Valéry the ideal attainment of the completely lucid mind. From his writings on Bach and Wagner, as well as Leonardo da Vinci, it is their almost superhuman ability to order their material into a work of structural unity that evokes his most intense admiration. The establishment of formal links between the separate parts imposes a pattern upon the material, which would otherwise reflect the 'accidental' nature of the world around and one's normal mental processes: 'pratiquer dans l'œuvre quelque ordonnance qui contrastât avec le méli-mélo de l'esprit . . . voilà ce que j'entends par *composition*.'[4] And thus the act of composition implies a creative tension between complexity and simplicity, as Valéry explains in a note to *Introduction à la méthode*:

> Notre pensée ne peut jamais être trop complexe, ni trop simple.
> Car le réel, qu'elle veut atteindre, ne peut être que d'une complexité *infinie* – inépuisable; et d'autre part, elle ne peut saisir, et se servir de ce qu'elle a saisi, que si elle lui a donné quelque figure *simple*.[5]

The advances in the techniques and construction of music caused Valéry to envy its capabilities, and often to exaggerate them. His ideal remained that of the musical composer lucidly assembling his score, but the reality which emerges from the *Cahiers* and poetry notebooks is more analogous to the musician composing at the piano:

Poète – Pianiste.
L'exécution sur soi-même
se considérer, s'assembler, s'accorder, s'attaquer, s'attendre et s'écouter comme un instrument; – comme résonateur d'un désir, comme présence, imminence de choses désirables.[6]

For Valéry there is no single 'method' of composition: it becomes clear that he employed a fundamentally experimental approach, trying out whatever developments suggested themselves to him. The drafts of the poems show a proliferation of material, as he adds to the complexity and density of the work, while the successive attempts to find a poetic form reflects the desire for a simplicity of structure that implies rather than explicitly states all the possibilities: one word suggests another, and Valéry will then seek a third which will stand for both. The poet's main concern is to sustain the poetic creation by whatever means possible, whether images, ideas, formal patterns, metre, rhyme or sonorous quality: 'La poésie exige une invention continuelle . . . La belle ne doit pas retomber au sol.'[7]

Si un écrivain n'est pas un sot, – il doit concevoir – sinon même esquisser, en chaque 'point' de son travail, une multiplicité de *solutions* possibles. Il doit considérer cet arbitraire comme possibilité même de son travail. Ce choix se fait ou non *sur le papier*.[8]

Valéry defined composition as the combination of separate parts, the bringing together of elements not normally so, which thereby imposes some kind of order over them. These elements are variously defined as energies, forces, forms, as well as ideas and images:

Composition. Poésie ou *Chaînes* . . . non seulement l'acte de joindre des parties, mais plus profondément de l'acte de concerter des énergies de formes très différentes, comme de *désirer* et *retenir, saisir* et *attendre*.[9]

Another time he isolates four distinct factors:

Art – Combinaisons sensorielles – agrément pur. consonnes
  Combinaisons énergétiques – attente. accumulation. réflexe
  Combinaisons sentimentales – souvenirs.
  Combinaisons intellectuelles – ordre.[10]

Valéry's notes attempt to break the process of composition down into several stages, sometimes classified according to psychological criteria, at others according to rather more mechanical principles of construction. The most useful classification of the entire process occurs in 1926:

1. Désordre initial. Eblouissement. vertige ou vide.
2. Tâtons. Ebauche d'un chemin – dans la masse mentale.
3. Actes nets.
4. Jugements. reculs.
5. Enrichissements.

Finally the poet stands back from his creation:

reprendre sa liberté à l'égard de ce qu'on fait et reposé, du haut, légèrement marquer de la canne les choses faibles, les choses lourdes, les choses inutiles, abattre, simplifier.[11]

The note indicates a fear, similar to Stravinsky's and Mallarmé's of the nothingness at the beginning of creation – 'la conscience a horreur de vide'[12] – and also a fine balance between the clear yet interrelated rôles of inspiration and conscious control. The emphasis is upon experimentation and intuition in item 2 and upon conscious criteria of choice in item 4; and yet it is only in the final stage that the poet sees his conscious mind as entirely separate from the work, dominating it and ordering it *retrospectively* rather than from the very outset. Remembering that the stages of composition represent a possible outline rather than a fixed pattern for each and every poem, the process will be analysed under five convenient headings: preparation prior to writing; beginnings; developments; construction; and finishing.

Preparation

'Désordre initial. Eblouissement. vertige ou vide.'

The preparation for writing a particular poem leads back, as Ince has pointed out, into the entire life and thought of the poet, both on general matters and on poetic principles. It is the stage of 'reflection and analysis, and not least, self-analysis', leading to 'an eventual integrated state of the poet where the benefits will arise spontaneously'.[13] Everything in the poet's experience contributes to make up the inspiration of a poem; indeed what appears as an inspiration may be a point of arrival rather than a point of departure. If it could be seen in sufficient detail, 'l'existence d'un artiste nous apparaîtrait, sans doute, comme une longue et constante préparation de quelque état suprême: nous assisterions à la construction d'un créateur'.[14] It is clear that in his maturity Valéry saw that lucid construction could never be enough on its own.

Il faut préparer un ouvrage jusqu'au point où il s'improvise et se fait tout seul.
L'improvisation spontanée a elle aussi sa préparation mais inconnue du créateur.[15]

Certain things are going on within the poet even before the first word emerges. It may be an inner desire to create, a sensitivity to the experience of poety ('l'état poétique') or a revelation about the nature of his own self:

une formule magique dont il ignore tout ce qu'elle lui ouvrira. une demeure, une cave et un labyrinthe qui lui était intime et inconnu.[16]

If a line or an idea occurs as an apparent surprise, it is perhaps precisely because its secret existence is suspected and desired by a primary level of consciousness; it works in the same way as the scent of a flower stirring one to seek its origin or

comme de l'or est dissous dans la mer. Si le liquide se sature et qu'un germe y soit jeté, tout s'oriente et s'éclaire.[17]

This idea, expressed poetically in *Le Vin Perdu*, was used earlier in a poem entitled *L'idée maîtresse*

J'étais dans ton ombre et dans ta composition
J'étais éparse, près et loin (comme une goutte de vin
    dans une tonne d'eau claire)
Dans ta substance . . .
Ton intelligence ordinaire s'étonnera elle-même
Elle trouvera de tels chemins que tu t'apparaîtras insensé
Tu diras ce qui te surprend. Tu te trouveras, ayant fait
Ton impossible.

The germ of a poetic idea crystallises, then, within a 'liquide' which is the total experience of the poet. A reaction is provoked among a number of 'circonstances présentes dans l'être de l'auteur'. These 'circonstances', combined in an original way, include:

la considération de soi, . . . la considération de quelque autre, . . . la considération de choses, . . . moi étant, subissant, s'ignorant, se percevant, . . . la présence des impressions immédiates ou récentes.[18]

The idea that creativity arises from the connection of previously disparate elements is not of course original; Koestler in his study *The Act of Creation* has charted it throughout history. But Valéry was very aware that unconscious forces were at work, and would deliberately contrive to get these forces working.

One of the ways was to consider formal patterns. On one occasion he planned a musical distribution of passages: 'Andante; Largo; Presto; Scherzo' with obvious symphonic intentions. He sought 'l'histoire qui donnera causes apparentes',[19] but did not, apparently, succeed. His plan for a 'symphonie pastorale dans le style classique' was however linked to the Narcisse theme and in a modified form led more fruitfully to the *Cantate du Narcisse*.[20] Another time he became preoccupied with the eight-syllable line after a discussion with Louÿs: 'il s'agit de donner un sens à cette expression'.[21]

Preparation for a poem occurs at the deepest, most secret level of the poet, reacting with more conscious, deliberate designs. For this to happen, Valéry stresses:

Il y a de merveilleuses coïncidences.[22]

But when it does the effect is startling:

> Perdu ce vin, ivres les ondes! . . .
> J'ai vu bondir dans l'air amer
> Les figures les plus profondes . . .   *Le Vin Perdu*

Beginnings

'Tâtons. Ebauche d'un chemin – dans la masse mentale.'

The urge to create materialises, then, in a fragment of verse, a 'vers donné' perhaps or an indication of a theme.

Composition

Le Bon Dieu / La Muse / nous donne pour rien le premier vers. Mais c'est à nous de faire le second qui doit rimer à celui-ci et ne pas être indigne de son frère surnaturel.[23]

The manuscripts show that this initial fragment is invariably followed on the same page by a number of additional words and phrases, scattered haphazardly often without concern for verse-form, as Valéry seeks to maintain the initial 'état poétique' by a kind of brainstorming:

d'abord tout jeter sur un papier - tout ce qui vient à propos de ce qui vint - aller loin, vite, au hasard - [24]

There may be no clear directions as yet, in some cases no stanza form, in others not so much as the indication of subject, only the sheer spontaneous suggestions arising from the poet and his reaction to his material, with each new word offering the possibility of new directions:

on n'y voit pas loin devant soi. Ce n'est pas en pleine lumière, mais par tâtonnements qu'on procède - avec des alternatives d'avancement brusque et sûr dans l'instant, et d'arrêts - d'impressions d'infranchissable.

   Le langage est un domaine *des plus accidentés* - à ce point de vue - Le Hasard![25]

A good example is offered in the first manuscript of *Les Grenades*, where an opening line is followed by two rather more tentative lines and a series of experiments with sounds and images as one association leads on to another.

Belles grenades entr'ouvertes
Par l'excès de votre (pensée) bonheur
Qui regorge de découvertes - éclate
                         crève
Belle fenêtre entrebaîllée   Belles grenades entrouvertes
                              toi
Belle grenade entrebaîllée j'aperçois un - secture structuré
    belles personnes   grains
        maillée
   blonde belle personne
Qui d'un bras d'autre moissonne
    cheveux
  une chevelure
      écrins
      chagrin

As he overcomes the tensions of the blank page, Valéry indicates that he can relax more and allow his reactions free rein, releasing them by a mental game with the memory. He repeats what is already written again and again, 'Comme si'il essayait de se souvenir de la suite encore à naître.' He acts as though the problem is already solved: 'tendre l'oreille pour se faire parler'.[26]

Le vers *suivant*, engendré par le *précédant*, – comme contenu dans lui; de sorte qu'il soit obtenu d'un précédant en écoutant celui-ci, qui a créé une Attente à laquelle quelque chose doit se répondre, soit immédiate, soit après quelques autres vers. Il y a une opération inverse.[27]

Confirming the experimental nature of his approach, Valéry writes:

ce qui est trouvé devant faire trouver encore. Cela et le *provisoire* sont les vérités de la composition.[28]

The initial fragment plunges the poet into a complex set of developments. Around each word and each idea he builds up a 'palette' of other related words; he uses free association: 'se placer dans les mots . . . laisser venir les mots appelés à divers titres';[29] he searches for related meanings: 'chercher les accords de mots';[30] and as he begins to group these words further reflex actions, called 'tropismes', occur:

Faire sa palette. Assembler, ordonner, regarder les éléments 'purs' idées – mots . . . Autour d'une 'idée' – d'un Mot – viennent par tropismes quantité d'autres – comme étrangers entre eux.[31]

The artist's palette provides his basic medium, as yet unorganised, but a potential ready for combination. The words and images represent scattered fragments of future ideas, with gaps that will need filling at later stages of composition: 'îles, points ou astres, sur lesquels se placera le moment d'écrire'.[32] The position of these first fragments in the final version is not important; they may remain at the beginning, or find a place in the middle or at the end. Indeed the words may not finally be used, their value remaining hidden as they extend the range of images and associations during the elaboration of more extended fragments, but are ultimately omitted. The manuscripts show pages covered with a proliferation of words, suggested one by another in all tones and contrasts. Some are explored etymologically, rediscovering previous meanings; others develop metaphors and comparisons; phonetically he assembles homonyms, rhymes and alliterations; semantically he builds up synonyms, derivatives, composite words; often there are changes between the nominal, adjectival or verbal form of words. As Nadal explains:

Les palettes, sommaires ou complexes, présentent des groupements harmoniques ou logiques de mots dont les effets et les actions réciproques constituent une sorte de première ébauche de création par la parole. Les jeux de sens et de sons menés autour d'un mot, d'un groupe de mots ou quelquefois d'une phrase dessinent les itinéraires imprévisibles de la pensée ou de l'image.[33]

Developments

'Actes nets. Jugements. reculs. Enrichissements.'

As all his material accumulates Valéry comes increasingly to the position where the master craftsman can begin to make his contribution. He may be presented with several lines, several stanzas even, rhyme and rhythm schemes, and lists of related ideas. He can stand back a little and see clearer guidelines for further action – perhaps a central theme, possible contrasts, and a whole range of specific images. He has to locate these parts within a larger section, 'la suite', and he uses all the means at his disposal to increase his analysis and to stimulate his inventiveness:

Reprendre ce pêle-mêle – chercher toutes les liaisons possibles. Compléter par système ce qui est incomplet mais ordonné. Telle chose fera une ligne, telle autre une page, tel mot l'ensemble.[34]

As possible developments become clearer the demands upon the poet's freedom become greater; he accepts certain restraints, and indeed even welcomes them as a spur to further discoveries. Presenting the two extremes, Valéry contrasts the 'vers donné' with the 'vers calculé' which has to match up to the former:

Les vers calculés sont ceux qui se présentent nécessairement sous forme de problèmes à résoudre – et qui ont pour conditions initiales d'abord les vers donnés et ensuite la rime, la syntaxe, le sens déjà engagés par ces donnés.[35]

But this does not mean that the solution is a calculated rational one: it simply means that the conditions which a line must meet in order to be acceptable are clearer in advance. He is adding to the 'circonstances présentes dans l'être de l'auteur'. He is helping his memory to find the word, or is preparing for a solution that may come later as an inspiration:

> N'accuse pas d'être avare
> Une Sage qui prépare
> Tant d'or et d'autorité:
> Par la sève solennelle
> Une espérance éternelle
> Monte à la maturité!   *Palme* stanza 6
>
> . . . Viendra l'heureuse surprise   stanza 8

The solution itself may however only be provisional. Valéry asserts the value of 'vers transitoires', which are lines only partially acceptable, but which act as a guide to finding the definitive line. The sets of restraints may themselves be purely temporary, and progress in the composition is seen in terms of a constant compromise between these changing restrictions and the new ideas which must fit into them, or may in fact gradually modify the whole conception of the poem.

Le travail habituel du vers, le tripotage qui mène à la perfection, conduit à s'accoutumer à des changements de mots, à des suppressions, à des substitutions, qui, par leur heureux succès assez fréquent, déplacent le point de vue de l'écrivain et lui font penser légitimement que l'objet initial, le dessein primitif de son poème ne sont pas essentiels; qu'on peut et que l'on doit les abandonner, si une chance qui en éloigne se présente, – que ce ne sont que des conditions de *commencement* – une première mise au jeu; et il arrive à place dans l'acte modificateur du langage, et même dans le langage même le principal de son attention. En somme il comprend que c'est la *fin qu'atteignent les moyens*, et non la fin que suggère le désir inarticulé et l'occasion primitive, ou l'émotion – qui est l'importante.[36]

Considering the importance which Valéry attributed to 'idées – mots' in forming his 'palette', it is not surprising that the development of images occupies a central rôle. The function of the image is not so much to illustrate or accentuate the main idea, as to form an integral part of the poem, fusing all the various conditions into a whole. In writing about *La Jeune Parque* he said:

je tenais essentiellement à ne pas verser dans l'abstraction mais, au contraire, à incarner dans une langue aussi imagée que possible et aussi musicale que possible, le personnage fictif que je créais.[37]

116

The attempts to 'find' the image, and the sonorous and rhythmic experimentation are part of the same process: the discovery of what it is the poet wants to say, the definition and realisation of the poetic state that moved him to begin to write.

Si peu d'écrivains suivent un chemin (non une idée) qui de petits pas en petits pas, monotones, mènent à une surprise précieuse; et de là, reconduit comme insensiblement à l'entrée.

J'ai voulu faire ceci dans l'ébauche de prose intitulée l'*Ange*, et qui était toute en redites partielles et en retardements; et en vérité je ne savais où j'allais; point d'idée à suivre fixant le *sujet narrable*, *résumable* de cet ouvrage; mais, au contraire, l'idée du seul cheminement, une manière de s'avancer étant le *but* vrai.[38]

As will be shown, the rôle of the theme is closely paralleled by the rôle of melody in music, and depends very much upon the range of associations which are built around the words.

Like a series of variations, he explores the effects of different rhythms on similar poetic ideas. Alongside the early versions of *La Dormeuse* is a passage using the alternation of alexandrine and octosyllable. An early sketch of *Au Platane* shows a plan for eight stanzas. Although some stanzas contain little more than odd words outlining projected contrasts or changes in person, the alternation of 12- and 6-syllable lines is quite clear. These rhythmic patterns, or 'bouts-rythmés', are jotted down quickly, roughly, to see what suggestions they provide:

6 heures. Je fais un poème de ma façon, par émission de vers de mètres différents et de mots quelconques – occupé seulement de la suite de ces mètres qui est le vrai sujet de mon attention et de mon poème.[39]

Rhymes are used in the same way. Valéry is aware of the objections that may be raised against composition by 'bouts-rimés', but reflecting that the masters themselves, Mallarmé and Hugo, had written by rhyme schemes, he emphasises the importance of the subtlety of the conditions laid down and the 'intelligence et précision des esprits'.[40] The notebooks show the use of rhyme in developing the Serpent theme for *La Jeune Parque*; Valéry explores the possibility of unusual effects arising from the juxtaposition of words such as 'sœur / possesseur, vertigineux / nœuds, enlacée / menacée, œil / orgueil, dispense / pense'.[41]

La rime a ce charme – elle et toutes les conditions conventionnelles – de faire venir une foule d'idées, c.à.d. de combinaisons auxquelles jamais on n'aurait songé. On se fait des pensées tout étrangères à sa pensée.[42]

Furthermore the rhymes are means of assuring the liaison of 'forme et fond' and of structuring the poem:

Comme les parnassiens écrivaient d'abord la colonne de leurs rimes (il y a une page d'*Hérodiade* ainsi préparée, et rien que rimes), et plus justement, je pense, je voudrais que l'on préparât la page de rhythmes et phrases car pour obtenir l'unité dans l'effet, il faut commencer par la distinction des indépendantes à priori.[43]

An equally important constraint for Valéry was the aural quality of the fragments. His notebooks are full of experiments with sound-patterns, with lists of words related through vowel or consonant sounds, producing for each poem his own dictionary of closely homophonous words. Some of his plans are for a careful symmetry of sounds, some for random development, while others resemble a form of code. The sounds are developed, modifying the meanings of the words with great liberty: 'ce frémissement fin de feuille ma présence – ce frémissement seul de source sa présence', 'il envahit cette ombre où je m'étais placée – il dévaste cette âme . . .'

It is important to emphasise the relative nature of each of these techniques. None of them works in isolation from the others, however much Valéry stresses them individually. Nor do they operate at different moments of the creative process. While it is necessary to break them down for the purpose of this analysis, their unity in practice must be reinstated, and the constant interrelation of inspiration and conscious control re-emphasised. At any time throughout the composition, the poet may be confronted with a 'trouvaille' as strong as any he started with. It may be the discovery of a word which then releases another:

Une correction heureuse, une solution vient impromptue, à la faveur d'un brusque coup d'œil sur la page mécontente et laissée.
    Tout se réveille. On était mal engagé. Tout reverdit.
    La solution nouvelle dégage un mot important, le rend libre – comme avec échecs un coup libère ce fou ou ce pion qui va pouvoir agir. Ce mot va venir ailleurs.[44]

Or it may be a whole line which is added in; he quotes two
lines from *Palme*

> L'or léger qu'elle murmure
> Sonne au simple doigt de l'air   stanza 4

as an example of such a discovery: 'il me souvient que je n'ai
pu mettre autre chose.' He struck upon the lines after several
unsatisfactory attempts:

l'esprit de l'auteur est chassé de position en position de combinaison en
combinaison. Donc   conditions – attentes
                           combinaisons – actes[45]

A similar example occurred towards the end of the composition of *La Jeune Parque* in the final three lines:

> Je te chéris, éclat qui semblais me connaître
> Et vers qui se soulève une vierge de sang
> Sous les espèces d'or d'un sein reconnaissant!

He wrote to Pierre Louÿs:

J'ajoute (pour Poétique) que ces 3 vers: 'Je te chéris, éclat . . . recon-
naissant', me sont venus il y a 15 jours, tout rôtis, de la Muse, sans
attente ni provocation, et dans la rue. Je leur ai fait une place.
   Et: il m'apparut de suite après, que leur admission immédiate, presque irréfléchie dans mon texte était le résultat de cette récente pro-
clamation des Droits de la Muse. Une espèce de suggestion m'a imposé
de ne pas avoir même l'idée de discuter.[46]

In fact the lines remained unchanged through several editions
of the poem up to 1927, showing the force of the 'Droits de
la Muse'. It was only several years later that the change was
made to the definitive version:

> Doux et puissant retour du délice de naître,
>
> Feu vers qui se soulève une vierge de sang
> Sous les espèces d'or d'un sein reconnaissant!

Construction

As the fragments increase and the stanzas take shape the poet
is faced with new problems, such as providing continuity
between the fragments and giving some overall shape to the
proliferation of material. In some cases the problem is one of
finding the central theme among the many possibilities, in

others of expanding and polishing what he has already written. Valéry generally refers to this overall form as 'orchestration' and 'la suite des phrases':

Ecrire en partition d'orchestre c'est-à-dire être contraint de percevoir ce
qui coexiste à chaque instant et ce qui procède en même temps que ce
qui est énoncé et dans son ombre.[47]

But though seeking 'une méthode de construction' and an
'orchestration généralisée',[48] the solutions found show a
diversity of techniques in line with the experimental approach
of the earlier stages. In particular, continuity and modulation
become major preoccupations.

Changes of tone and theme are sometimes quite marked
between the different versions. In the first version of *Le Serpent*, for example, only the nihilistic and seductive aspects
are present, while the characteristic features of a burlesque,
mocking tone and an exaggerated sonority are entirely miss-
ing. An early version of *Les Pas* included the portrayal of a
fearsome awakening

> Dans un éveil terrible et tendre
> Où paraît tout ce qui n'est pas . . .
>
> fureurs
> Surgi des drames de ma couche
> Je sens mon spectre hors de mes draps
> Aux ténèbres je tends ma bouche
> Donne-moi ce que tu voudras
>
> (*Cahier Charmes* I f. 30)

It is only when a more appropriately tender tone is found
that the thematic unity of the poem is developed.

Particularly with some of the longer poems, the overall
shape seems to have presented Valéry with some difficulties.
Of the sketches for *La Jeune Parque* he wrote:

J'ai là une sorte de poème qui ne veut s'achever . . . Sans 'sujets', sans
nom, sans âge certain, hydre infiniment extensible, qui se peut aussi
couper en morceaux . . . un train d'alexandrins . . . un serpent de
trucks.[49]

The longer poems tended to be written in independent sections; the problem of composition was to establish a series of
different sections modulating from one to another:

La Jeune Parque fut une recherche, littéralement indéfinie, de ce qu'on pourrait tenter en poésie qui fût analogue à ce qu'on nomme 'modulation', en musique. Les 'passages' m'ont donné beaucoup de mal.[50]

Esthetica mea (grand art)
Modulation. Cette idée-image m'a passionné – il y a 40 ans.
Un modèle est ce passage de saison en saison.
Mais la vraie notion appartient à la sensibilité. Passage insensible par une succession composée, non continue et non discontinue – changement sensible après qu'il s'est produit.
Evitement des seuils. La voix. La galbe du corps.[51]

Sometimes, said Valéry, the need to make the transition produced in the poet 'une idée charmante, touchante, "profondément humaine"'.[52] Such an instance was the theme of Spring in *La Jeune Parque*: 'J'ai même été forcé, pour *attendrir* un peu le poème, d'y introduire des morceaux non prévus et faits après coup. Tout ce qui est sexuel est surajouté.'[53] But the theme of course arose out of all that had been written before; far from being gratuitously grafted on at the end, it is of major importance and in its final position introduces the theme of maternity and the Parque's subsequent rejection of the 'exécrable harmonie!': 'Chaque baiser présage une neuve agonie . . .' From the need to modulate for the sake of the construction and the theme, a development in the personality of the subject takes place:

comme la suite toujours possible est l'homme même, ou la vie d'homme, ce besoin *formel* trouve une réponse – fortuite ou heureuse chez l'auteur – et *vivante*, une fois mise en place, pour le lecteur.[54]

If some transitions form a vital part of the structure of the poems, others are deliberately omitted. In the case of the Parque we are presented with a succession of different moments in her life, of different 'present' times, without the narrative explanation of how she got from one place to another. Indeed the silences themselves are built into the construction. Different lengths are indicated (three points of suspension, a break in a line, a break between two lines, and a larger break between sections); these silences have an evocative and dramatic effect which involve the reader's participation in reconstructing them.

Valéry clearly rejected any narrative elements in poetry

and thus any unity brought by the sequence of events or logical developments of ideas was seen as quite arbitrary.

Ni la chronologie d'un récit, ni la pure succession de situations, ni le développement 'logique' des 'idées', ni même celui d'un 'sentiment', ne suffisent à donner à un poème l'unité . . . substantielle, la continuité, l'indivisibilité qui en feraient le 'corps glorieux et incorruptible' que l'on peut concevoir.[55]

While the transitions were successfully achieved in *La Jeune Parque*, adding depth and continuity to the whole, in other poems these problems were never completely resolved, as indicated by the titles of *Fragments du Narcisse*, and *Ebauche d'un Serpent*. It would seem however, from Valéry's own statements, that *Narcisse* represented an attempt to tackle the composition of a long sustained poem from a different angle. Removed from the dramatic complexities of *La Jeune Parque* and the recitative quality of her monologue, it seeks unity in the calm unfolding of a soliloquy, in the 'continuité musicale', as is evident in its form with blocks of alexandrines and, with few exceptions, a succession of rhyming couplets, *a a b b c c. . . .*[56]

The importance of continuity and modulation was just as evident in the poems organised into stanzas, and particularly so in the longer ones. In the same article quoted above, Valéry proposes the linking of stanzas into a continuous pattern as a possible solution:

Il existe cependant un moyen de résoudre sans des peines infinies ce problème de la composition, si subtil et si difficile à énoncer que nombre de grands poètes semblent ne pas en avoir conscience: l'emploi de strophes, mais de strophes qui s'enchaînent et puissent donner l'impression d'une suite de magiques transformations de la même substance émotive.[57]

In many cases the composition proceeded by a process of internal development from one version to another, as one stanza split and generated others as extensions or contrasts. Of the longer poems, *Cantique des Colonnes*, *Le Rameur* and *Le Cimetière marin* stand out for their overall composition. In the first two the subjects readily lend themselves to a slow rhythmic progression which is apparently unending. In *Can-*

tique the structure arose from within stanzas already written. From the stanza eventually placed sixth in the final version. Valéry developed stanzas 7 and 8, evoking the origins of the stone columns and how they have been brought to a state of glistening beauty. Similarly stanzas 10 and 11 are an extension of stanza 9 presenting a 'chant' of their present joy and charm which though sensual is divine and chaste. The early version of the poem is rearranged to bring these two parts immediately next to each other, contrasting the past and the present of the columns.

Much more rearrangement took place in *Le Cimetière marin*. The stages of composition have been analysed in detail by L. J. Austin who shows that from an early version of 7 stanzas, five remained almost unchanged and in fact shape the final poem. These five are, using the numbers of the final version, stanza 1 ('Ce toit tranquille'), 13 ('Les morts cachés sont bien dans cette terre'), 14 ('Tu n'as que moi pour contenir tes craintes'), 21 ('Zénon! Cruel Zénon!) and 24 ('Le vent se lève! . . . Il faut tenter de vivre!'). As the composition proceeded Valéry developed ideas from each of these stanzas, extending the image or contrasting it, and subsequently reordering the stanzas. For example, from stanza 1, with its image of the sea, its glistening surface and the calm contemplation, he developed stanza 8 as an opposing balance: an isolated observer, looking inwards to the depth of his being as if surveying a vast inner sea: 'O pour moi seul, à moi seul, en moi-même . . .' Alongside the draft of stanza 3 ('Stable trésor, temple simple à Minerve') he contrasted this calmness with the vigorous stormy scene that formed stanza 23: 'Oui, grande mer de délires douée . . .'

Already in the early version Valéry had established the framework of the poem with its movement from sensation to abstraction and back to sensation; the major themes of the sea, the sun and death were also evident. But from this point there is no linear development: each idea is taken as far as possible free from temporal or logical restrictions and its place in the poem assessed afterwards. Each stanza has its own internal perfection, its own form and logic:

Quand tu fais un ouvrage exécuté, trouve d'abord une partie que tu portes au plus haut point de beauté afin qu'elle te serve de désir et de condition de perfection de toutes les autres, qui ne voudront lui être inférieures.[58]

All these factors combined to make a reordering of stanzas possible according to the effect desired. The most drastic changes occurred between stanzas 4 and 9, from the first publication in *N.R.F.* to the definitive version. Within the overall movement from sea to cemetery, the problem was where to place the peak of admiration and identification ('Temple du Temps . . .') and the moment of abstraction and questioning which breaks the previous unity of observer and scene ('Sais-tu, fausse captive . . .'). In fact the *N.R.F.* version shows the order of stanzas as 1, 2, 3, 9, 5, 4, 6, 8. It was perhaps in this work that Valéry came closest to his orchesttral ideal – 'orchestrer = disposer'[59] – precisely because of the perfection of each stanza, and the symmetrical developments and contrasts. Moreover with the fusion of concrete and abstract and the use of symbolic images rather than argument, he was able to express poetically his early ideas on the relativity of mental states:

Dans le Cim. marin, il me souvient que je formai et plaçai des strophes, comme on fait de masses, de couleurs, ou d'atomes – strophes suggérées dans leur tonalité par l'équilibre général . . .
D'où quelque hésitation sur les placements . . .
Ainsi de la strophe Zénon, – introduite pour *philosopher* le personnage virtuel – la *Personne-qui-chante*. Mais ce système de composition traite la 'pensée' en moyen . . . la 'pensée' tenue pour *partie* d'une transformation cachée.[60]

It is striking that the intention to 'philosophise' was clear from the beginning, for the Zénon stanza was one of the first seven which he wrote.

A note written alongside these remarks suggests a similar process for the composition of the *Serpent*. Each section of the early version is developed into a group of two or three stanzas of a fair degree of perfection; different time perspectives are introduced, leading to further groups of stanzas; like building-blocks the groups are moved, inverted and ordered so that some overall shape and development of argument is

constructed; and as the blocks are ordered, gaps in the structure become evident and the need for some new transitional
section emerges.

The problems of transition and organisation arose too in
the final stages of composition of *La Pythie*. Valéry was reasonably sure of the opening sequence and the latter part of
the Pythie's words, but was far less certain how to construct
the first two-thirds of her speech, stanzas 4 to 13. With the
seventh version of the poem certain groupings of stanzas
begin to clarify, indicating the different moods and reactions
of the Pythie: defiance (5 and 4), withdrawal to a blissful
past (9 and 10); the horror of the present situation (12 and
13); acceptance and submission (6 and 7), although Valéry
is still unsure of their position relative to each other. Stanza
11 is written initially to develop the rites of preparation in
stanza 12; the modulations are those of music and the changes
she herself is undergoing in her present agony, as the draft
MS. shows: 'Hélas être méconnaissable modulation du temps
de vous méconnaître . . .' However its value as a transitional
stanza bringing the Pythie back from her reminiscences to
the present situation becomes apparent to Valéry and subsequent plans show stanzas 9 and 10 followed immediately
by 11, then 12 and 13. The structural problem is now more
clear: the need for a transition in the opposite direction,
from the acceptance of stanzas 6 and 7 back to the past of
stanzas 9 and 10 where she recalls her former happiness. In
one plan of stanza numbers the division between stanzas 7
and 9 is marked by a double line; and alongside stanza 9 of
the seventh version Valéry writes '8 à faire'. The intention is
clear in the manuscript:

O sombre, o folle, o sage, ô
Tourne toi plutôt
voir
pouvoir

Ecoute
Sombre, folle
    A toi même sombre étrangère
. . .
Retourne toi vers   époque
    D'autres   que les tiens   (f. 124)

The stanza is then formed from this need for a transition and another part of a stanza which until now has been placed later in the poem:

> Insensible, invisible Père
> Je te hais de tous mes tronçons
> Mais crains le ressort de vipère
> De mon cœur noué de frissons

Of the various plans, only the last two include stanza 8, and though the final one shows the published order of stanzas, the penultimate one (f. 94) presents an extraordinary attempt to reshape the poem. It reveals a final hesitation over the ordering of the Pythie's speech and involves quite a radical restructuring: it is undoubtedly the most significant example of this particular technique of composition, for the entire development from stanzas 8-23 is changed. Stanzas 1-7 remain in their normal order (with 5 and 4 reversed as in many versions); stanza 8 follows to announce the transition back to the past but is succeeded by stanza 13 ('Qu'ai-je donc fait') no doubt because the references to virginity were considered appropriate to her former innocence and happiness; then follows stanza 11 ('Hélas! ô roses, toute lyre / Contient la modulation') but with the modulation now working in the opposite direction, from present back to past; then stanzas 9 and 10 ('Mon cher corps' and 'Toi mon épaule') are used and the movement back to the present is effected by stanza 12 which recounts the preparations for the rites. The reordering of the second part is less satisfactory and offers two series of stanzas in reverse order: 14, 18, 16, 15, 21, 20, 19, 22, 23. The movement is abrupt from 'Pourquoi, puissance Créatrice' to the tears, the rejection of divine light, the plea for calm, the willing acceptance and the approach of the final crisis. But rather than discussing the advantages and disadvantages of the placing of particular stanzas, it is important to recognise the implications of this plan; the very fact that he could contemplate and experiment with such a different presentation underlines that the chronological development, the unfolding of the 'story' is much less important in the finished work than the resonance of each of the stanzas and its interconnections; if certain sections remain constant, they seldom comprise more than two or three stanzas and may in any case change their position relative to each other; above all each stanza carries with it the implications of the others, so that the poem becomes a construction of different melodic lines, theme and counter-theme combining not so much sequentially as in a manner which is characteristic of the polyphony of modern music.

With the shorter poems the construction is tackled in a rather different fashion. Instead of ordering groups of complete stanzas, the problem is to construct the thematic development within the pattern of lines and stanzas; sometimes this may mean reducing rather than expanding the material, so that each word and line becomes more highly charged with poetic meaning, and the structure of lines more carefully balanced. Several of the shorter poems follow the sonnet form. From about 1910 Valéry undertook a detailed study of the literary use of the sonnet from Petrarch onwards, and he developed a clear conception of the internal balance which he sought:

Il y a d'abord une condition commune aux 4 éléments
(1) A, B, C, D = 0
Il y a une condition des quatrains
(2) A, B = 0
et une des tercets
(3) C, D = 0
Il y a une asymétrie des quatrains
(4) A + B = 0
et des tercets
(5) C + D = 0

Les mêmes rimes aux quatrains ont une signification qu'il faut trouver. *Faire le sonnet, c'est trouver cette signification* – c'est trouver une des expressions ou solutions de cette relation, *mêmes rimes.*
(Un bon sonnet ferait sentir qu'il *fallait* que les deux quatrains rimassent entre eux.)[61]

With most of the fourteen-line poems in *Charmes* Valéry seems to have decided upon this form at an early stage: it was after all a form that preoccupied him even more in the *Vers Anciens. La Ceinture* presents an interesting exception: an early version outlined 5 stanzas of four lines each, and the intention is confirmed by a separate list of the poems in which Valéry indicated twenty lines for this poem. The theme was clear, with the first three stanzas very similar to the final version, a fourth fragmentary stanza and a fifth almost complete; but the form was evidently discovered late in the process of composition.

> Cette ceinture vagabonde,
> Dont joue un corps aérien
> Est-elle pas le seul lien
> Qui me rattacherait au monde? (stanza 3)

> Absent, présent, toujours plus seul   je suis le seul
> Et sombre . . .   espoir
> Car . . .
> Ta . . .   (stanza 4)

> Le songe prêt à se dissoudre
> Plus mollement se berce encor
> Dans la tristesse du trésor
> Une ceinture se . . .   (stanza 5)

The sketch for stanza 4 suggested the introduction of the first person singular, as the observer identifies himself separate from the experience; also some form of contrast is indicated, and the observer's use of direct address instead of the third person. The elimination of six lines, the evocative use of 'linceul' (shroud, echoing 'ceinture', refers both to poet and scene, suggesting death, sorrow and isolation), and the fusion of opposites in the final distich, all contribute to a dramatic close to the poem:

> Absent, présent . . . Je suis bien seul,
> Et sombre, ô suave linceul.

After such an incisive shift of emphasis any further development seems like a superfluous gloss on the poem.

The technique of suddenly changing the perspective to the first person heightens the tension and at the same time personalises the experience: the reader becomes involved in the same process of isolation and observation as the poet himself. The technique is used in *La Dormeuse* ('ta forme veille, et mes yeux sont ouverts') and in a somewhat similar way in *Les Pas* too ('Car j'ai vécu de vous attendre, / Et mon cœur n'était que vos pas'). The changes in perspective and variations in person are an integral part of the construction of the poems, creating a sense of drama and tension in even the shortest piece, and the manuscripts confirm that Valéry often changed the personal pronouns or possessive adjectives in order to achieve such effects.

Finishing

'reprendre sa liberté . . . marquer de la canne les choses faibles, les choses lourdes, les choses inutiles, abattre, simplifier.'

As has been seen already with *La Ceinture*, the construction of a poem may be aided as much by the suppression of certain material as by new developments. This is hardly surprising when at every stage Valéry has been concerned to exhaust all the possibilities of an idea. The intentions of the poet are revealed both through what he accepts and through what he rejects, for the same criteria of choice are involved in either decision. However he has arrived at his material, it is his judgement in selecting that which best expresses his poetic experience which ultimately counts. As with the final lines of *La Jeune Parque*, this judgement may only assert itself several years later. L. J. Austin stresses the importance of this faculty in the composition of *Le Cimetière marin*: 'Par un travail acharné, il accepte ou rejette, il enrichit ou il épure, selon les conditions dures et complexes auxquelles il se soumet volontairement, les images qui surgissent innombrables dans son esprit.'[62]

Certain of the original words – the 'îles, points ou astres' which have precipitated his imagination – are deliberately omitted:

Peut-être ces mots ne seront-ils pas prononcés. Les plus importants ne le sont pas. Certains ont un rôle toujours caché.
Les plus importants ne sont pas du tout celles que mon écrit représentera de son mieux, ni même celles qu'il suggérera.[63]

In *Les Pas* the allegorical references to Psyché as a source of inspiration are deleted. *Intérieur* was written straight off with few variations; but the final two lines come too close to offering an explanation of the poem:

Elle met une femme au milieu de ces murs
      la rêverie heureuse   décence
Et dans la verrerie errant avec [aisance]
Passe entre mes regards sans briser leur absence
L'imprévu familier de ce risque indirect
Le donne et le refuse à l'étrange intellect
    mêle
           parmis la pensée   élément
              la rêverie   ornement   d'innocence
                sévère[64]

In the final version the description and intellectuality are replaced by an image rich in associations of 'absence' and 'présence', perhaps suggested by 'verrerie'; instead of the woman passing about the room among the glassware, her own presence acts like a fine glass in the rays of the sun: though transparent itself, it makes the sun-rays visible:

Comme passe le verre au travers du soleil
Et de la raison pure épargne l'appareil.

The manuscripts of *La Pythie* show a similar process applied to entire stanzas. In almost every draft, from the second to the seventh and penultimate version, Valéry had shown the transformation of the Pythie's voice into 'Saint Langage', expressing directly the words of divine wisdom:

Je suis la parole et la reine
Simple en dépit de mes joyaux
Pathétique et pourtant sereine.

She rises like a goddess out of the water, evoking the dawn of a new language in a manner that recalls *Aurore*:

Comme la nageuse s'enivre
Presque debout dans le pur ressort essor
Rejaillissante . . . délivre
L'aisselle et son creux (nid) d'or
Je suis enfin sauve des ondes
Et j'élève au regard des mondes
L'éblouissement de l'anneau.

But as the central section of the poem developed, where the Pythie's own words express her reaction to what is happening, so towards the end of the composition Valéry reduced the final section, preferring to hint at the 'Saint Langage' briefly rather than expand upon the divine words: no doubt the difficulty of sustaining the tone may explain the decision in part, but there are some fine passages among the drafts; above all it would seem to be a matter of balance and structure, achieving a shape that is totally satisfying in the brevity of its conclusion.[65]

In the composition of *Ebauche d'un Serpent* certain key final lines were taken from an early phase of *La Jeune Parque* and then eventually omitted in the final version. A manuscript of the *Parque* contains

> Et de ma queue –
> Eternellement le bout mordre.

The versions of the *Serpent* of 1921 and 1922 end with:

> Et parmi l'étincellement
> De sa queue éternellement
> Eternellement le bout mordre.

As Lawler comments, 'Il nous semble que voilà déjà le dessein essentiel du poème; Valéry écrivit peut-être *L'Ebauche* autour de ce vers en se réservant le plaisir sophistique de l'effacer de la version définitive sept ans plus tard.'[66] In each of the cases discussed, it can be seen that Valéry has replaced an explanation, a description or an ending that he felt to be too obvious, with an image that takes on both concrete and symbolic value.

Valéry often made the point that he never considered a poem to be finished: publication, he maintained, took place at an arbitrary point in the development. It did not even necessarily halt the process, as the changes to *Le Cimetière marin* in subsequent publications reveal, though, as with *Eté*, a publisher's deadline can present the incentive to finish off.

Du côté de l'auteur – Variantes –
Un poème n'est jamais achevé. C'est toujours un accident
qui le termine, c.à d. qui la donne au public.
Ce sont la lassitude, la demande de l'editeur, – la poussée d'un autre poème.
Mais jamais l'état même de l'ouvrage, si l'auteur n'est pas un sot ne montre qu'il ne pourrait être poussé changé.
Je conçois, quant à moi, que le même sujet presque les mêmes mots pourraient être repris indéfiniment et occuper toute une vie.
'Perfection'
C'est *travail*.[67]

It is not surprising that a poet with such rigorous standards found it hard ever to feel completely satisfied with his work, but the negative nature of some of his decisions is revealing. With *La Ceinture* it was the elimination rather than the addition of material which produced the tight self-contained structure he had been seeking. In other cases, only too well aware of the haphazard, pragmatic nature of his composition, it was only when he felt all his traces to be well covered that he could feel that the poem was finished. The richness of imagery, the fluidity of rhythm, the obliqueness of his themes all too often had much humbler origins which Valéry was naturally reluctant to reveal. His experience of Mallarmé's salon, his years of individual study, his preoccupation with theories of form, had all led him to make an instinctive link between the perfection and the inaccessibility of a work, an attitude that is only reinforced by his reference to a work of the difficulty and complexity of *La Jeune Parque* as a mere exercise.

Le travail du poète . . . est en grande partie de brouiller et de cacher les origines vraies. De les cacher à lui-même. Ce qu'on appelle perfection d'un ouvrage n'est que la dissimulation de sa vraie génération. Achever, (en ce sens) c'est escamoter les traces de travail, les bavures et tâtonnements, rendre aussi inintelligible que possible le procédé de génération, rendre inaccessible l'approche, supprimer les coups voisins du but les plus probables.[68]

Valéry's writings constantly reveal his intellectualism: when examining the notebooks of Hugo and his sketches for *Le Cheval* he is taken with the idea of writing 'le poème de ce Poème';[69] his acceptance of inspiration is never quite wholehearted; his claims for a formal method are always vigorously argued; and as he points out 'L'objet général de ma tendance intellectuelle a été de substituer le conscient à l'inconscient dans les travaux de construction.'[70] And yet his practice displays a profoundly experimental and human approach that places the concrete image at the heart of his experience. At every moment the whole range of the poet's emotional and intellectual faculties are called into action: each experiment is a step towards self-discovery. The position of the poet is compared to 'le compositeur de musique "savante"'.[71] Like a musician sustaining several lines of simultaneous counterpoint he is constructing, ordering and assembling material of considerable complexity.

Composition above all involves combination: each element of the poetic experience must be brought to take its part in the larger work, whether through analysis, chance or inspiration. For figuratively:

Ce vers est *là*, *pour* la logique
Celui-ci *pour* motiver empiriquement
Celui-là pour rimer avec l'autre
Cet autre pour satisfaire ou tromper une attente. Surprendre ou combler ou préparer – c. à d. se réfère au fonctionnement. Chacun sa fonction.[72]

Freed from 'l'ère d'autorité' when words are restricted to the pre-existing meanings from life, his inventiveness takes off from the reworking of his own material. 'Il ne s'agit plus en effect de préhension du réel par un mode de vision ou d'expression directe du monde, mais par un mode inventif de la matière elle-même des mots.'[73] Or in the words of *Prose (pour des Esseintes)*

> Car j'installe, par la science,
> L'hymne des cœurs spirituels
> En l'œuvre de ma patience,
> Atlas, herbiers et rituels.

The 'palettes', the 'bouts-rimés', the 'vers trouvés', as well as the more extended fragments are all in a sense preparatory work for the invention of the perfect simplicity of the final form. If many of the origins are humble and ordinary and the successive approximations patiently accumulated, the innumerable drafts and reworkings reveal an inspirational force and an extraordinary capacity for imaginative leaps that is fascinating in its demonstration of the creative process at work.

J'ai été extrêmement frappé, plus que je n'en fus surpris, de voir, dans plus d'un cas, l'excellent, le parfait ne s'établir que sur les ruines, jusqu'ici inconnues de textes successifs, parfois assez médiocres. Mais je sais par expérience à quel point les reprises infinies sont la condition de l'efficace et de la pureté finales. Rien, d'ailleurs, n'est plus agréable, à mon avis, que de travailler sur une ébauche qui nous force, sans doute, à réagir contre l'imperfection que nous sentons, et n'ayant plus à penser à remplir le 'vide papier', où siège le vertige du commencement.[74]

In writing his poetry Valéry used an astonishingly wide variety of techniques, developing images, rhythms, or sonority, establishing certain criteria at one stage, only to discard them later, experimenting with different sections, extending the metaphors and building up the range of associations, all the time working towards a structure of considerable density. At each stage fresh images spring up which encompass all those written before and extend them in a new direction, generally in a still more concrete, and yet symbolically charged, form. For it is ultimately the gradual process of ordering experience which represents the poet's most human achievement:

La composition est ce qu'il y a de plus *humain* dans les arts. La nature n'offre que des systèmes au hasard; et il faut chercher un lien qui donne quelque relation entre un ensemble et ses parties. Ceci exige l'homme.[75]

6

MELODY

La mélodie est une idée inséparable d'une forme.

MS. Poésie f. I^{vo}

La mélodie est une attente organisée . . . mélos est suite de notes suggérant entr'elles d'autres liaisons que les liaisons données – et ceci selon une loi de minimum comme la mémoire. Mélos = mémoire à l'état naissant.

XII, 1928, p. 705.

Valéry's analysis of melody reveals a close analogy between the function of melody in music and the rôle of a theme or image in poetry. He is concerned particularly with the way that both help to organise the shape of the entire work, and it will be shown that he uses the expression 'the melody of a poem' to refer to the structure of its themes. After passing briefly over his musical analysis in order to draw out the more revealing implications for his poetry, the rôle of melody in the composition of *Les Pas* will be studied.

In the early volumes of the *Cahiers* between about 1900 and 1906 Valéry attempts to define 'melody' in terms of physiological and psychological criteria: he studies the aspects of vocal production, acoustics and intervals, as well as the effect upon the listener, the relationship with memory and the similarities with the working of dreams.[1] Between 1912 and 1917 he again shows considerable interest in the subject, especially in connection with poetry, and he develops some of these ideas in his later notes on poetics.

He sees melody as a series of notes of an established unity, which imposes itself upon the memory:

Mélodie est la suite de notes qui peut se remplacer par un seul *signe* par la mémoire et être réveillée par ce signe auquel elle obéit en tant que développement.

135

Une suite est donc ici entièrement déterminée par un élément *indivisible*, donné.

Propriété capitale de la mémoire.[2]

Each note is relative to those that precede and follow it.

Il y a une mélodie quand la 3me note restreint la possibilité de la 4me. Ce qui rapprocherait la mélodie de la *phrase*.[3]

La mélodie.

C'est l'état de ne pas distinguer le point sonore *qui est* de celui qui va suivre.

Chaque point (de la mélodie) est défini à la fois comme être et comme relation d'autres points.[4]

He refuses any suggestion that melody is simply a pattern of sounds, in music or in poetry: 'Une mélodie n'est pas une pluralité de notes, ni une phrase une pluralité de mots . . . Une phrase réelle fait toujours partie d'un certain dialogue.'[5] The notes of a series act as stimuli: they excite the listener to expect one sound rather than another, each resolution leading on to the next and creating a recognisable whole.

The successful resolution, from note to note, depends upon some reference system, upon the 'préexistence d'un ordre d'un classement'.[6] This may be simply the recollection of a tune heard before, but this in turn depends upon one's aural memory and 'le souvenir des notes non entendues – sous entendues – leurs harmonies'.[7] The complete series of individual notes form together and operate as a single unit whose movement towards resolution is irresistible – 'la mélodie est ce qui ne peut s'interrompre'[8] – and thus becomes, in effect, recognisable, evocative and intelligible:

Il y a mélodie lorsque l'ordre des notes c.à d. la relation entre leur position et leur nature (hauteur) peut d'*autre part* figurer pour l'intuition un état autre qu'auditif, une succession continue d'états mentaux, une transition psychique générale.[9]

Melody, like rhythm, is one of the more easily identifiable components of music, and as such appears to provide a point of stability within the changing flow of music. The listener can recreate the melody for himself more easily than, say, harmony. It can help him to identify a composition, it can make a 'difficult' work more acceptable and can eventually help the listener to grasp the shape of the whole work.

La mélodie intervenant dans le chaos donne l'impression de retrouver l'*intelligible* . . . J'ai noté cet *effet* hier au conservatoire – en vue d'y penser (et me voir y pensant) – (Symphonie en la) Tout à coup – *lumière* – chemin, forme, Mélos, et complaisance.[10]

Through the process of recognition and identification the emotions of the listener are called into play as the melody provokes a 'disposition de l'âme'.[11] 'Les mélodies évoquent, provoquent des *actes* soit réalisables ou externes, soit subis ou internes.'[12] The shape of the melodic line, and the tensions and releases of the harmony, take on the shape of particular reactions in the context of the listener's musical experience: 'Mélos, le contour d'une émotion.'[13] Melody in fact acquires a kind of meaning relative to the structure of the whole. Valéry compares this to the temporary meaning attributed to an idea or mental state, which he sees as a point of stability within the constantly modifying pattern of mental activity.

Une mélodie est un segment continu – une unité – *composée* au regard des organes – *solide* à l'égard de la mémoire et de l'interprétation ou compréhension.[14]

From this brief survey of Valéry's analysis of melody, it is possible to see the importance he attached to its poetic equivalent. He saw the implications for poetry very early; around 1893 he wrote to Pierre Féline:

la notion de l'idée proprement poétique a tendu à se préciser en moi. Il y a une relation profonde, certaine, mais très cachée pour la conscience claire entre les *idées* du langage et celles qu'on remarque en musique (thèmes, mélodies).[15]

This interest was certainly more than theoretical. In an important passage on the composition of *La Jeune Parque* Valéry described the development from an initial melody:

J'ai pensé à Gluck. J'ai joué avec deux doigts. A l'inverse de Lulli au Th. Français j'ai mis des notes sur le S. d'A. [le songe d'Athalie]
j'ai supposé une mélodie, essayé d'attarder, de ritardare, d'enchaîner, de couper, d'*intervenir* – de conclure, de résoudre – et ceci dans le sens comme dans le son.[16]

The music for Racine's play was written by J.-B. Moreau, not Lully. Only the choral parts were set to music, while the rest of the play, including the account of Athalie's dream (Act II, scene 5) was spoken. Valéry is clearly implying that, unlike the composer, he has orchestrated the theme of a sleeping woman. It is important to emphasise that Valéry does not say that the pattern of sounds in the poem forms a musical accompaniment to the meaning, like notes added to words. Indeed the last phrase, 'et ceci dans le sens comme dans le son', appears to lay particular emphasis upon the meaning of the words and upon the thematic development. The melodic theme is not a simple linear statement of the 'message' or idea: it is the shape of the idea as it emerges within the structure of the poem, prompting as it unfolds various hypotheses in the reader as to its ultimate direction, for 'la mélodie est une attente organisée'.[17] The multiple associations of the words, the variations in syntax, the interruption of episodes break down any single linear development and focus attention upon the way in which the melody develops, upon the various attempts 'd'attarder, de ritardare, d'enchaîner, de couper, d'intervenir'. This view is evident in a note which discusses Mallarmé's sonnets '*Le vierge – Le silence déjà* etc.':

si l'on observe l'attaque en musique, on trouve souvent qu'elle se fait par notes ou accords qui ne se composent en dessin mélodique qu'au bout de quelques mesures. Semblent d'abord sans lien autre que la succession. Comme des couleurs distinctes se manifesteraient ça et là sur une toile – et donc comme formant un simultané sans signification mais suggérant un besoin d'explication et de liaison – et une attente déjà créatrice d'ébauches. La suite éclaire ceci et profite de ses demandes dans lesquelles il y a déjà la substance de la réponse.
Je compare à ceci l'effet d'*obscurité* ou plutôt de *compréhension dif-férée* obtenu par M. dans ces poèmes. Leurs premiers mots semblent rapprochés au hasard – mais leur résonance en est plus sensible, se développant sans produit *significatif*, d'abord, et étant accusée par la force du vers qui agit seule et s'impose par soi seule à la sensibilité, s'introduisant par les voies de l'univers de l'ouïe, et jouant sur le voisin-age *comme accidentel* des éléments de signification – *faisant attendre et désirer* quelque résolution-, une combinaison brusque en Idée ...[18]

In relation to poetry, then, the term 'melody' is used to refer to the central theme or images of the poem, around which the developments and contrasts are built. In the early stages of composition the melody may be as yet unformed, or only partially complete, consisting of a few fragments and the related ideas which they provoke. It may even at this stage consist only of a single line, 'un don des dieux': 'Les thèmes ou mélodies en poésie, ce sont les vers *trouvés* qui s'opposent aux vers *cherchés*.'[19] The distinction between an inspired and a constructed line is not sharply contradictory: the 'vers trouvé' may itself be a response to a certain expectation. 'Trouver un vers, une mélodie, c'est entendre – attendre. Et alors – on reçoit toujours.'[20] The awaited response comes perhaps most easily when the writer is off his guard, but it is recognised as part of himself: 'car j'ai vécu de vous attendre, / Et mon cœur n'était que vos pas.'[21]

The theme, beginning perhaps with a line as in *La Pythie*, or a collection of fragments, is not completely formulated until the response which it seems to demand is fully developed:

Ego Scripto. Les *fragments – germes*
J'ai besoin de *recevoir* un thème pour avoir envie ou prétexte à *faire* des vers.

Qu'est-ce que j'entends par *thème*?
C'est au sens musical . . . un élément de discours, un *vers*, qui suppose *une suite*, un complément, un reste, un manque, un désir, un *besoin*, une différentielle. D'autres fois un dénouement, une scène.

Donc l'incomplet – qui naît de *rien*, d'un côté et tout l'implexe encore *muet*, de l'*autre*.[22]

One example of thematic development can be seen in the manuscripts of *La Jeune Parque* in connection with the passage towards the end of the poem when she slips into the second sleep in the early hours of the morning, 'Délicieux linceuls, mon désordre tiède' (lines 465ff.). Valéry initially outlined the problem he was facing in these terms:

Peindre dans cet endroit de ce poème – cette mort modulée, par substitutions insensibles, indolores – comme *musicale*, comme un passage du double au simple, un retrait par dessous . . . par voie réversible.

Sans que l'on puisse dire à tel moment il y a quelque chose de changé. – Les sensations se font images, le présent se brouille avec le passeé.

Les substitutions d'idées se mêlent de variations d'idées, même de leur altération vers l'informe, le non-significatif – le moi-même sans référence, – la connaissance fait place à l'existence, l'autre à moi et c'est la mort même . . .[23]

He proceeds to draw up a plan of the progression of psychological and physical states in a fairly schematic way, though fragments of lines begin to emerge as his composition moves from 'l'incomplet' to 'l'implexe', continuing the 'vers donnés' with analytical guides, and gradually giving melodic shape to the section. One manuscript for example lists some of the stages from waking to sleep: 'A faiblesse . . . fatigue . . . B désintéret lâcher . . .   C retrait   confusion . . . mélange   D résultat – étrange être . . . achevé – révolue – absolue   Final – arpeggiando.' In the next MS. each of these sections is taken up in detail, the analysis is extended, fragments are noted, rhymes suggested and lines begin to emerge. The proliferation of material is such that it is possible to give here only a sample of some of the developments for sections B and C:

B   Désintérêt – lâche – partiel local   arrêts gradués par degrés
                                                                    cède
         Retrait   trop
                                              Délicieux linceuls désorde si
                                                            tiède – couche
              intérieur – De mes appartements   caprices
                                      où de mon coeur baignant

C   Mélange – mélange – confusion   les battements
       Substitution – Modulation   autre   module   le même   l'Autre
                                                  adule
                            méconnue

. . .   Couche où je me répands m'interroge et me cède
                 Où de mon cœur noyer les battements

The comparison of different versions of a poem reveals how certain snatches of melody are developed. They may be present from the beginning, but their function in the whole work may be less clear at separate stages because of the different directions which the poem takes. The different versions of *Les Pas* offer a particularly good example as the initial lines remain virtually unchanged even though their position alters. The *Cahier Voilier* contains a thirty line draft which begins with these lines:

         Personne pure ombre divine
         Qu'ils sont doux tes pas inconnus
         Si tous les biens que je devine
         Sont sur   de pieds nus
         Dans la nuit favorable et tendre
         Où seul vit ce qui ne meurt pas
         Viens

Melody

The lines present the gentle steps of a godlike figure promising great gifts and pleasure, though as yet it is not clear who the figure is nor whose the voice that calls. The purity and divinity are emphasised and the element of mystery accentuated by the rhyme 'divine / devine'; but the awe is overlaid with a strong sensual impression, not only in 'biens', but in the determination to rhyme 'pieds nus' with 'inconnus' even though the rest of line 4 is uncertain. This is reinforced by the shift from 'pas' in line 2 to 'pieds' in line 4, from the rhythmic sound of the footsteps to the physical presence. These opening lines fuse the reaction of awe, anticipation and sensuality.

From this initial melody many developments can be seen to occur in subsequent lines. In one case the pure divine character adopts the sensual and intellectual qualities of the goddess Psyché:

> Psyché de tes lèvres avancées
> Tu présentes sans l'apaiser
> A la soif des pures pensées
> . . . de ton baiser . . .   8–11

with alternative forms tried out later:

> Je pressens ta lèvre avancée
> Vers l'habitant de ma pensée   21–2
> Psyché de tes lèvres tendues . . .
> La nourriture d'un baiser   26–7

The change of images from 'soif' to 'nourriture' is particularly noticeable; from Psyché's failure to quench his intellectual thirst Valéry moves to the kiss that will appease his appetite and provide succour and consolation.

In addition to the changes in the godlike figure, Valéry develops different reactions in the poet. Recalling the drama of self-knowledge and sexual awareness in *La Jeune Parque*, for which Pierre Louÿs had offered the title *Psyché*, there is a movement of opposition and rejection: ' . . . je te refuse / Une sagesse dont je meurs'. He presents the counterpart of the feelings, the paradox of love and death, consciousness and unconsciousness; the 'biens' suggest an opposite development:

> . . . mon âme devine
> Sous le silence d'un linceul . . .   15–16

This sombre note becomes still more explicit at the end of the first draft, recalling ideas from the first four lines ('ombre', 'nus') in a quite different tone:

> Sur le silence sont
> Soyeusement d'une ombre nue
> Le venir même d'un frisson . . .   28–30

The most striking development though is of the slow rhythmic approach of the 'pas' themselves and the poet's intimate relation to them. After the experiments, hesitations and possibilities of lines 5–16, the four lines 17–20 seem to represent precisely those 'vers trouvés' awaited eagerly:

> Tes pas fille de mon silence
> Saintement lentement placés
> Vers le lit de mon indolence / vigilance
> Comptent / procèdent muets et glacés . . .

In the second version these lines are moved, with minor changes, to become stanza 1 and provide the principal melody of the poem. With the main theme now established Valéry is able to proceed with the poem, reorganising the lines, fusing the images and omitting the reference to Psyché. It is as though the opening lines of the first draft ('Personne pure ombre divine . . .') were felt to be a melodic development which needed a reason or justification. With 'Tes pas fille de mon silence . . .' now established as the main theme, these lines could find their context, taking their place in the second stanza, so that the delighted reactions of the writer form a counter-theme to the presentation of the 'pas'.

> enfant
> Tes pas, fille de mon silence
> Saintement, lentement placés,
> Vers le lit de ma vigilance
> Procèdent muets et glacés.
>
> Personne pure, ombre divine,
> Qu'ils sont doux, tes pas retenus!
>   Quand   maux
> Ah! tous les dons que je devine
> Viennent à moi sur ces pieds nus!
>
> *Cahier Charmes* I f. 30

Melody

A variant for the first line is noted: 'fille / enfant', becoming in the final version 'enfants de mon silence'. Instead of centering attention on the approaching figure, the reader's attention is focused on the creative rôle of the observer: the movement of the figure is a part of himself, unformed, unable to express itself alone and depending upon his silent attention to bring it to life.

In the second version Valéry still proposes to develop the counter-melody, the theme of death and anxiety, the feelings of mystery, uncertainty and awe before the divine and the drama of the inner struggle brought from sleep to consciousness. Two stanzas balance the opening two, while a variant for line 7

Quand tous les maux que je devine

indicates a possible transition.

Ne hâte pas la marche tendre
Dans un éveil terrible et tendre
Où paraît tout ce qui n'est pas

Eternelle
J'aime ce vol
qui
Ma certitude

Ne te hâte pas
Ne hâte pas

C'est mon art que de les attendre

C'est mon cœur qui compte les pas

fureurs
Surgi des drames de ma couche

Je sens mon spectre hors de mes draps
offert
Aux ténèbres je tends ma bouche

Donne moi ce que tu voudras

Cahier Charmes I f. 30

The fifth stanza is largely formed from a fusion of lines already scattered in the first draft; lines 8–11, 21–2 and 26–7 become:

Si, de tes lèvres avancées,
Tu présentes pour l'apaiser,
A l'habitant de mes pensées
La nourriture d'un baiser,

The interlocking rôles of sonority and rhythm are evident in the changes: 'Psyché' is replaced by 'Si', a conditional movement already suggested by line 3 of the first draft and a means of creating tension and suspense. 'Tu présentes sans

143

l'apaiser' becomes 'Tu présentes pour l'apaiser' (and subsequently 'Tu prépares pour l'apaiser'), a thematic modification, as commented above, and a movement from the predominant sibilants to the consonant *p*. The need to provide some resolution to the conditional leads Valéry to amend the order of stanzas, encircling this one and arrowing it in between stanzas 4 and 5.

However the variants to stanza 3 already seem to modify the tone, attenuating the emphasis upon struggle in favour of a timeless note of peace. The sombre tone is abandoned in the final version with the suppression of stanza 4 ('Surgi des dramas de ma couche') and the reversal of the order of stanzas 3 and 5: stanza 3 of the second draft becomes stanza 4 of the final version, forming now a conclusion to the poem with the discovery of the second line 'Douceur d'être et de n'être pas'. The poet joyfully accepts the union of self and mistress, of conscious and subconscious 'sensibilité', of the writer and his own inner inspiration. He creates a total harmony which is expressed in the echo of the opening in the final stanza. It is interesting to see how, having adopted this development, the last two lines of the stanza change their impact in the different context. Where in the second version the lines rang with dread and determination, they are now transformed into an expression of joyful identification and anticipation. The change from separation to acceptance is reinforced by the move from indirect to direct address: 'les' → 'vous' and 'ces' → 'vos'.

> Ne hâte pas cet acte tendre,
> Douceur d'être et de n'être pas,
> Car j'ai vécu de vous attendre
> Et mon cœur n'était que vos pas.

The structure of the completed poem is built around the approach of the footsteps and the reactions of the observer, as a melody and counter-melody which develop, oppose and unite. The first stanza describes the approach of the footsteps: though dependent upon him and his inner attention they are remote, indistinct and majestic ('muets et glacés'). 'Tes pas' are answered by 'mon silence . . . ma vigilance'. The second stanza evokes the presence of the divine figure, the joyful anticipation of the poet and his delight in her approaching physical person. 'Tes pas' now inspire a more positive reaction: 'Qu'ils sont doux'; 'ces pieds nus' as they near the poet lead him to think of 'tous les dons que je devine'. The perspective widens in the third stanza, upwards to the sensual figure of the woman. She is no longer cold and remote, but offers comfort and love. She is evoked by 'Tes lèvres' which appeal to his deep unconscious self, 'l'habitant de mes pensées'; and the two persons are fused in 'la nourriture d'un baiser' and 'cet acte tendre'. The tension is heightened at this point by the construction: the third stanza depends upon 'Si', leading, after 'un baiser', to the release and calm of the fourth stanza. The 'pas' are no longer like those of children or a mistress, but have reached maturity, and evoke tenderness, respect and identification: 'vos pas' are now part of 'mon cœur'.

It is evident then that melody plays a major rôle in the composition of Valéry's poetry. It represents the central thematic image or given line around which the whole poem is structured. The initial stimulus may for Valéry be typically sensual and this is then developed with scrupulous attention to detail and untiring awareness of its intellectual implications. Its position in the final work may bear little relation to the order of composition for it has generated material in all directions: a scene, a situation, a justification, an expansion or a contrast. The compositional care and attention of the poet are such that these differences are not apparent within the smooth coherence of the whole. Valéry attempts a variety of developments to establish the theme and counter-theme. As the density of meaning is furthered, the themes are sorted, re-ordered and rejected so that they shape the entire work, achieving a tightly balanced structure. The study of the drafts shows that the process of composition is not merely the filling out of an idea, but is its very elaboration. The process, described by Ireland in relation to *La Jeune Parque*, applies equally here:

The subject, for Valéry, is produced by the poem, not the poem by the subject. Indeed, starting with what were really musical considerations and working with the ends of music always in view, Valéry found his poem developing a subject almost, – to put the matter very strongly, in spite of himself.[24]

The expansion of meaning is, of course, an integral part of this thematic development, each of the components of the theme taking on more subtle layers of association. If the themes are the melodic lines, then the words are the individual notes that form the melody, and it is to the way that these 'notes' become more highly charged with harmonic associations that attention must now be turned, for, as Valéry said, 'Peut-être, un des dons du poète, et le plus pur, rare, c'est comme la *mélodie des associations d'idées.*'[25]

7

LES HARMONIQUES

Salut! encore endormies
A vos sourires jumeaux,
Similitudes amies
Qui brillez parmi les mots.

Aurore

Much of the envy of music arose, for the nineteenth-century poets, from its harmonic power, from the fact that notes can be played simultaneously in infinite combinations giving a sense of order and logic to a work and extending its range of suggestion. To the non-specialist such as Valéry, harmony seemed a secret language, capable of expanding indefinitely the artist's power of expression. He described the effects of chords as 'spatial' for example, as they seem to extend the area round the notes of a melody adding atmosphere and suggesting a transition in time:

Pourquoi les musiciens usent-ils de l'harmonie, enrichissent-ils la suite linéaire par des soutiens plus ou moins enchaînés entre eux? Il me semble que ces pièces d'architecture, accords etc. ont comme pour fonction de suggérer tout l'*espace*, c.à d. toutes choses qui entourent la chose dont on s'occupe principalement, milieu et réserve d'où le passé et l'avenir aussi peuvent sortir.
Puis les accords leur servent de transition auditive, de points multiples.[1]

La sensation des accords en musique est quasi-spatiale-accommodation. Qu'est-ce que l'intervalle de 2 sons? *Sons* sont des sens-auditives qui engendrent perception d'*intervalle*. Et non, les bruits. Les bruits ne se construisent pas . . .
Ainsi 1° intervalle de 'temps' 2° intervalle de hauteur. Ce terme de haut et de bas exprime des directions d'efforts relatifs moteurs.[2]

The harmonic system of any musical tradition provides a set of guidelines for combining the notes by reference to tonality: 'Harmonie – préexistence d'un ordre de classement.'[3]

But the developments in harmonic style introduced by Debussy sought to break away from the classical procedure of harmonic succession based on the relationship of tonic and subdominant. His music has a sense of indefiniteness, a vagueness of tonal relationship created by the lack of cadential harmony.[4] The suggestive nature of his music exemplifies Mallarmé's attempt to 'peindre non la chose mais l'effet qu'elle produit'.[5] Mallarmé saw that the words of a poem can reflect one upon the other so that a system of relationships may be established giving them the quality of a musical scale:

Ce à quoi nous devons viser surtout est que, dans le poème, les mots – qui sont déjà assez eux pour ne plus recevoir d'impression du dehors – se reflètent les uns sur les autres jusqu'à paraître ne plus avoir leur couleur propre mais n'être que les transitions d'une gamme.[6]

He sought not simply an accumulation of beautiful sounds as the Parnassiens had done but a synthesis of effects, a fusion of qualities into the 'mot total, incantatoire'.[7]

In a deliberate attempt to give poetry some of the expressive effect of music the notion of 'harmony' is very important in Valéry's work. But there are certain distinctions to be made between harmony in poetry and in music, and it is essential to try to clarify the different semantic connotations of the term for Valéry, particularly since he uses the adjective 'harmonique' or the plural noun 'les harmoniques' more often than the noun 'l'harmonie'. Musical harmony depends upon the possibility of combining notes simultaneously and forming a sequence from these combinations of sounds; but the words of a poem are not notes which are actually sounded at the same time as each other and this crucial distinction must be recognised from the outset.[8] Although a strict parallel may not be established, a different form of simultaneity may however arise from the multiple facets of a single word in its poetic context, assisted by the recollection of words previously read, the visual scanning of the page and the latent experience of the reader. The single word is composed of a sound and a meaning which may or may not be related in the particular instance; its sound may combine with a pattern of vowels and consonants extending over several words; its accent and timbre may form part of a larger rhythmic movement; its declamatory effect may convey a sense of drama; its meaning may form part of a thematic movement which establishes a contrapuntal effect in contrast to the principal theme. But, except in a rather general way, simultaneity does not in itself make for harmony and one must beware of identifying these wider connections as the poetic equivalent of chordal harmony. The difficulties are compounded by a degree of vagueness in Valéry's use of the terminology.

In one sense, the most general, harmony involves everything; it implies a relationship between all the constitutent parts of the poem:

En parlant de composition, je songe à des poèmes dans lesquels on tâcherait de joindre la complexité savante de la musique en introduisant systématiquement entre leurs parties des rapports 'harmoniques', des symétries, des contrastes, des correspondances.[9]

In another sense Valéry uses 'les harmoniques' to refer more specifically to the timbre of the sounds:

éprouvez à loisir, écoutez jusqu'aux harmoniques les timbres de Racine, les nuances, les reflets réciproques de ses voyelles, les actes nets et purs, les liens souples de ses consonnes et de leurs ajustements.[10]

But above all, and with rather more consistencey than the two previous quotations might indicate, he uses the term 'les harmoniques' to refer to the different levels of meaning of a single word and the combination of associations which it may stir:

La forme littéraire ressemble beaucoup au timbre. Elle est due aux harmoniques - c'est-à-dire à ce fait qu'une idée peut être exprimée en même temps que plusieurs idées accessoires.[11]

And it is with this aspect therefore that the present chapter is concerned.

The constant exploration of poetic association is a fundamental characteristic of Valéry's musical style, with each word combining a number of different balancing and contrasting rôles. Each word and image is in Valéry's term 'multivalent' and this is an expression of a particular understanding of the poetic experience. It is, he says, not about argument or logic; it is about reaction and suggestibility and is concerned to stir and extend the associations of a particular experience:

> La poésie, en fabrication ou en action, fait appel à des propriétés ψ que l'usage ordinaire du discours fait au contraire oublier, *résorbe*.
> En particulier, le *Vers* est autre chose encore qu'une condition auditivo-motrice. Il entraîne des effets d'interférence sémantique (qu'on trouve aussi dans la prose à l'état accidentel). Comme l'assonance ou l'allitération font des syllabes successives, un composé neuf – ainsi les idées pressées donnent, en outre de la signification résultante, des effets de résonance.[12]

> Résonance. En un instant, l'âme assemble les éléments, souvenirs, images etc. qui renforcent l'objet-idée à peine éveillé qui est un élément de sensibilité profonde.[13]

Words may refer directly to 'les êtres, les choses, les événements et les actes' of 'le monde sensible'; but this specific reference carries with it the harmonics or overtones that are suggested by associations, by previous uses, by synonyms and homonyms; all combine together 'dans une relation indéfinissable, mais merveilleusement juste, avec les modes et les lois de notre sensibilité générale'.[14]

> Alors, ces objets et ces êtres connus changent en quelque sorte de valeur. Ils s'appellent les uns les autres, ils s'associent tout autrement que dans les conditions ordinaires. Ils se trouvent . . . musicalisés, devenus commensurables, résonants l'un par l'autre. L'univers poétique ainsi défini présente de grandes analogies avec l'univers du rêve.[15]

> Harmoniques . . . constitution d'un état *intrinsèque* – sans référence au réel, sans fin à atteindre – *même quand une représentation du réel est employé*. Ce réel devient alors partie d'un système harmonique.[16]

Poetry has always been concerned to build up associations, but what distinguishes the emphasis of Valéry and his contemporaries is the extent to which these associations are developed, and the relative unimportance of the primary specific reference. Valéry explained to Lefèvre that Rimbaud's poetry presents the discovery of 'tout un domaine littéraire dans les harmoniques de nos sensations';[17] and indeed he later wrote of Rimbaud creating 'une sorte d'*incohérence harmonique* . . . des dissonances étonnamment exactes et de complémentaires verbales – ceci sur un fond 'observation sensorielle'.[18] Taking an example from Villiers de l'Isle Adam,

Valéry distinguishes between the immediate specific meaning, 'le sens local', and the effects of the overtones of the words, 'la valeur de résonance, la valeur de combinaison des résonances ou de "reflets" de voisinage':

'Clarté déserte'   (Villiers)

Ce que je nommerais *résonance significative* est la production *par* l'intervalle entre les valeurs des mots joints.
C'est l'hiatus qui produit.[19]

An early *Cahier* provides one of the rare examples of Valéry's poetic analysis as he picks out himsef the associations of a line, identifying the fundamental notes and the harmonics:

harmoniques –
cf.   'une profonde intarissable sibylle'
      profonde + intarissable ≡ source, eau
      et source + sibylle   ≡ tableau vague
      source sibylline
      voix chuchotement eau
Or les notes fondamentales sont les trois mots écrits en dessus.[20]

For Mallarmé and Valéry the organisation of the associations became the very subject of the poem. They sought the fullest possible exploitation of the harmonics and their integration into the formal structure of the work: 'La nécessité poétique . . . inséparable de la forme sensible est d'engendrer en nous un *monde* – ou un *mode d'existence* – tout harmonique.'[21] Still more revealing from the point of view of composition is an analysis of Mallarmé's use of metaphor. Like a painter, Mallarmé was aware that 'chaque objet de la vue est virtuellement chargé des reflets des objets voisins'.[22] In the same way a mental image excites a range of similar, complementary and contrasting images which constitute 'un domaine de possibilités harmoniques'. When developed to the full they form 'le domaine de la Spiritualité ou de la Poésie'; poetry is the attempt to control and order the associations:

on *écrit* par harmoniques, de métaphore en métaphore . . . D'où ce *glissando* de métaphore en métaphore chez Mallarmé. 'La *chevelure* – vol – flamme' etc. relayé par sonorités, allitérations.
Ceci du reste, obtenu certainement par étapes, reprises successives, contractions des relations.[23]

Indeed for Valéry, aspiring to 'la poésie pure', these combinations and internal associations may construct, like the music of Bach, 'un sentiment sans modèle . . . dont toute la beauté consiste dans ses combinaisons'.[24] In the notes for a lecture on 'poésie pure' Valéry speculates on the possibility of works in which 'les relations des significations seraient elles-mêmes perpétuellement pareilles à des rapports harmoniques'.[25] He recognises this to be an unrealisable ideal, but the deliberate exploitation of the harmonic possibilities of words forms a major part of his compositional techniques, achieved, as he says, 'par étapes, reprises successives, contractions des relations'. It is therefore appropriate to turn now to an examination of the manuscripts and the poems for evidence of these 'rapports harmoniques'.

In the early stages of composition the associations of each word are explored in building up the poetic 'palette', as these are extended and deepened at each successive redraft. Even when the poem is well advanced Valéry explores the resonances of words within himself as a means of generating further internal developments of the poem:

Je travaille une strophe - je suis non satisfait dix fois, vingt fois mais à y revenir sans cesse je me familiarise non avec mon texte, - mais avec ses possibilités, ses harmoniques.
    L'idée initiale, les mots posés, tout cela importe peu. Et c'est précisément cette liberté qui est poésie et qui fait de ma présence une sorte de matière plastique.[26]

Using like Racine a restricted range of vocabulary,[27] Valéry exploits to the full the suggestive power of the words so that each becomes highly charged with meaning. Simile and comparison are replaced by a systematic use of metaphor; one of the terms of the comparison is omitted, so that only the image to which it is compared is present in the poem - the impression is conveyed and the object is implied.

Dans [le Symbolisme] la métaphore continue n'a pas de terme principal. Il y a perpetuel échange entre les termes de comparaison, et souvent, par une généralisation très naturelle, l'un des termes est supprimé, pour ne laisser, arrangé avec l'autre terme, que son attribut, ou sa fonction. Le terme conservé est modifié par la présence cachée du terme supprimé.
    Comme dans la musique moderne, harmonie et mélodie communiquent continuellement, se soulagent l'une l'autre, s'engendrent.[28]

This deliberate expansion of the harmonic range of the poetic expression can be demonstrated by comparing the first sketches and the final version, observing the gradual accumulation of resonances to the line. In stanza 10 of the final version of *La Pythie* she addresses herself thus:

> Toi, mon épaule, où l'or se joue
> D'une fontaine de noirceur,
> J'aimais de te joindre ma joue
> Fondue à sa même douceur! . . .

The lines convey the innocence of the Pythie's youthful life, at one with her own body, free from shame, delighting in her own gentle sensuality. The first and second lines in particular show a concentrated use of metaphor: the golden light of the sun playing on the dark water of a spring, the glistening of light and dark, the tresses of hair falling over the shoulder, the movement of hair, the purity of the spring, the secret darkness of the depths: all these suggestions arise from the transposition of 'or' for light, 'fontaine' for hair.[29]

The first draft shows a much more straightforward description and a more 'prose-like' syntax:

> Sur mon épaule où l'air secoue
> Une ⌊fontaine⌋ de noirceur
> Parfois   j'inclinais une joue
>   je cherchais de mes regards
> Et je caressais ma douceur
>   la   de mon épaule
> (*La Pythie, Cahier Charmes* II f. 23)

The image of the spring, a harmonic of 'hair', is present from the start, underlined for retention. But the other lines are essentially a series of descriptive verbal phrases 'où l'air secoue . . . parfois j'inclinais . . . je cherchais . . . et je caressais'. Second draft:

>   se dénoue
> Sur mon épaule où [l'air] secoue
> Une fontaine de noirceur
>   j'inclinais l'ombre de ma
> Je faisais venir ma joue
> Et je [caressais] ma douceur
>   connaissais
> (*Cahier Charmes* II f. 23)

The harmonic resonances of the second line spill over now to the other lines, building up a pattern of inter-relationships: 'ils s'appellent les uns les autres . . . ils se trouvent musicalisés'. The unstated image of the hair prompts 'se dénoue'; 'fontaine de noirceur' now suggests 'l'ombre de ma' for line 3; and the relation between 'corps' and 'esprit' arises with 'connaissais' for 'caressais'. The successive versions demonstrate Valéry's attempts to compress the lines, adding in as much material as possible, eliminating the sequence of clauses by weaving the syntax of the lines together: he is determined to give the lines as much harmonic richness as possible, exploiting the opportunities of each syllable:

line 1	Sur mon épaule où l'or dénoue
	Sur mon épaule où l'air dénoue
	A mon épaule où l'or se joue
	Toi mon épaule où l'or se joue
line 3:	J'inclinais l'ombre de ma joue
	J'aimais jadis fondre ma joue
	<div align="center">presser</div>
	Jadis, j'aimais presser ma joue
	Que j'aimais de fondre ma joue
	Que j'aimais de te fondre ma joue
	<div align="right">(4th–7th stages of poem)</div>

'Connaissais' is rejected because he is evoking here a state that precedes consciousness; the search for unity and a caressing sensuality can be seen in the alternative verbs he tries: 'j'inclinais', 'j'aimais presser', 'j'aimais fondre', 'rejoindre'. By the sixth version the image of cheek and shoulder pressed together as a symbol of the unity of the self is clearly evoked by the use of 'fondre':

> Que j'aimais de fondre ma joue
> Et de rejoindre ma douceur

Moreover the resonances of 'fondre' link up with other words in the stanza: the idea of warmth in 'l'or', the idea of a melting liquid in 'fontaine', the idea of fusion in 'rejoindre', as well as the implication of tenderness in the reflexive form 'se fondre'. But it must be admitted that the fourth line seems weak and loosely connected: '*Et de* rejoindre . . .' By a change of syntax and variation of personal pronouns Valéry

seeks in the seventh version of the poem to create the effect
of oneness in the very structure of the lines, so that the harmonics and the syntax become identified:

> Toi, mon épaule où l'or se joue
> D'une fontaine de noirceur
> [Que] j'aimais de te fondre ma joue   Je t'aimais
>   te lui   sa ta
> Et de [re] joindre [ma] douceur   Fondue à ton
>   autre douceur

The past participle 'fondue' incorporates the fourth line into
the structure of the main clause, making a single unit. 'Autre'
is used because it is separate from her present self; but this is
already conveyed in the imperfect tense and the personal pronouns, so 'même' will be used to reinforce the unity in the
past. And so from a series of verbal phrases in the first person, Valéry has constructed around the harmonics a single,
compressed image, rich in association, characteristically
employing all three personal pronouns, fusing 'épaule', 'fontaine' and 'joue' into a single statement where each sounds
with the resonance of the others: it is as close as poetry may
come to chordal harmony. In such a way the poet is able to
achieve the evocative language of the musician:

L'art de dire autre chose que ce qu'on dit – c'est l'harmonie musicale.
En littérature – allusion soit par épithètes, soit par *fausses propositions*,
qui soient incohérentes ou irréalisables *à la lettre* et intelligibles par
transposition.[30]

Many other examples are to be found of this systematic
use of metaphor; the use of 'argile' for the body, at once tactile and sensitive

> Vers mes sens lumineux nageait ma blonde argile
> > *La Jeune Parque*

> Et vos partages indicibles
> D'une argile en îles sensibles   *La Pythie*

'sépulcre' for the death-like sleep of the woman's body:

> Mais à peine abattu sur le sépulcre bas
> > *La Fausse Morte*

'pierres' for the rigid position of the body locked in regular
movement:

. . . par le mouvement qui me revêt de pierres.   *Le Rameur*

Guiraud has shown how Valéry achieves a fusion of the two terms of a comparison by the relatively frequent use of the preposition 'de', coupled with a relatively infrequent use of 'comme'.[31] Valéry creates an identification of qualities which is immediately striking and demands an imaginative leap on the part of the reader. *La Jeune Parque* uses for example 'cette gorge de miel', 'le vent d'or', 'une grotte de crainte', 'un aromatique avenir de fumée' and *Fragments du Narcisse* shows 'cils de soie', 'corps de lune et de rosée', 'pente de pourpre' among many others. A fusion of qualities is achieved which avoids the need for a more overtly stated comparison or a subordinate clause. Examination of the manuscripts confirms this process: it shows that while the specific comparison with 'comme' figures often in the early drafts, it tends to be eliminated during composition. There are several examples from *La Pythie*:

	Gesticule dans la tourmente	
	Odorante comme un nageur	f. 95
→	Parmi l'odorante tourmente	
	Prodigue un fantôme nageur	st. 2
	Me faire toute comme	f. 99vo
	il trouble comme une matrice	f. 98
→	Dans cette vierge pour matrice	st. 14
	comme bleu	
	Ils m'ont reconnue une stigmate	f. 121
→	Ils m'ont connue aux bleus stigmates	st. 12

'Comme' is not used at all in the final version of *La Dormeuse*, but occurs many times in the manuscripts:

Comme en forme sur les nuits la sagesse endormie	f. 71
Comme en peint sur les nuits la sagesse endormie	*Charmes* II
Comme avec regret une âme raffermie	f. 22vo
A cette heure où les uns et les autres	
sont en toi comme dans une urne	,,
Forme comme la mer faussement endormie	f. 73
Femme comme la mer faussement endormie	f. 74
accalmie	

D'un corps baigné de linge et une croupe accalmie f. 76
Que baigne comme
Dormeuse comme une courbe f. 80vo
Comme seuil grâcieux d'une aveugle ennemie f. 82vo

A still more complete form of identification is the use of direct address and apposition: the object or experience become quite inseparable from the reactions provoked in the poet and can only be reconstructed through a sympathetic response to these reactions:

> . . . mon cher corps, temple qui me sépares
> De ma divinité *F. du Narcisse*
> Tes pas, enfants de mon silence *Les Pas*
> Soleil, soleil! . . . Faute éclatante! *E. d'un Serpent*

One further means of extending the range of associations is the consistent use of etymological meanings. Many of the apparent difficulties of comprehension are resolved by an understanding of the original meanings of the words. Thus 'une image vaine' from the Latin 'vanus' means empty, 'colombes sublimes' again from Latin means high. This feature has been studied in detail by A. Henry who has classified the words according to their derivations.[32] The reference to the stars in *La Jeune Parque*, 'Tout-puissants étrangers, inévitables astres' seems obscure without the etymological meaning of exterior and distant for 'étrangers' (from 'extranei') and inescapable for 'inévitables'. In the following section of the poem the divisions within the self are referred to:

> Dieux! Dans ma lourde plaie une secrète sœur
> Brûle, qui se préfère à l'extrême attentive.

'Lourde' from 'luridus' means pale or yellow as well as heavy. The 'secrète sœur' is hidden from her, unknown, mysterious and sensual; the etymological meaning 'separate' reinforces the sense of division within her. 'Se préfère' (from 'praeferre') means to present herself, put herself forward, hence to confront the other self. The intellect is supremely attentive, aspiring towards an absolute, 'extrême' recalling 'diaments extrêmes' of line 2. The etymological meanings, though in some cases quite remote from current meanings, add further perspectives to the interpretation of the lines. In the *Vers*

Anciens there is a tendency, as Guiraud remarks, for the original meanings to replace all others:

Le procédé est appliqué systématiquement dans les *Vers Anciens*. Il y est souvent un peu voyant, un peu cru. On prend le mot dans son son sens étymologique, mais en lui donnant une signification qu'il avait perdue ou même qu'il n'a jamais eue, on lui retire celle qu'il avait acquise par la suite. A remplacer 'jeune fille' par 'pucelle' on n'a rien gagné sinon en hermétisme et préciosité.

Beaucoup plus subtilement, à partir de *La Jeune Parque*, Valéry s'attache à faire revivre les valeurs primitives du mot sans écarter leurs valeurs actuelles.

Il s'agit moins de créer un mot nouveau, que d'étendre le domaine sémantique d'un mot connu et d'en prolonger les harmoniques.[33]

Valéry believed that these harmonics constitute the essence of the poetic experience and that the poet's ability to explore and evoke the mysterious world of suggestion and association gave him a new powerful understanding. For the harmonics have their root in our deep motives and drives, our primitive sensations as well as our memories and conscious associations.

> . . . Je vais cherchant
> Dans ma forêt sensuelle
> Les oracles de mon chant.   *Aurore*

The process is at once analysed and illustrated in *Dialogue de l'Arbre* when Lucrèce's praise of the beech tree brings Tityre to think of love. Describing the inner source of the 'harmoniques' Lucrèce says:

Ma parole, Tityre, a donc touché ce point, ce nœud profond de l'être, où l'unité réside et d'où rayonne en nous, éclairant l'univers d'une même pensée, tout le trésor secret de ses similitudes . . . Chante-moi plutôt cette métamorphose . . . Comment dans ton esprit, une plante croissante te fit songer d'amour, ce besoin de plaisir?

TITYRE

L'Arbre et l'Amour, tous deux, peuvent dans nos esprits se joindre en une idée. L'un et l'autre sont chose qui, d'un germe imperceptiblement née, grandit et se fortifie, et se déploie et se ramifie; mais autant elle s'élève vers le ciel (ou vers le bonheur) autant doit-elle descendre dans l'obscure substance de ce que nous sommes sans le savoir.[34]

Charmes is characterised by the richness of metaphor, with a fusion of concrete and abstract, sensual and spiritual imagery. In a number of cases Valéry began with description and comparison and throughout the process of composition pared down the lines leaving perhaps only one term of the comparison while extending the other associations much further. The process of building up the layers of harmonics and weaving them into the structure of the poem can be clearly seen in *Cantique des Colonnes*: it is not proposed to study here the harmonic implications of the whole poem, but rather, by focussing upon the opening sections, to provide an example of the way that Valéry expands the harmonic range as the words reflect back upon each other and new material enriches the associations of what has already been written.

The first draft of 12 lines is inscribed within a sketch of the capital of a column and presents already the main theme:

> Douces colonnes, ô
> Chapeaux ornés de jour
> Garnis de vrais oiseaux
> Qui marchent sur le tour;
>
> Douces colonnes, ô
> L'orchestre de fuseaux
> [Haute fôret sans arbres
> Qui ne devez qu'au marbres . . .]
>
> Que portez-vous là-haut
> A l'azur sans défaut
> Nos entières jeunesses
>   antiques
> Fronts purs et belles ombres
>   Le temps couleur de miel
>   jour
>   . . . Loin du ciel

Already the harmonics are rich and interrelated but the poem consists largely of a series of descriptions of the columns. They are portrayed as 'chapeaux', 'l'orchestre' and 'Haute forêt' and are seen with birds perched on the top. Their place in the light, their reach up to the sky is indicated and brief reference is made to their origins. The overall effect is mainly visual; the references are essentially one-dimensional.

'Douces' in the first line immediately surprises by its application to stone columns; though made of hard material they may be soft in shape with their rounded contours. The description of the columns as 'chapeaux' in line 2 presents another striking image. Derived from 'chapiteaux', it suggests

159

the architectural decoration at the top of the columns, jutting out like the brim of a hat. The reference is an apostrophe and makes a direct if somewhat unusual comparison between column and hat. The qualifications of lines 2–3 are related grammatically to 'chapeaux' and indicate the light of day and the birds walking around on top. Stanza 2 addresses the columns as 'l'orchestre des fuseaux'; visually they resemble a row of spindles or a range of organ pipes; it introduces the important notion of their sonorous quality, but for the moment the visual aspects dominate, as lines 7–8 show with the comparison to rows of tree-trunks in a forest. Stanza 3, developing the idea of 'ornés de jour', presents the visual perfection of the columns in the light and their reach upward into the sky; and it indicates most importantly the poet's intention to give voice to the columns.

Already in this first draft the essential ideas are present – the columns as a visual form, the sky, the birds, the movement, the voice of the columns. In the second version Valéry builds upon these ideas, extending the range of implications enormously and linking them all together.

The second version of the poem appears in the notebook of *Charmes* entitled 'P.V. Petits poèmes. MCMXVII'. It is set out on the page in three columns which represent visually the subject of the poem: there are five stanzas in each column, although the third column has some stanzas with only a single line. The first ten lines of the first draft have now produced five stanzas (stanzas 1, 2, 3, 4, 6 of the final version), while the last two lines and the marginal note lead to a further two stanzas (stanzas 12 and 13).[35] The manuscript shows also a proliferation of ideas, new stanzas and sketches which are like harmonic extensions of these openings (stanzas 16, 9, two stanzas subsequently omitted and sketches for 14, 10, 7, 18).

The most significant discovery is the association of the columns and female figures, hinted at in the final line of the first draft; it is an additional harmonic of the columns, but one which reflects back and acts as an unstated unifying image. 'Douces' suggests the smoothness to touch, the softness of skin. The change from 'ô / Chapeaux' to 'aux / Chapeaux' makes the comparison between columns and hats less direct, places it in effect further up the range of harmonics; the female presence is now implied by the association with a woman wearing an elaborately decorated hat: if 'colonnes' is the fundamental note and 'chapeaux' an upper harmonic, the intervening harmonics 'femmes' and 'chapiteaux', though stronger, are implicit rather than explicit.[36]

The birds, as in the first version, move around on the inanimate stone, contrasting figures of life, lightness and song (made explicit in this second draft with 'Chantant sur le contour'). Valéry seems to wish to stress this aspect as he adds to line 4 'Bougeant vivant', and writes in the third version 'Qui vivent sur le tour'; all these alternatives would tend to confirm the literal meaning of 'vrais oiseaux'. But Valéry's untypical use of the adjective warns perhaps that other intentions are implied: they may be real decorations on the hats, real carving, immortal ornaments in stone which suggest for all time song and flight rather than actually singing and flying, and therefore inevitably dying. It is interesting to note that he returns to his first formulation 'Qui marchent sur le tour' for the published version, no doubt for the link with 'Nous marchons dans le temps' in the final stanza. But for the moment the birds are there as a symbol of the link between the columns and the sky.

In the second stanza attention now turns to the sonorous quality of the columns. Visually they resemble a row of pipes, but the song of the birds, the sound of the wind through the columns and the suggestion of the temple built by the sound of Orpheus' lyre convey the aural impression of an orchestra of sound, the harmony of the music and the proportions of the columns raised to the heavens becoming part of the harmony of the spheres.

> Le dieu chante, et selon le rythme tout-puissant,
> S'élèvent au soleil les fabuleuses pierres
> Et l'on voit grandir vers l'azur incandescent
> Les hauts murs d'or harmonieux d'un sanctuaire.
>
> *Orphée*, 1891

The addition in the second version of 'Chacun immole son / Silence à l'unisson' recalls the 'Musicienne du silence' of Mallarmé's *Sainte*. The visual and aural associations are overlaid with the abstract idea of their united dedication to the music of silence, while the sonority itself is conveyed in the disposition of the rhymes – both masculine and exceptionally *aabb*.

Stanza 3 affirms the upward aspiration of the columns; it is not just the birds which are able to fly up into the sky but the graceful architectural harmony which aspires to purity and beauty. Their relationship to the light is reversed: while the light reaches down to them in stanza 1 ('ornés/carrés/ garnis de jour'), here it is they who reach up, arms extended into the sky ('Que portez-vous si haut . . .'). The capitals are the point of contact between the man-made and the heavenly, the vital link between the columns and the radiant light, an idea developed later as:

> Sur nous tombe et s'endort
> Un dieu couleur de miel

Stanza 4 takes up the musical reference of unison from the second stanza: 'Nous chantons à la fois . . . O seule et sage voix / Qui chantes pour les yeux'. With a single voice and with a divine wisdom drawn from the skies they create a visual song. The music depends upon the divine insight of the gods, but is there for man – the questioning poet of lines 9–10 – to behold.

This section of the poem is completed in the third version by stanza 5 which brings together the images in a climax of associations:

> Nos hymnes sont candides
> Et toute la fierté
> De nos forces limpides
> Ecoute la clarté[37]

'Observe the pure sounds of the music' the columns sing out. Initially called *Petit Chœur des Colonnes*, then *Complainte des Colonnes*, Valéry finally arrived at the religious implications of the Canticle. With 'Nos hymnes sont candides' ('Vois quels hymnes candides / Quelle sonorité' in the final version) the reference to music and the sky are bathed in the religious

tone of adoration and worship, culminating the images of the
orchestra, the sacrifice ('immole') and the unison of stanza 2,
the ascendancy, purity and grace of stanza 3, the heavens
and the single voice of wisdom of stanza 4. 'Candides' while
describing their innocence, also implies the sincerity and
purity of the song; this is matched by the whiteness of the
stone polished in the light of the sun and the moon in a
stanza which is added (st. 8, drafted in *Cahier Charmes* I f.
31vo). 'Candides' is associated too with 'limpides' and 'clarté'
so that the three elements – the song, the columns, and the
sky – music, architecture and space – are fused into one
symbol of clear transparent light. Daylight itself is a symbol
of the divine. Music and architecture are drawn from the
same divinely inspired harmonious source, and their qualities
transposed: music becomes spatial while architecture acquires
sound, pitch, volume and subsequently movement.

It is not intended to study here the structure of the whole
poem but some idea of the generation of the sections can be
gained from a schematic outline of the stages (using the stanza
numbers of the final poem)

1st version		2nd version		3rd version[38]		
1						
2 (11.1–2)	→	2				
3 (11.1–2)	→	3				
		4	→	5		
2 (11.3–4)	→	6	→	7	→	8
				10	→	11
3 (11.3–4)	→	12				
Marginal note	→	13	→	14		
		16	→	17		
		9				

It is important to recognise that the harmonics, so carefully
built up in the opening stanzas, are not left fixed for the rest
of the poem. Often they serve to set up further tensions and
paradoxes. The two lines deleted from the first draft ('Haute
forêt sans arbres / Qui ne devez qu'aux marbres') suggests the
origins of the columns; this is developed in stanza 6 'Si
froides et dorées / Nous fûmes de nos lits / Par le ciseau
tirées, / Pour devenir ces lys!'). And in the final version

Valéry achieves a successful modulation into this section of the poem by the change of the fourth line of stanza 5 to 'Tirent de la clarté'. The idea of 'silent music' in stanza 2 is developed in a series of negatives in stanzas 9, 10 and 11. Though acquiring personal characteristics, and though visually and aurally appealing, the columns are deprived of their senses and means of expression as individuals. They are 'sans genoux', 'sans figures', they have 'le nez sous le bandeau', 'riches oreilles sourdes', 'les yeux noirs' ('bandeau' and 'oreilles' meaning architecturally the entablature and the volutes). They are not separate humans, they are unable to appreciate the very qualities they are, as a whole, creating. And again, though 'sans genoux', they dance and move with careful measured pace in stanzas 15 and 16. They become in fact the idealised embodiment of perfect movement and like Mallarmé's 'absence de rose', a negation, a purity which can, at best, inspire the attempts of mortals:

> La belle devant nous
> Se sent les jambes pures   (stanza 9)

Gradually all the qualities which started as decorations or additions to the columns are appropriated as integral parts: they acquire life, speech and feminine grace; they acquire light, song and movement; and they acquire the abstract qualities of music, architecture and divine harmony.

The rôle of harmonics in the process of composition is clearly crucial. The care and attention which Valéry gives to the extension of associations of meaning create, from a restricted number of fundamental notes, a web of harmonics that is highly charged with symbolic meaning. The metaphor takes over as the basic material of the poet's language and leads away from any direct reference to still further metaphors. Valéry has achieved precisely that 'glissando de métaphore en métaphore' he admired in Mallarmé.

Elément capital de la poésie – ce sont les images et mouvements harmoniques à l'idée directrice, la renforçant comme latéralement inutiles au sens, nécessaires pour former un être vivant tout entier. être qui pour pensée a le sens strict du poème l'effet des vers, la vie entière – l'objet

164

du poète étant de substituer une vie à une vie à l'occasion d'une idée ou sens.[39]

Dans aucun art, rien n'est fait, tant que le *chantant* n'a pas été trouvé c.à d. la *température* à laquelle les transformations ou substitutions, les parties diverses sont harmoniques – sonnantes – préparés – préparant – héritant de l'énergie les unes des autres.[40]

8

RHYTHM

Pour bien rythmer, essayer son vers en *musique* . . . Ce procédé donne bien les temps, les mouvements.

VI, 1916, p. 197

La poésie est une danse. Le vers est une manière de dire – comme les pas de danse sont manière de se mouvoir.

XV, 1932, p. 918

It is significant that Valéry should relate his analysis of rhythm to dance and ballet rather more than to orchestral music. Certainly he could not help being impressed by the dynamic movement of Wagner and Beethoven, but their dramatic effects were a long way from the fluidity and intricacy of rhythm sought in poetry. And though familiar with the music of his contemporaries, it was to the choreographic expression of musical rhythm that Valéry turned in seeking a model for poetry.

Poésie, tu es danse. Danse, tu demandes la grâce. Mais la *grâce* ne peut paraître *dans les actes difficiles*, si la plus grande *force* n'est pas acquise, tout d'abord.[1]

Poetry then emphasises rhythmic expression for its own sake, as part of the total 'charme', a quality which distiguishes poetry and dance on the one hand from speech and walking on the other:

La *danse* et le *Chant* semblent réponses à des besoins d'origine centrale; énergétiques purs . . . la phase fonctionnelle . . . *fin et moyen* d'elle-même.[2]

Valéry's interest in rhythm lies in its special implications for 'le fonctionnement de l'esprit'. Rhythm implies a particular relationship distinct from other states and full of apparent paradoxes. Though a function of time, it has the power to abolish time, and though demanding the association of the self with rhythm, it has the power to suspend reflective consciousness:

La musique (le 'rythme') est un autre 'Temps'[3]

Rythme et *conscience s'excluant.* Conscience se cherche une fin. Mais Rythme se demande et se répond. Mais Mélos les compose.[4]

Above all rhythm has the capacity to involve the whole being, as an expression of the 'sensibilité', the physical, walking, dancing, breathing self, the self of love and the emotions: 'Le rythme. Loi de la sensibilité.'[5]

L'Etat du rythme. Etat conservatif . . .
Il modifie singulièrement les catégories du temps. Le danseur ne va nulle part. Le but, la cause, l'être, l'acte, l'effet sont ici mis et enchaînés, comme les valeurs d'une période. Ils se succèdent sans se détruire comme les faces d'un même objet, comme si ces substitutions formaient un groupe.[6]

Un vers est bien rythmé quand les rythmes qui le composent (ou le décomposent) se peuvent succéder et enchaîner, les mouvement qu'ils supposent et font *naître* d'accord avec le sens, peignant les effets physiologiques musculaires du sens: ni faux ni automatiques.[7]

By a process of identification the listener is led to produce the rhythmic pattern himself, associating with the sounds perceived, so that the effect is physical and muscular as well as aural and mental.

Le rythme est un mode de changement qui excite l'*imitation* de lui-même par l'appareil lui-même qui l'a produit – et puis par d'autres systèmes, du même individu, ou d'*autres individus*, qui se synchronisent, et *se font un seul.*[8]

The consciousness of the listener is thus caught up in a pattern of expectancy in which he is anticipating what is to come according to 'laws' derived from what he has already heard. 'Tout le rythme est fondé sur l'attente.'[9] Repetition is therefore seen as one of the results of rhythm, rather than a cause: 'La répétition, dont on fait à tort un caractère de *rythme*, en est au contraire une conséquence.'[10]

Rhythm was seen by Mallarmé as a necessary part of the poetic experience, and indeed as one of the distinctive features capable of transforming everyday language into poetry: 'Le vers est partout dans la langue où il y a rythme.'[11] Valéry equally identified the fascination created by a feeling of pulse as essential to the spell of poetry. It is the rhythmic combination of 'sons purs' which brings poetry close to the quality of song:

Une chose est *poétique* quand elle fait chanter . . . quand ses effets sur l'être sont de la nature d'un chant . . .
C'est ce qui ne peut s'exprimer sans rythme.
Le rythme n'est que synchronisme, résonnance.[12]

In *L'Ame et la Danse* the walk of the dancer appears to Eryximaque as 'le suprême de son art . . . A la lumière de ses jambes, nos mouvements immédiats nous apparaissent des miracles.'[13] In the same way poetry seeks to become 'la marche de la voix'.[14] As Athikté dances, the virtuosity of her performance is translated into the leaps and turns of Phèdre's language:

Par les Muses, jamais pieds n'ont fait à mes lèvres plus d'envie!

SOCRATE
Voici donc que tes lèvres sont envieuses de la volubilité de ces pieds prodigieux! Tu aimerais de sentir leurs ailes à tes paroles, et d'orner ce que tu dirais de figures aussi vives que leurs bonds![15]

It is precisely this effect that is sought in poetry, conveying the rhythm of movement, act and gesture by the articulation of the voice, the placing of regular beats, points of emphasis, mute -*e*s and the variation of rhythmic groups across the whole stanza. Valéry notes the importance of 'ce souci de la construction de la strophe, qui conduit à suivre de l'oreille (intime) la variation de l'acte de la *marche de la voix* ou *par la voix* avec ses pas et ses glissements sur muettes. Je dis: marche, mais il y a danse et nage aussi et une certaine "mimique".'[16]

The desire for a sustained rhythmic structure was one of the reasons for Valéry's preference of regular verse forms. The pattern of the lines provides an 'espace vide, mûr à décorer'[17] and the rhyme scheme extends this property to the couplet and the stanza, thereby creating a sense of anticipation in the listener.

Rimes. Les critiques de la rime ne songent pas qu'il y a la manière de s'en servir. Ils ne savent pas qu'elle *rythme* un discours. Il faut en général que deux vers qui riment l'un avec l'autre soient très *différents de structure*.[18]

The regularity of form allows a sense of pulse, against which the poet may establish the rhythmic variations: there is a kind of tension between the two which gives Valéry's mature poetry its sense of rhythmic vitality. By the use of enjambement, the positioning of the caesura, the use of the mute -*e* and the weaving of the syntactic structure through the lines and even over several stanzas, a taut, springy rhythmic movement is created.

The rhythm operates then within the context of the whole poem, not as an empty shell:

Il n'y a rien de général en cette matière, *il n'y a pas deux vers comparables.* Le squelette d'un vers n'est pas un vers.[19]

The warning applies specifically to the critic, to the 'phonéticiens de la poésie moderne [qui] n'ont pas fait, ni fait faire l'ombre d'un beau vers'. The poet, on the other hand may indeed use the rhythmic skeleton of a line in order to create quite deliberately another line of his own:

Il y a des vers qui sont des traductions rythmiques d'autres vers, et faits par une mémore de ces derniers servant de modèles. Tous les mots sont autres et c'est le même vers.[20]

Recognition of the rhythm of a particular line is not therefore simply a matter of counting syllables: the specific context of the line has to be considered: 'l'oreille pure ne sait pas compter . . . on ressent au 3e vers qu'il y a une *possibilité – besoin de continuer*'.[21] Valéry did of course use other verse forms, including vers libre, but seems always to have returned to the framework of regular forms of French prosody: 'Toutes les fois qu'on veut varier on retombe au vers régulier.'[22]

Rhythm then plays its part in structuring the whole poem, establishing balance and contrasts between parts, a rhythm that is not just an effect of sound and emphasis, but is extended to the meanings and relationships of the sections. For Mallarmé music was an expression of the 'Idée, ou rythme entre des rapports'.[23] Valéry expresses essentially the same idea from a compositional point of view:

Musical techniques in Valéry's poetry

Inspiration: Axiome: Ce qui est provoqué par le mouvement du rythme, vaut en *significations comme* vaut le rythme (en mouvement). Ce rythme n'est pas nécessairement phonique. Mais consiste dans les relations intrinsèques - compensations etc. - cf. images, métaphores - ce sont les complémentaires.[24]

Rhythm in movement; rhythm of ideas; Valéry even extends the concept in an architectural sense to rhythm in space: all are basically attempts to get closer to the musical experience that is easily recognised, but much less easily defined. This difficulty is indicated in an ironical note in 'Question de Poésie': 'J'ai lu ou j'ai forgé vingt définitions du *Rythme*, dont je n'adopte aucune.'[25] In poetry rhythm is not reducible to any single feature, but is related to metre, accent, repetition, timbre, the division of the line, and above all the meaning of a particular poem, for there can be no rhythmic patterns separate from the poetic context. In this chapter Valéry's understanding and use of rhythm will be analysed, firstly in relation to the composition of *Le Cimetière marin* and *Au Platane*; then in relation to his early and later poetry; and finally in the particular example of *La Fausse morte*.

Several times Valéry refers to rhythm not only as an essential part of the poetic experience, but as a major source of poetic inspiration. The most celebrated instance was the composition of *Le Cimetière marin*, which has provoked much critical debate. In the account of a conversation with Lefèvre, Valéry makes two important points: that the poem was begun while he was still working on *La Jeune Parque*, and that the initial inspiration for the poem came as some lines in a decasyllabic rhythm:

J'avais fait quelques strophes du *Cimetière marin* pendant que je composais la *Jeune Parque*.
Il est né, comme la plupart de mes poèmes, de la présence en mon esprit d'un certain rythme. Je me suis étonné, un matin, de trouver dans ma tête des vers décasyllabiques.[26]

The similarities between the two poems are manifest: the figure standing by the sea, totally preoccupied with problems of life and death, aware of the changing states of mind and the complex relationship to the environment. In generalising

170

the importance of rhythm in his poems, Valéry is confirming the impression of vitality in *Charmes*. The final sentence of the above quotation is crucial in establishing the starting point of the poem and may usefully be compared to his statement in the article 'Au sujet du *Cimetière marin*':

. . . je n'ai pas *voulu dire*, mais *voulu faire*, et . . . ce fut l'intention de *faire* qui *a voulu* ce que j'ai *dit*. . .

Quant au *Cimetière marin*, cette intention ne fut d'abord qu'une figure rythmique vide, ou remplie de syllabes vaines, qui me vint obséder quelque temps. J'observai que cette figure était décasyllabique, et je me fis quelques réflexions sur ce type fort peu employé dans la poésie moderne[27]

The manuscripts of *Le Cimetière marin* reveal that this rhythmic figure arose from the addition of two syllables to a line from *La Pythie*:[28]

$$10 = 5 + 5 = 6 + 4 = 4 + 6 = 4 + 4 + 2$$

[Honneur des hommes] | Saint langage | aurore
Idéale mer, Océan sonore
         rumeur au
Chaleur tranquille et [douceur] du soleil
Qui se balance et [frappe] et t'illumine
            silence et
  Toute
[D'une] volupté pleine de sommeil
Sur toutes si la lune change chemins
C'est toi désir c'est toi qui   a   c
      immortalité   a   b
Quand l'[immobilité] toute lancée   b   c
Le crâne vide et le rire éternel   c   b
Veut consoler une vie ignorée   b   a
Il [montre]   c   b
    de la mort fait un sein maternel
Elle fait l'ombre –
Le beau
    Mensonge noble et très pieux ru [-se ?]

Written at the foot of the page, upside down:

à l'aide des mots trouver rythme
à l'aide des rythmes trouver la phrase
à l'aide des phrases alliter –

C'est comme *peut* se faire les vers[29]

This remarkable page of manuscript provides ample justification for Valéry's assertions: 'Honneur des hommes' is crossed out and the other three words subsequently abandoned, confirming that the initial syllables were 'vaines' rather than 'vides'; but the rhythmic division of the line is indicated by vertical strokes and a second decasyllabic line is written, rhyming with the first. Valéry becomes aware of the rhythmic possibilities as he explores the different internal divisions of the decasyllabic line. Further lines are written which are very hesitant, uncertain in form, but, as the figure to the right demonstrates, he envisaged a six-line stanza even though the actual disposition of rhymes is not yet decided. The rhythmic impetus for this passage does indeed appear very strong and is confirmed by the comments pencilled in at the foot of the MS. An analysis of the thematic development would demand a detailed consideration of the sequence of early manuscripts; but it is interesting to note from this draft alone that while the first stanza sketched might present another moment in the consciousness of the Parque as she looks out over the sea in the light of dawn, the second affirms her 'refus de l'absolu' and the drawing back from death.[30]

Much of the critical debate has focused upon the claims for the principle of formal composition which Valéry appears to make in 'Au sujet du *Cimetière marin*', as though the rhythmic pattern itself 'demanded' a particular subject:

Entre les strophes, des contrastes ou des correspondances devaient être institués. Cette dernière condition exigea bientôt que le poème possible fût un monologue de 'moi', dans lequel les thèmes les plus simples et les plus constants de ma vie affective et intellectuelle . . . fussent appelés, tramés, opposés.[31]

As the MS. shows, Valéry's 'exigea bientôt' is soon indeed: the sea is evoked in the second line written, the 'monologue de "moi"' indicated already in the seventh line ('C'est toi désir c'est toi qui') and the theme of death explicit in the second stanza. Clearly Valéry is not claiming that the rhythmic figure was entirely devoid of content: the thematic context is established from the beginning but is as yet unexceptional – rooted in his own experience and that of *La Jeune Parque*, and composed of words that are not ultimately used – while the initial concerns, the circumstances of the poetic moment, are focused upon the rhythmic impetus, the metre, the verse form, the alliteration. Furthermore the need for contrasts and developments was not considered by Valéry an abstract formal demand but the most human of all, for man above all is typified by the continual changes of consciousness: 'la suite toujours possible est l'homme même, ou la vie d'homme'.[32] If Valéry gives the impression of a certain inevitability about the composition, it was because the combination of factors must, in retrospect, have appeared so: the particular initial lines, the decasyllabic rhythm and the formal concerns, the idea of a mature examination of the themes of the adolescent Parque, as well as his 'démon de la généralisation'. The rhythm triggered the release of all these factors and inspired him to *want* to write a poem, just as some twenty years later he was taken with the idea of a musical composition arising from the rhythm of walking:

Hier, en marchant, curieuse invasion de moi par une sorte de composition musicale – ou plutôt d'*état composant*, construisant avec un modèle architectural dans l'esprit des masses – fondations – parallèles.
On pouvait en faire un conte – La symphonie du 28 juin.[33]

A further illustration of the importance of rhythm in composition is provided by the first version of *Au Platane*. It was written in 1918 near Avranche 'dans une campagne plantée des plus beaux arbres que j'aie vues . . . dans cette riche région où le grand arbre pousse comme l'herbe, où l'herbe est d'une force et d'une facilité incroyables, où la puissance végétale est comme inépuisable'.[34] The first version, apparently written quickly, comprises four stanzas and the outline for four others.

1. Tu penches haut platane et te proposes nu
        Ton corps très pur se livre
   Mais ta splendeur est prise et ton pied retenu
        Ton vol ne . . . suivre.
2. Tu n'iras pas plus loin que Cybèle ne veut
        Si ton désir s'exalte
   Arbre, élève-toi – mais . . . rompre le vœu
        De l'éternelle halte.
3. Tu n'iras pas plus loin, ô semblable à la mer
4. Mais de tes bras plus durs que les bras animaux
        Tu . . .

Musical techniques in Valéry's poetry

> Tu places dans l'azur le tourment des maux
>> Que le désir fait naître.
> 5. Tu t'offres, grand platane et te proposes nu
>> . . .
> Mais . . .
>> La place de ton ombre
> 6. Et tu gémis . . .
>> Cependant . . .
> Ton corps poli . . .
>> . . .
> 7. Le tremble . . . le charme et le hêtre formé
>> De quatre jeunes femmes
> Ne sont pas plus heureux et dans l'air embaumé
>> Ne mêlent pas leurs âmes.
> 8. Tourment . . . par l'âpre tramontane

The alternation of lines of twelve and six syllables is clear in this framework for eight stanzas. The rhythm has at this stage the dominant rôle, carrying the poet forward, leaving gaps to be filled at a later stage. The details are for the moment less important than the alternation of the rhythm and the opposition and contrast this is intended to convey, outlined sometimes merely by a conjunction: 'Mais . . .', 'Et tu gémis . . .', 'Cependant . . .'. Already the idea of departure and flight in the alexandrines ('Arbre, éléve-toi . . .', 'la mer', 'l'azur', 'l'air embaumé', 'l'âpre tramontane') is contrasted with the limitations and restrictions in the hexasyllabic lines ('ton corps', 'l'éternelle halte', 'la place de ton ombre'). Rhymes have been sketched in even though the preceding part of the line is incomplete. The result is a spontaneous rhythmic development illustrating Valéry's call: 'd'abord tout jeter sur un papier – tout ce qui vient à propos de ce qui vint – aller loin, vite, au hasard'.[35]

The evolution of Valéry's rhythmic style is very noticeable between the early and the later poems. In *Album de Vers Anciens* the rhythm is gentle and unobtrusive. Following the Parnassien example, Valéry tends to place the important word at the end of the line. With the exception of *Le Bois Amical*, *Vue* and *L'amateur de poèmes*, all are alexandrines with a fluid and generally unaccentuated rhythm composed of long, sparsely punctuated sentences spanning whole stanzas. The long phrases and expanded syntax create a sense of tension: the meaning is suspended while the phrase winds in and out of the pattern of lines, and resolution comes only with the full stop with which the stanza usually ends. The first two stanzas of *Au Bois Dormant* illustrate the point clearly:

> La princesse, dans un palais de rose pure,
> Sous les murmures, sous la mobile ombre dort,
> Et de corail ébauche une parole obscure
> Quand les oiseaux perdus mordent ses bagues d'or.
>
> Elle n'écoute ni les gouttes, dans leurs chutes,
> Tinter d'un siècle vide au lointain le trésor,
> Ni, sur la forêt vague, un vent fondu de flûtes
> Déchirer la rumeur d'une phrase de cor.

Certainly there are exceptions to this rhythmic fluidity: the rhythm of the spinning-wheel in *La Fileuse*; or the forms of dramatic address which stand out from the rest of the poem:

> Azur! c'est moi ...   *Hélène*

> ... Je compose en esprit, sous les myrtes, Orphée
> L'Admirable! ...   *Orphée*

The movement of the sea and the opening address to nature in *Eté* present perhaps the most vigorous, controlled rhythmic effect:

> Eté, roche d'air pur, et toi, ardente ruche,
> O mer! Eparpillée en mille mouches sur
> Les touffes d'une chair fraîche comme une cruche,
> Et jusque dans la bouche où bourdonne l'azur.

With *La Jeune Parque* a much greater variety of rhythm is found within the alexandrine. The changes in the mood of the Parque, her anxiety, despair, exhilaration, resignation are all conveyed in appropriately different rhythms. Exclamations and silences abound, the lines broken up in every conceivable manner, with 'points de suspension' placing the caesura at the beginning or the end of the line even.

> Salut! Divinités par la rose et le sel,
> Et les premiers jouets de la jeune lumière,
> Iles! ...   348–50

> Non, vous ne tiendrez pas de moi la vie! . . . Allez,
> Spectres, soupirs de la nuit vainement exhalés.　　271-2

At moments of great agitation the structure of the alexandrine momentarily breaks down: a silence, full of thought and foreboding intervenes even in the middle of a line.

> Quelle résisterait, mortelle, à ces remous?
> Quelle mortelle?
> 　　　　　　Moi si pure, mes genoux
> Pressentent les terreurs de genoux sans défense . . .　　243-5

The bewilderment at her second awakening appears to disrupt the structure of the lines completely; but read aloud, the alexandrine is still maintained, only filled out with silence, tension and confusion:

> Regarde: un bras très pur est vu, qui se dénude.
> Je te revois, mon bras . . . Tu portes l'aube . . .
> 　　　　　　　　　　　　　　　　O rude
> Réveil d'une victime inachevée . . . et seuil
> Si doux . . . si clair, que flatte, affleurement d'écueil,
> L'onde basse, et que lave une houle amortie! . . .　　333-7

The effect is vigorous, dramatic and very impressive. And yet the rhythm of *La Jeune Parque* in general is still restrained in comparison to *Charmes*. Partly it is the nature of the subject, for until her rejection of past thoughts in the light of dawn ('Non, non! . . . N'irrite plus cette réminiscence!') she is for the most part overwhelmed by experience, taken up and blown one way and another by the force of the different ideas. Though exclamatory in certain sections, the rhythm is essentially submissive. Partly too the difficulty of the task was enormous, and the desire for a Racinian type of continuity imposed demanding conditions.

It was only after the successful completion of *La Jeune Parque* that Valéry developed into the confident rhythmic poet of *Charmes*. After the long effort of hard work 'on s'ébroue! on a ôté les bottes plombées, et l'on danse'.[36] He was, he said, in a state of 'virtuosité aiguë',[37] and found that the poems *Aurore* and *Palme* were written easily and quickly. He turned to a variety of poetic forms, as if intent on mastering each of the different poetic traditions. In a letter to Jacques Doucet he described *Charmes* as 'un ensemble d'ex-

périences prosodiques', and as Lawler comments, 'Valéry se
voulait maître en rythmes, en rimes, en formes fixes après la
longue ascèse des alexandrins de la *Parque*, et son recueil
constitue à cet égard le manuel du parfait rhétoriqueur.'[38]
Many of the forms date from the sixteenth century; though
several of the poems are sonnets they each follow different
schemes of rhyme or division of lines. Some of the poems
arose out of a deliberate concern with verse form: *La Pythie*
from a discussion with Louÿs on the octosyllable, the seven-
syllable line from an admiration for Ronsard and Hugo. And
the ten-line stanza, though in the tradition of Ronsard, Malherbe and Lamartine, is used to particular effect, achieving,
as Porché has remarked, 'un mouvement original qui communique à la pensée, même abstraite, l'allure d'un message
urgent'. A feeling of 'dynamisme puissant' is created by the
'rythme précipité' combined with 'la densité des phrases'.[39]

What is striking is Valéry's ability to master the different
forms with such confident, vigorous rhythms that they seem
to be breaking out of the structure of the poems. He observes
the traditions of French prosody not only to exploit and
reinvigorate the richness of that tradition, but as a spur to
greater creativity: 'Je suis libre, donc je m'enchaîne.'[40] The
most effective example of the relationship between rhythm
and metre is provided by the two poems with five-syllable
lines, *Le Sylphe* and *L'Insinuant*, both in their different ways
'poèmes séducteurs'. The contrast in rhythm could hardly be
greater between the light, playful, song-like quality of the
former and the slow, devious serpentine trance of the latter,
illustrating Valéry's note in the *Cahiers*:

Vers réguliers – Rythme etc. rendent possible de faire des vers très longs
et très brefs dans le *même nombre de syllabes*.[41]

> Ni vu ni connu
> Je suis le parfum
> Vivant et défunt
> Dans le vent venu!   *Le Sylphe*
>
> O Courbes, méandre,
> Secrets du menteur,
> Est-il art plus tendre
> Que cette lenteur?   *L'Insinuant*

Rhythm, then, becomes an increasingly important poetic technique for Valéry in his mature verse. The poetry of *Charmes* is vibrant with strong, springy rhythms that show him to be skilled in a variety of effects. And when peaceful and gentle, the rhythm is far more relaxed than in the earlier poems, as with the slow simplicity of *Fragments du Narcisse*, especially in the second fragment. The techniques are numerous: the accentuation that arises from word-order such as placing the adjective before the noun; the use of the rhythmic group 1–5; the use of exclamation, question, apostrophe and inversion; the dramatic use of enjambement; and the full exploitation of the mute -e.[42] The mute -e has the value of a silence, but has also the effect of strengthening the other vowels in the line, usually, though not always, the preceding vowel ('Iles! . . . Ruches bientôt'). It permits freedom of interpretation and variation of intensity within the line; combined with the 'consonnes continues' it achieves a slower, more reflective pace: as Valéry himself wrote, all these effects may arise from

l'e muet, qui tantôt existe, tantôt ne se fait presque point sentir s'il ne s'efface entièrement et qui procure tant d'effets subtils de silences élémentaires ou qui termine ou prolonge tant de mots par une sorte d'ombre que semble jeter après elle une syllable accentuée.[43]

La Fausse Morte

By way of conclusion, the interconnection of rhythm with timbre and poetic context is best illustrated by a detailed analysis where it is possible to demonstrate the precise effects contributed by quite specific points of style. The composition began, surprisingly perhaps, with an indication of a mood, a moment of peace between lovers:

```
                      du │ dernier │  moment de l'âme
        [Hu] Que    d'un reste          extrême paix
                   Humblement, tendrement
            Sur le tombeau charmant,   sur le doux monument
                sonnait dans
            Où sonne de ton cœur une heure prodiguée,    déja⁴⁴
```

He is seeking the expression of time suspended in a moment of ultimate calm, underlining significantly the words 'dernier' and 'extrême paix'. But though he has discovered a web of sound to convey this effect, there is clearly an initial problem in finding the appropriate form, and this first sketch shows his rhythmic uncertainty. After the movement of 6 / 12, a second alexandrine seems to re-establish the regular metric pulse, both in its rhythm and its reference to 'une heure prodiguée'.

He indicates a readjustment to the opening and the rhythmic pattern becomes clearer as he begins again, finding all at once the form for the poem. 'Humblement, tendrement' now begins the alexandrine, 'sur le doux monument' spilling over to make line 2 and creating a sinuous rhythm evocative of 'l'extrême paix', as though 18 syllables in length:

Humblement tendrement, sur le tombeau charmant

Sur le doux monument

des restes   blancheur
Que d'ombres de parfums   –   –   et d'amour prodiguée
de   les derniers moments d'une amour prodiguée

Forme ta grâce fatiguée,

Je meurs, je meurs sur toi, je tombe et je m'abats,
en

Though there is considerable uncertainty over the words for line 3, the rhythmic variation is clear; the two dashes after 'parfums' would seem to suggest that Valéry first wrote

Que d'ombres de parfums   –   –
Forme ta grâce fatiguée

in order to establish the rhythm and then returned to add 'et d'amour prodiguée' and other variants. Of course the two mute -es of line 4 ('Forme ta grâce') make it into an octosyllable and this pattern 12 / 6 / 12 / 8 / 12 is maintained in a second draft *Cahier Charmes* I f. 16.

After the apparent length of the first stanza and the rhythmic diversity of line 5 broken up into four distinct phrases, the alexandrines of stanza 2 take on a positively sprightly rhythm: the absence of punctuation in lines 6 and 7 and the more rapid reawakening in the four and a half, rather than five and a half, lines written at first make this quite clear:

Mais à peine abattu sur le sépulcre bas
Que la morte apparente en qui revient la vie
                              les referme
        rouvre les yeux
                         me sourit
Frémit, m'attire à soi   et me mord
Et m'arrache toujours une nouvelle mort
        Plus précieuse que la vie.

The additions made to this manuscript seek to retard the awakening by an expansion of the phrase 'à peine . . .' and a development of the image of 'le sépulchre bas'. One alternative suggests La Dormeuse: 'd'où l'âme semble absente et – – revie'; and a second, recalls 'l'âme absente occupée aux enfers': 'Dont la calme étendue / close torpeur / change   au néant me convie'; other variants suggest 'Dont la close étendue / belle torpeur / belle pâleur   au néant / aux ombres me convie'. Perhaps of most interest rhythmically is the version in the Cahier Voilier where the poem begins:

Humblement, tendrement,
Sur le tombeau charmant,
Sur l'insensible monument . . .

giving a pattern of lines in the first stanza 6 / 6 / 8 / 12 / 8 / 12.

Though apparently much less regular than the other poems of Charmes, the pattern which he finally adopts, 12 / 8 / 12 / 8 / 12 . . . , is related to some of the poems of La Fontaine, and to erotic epigrams in Latin; it is certainly used for deliberate effect and displays a feeling of inevitability and total formal control.

Humblement, tendrement, sur le tombeau charmant,
        Sur l'insensible monument,
Que d'ombres, d'abandons, et d'amour prodiguée,
        Forme ta grâce fatiguée,
Je meurs, je meurs sur toi, je tombe et je m'abats,

Mais à peine abattu sur le sépulcre bas,
Dont la close étendue aux cendres me convie,
Cette morte apparente, en qui revient la vie,
Frémit, rouvre les yeux, m'illumine et me mord,
Et m'arrache toujours une nouvelle mort
        Plus précieuse que la vie.

But the pattern is itself broken up internally, illustrating the notes made in the *Cahiers* on the technique of varying the caesura

Prépare tes poèmes par rythmes dans un rythme

Alexandrin = 6.2.4
7.5[45]

Les rapports de la *phrase* avec le vers c'est-à-dire des deux divisions indépendantes du discours
Le vers coupe la phrase en éléments   La Phrase coupe autrement de sorte qu'on a par exemple 12 + 12 + . . . = 5 + 4 + 9 + 3 + 11 . . . = 5 + 4 + (3 + 6) + . . .[46]

La Fausse Morte is in fact broken up as follows:

3.3.6 / 8 / 3.3.6 / 8 / 2.4.2.4
6.6 / 6.6 / 6.6 / 2.4.3.3 / 6.6 / 8

Referred to as a 'poème indiscret; un peu trop clair' by Alain[47] it presents indeed the drama of the poet and a woman, but is also about the poet and his poem, the artist and formal beauty, the self and its own creations. The first five lines present the sexual embrace of the poet and the woman who is identified at first as 'le tombeau charmant'. It is less a comparison with death-like beauty than one of devotion and admiration before some awe-inspiring object that remains remote and mysterious to him. The full implications of death are not revealed until the final two lines of the poem. 'Charmant' recalls the magical spell cast by the whole collection of *Charmes*. The initial approach is hesitant and gradual and the breaks in the line show the tentative movement leading into the second line, so that the octosyllabic has a longer, more continuous rhythm than the alexandrine. This is reinforced by the internal rhyme of '-ment', making the two lines seem almost like four increasingly long lines, focusing the lingering devotion 'Sur l'insensible monument', giving a sense of space and timelessness to the lines; the absence of a strong tonic accent is achieved by the movement of the lines combining with the 'musique verbale': a murmuring sequence of nasal vowels, a predominance of 'consonnes liquides' and a number of internal rhymes creating a somewhat indistinct sonority against which the single 'i' rings out with extraordinary length.

Humblement, tendrement, sur le tombeau charmant
BL M   T DR M   S R L T B   CH RM
un e an an e an u e on o   a an

Sur l'insensible monument
S R L S S B L M N M
u   in ani e   o u an

There are only two plosives in an initial position ('*t*endrement, *t*ombeau'); the others are medial and the plosive effect weakened by the combination with -L, -R or nasals. 'H*umb*lement . . . *tendr*ement . . . *tomb*eau . . . insensi*b*le'.

The same rhythmic pattern (3.3.6 / 8) is repeated in lines 3 and 4, as the approach becomes more personalised and human, the shadows becoming more physically suggestive and alluring, the devotion becoming love. The death evoked is seen to be like that of a sleep that is both graceful to watch (cf. 'charmant') and implies that grace that she is able to bestow. The body is a monument to a part of the self that is absent. 'Abandon' conveys the lifeless surrender as if to sleep, but with 'amour prodiguée' indicates the unrestrained nature of the instincts that are now dormant. The effect of the alternating lines is here quite different from *Au Platane*, where a clear rhythmic contrast is achieved from one line to the next, the two alexandrines rhyming and the two hexameters rhyming to give an *a b a b* pattern. In *La Fausse Morte* the rhyme scheme is *a a b b* and the octosyllable has the effect of prolonging the alexandrine, abolishing the rhythmic pulse of the metre, suspending the passage of time. The repeated pattern 3.3.6 / 8 achieves in the first four lines a kind of rhythmic cadence as if indicating breath-marks. It leads with increasing tension to the rhythmic climax and relaxation of the fifth line. Here the rhythm is broken into shorter units: 2.4.2.4. But the absence of a comma in the second hemistich produces a long *decelerando* in the line. The strong accent on the long vowels 'meurs', 'meurs', 'tombe', 'm'abats' makes the silences between as long as the words themselves. The first three lines addressed the woman indirectly in the third person; in line four the poet moves to the direct address of the second person; and here he identifies himself in the first person. 'Je' is repeated four times. The eye of the poet, the consciousness that has been previously implied becomes dominant; it reaches the moment of self-assertion which is paradoxically the death of the self.

Continuity with the second stanza is maintained by the rhyme and the comma rather than full stop at the end of line 5. But after the intense timeless quality of the first stanza and the variety of rhythmic pattern, the second stanza changes pace with a succession of alexandrines which run on without being broken into shorter phrases: the lines are faster and the pulse of time is reestablished. The effect is complex, for after 'Mais à peine' lines 6 and 7 offer a brief recapitulation of the opening theme, though now in a secondary rôle. They evoke again the restfulness and stillness; the deathly state of the woman has involved the death of the poet as well and a series of words deny all movement: 'abattu', 'sépulcre', 'close', 'cendres', 'morte'. Yet the effect is different from stanza 1, and lies more in the unaccentuated sweep of the lines: apart from 'close' and 'cendres' the vowels tend to be short and there are eleven plosives in lines 6 and 7 alone, eight of which are followed immediately by a vowel, only three softened by -l or -r.[48] This creates a steady, even passage through lines 6 and 7, in one single movement: it is a transition passage, emphasized by the rhymes: line 5 rhymes with 6 ('m'abats / bas'), 6 with 7 at the caesura ('abattu / étendue') and 7 with 8 ('convie / vie').

But the phrase beginning 'à peine' is a subordinate (a syntactic 'mise en abîme' of phrase within clause within sentence, which in turn provokes a further subordinate 'Dont la close étendue . . .' descending to the depths of 'les cendres'): it can offer only provisional respite from the whole inexorable movement. By line 8 the flow of the rhythm begins to be disturbed: 'apparente' at the caesura sets a note of doubt; the comma strongly divides the line 6.6; with mounting tension the second hemistich – yet another subordinate, delaying still further the main verb – presents the reawakening; the suspense of 'Mais' must be resolved:

> Mais . . .
> . . .
> Cette morte apparente . . .
> Frémit

The full dramatic significance of the extra line which Valéry introduced into the second stanza can now be appreciated. 'Frémit' at the beginning of line 9, with its strongly accented and vibrant vowels, conveys the sudden start back to life; 'les yeux' emphasize that it is now the woman's eyes which are open and dominant. Creatively, assertively she enlightens the poet on his own death and her freedom from his dominance. The death of the poet in line 5 is echoed now by the assertion of life and energy of the woman and the line increases in intensity, reaching its climax at the end with 'me mord'. After the deliberate delays of the first three lines of this stanza, 'Frémit' introduces the resolution and leaves us quivering with anticipation for the finale of four massive chords:

Frémit, . . .   rouvre les yeux, . . .   m'illumine . . .   et me mord,

The unbroken rhythm of the last two lines, an alexandrine and an octosyllable flowing into each other, is like the final expiration of the poet's own breath: he is reaching the point of separation and the syntax, sustained through many clauses over eleven lines, resolves finally with the full emphasis, after 'mord' and 'mort', falling upon 'précieuse' – lengthened by the diaeresis, and still more so by the mute -e – which is followed by the brief concluding phrase 'que la vie'. Yet again he is reminded of the interdependence of life and death, and finds peace and relaxation in the knowledge that the life he has created has become fully independent from him.

It can be appreciated, then, that rhythm plays a very significant part both in the composition and in the reading of Valéry's poetry: the pace, the phrasing, the breath-marks, the accents, are essential features of the rhythm of *La Fausse Morte*, inseparable from the meaning, the sounds, the metre, the use of mute -*e*, the placing of the caesura. Valéry often regretted that poetry lacked 'une notation de la *diction*' as a means of indicating 'allure, accent'; he expressed severe reservations over any attempt to translate poetry as 'le texte nu' into a passage of prose while ignoring the changes of tone, the forms of address, the voice of the poem itself. The above analysis, it is suggested, sets forth the principles of the critical method which Valéry himself proposed, wherein it is the reader's responsibility 'de compléter le texte donné par les indications de mouvements, d'intensités et de rythmes que le texte . . . suggère, et qui . . . doivent en lui donner tout son effet'.[49]

9

LA MUSIQUE VERBALE

La poésie . . . Appel à la *sonorité* totale, il s'agit 'd'expliquer' ce
qui chante, ce qui fait chanter, ce qui rend chantant.

XII, 1938, p. 918

La difficulté de la poésie est de trouver des paroles qui soient en
même temps musique par elles-même et musique par analogie.
Musique dans la sensation et musique dans leur sens.

XI, 1924, p. 778

Except perhaps for the vividness of imagery, it is the sound
of Valéry's poetry which forms the most striking first impression.
The fluidity, the suppleness and the insistence of the
sonorous patterns have a fascination of their own that is
immediately apparent on any page of *La Jeune Parque* or
Charmes. However often the poems are reread, however
many other impressions and analyses are built up, a reading
of the poems can never become a purely intellectual affair,
for the reader is inevitably led to form the sounds himself or
herself and add the vocal pleasure of the lines to his or her
understanding of the themes and images. The poems admirably
meet Valéry's own criteria of fine verse:

Un beau vers renaît indéfiniment de ses cendres, il redevient, – comme
l'effet de son effet, – cause harmonique de soi-même.[1]

In the words of J. Supervielle, Valéry's poetry presents an
'elixir de sonorités'.[2]

The quality of the sound is so important that Valéry sees it
as a defining characteristic of poetry.

La musique se reconnaît déjà, et s'impose par le son qui est une étrangeté de pureté au milieu des bruits: le poète doit à chaque fois tirer des
mots accoutumés leur aspect de son pur, et faire tellement que faire le
son suffit déjà à faire un poète.[3]

On a number of occasions Valéry drew the comparison

with music, because a single note is sufficient to evoke 'l'univers musical'. A noise, he says, will only make one think of a single event, while a musical sound will evoke a new realm of experience: the purity allows for combinations, developments and contrasts that stir the reactions of the listener.

vous auriez la sensation d'un commencement, le commencement d'un monde; une atmosphère tout autre serait sur-le-champ créée, un ordre nouveau s'annoncerait, et vous-mêmes, vous vous *organiseriez* inconsciemment pour l'accueillir. L'univers musical était donc en vous avec tous ses rapports et ses proportions.[4]

The poet does not have the advantages of the musician, for he has to create his 'univers poétique' from language: 'Le poète est obligé de créer le "son" que le musicien n'a pas à élaborer.'[5] Though the techniques of poetry are limited in comparison with the range of notes and tempi possible in music, the purity of sound remains a constant ideal, the clear marking of 'l'enchaînement des sons . . . leur totalisation auditive et non leur somme significative'[6] a major preoccupation for Valéry.

Attempts have been made to compare the succession of vowel sounds to a melody composed of notes, but Valéry recognised the limitations of this and proposed a more accurate analogy: the recitation of poetry is 'une construction dans le temps qui est assez analogue à une mélodie mais ici les timbres (voyelles) au lieu de hauteurs'.[7] 'Le mot correspond au timbre.'[8] This idea is not paradoxically without its musical counterpart, in Debussy and Webern for example. But in general the French language has been considered lacking in musical characteristics compared to other European languages. A high degree of artifice is necessary to make the musicality evident, so that the music of poetry is a direction, an aspiration, a suggestion of what might happen rather than an actual fact: 'le français est musical . . . plus en suggérant un air sur lequel les paroles se chanteraient que formant soi seul une véritable musique'.[9]

The subject of the poet's use of sound is large and complex and Valéry continually returned to examine all its aspects in the *Cahiers*. To begin with in this chapter the rôle of sound in the process of composition will be analysed, followed by a study of 'la continuité musicale' in the poems; finally Valéry's approach to the problem of the relationship between sound and meaning will be considered.

In 'Le Prince et la Jeune Parque' Valéry relates how, before any idea for a poem started to develop, he found himself acutely aware of the sounds of language.

> Je m'aperçus que je redevenais sensible à ce qui sonne dans les propos. Je m'attardais à percevoir la musique de la parole. Les mots que j'entendais ébranlaient en moi je ne sais quelles dépendances harmoniques et quelle présence implicite de rythmes imminents.[10]

The sounds present themselves in a quite unordered fashion. The poet is aware of all the possibilities of timbres and their combinations; he explores the different suggestions, selecting those combinations which are particularly appealing, and is seduced by the 'divines murmures de la voix intérieure'.[11] This inner voice of the poet is an active participant in the selection of words: the fascination with sounds which, in the finished poem inspires the reader to continually recreate the aural pattern, begins with the poet's awareness of sound for itself:

> . . . je sens assez nettement se former ou se chercher mes vers dans une région de l'appareil vocal-auditif et moyennant une certaine attitude de cet appareil (en tant qu'il est capable de modifications musculaires)[12]

It is evident that different poets can have different 'voices': not simply because of a different musical register as Valéry suggested at one point – 'poètes ténors, ut^2–si^3 poètes contraltos fa^2-fa^4'[13] – but because the poet's individual selection of sounds from among all the possibilities offered provides characteristic features of a highly personal nature. Valéry felt himself to be a specialist in the sounds *é, è, ê*.[14]

> La voix de *chacun* évite plutôt certains mots et certaines articulations de *tons*, en recherche d'autres; ne peut souffrir telles duretés, affectionne telles résistances ou telles facilités.[15]

Still this acute sensibility to the quality of sound remains a long way from the first attempts at poetic composition. It serves more as a preparation of the poet's faculties and marked for Valéry a revival of interest in poetry as a diversion from the problems of abstract analysis which are most predominant in the *Cahiers*. Just as the sounds of an orchestra tuning up are not music, equally 'tout ce qui vibre n'est pas bon'.[16] The initial exhileration with sound may indeed have produced some 'purs fragments' but soon the abstract problems returned both as problems of poetic composition and as the very material from which his poetic themes were hewed.

As work on the drafts progresses the 'voix intérieure' came to adopt an evaluative rôle: '(elle) me sert de repère'.[17] This inner voice selects the sounds and orders them, creates a pattern that is not evident in the sonorous disorder of everyday language, and helps to decide which possible developments to accept into the poem. It is particularly important in establishing a continually even texture of sound, an aspect of Racine which inspired Valéry's deep admiration:

Racine procède par de très délicates substitutions de l'idée qu'il s'est donnée pour thème. Il la séduit au chant qu'il veut rejoindre. Il n'abandonne jamais la ligne de son discours.[18]

Valéry constantly returned to the idea of allowing sound to take over the process of composition. The following note, written in 1940 when he was working on *Mon Faust*, marks a revived interest in formal composition, but reveals the extent to which it was an ideal rather than an account of his own poetic practice:

Je voudrais commencer une fois par un *mot isolé*, substantif ou qualificatif comme pour donner à entendre un *son* dont on laisse s'épanouir la résonnance, les harmoniques. Puis les reprendre, et comme chercher dans cette atmosphère une direction, et particulariser jusqu'à ... *comme trouver la voie des combinaisons complètes* qui constitueront l'ouvrage.[19]

The experience of *Charmes* shows the constant preoccupation with sound throughout the entire process of composition. Initially the associations of vowels and consonants help the poet to build up his 'palette'. The lists of words with associated sounds constitute the basic material from which the poem is assembled. In some cases a particular sound has been used as the basis for a whole stanza, providing an underlying tone, or bass note, linking the various elements together. The various groups of syllables were noted alongside the stanzas of an early version of *La Pythie*, next to stanza three of *Le Cimetière marin* Valéry wrote an *s* in an early draft. In fact the stanza is built around this sound, and the major themes emerge from it: 'Stable trésor', 'temple simple', 'Masse de calme', 'visible réserve', 'eau sourcilleuse', 'sommeil', 'silence', 'édifice'.[20]

As the composition advances particular problems arise, and the sound becomes one of the conditions which have to be satisfied.

Pour l'harmonie du vers, je cherche et tatonne au moyen de mots inexistants, de sons verbaux inventés par le besoin même de l'oreille – et auxquels, une fois trouvés, il faut substituer les mots vrais qui s'en rapprochent le plus. Ceci est général. Nous cherchons au moyen du besoin même.[21]

An example of this is provided by an early version of *La Fausse Morte*. Line 9 was incomplete, but Valéry indicated the sound pattern he was seeking:

> Tréssaille, s'illumine et m . . . et m . . .
> → Frémit, rouvre les yeux, m'illumine et me mord.

This alliteration recalls the persistent sound of the first stanza 'Je meurs, je meurs sur toi', as well as references to the woman as 'monument' and 'morte'; the increased intensity of sound and the more frequent repetition of the letter *m* give dramatic shape to the line.

In some cases the reworking of the line is largely a question of a more fluid arrangement of sound:

> Commande au plein sommeil l'onde l'ampleur
> → Quand de ce plein sommeil l'onde grave et l'ampleur
> *La Dormeuse*

In many more cases a change of image is involved:

> Autel amas doré d'offres et d'abandons
> → Dormeuse, amas doré d'ombres et d'abandons.

In certain circumstances the fluid movement is deliberately broken, as in stanza 5 of *La Pythie* where a more punctuated, violent sound is called for to evoke the sounds of struggle, blasphemy and tirade. A comparison of two versions shows the following changes:

> Dont les combats tordent ma langue
> La fait vibrer d'une harangue
> Si différente de mes vœux   (*Cahier Voilier*)

> Dont les éclats hachent ma langue
> La fait brandir une harangue
> Brisant la bave et les cheveux
>   (*Cahier Charmes* I f. 36)

In spite of its meaning the first version slides fluently over the tongue. In the second 'les éclats hachent', with the hiatus, the prominence of 'hachent', the ugliness of the internal rhyme, conveys the violence of her language; the *a* continues to reverberate through the lines, and '*les é*clats h*ach*ent' is echoed in '*la* b*ave et les ch*eveux'; the plosive *b* is used to full effect, especially in combination with *r*, and, in the change from 'vibrer' to 'brandir', is brought forward to the initial position, lengthening the following vowel, as again in 'Brisant'; and behind all these emphatic and vigorous sounds lies the moaning insistence of the nasals in 'ma langue', 'brandir', 'harangue' and 'Brisant'.

Valéry's concern for the verbal music may thus inspire him to seek greater sonorous variety, avoiding the easier, more obvious forms of assonance which can sometimes be seen in earlier drafts. In the first sketch for stanza 4 of *La Pythie*, Valéry wrote:

> Et de tout mon corps l'arc obscène
> Semble se tendre pour darder,

and changed the second line to

> Tendre à se rompre pour darder
>   (*Cahier Pythie* f. 97)

The change is partly syntactic, but also replaces the assonance of the nasal vowels by a line that avoids repetition, except for the underlying and more subtle unity of the five *r* sounds: the effect of the wide range of vowels and the dental consonants is that the very process of articulating the line conveys the tension and extremity of her situation.

Musical techniques in Valéry's poetry

The relationship between sound and rhythm can be observed in two examples demonstrating a quite distinct approach
to composition. In one case Valéry starts with a rather prose-
like statement for the last lines of 'Honneur des Hommes,
saint Langage':

> Voici parler une Sagesse
> Si pure sonner une voix
> Que l'on connaît quand elle sonne
> Qu'elle n'est la voix de personne
> Sinon des ondes et des bois.　　　(*Pythie* f. 99)

The changes which he makes reveal a tightening of the syntax,
a controlled alliteration and a sustained rhythm which resolves on to the final line, changes which effectively transform
the prose into poetry:

> Et sonner une telle voix
> Qui se connaît quand elle sonne
> N'être plus la voix de personne
> Tant que des ondes et des bois.　　　(f. 99)

In another case Valéry does not start with a statement but
with a series of rhyming words from which he attempts to
formulate his lines; he clearly has a set of sounds in mind and
indeed uses these to suggest new words, enriching the substance as he incorporates the new ideas; the words are like
notes that he tries out in different combinations to find the
shape of the phrase. The passage in question forms the second
part of stanza 3:

> 　　　malice　maudite
> Ah! [supplice], quels maux je souffre
> Toute ma nature est un gouffre
> Et [ton] ce [corps]　　est pétri
> Par une puissance adultère
> Ah! quel poison ne peut se taire
> 　　　[mal me fait ce mystère]
> Quel mal me veut ce grand Esprit　　　(f. 97)

Alongside there are a series of alternatives:

> Et dans ce　—　meurtri
> Une intelligence adultère
> Torture un corps qui veut se taire
> Une langue qui veut taire
> Ce mal que lui veut ton Esprit

192

La musique verbale

> Je me perds dans ce corps meurtri
> J'ai fini j'ai — —

Among a palette of rhyming words that eventually found a place in stanzas 2, 3 and 12, he rewrites the lines attempting yet again a slightly different form.

> Ah   quels mx je souffre
> Toute ma nature est un gouffre
> [Mon corps]   Entrouverte aux esprits
>   ricane
> Une intelligence adultère
> Dans
> Exerce un corps qu'elle a compris
> perce   (f. 121)

Apart from the variant 'Je suis entrouverte aux esprits' (B.N. VRY MS. 1841), Valéry moves next to the definitive version:

> – Ah! maudite! . . . Quels maux je souffre!
> Toute ma nature est un gouffre!
> Hélas! Entr'ouverte aux esprits,
> J'ai perdu mon propre mystère! . . .
> Une Intelligence adultère
> Exerce un corps qu'elle a compris!

In some instances little more than the similarity of rhyme persists through different versions:

> Sonnes-tu le . . . de l'avenir?
> Ou sont-ce les bruits de ma roche
> Suis-je déjà . . . si proche
> De la terre, où je dois m'unir
>   (. . . temps de finir)
>   (MS. of *La Pythie*,
>   *Cahier Voilier*)

> Que dites-vous de l'avenir
> Battez en moi, bruits d'une roche
> Attaquant l'heure la plus proche
> Suis-je ma tombe, ou toute proche
> Mes deux natures vont s'unir!   (variant)

> Que dites-vous de l'avenir!
> Frappez, frappez, dans une roche,
> Abattez l'heure la plus proche . . .
> Mes deux natures vont s'unir!
>   (final version st. 19)

The rhyme-scheme was clearly of great importance, not only in the images presented, nor simply in their conformity to the pattern *ababccdeed*. Valéry had found a pattern which brought the rhymes together in a closely interrelated fashion: '. . . ces fleuves/ . . . sont ici/ . . . les neuves/ . . . merci/ . . . aurores/ . . . sonores/ . . . avenir/ . . . une roche/ . . . plus proche/ . . . vont s'unir', The rhymes are rich and have sounds in common with other rhymes. Thus 'sonores' rhymes with 'aurores' and has the *r* sound in common with five of the other eight lines. 'Avenir' rhymes with 'vont s'unir', has the *r* of 'merci, aurore, sonores, roche, proche', the *i* of 'ici, merci' and the '-ve-' reversed from 'fleuves, neuves'. Rhyme b ('sont ici') is echoed in three ways by line 10 ('vont s'unir'): it has the *i*, the *s* and the *ont*.

The attempts for the beginning of the third line of *Le Cimetière marin* reveal a process whereby sound, image and harmonics are built up together in ever more complete fashion, encompassing all previous attempts.

Midi le juste y compose de feux.

The first version was 'L'or maritime y compose de feux', but a number of alternatives were tried: 'Le milieu du jour: l'or sublime; un songe d'or; Le pur solstice; Midi sublime; Midi le pur; Midi suprême; le même; le morne; le calme.' Lawler suggests that the definitive word was inspired by a line written for stanza 6 'Je te soutiens admirable justice'. The variants form groups among themselves. The first derive from the image of the golden light of the sun on the sea and the alliteration of *p* with 'pins palpite' in line 2; the next attempts use the same epithets with 'Midi'; then follow attempts to create an alliterative effect with 'Midi'. The final version not only presents a more arresting image, it includes all the other meanings, the sun precisely balanced at its zenith, the supremacy of the sun, the associations of consciousness and wisdom; it also abandons any attempt at obvious alliteration. Its effect is more subtle, in echoing the *t* sounds of the first two lines, charged with quivering tension, and in conveying the precision by the closed vowels *i* and *u*.

In works of such complexity as Valéry's, the need for unity is essential. Like Gluck, Valéry was concerned to achieve 'la divine continuité'.[22] In Gluck this is achieved by the constant instrumental accompaniment, in Valéry by the perpetual modulation of sound, the 'continuité de beau son',[23] extended within the lines, from one line to the next, and over the whole stanza and poem. Valéry himself was unimpressed by the analyses of phoneticians and similar scientific attempts to describe the use of sound in poetry: 'nous avons beau compter les pas de la déesse, en noter la fréquence et la longueur *moyenne*, nous n'en tirons pas le secret de sa grâce instantanée'.[24] The danger of such methods, he said, lay in presenting as a single simultaneous event what is really a succession of mutually related effects. In reading the poem the words present a continually changing series of moments:

l'instant . . . est à la fois sensation et attente-sensation qui dépend d'ailleurs d'un choc et d'une modification de l'état choqué par les états antérieurs.[25]

By a variety of techniques, suited to the circumstances, Valéry aims to achieve an uninterrupted flow of sound across the whole poem, to which every part contributes. For 'la structure successive de ces actes d'articulation . . . fait le dessin du discours'.[26]

Rhyme has been identified as an important factor of composition, even when the rest of the line was blank. Indeed Guiraud has shown that 'Valéry, avant du Bellay, Vigny et Ronsard, est celui de nos poètes qui rime le plus richement.'[27] One need only open the collection at random to discover rhymes of uncommon richness: 'buvait-duvet', 'Intelligence-négligence', 'son essence-connaissance' (*Poésie*); 'éternité-divinité', 'jeunesses-finesses', 'éveillées-appareillées' (*Cantique*); 'hantées-enchantées', 'consentir-mentir', 'tacite-tel site' (*Narcisse*). But even this richness was not sufficient for Valéry, who disliked the 'rime riche' on its own:

La rime riche tend à détruire l'*unité* d'impression – cf. Hugo – Car elle amène des solutions *extérieures*, qui valent pour le cas particulier, mais qui englobent, dans la suite, des éléments trop éloignés. Il est vain de rimer si le reste du vers n'est pas musical.[28]

This musical unity for Valéry had to be expressed not just by a formal correspondence at the end of each line, but by an extension of the rhyme through alliteration, assonance and similarity of timbre. Valéry exploited traditional prosody to the full and even employed techniques generally avoided or proscribed. His poetry shows a systematic use of the 'vers léonin', the homophony of the rhyme and caesura, which is established upon vowels and consonants together, upon both alone, and also upon closely related timbres.

> Que fais-tu, hérissée, et cette main glacée
> > *La Jeune Parque*

> Amèrement *la même* . . .
> > Un miroir de *la mer*
> > *La Jeune Parque*

> Vous me le *murmurez r*amures! . . . O *rumeur*
> > *F. du Narcisse*

Including the similar timbres, one out of every four lines in *La Jeune Parque* and *Narcisse* can be considered a 'vers léonin'.[29]

The 'rime renforcée', the rhyme of two caesuras, is exploited to a similar degree, one fifth of the lines in the *Jeune Parque* and over a quarter in *Narcisse*.

> Onde, sur qui les *ans* passant comme des nus,
> Que de choses pour*tant* doivent t'être connues.   *Narcisse*

> Tu triomphes, ô p*aix* plus puissant qu'un pleur,
> Quand de ce plein somm*eil* l'onde grave et l'ampleur
> > *Dormeuse*

On some occasions the caesuras establish a counter-rhyme within the line, as in these four lines from *Narcisse*:

> Prenant à vos regards cette parfaite proie,
> Du monstre de s'aimer faites-vous un captif;
> Dans les errants filets de vos longs cils de soie
> Son gracieux éclat vous retienne pensif;

The main rhyme is *abab*, while the caesuras rhyme *a'b'b'a'*. It was seen that a similar procedure effects the transition between stanzas in *La Fausse Morte*.

In addition to the richness of rhyme and the internal rhymes within the lines, there is the process of extending the correspondences of sounds backwards into the penultimate or even antepenultimate syllables. Thus for example 'volonté–

volupté', 'ma fille–famille'. Indeed he extends the similarities
of sound so far back that the rhyme appears to encompass
the whole line, a phenomenon known as 'olorimisme'. Guiraud is undoubtedly correct in asserting that 'tous les vers de
Valéry tendent à l'olorimisme'.[30]

The traditional rules of prosody assert that the masculine
and feminine rhymes should not be assonant. Valéry on the
contrary systematically sought partial assonance and alliteration of the rhymes. The poetry of *Charmes* shows a consistent search for closeness of rhyme that serves to link whole
lines and entire stanzas. The first two stanzas of *L'Abeille*
show considerable similarity of timbre: '. . . mortelle, . . .
abeille, . . . corbeille, . . . dentelle. . . . belle, . . . sommeille,
. . . vermeille, . . . rebelle'. The whole of *Le Sylphe* seems
built around the two dominant sounds of the first line, *i* and *u*.

stanza 1	Ni vu ni connu, . . . parfum, . . . défunt, . . . venu.
stanza 2	. . . connu,. . . génie, . . . venu, . . . finie.
stanza 3	. . . compris,. . . esprits, . . . promises.
stanza 4	. . . connu,. . . sein nu, . . . chemises.

These effects are used of course with specific intentions, conveying the continual motion, the movement around a fixed
point that the poems portray, both literally in the movement
of the animals and metaphorically in the sense of the conscious mind turned upon itself.

Cantique des Colonnes achieves a similar effect for the purpose of establishing the unity, regularity and conformity of
the columns: their beauty is not individual but achieved as a
group. Indeed one half of all the rhymes are based upon the
range of vowels *é*, *è*, *i* or their combinations; a third of the
rhymes are based on *o*, *ou*, *on*. The overall impression is of
two major rhymes linking whole stanzas rather than single
lines to each other. One series:

stanza 5	. . . candides, . . . sonorité, . . . limpides, . . . clarté.
stanza 6	. . . et dorés, . . . lits, . . . tirées, . . . lys.
stanza 16	. . . dix, . . . passées, . . . jadis, . . . assez

the other series:

| stanza 1 | . . . aux, . . . jour, . . . oiseaux, . . . tour. |
| stanza 2 | . . . ô, . . . fuseaux, . . . son, . . . unisson. |

stanza 14   . . . Jour, . . . offrons, . . . amour, . . . fronts.
stanza 17   . . . amours, . . . monde, . . . jour, . . . onde.

The assonance of rhymes is in fact a particular, more noticeable case of the unity of timbre achieved throughout the whole verbal texture of the poems. The use of enjambement is marked, often emphasised, by the use of 'rime enchaînée' at the beginning of the following line. The echo effect of *Narcisse* is well known:

> Les efforts mêmes de l'amour
> Ne le sauraient de l'onde extraire qu'il n'expire . . .
> PIRE.
>   Pire? . . .
>   Quelqu'un redit *Pire* . . .

but occurs frequently elsewhere:

> Entre moi-même et l'onde, et mon âme, et les dieux! . . .
>   Adieu . . .   *Narcisse*

>   Je sens dans l'arbre de ma vie
>   La mort monter de mes ta*lons*!
>   Le *long* de ma ligne frileuse   *La Pythie*

> Qui *pleure* là, sinon le vent simple, à cette *heure*
> *Seule*, avec diaments extrêmes? . . . Mais qui *pleure*,
> *Si p*roche de moi-même au moment de *pleurer*?
>   *La J. Parque*

The rhyme and the 'rejet' present a delicate progression of modulating sounds weaving a pattern around the regular framework of the alexandrine, as in these four lines, again from *La Jeune Parque*. They are written in italics, in parenthesis, the only lines not spoken by the Parque herself:

> (*La p*orte basse c'est une bague . . . où la *gaze*
> *Passe* . . . Tout meurt, tout rit dans la gorge qui *ja*se . . .
> *L'ois*eau boit sur ta bouche et tu ne peux le *voir* . . .
> *V*iens plus bas, parle bas . . . Le noir n'est pas si n*oir* . . .)

The unity of sound is extended over the whole poem by the selection of a particular register of timbres appropriate to the theme. Guiraud has shown the entirely different range of consonants and vowels in *La Dormeuse* compared to *Les Grenades*: in the former the labial sounds *b*, *m*, *p*, *f* and the nasal and 'grave' vowels predominate, creating a quiet and languid atmosphere through words such as 'endormie, accalmie, ombres'; in the latter these sounds occur much less frequently and instead the gutteral consonants *g*, *k*, *r* and the clear vowels predominate bringing out the hard crystalline quality of the 'dures grenades entr'ouvertes' and of 'L'or sec de l'écorce'.

The modulation of one sound to another over a number of lines or even an entire poem is difficult to assess, for a sound pattern gives a very unsatisfactory picture of the changing effects. A pattern appears static, whereas the main feature of the modulation of sound is that it is a dynamic movement based on development, contrast and anticipation. A small example will illustrate the complexity and skill of Valéry's effects. The passage in question is the rhythmic phrase beginning 'J'étais l'égale et l'épouse du jour' which needs to be placed in the context of this section of the poem.

> Harmonieuse MOI, différente d'un songe,
> Femme flexible et ferme aux silences suivis
> D'actes purs! . . . Front limpide, et par ondes ravis,
> Si loin que le vent vague et velu les achève,
> Longs brins légers qu'au large un vol mêle et soulève,
> Dites! . . . J'étais l'égale et l'épouse du jour,
> Seul support souriant que je formais d'amour
> A la toute-puissante altitude adorée . . .   102–9

The passage is the first moment of lightness in the poem as the Parque reminisces about her youth and innocence. So far the reader has suffered with her the anxious awakening, the struggle with the serpent, and the awareness of the strength of division within herself. With relief she escapes from the nightmare world of dreams into her own past. Three long rhythmic phrases presented here convey the youthful intensity that is at once breathless, eager and untroubled. The modulation of sound is prepared by the shift from *f* to *v*, from *i* to *è*. The unbroken rhythm of line 106 gives 'Dites!' at the beginning of line 107 full dramatic effect, after which a light skipping rhythm takes off. The *é* and *è* sounds of 107 effect a gradual modulation through 'étais l'égale et l'épouse' introducing the *ou* and *u* sounds at the end of the line. The variation of *ou* and *u* continues in 108, where they contribute the main vocalic sound, a pedal-point of continuity while the consonants shift to *s*. The word 'amour' picks up the *a* sound of 'égale' and prepares its predominance in the following line, where it intermingles still with *ou* and *u*, ending with the initial *é*. The vowels act like held notes while the consonants change, and then the consonants are held while the vowels change; the movement from *é* to *ou* to *u* to *a,* supports and reacts to the movement from *l* to *s* to *m* to *t* and *d*. In the last line the consonants are mainly the dentals, while the vowels change through the whole range of open, closed and nasal: *ou - i - an - i - u - a - o - é*. The passage uses a wide range of consonants and vowels, demands great agility of delivery, has a supple elastic rhythm and a series of over-lapping symmetries, which are all totally appropriate to the theme and quite memorable. The modulations indeed are still to be heard in the rhyme five lines later: '. . . dorée / O pau-pières . . . trésor, / . . . d'or / Poreuse . . . m'enclore / . . . dévore.'

The modulating pattern continues through the whole poem. Changes occur at moments of anguish, uncertainty or lyri-cism, but the continual attention to the form of speech gives a sense of consistency to the many developments, provides an aesthetic sense of unity, and assures the reader that the Parque who stands on the sea shore at the end is, in spite of her different outlook and understanding, still the same per-son who awoke in confusion.

Valéry himself was a harsh judge of his achievements and has indicated only a few passages with which he was particu-larly pleased. He noted in the *Cahiers* as 'les vers qui m'ont donné la sensation de se faire par la continuité et de la pro-duire en retour' two lines from *La Jeune Parque*

> O n'aurait-il fallu folle, que j'accomplisse
>
> A l'extrême de l'être, et belle de faiblesse

Celui-ci fait sur les *è graves* que j'aime tant (cf. *Anne*: Tette dans la ténèbre . . .)[31]

One other passage was felt by Valéry to be equally admir-able, the eight lines from *Fragments du Narcisse* beginning 'O douceur de survivre à la force du jour . . .', which he described to Jean de Latour as 'ceux qui m'ont coûté le plus de travail et que je considère comme les plus parfaits de tous ceux que j'ai écrits.'[32] The lines portray the setting of the sun and evoke the feelings of enchantment, splendour and contemplative pleasure in terms of a pastoral scene, rich in colour and with erotic overtones. The emotion of Narcisse's attempted communion with the self is seen in terms of a sunset, itself an abstraction ('survivre à la force du jour') that becomes gradually personified in the form of a woman withdrawing from her lover, until, merging into the darkness, the image of 'le soir' is reasserted, though as no more of a reality than 'un songe'. The skill of the 'musique verbale' is consummate, achieving a gently modulating pattern that casts its own spell on the reader, combining the alliteration and assonance of certain key sounds with subtly varying rhythms and internal rhymes which build up to the combination of nasals in the final two lines. The 'musique verbale' is not, cannot be, that of music; but it can, like music, convey the sheer beauty of sound, exert a fascination that is quite particular:

> O douceur de survivre à la force du jour,
> Quand elle se retire enfin rose d'amour,
> Encore un peu brûlante, et lasse, mais comblée,
> Et de tant de trésors tendrement accablée
> Par de tels souvenirs qu'ils empourprent sa mort,
> Et qu'ils la font heureuse agenouiller dans l'or,
> Puis s'étendre, se fondre, et perdre sa vendange,
> Et s'éteindre en un songe en qui le soir se change.

At the fiftieth anniversary of the Lamoureux concerts Valéry emphasised the importance of music to the symbolist poets: just as music is organised sound rather than random noise, poetry seeks a unity of expression and meaning that distinguishes it from the essentially communicative language of everyday speech.

Comme la musique, dans ses débuts, a divisé les impressions de l'ouïe, . . . ainsi la Poésie s'est efforcée, parfois très laborieusement, parfois très dangereusement, de distinguer (de son mieux) dans le langage, des expressions dans lesquelles le sens, le rythme, les sonorités de la voix, le mouvement s'accordent et se renforcent, tandis qu'elle s'essayait au contraire à proscrire les expressions dans lesquelles le sens est indépendant de la forme musicale, de toute valeur auditive.[33]

But while the comparison excited his admiration and established an ideal for poetry, it did in a sense serve to emphasise the difference between the medium of the poet and the musician. The poet is struck by the arbitrary nature of the link between the sound and the meaning of a word, but seeks to create the impression of some necessary and vital connection:

Axiomes de poésie.
(a) il y a une musique des paroles
(b) il n'y a aucun rapport rationnel – c.à d. exprimable généralement entre le son et le sens
(c) il est possible de construire un discours à double loi – un système de signes successifs à doubles effets – c.à d. une suite ayant une loi sensible et d'autre part engendrant par sommations de significations partielles, un état significatif, des choses, des actes imaginés etc. [34]

Though a continual preoccupation of all poets, the problem of sound and meaning was an essential part of aesthetics in the second half of the nineteenth century. Poetry aimed not so much to describe experience as to convey the very sensation of experience: the metaphor took over from the simile: the sounds of Baudelaire's *Correspondances* sought to actually evoke and prolong the experience of 'une ténébreuse et profonde unité'. Baudelaire suggests that this is achieved in the same way as in music; in his article on Wagner he compares his own reactions to the prelude to *Lohengrin* with those of Liszt and Wagner himself, arguing that:

la véritable musique suggère des idées analogues dans des cerveaux différents. . . . car ce qui serait vraiment surprenant, c'est que le son *ne pût pas* suggérer la couleur, que les couleurs *ne pussent pas* donner l'idée d'une mélodie et que le son et la couleur fussent impropres à traduire des idées. [35]

But the metaphysical totality of experience remained a distant ideal when the poet was confronted with the properties of everyday language. His basic material demanded considerable attention and work to be transformed. Mallarmé regretted in *Crise de Vers* 'que le discours défaille à exprimer les objets par les touches y répondant en coloris ou en allure, lesquelles existent en l'instrument de la voix'. [36] The problem is immediately faced with such basic words as day and night:

à côte d'*ombre* opaque, *ténèbres* se fonce peu; quelle déception devant la perversité conférant à *jour*, comme à *nuit*, contradictoirement des timbres obscurs ici, là clairs.[37]

The solution, as shown by a comparison of two versions of *Victorieusement fui le suicide beau*, was to surround a word like 'minuit' with others that darken the effect through their meaning and their longer 'darker' vowels:

> Quand de tout ce coucher pas même un cher lambeau
> Ne reste, il est minuit, dans la main du poète   (1885)

> Quoi! de tout cet éclat pas même le lambeau
> S'attarde, il est minuit, à l'ombre qui nous fête   (1887)

Valéry discussed the question of sound and sense at great length, both in the *Cahiers* and in his published work. He developed the celebrated image of the poetic pendulum, which has in turn provoked much critical discussion as to the relative importance of sound.

Vous trouverez qu'à chaque vers, la signification qui se produit en vous, loin de détruire la forme musicale qui vous a été communiquée, redemande cette forme. Le pendule vivant qui est descendu du *son* vers le *sens* tend à remonter vers son point de départ sensible, comme si le sens même qui se propose à votre esprit ne trouvait d'autre issue, d'autre expression, d'autre réponse que cette musique qui lui a donné naissance.[38]

It emerges, particularly from Valéry's published work, that the indivisibility of sound and sense is an ideal to which the poet aspires whatever the difficulties, although he is rather more reluctant to discuss the practical measures to achieve this. From the notes in the *Cahiers*, however, it is possible to distinguish three approaches to the problem: an imitation in the sound of the meaning conveyed by a word or a line; an apt and apparently indivisible relationship between the sound and meaning which centres around some key word or words; and the absence of any apparent relationship between the pattern of sound and the meaning.

The first of these techniques was called 'harmonie imitative' and seems generally to have met with Valéry's disapproval: 'Cette harmonie ne doit pas être définissable. Quand elle l'est c'est l'harmonie *imitative* – et ce n'est pas bien.'[39] In such cases the sounds are put in a position of diminished importance compared to the meaning, creating an imbalanced effect. Imitation can only serve to reinforce the element of sense transmitted, 'l'imitation dans les arts considérée comme *compréhension*'.[40] And as such it verges on the purely onomatopoeic effect:

Harmonie imitative, fleurs artificielles, statues peintes, figures de cire, *C'est imiter par des sons ce qui est déjà sons.* Vouloir faire confondre, tromper l'œil ou l'oreille. Au lieu de copier les lois dans un autre système.[41]

Valéry qualified the line of La Fontaine

Prends ce pic et me romps ce caillou qui me nuit

as a 'vers d'harmonie quasi imitative',[42] and presumably, therefore, disapproved. But the same charge could perhaps equally be applied to lines of Valéry himself. The exaggerated effects of *Ebauche d'un Serpent* are, by his own admission, deliberate. And yet what is to be made of lines such as

Bois qui bourdonnerez de bêtes et d'idées,
D'hymnes d'hommes comblés des dons du juste éther

with its proliferation of alliterations and the onomatopoeic effect of bells? The lines, taken from the passage evoking the 'Iles' in *La Jeune Parque* are the high point of the incantation. But the alliteration and assonance do seem overdone, perhaps too obvious, and detracting thereby from the unity of the passage. Berne-Joffroy elaborates a principle which seems an appropriate measure for such cases: 'dès que le procédé se fait visible, il perd de son efficience'.[43] This principle echoes Valéry's own: 'Le meilleur ouvrage est celui qui garde son secret le plus longtemps'[44] and reasserts the desirability of a subtle, sometimes indefinable, albeit certain, relationship between sound and meaning.

The second technique used by Valéry is 'une tentative de faire de l'harmonie, et même de la faire sentir presque génératrice de la signification ou mélodie'.[45] The harmony is generated 'au moyen de la matière du langage, ou par la *distribution* de cette matière'.[46] The sounds which occur in certain words of key significance are prolonged through the sonorous pattern of the line. Thus, by extending the sounds

of words which are important for the meaning, other parts
of speech like articles and conjunctions, which do not immediately relate to any special image, become involved in the
expressive effect.[47]

The principle of a key word directing the expression
through a continuation of its sounds can be simple, or can
produce quite complex effects, as in the opening of *La Jeune
Parque*:

> Qui pleure là, sinon le vent simple, à cette heure
> Seule, avec diamants extrêmes? . . . Mais qui pleure,
> Si proche de moi-même au moment de pleurer?

The major sounds occur in the first two words 'Qui pleure'
and introduce immediately the dominant themes of these
lines: the sobbing and the question of identity. The insistent
questioning runs through the words 'Qui . . . sinon . . . qui . . .
si . . .' The word 'pleure' (or 'pleurer') appears three times in
emphatic positions. The *pl* and *eu* sounds take on qualities
that make them seem particularly suited to express the sobbing which the Parque hears. The plosive labials and the vowels
are aided by the irregular rhythm of the first two lines; they
are divided 4.5.3/1.8.3, but the enjambement tends to make
'à cette heure / Seule' into one group, and the final group is
separated by the silence of the 'points de suspension'.

It is more difficult however to identify any immediate
expressive effect in the other sounds, the *s* of lines 1 and 2
which gradually gives way to *m* in line 3. The Parque wakes
hearing some distant, exterior sound, which she thinks for a
moment might be the wind: can the *s*-es be associated then
with the wind? But of course it is not the wind she is actually
hearing, only something like it. The sounds themselves play
a deliberately ambiguous rôle. It is clear that at first she hears
a distinct sound that seems to be coming from outside the
small centre of awakened consciousness; after a silence the
sound seems nearer: 'proche de moi-même'. 'Moi-même' is
especially significant with its three *m* sounds, giving an effect
of interiorisation to them: corresponding to the shift in
meaning from exterior to interior is the change from clear-
sounding fricatives to the nasals.

Thus the *œ* and *s* sounds become associated with the sobbing through the key word 'pleure' and the surrounding of
'vent' with sibilants, in much the same way as Mallarmé
darkened 'minuit'. But here, as in all his poetry, Valéry is not
so much concerned with imitating the sound, as with conveying the effect, creating with words an experience which provokes the same kinds of responses. The lines convey the sensation of persistent questioning, of rustling wind, of a distant
dissociated identity, and a close, more intimate presence.

The sounds of nature are only present to a rather limited
extent in Valéry's poetry. But throughout the poems ring the
song, speech and exclamation of the human voice, conveying
orally the light, rhythm, movement and tactile nature of
experience.

The visual perfection and unity of the columns in *Cantique
des Colonnes* is expressed by the unity and clarity of sound:

> Pour affronter la lune,
> La lune et le soleil,
> On nous polit chacune
> Comme ongle de l'orteil!

As blocks of regular white stone, the columns are placed in
the light of the sun and moon, taking on the deep brilliance
of these sources of light. The purity of the light arises from
the smoothness of their finish; 'polit' and the succession of *l*
sounds give the stanza a tactile sense of the evenness of the
surface.

The gentle restrained movement of the woman in *Intérieur*
is expressed through the soft unemphatic sounds, especially
from 'molles chaînes' which describes the look in her eyes,
the heavy languid eyelashes, the decoration, the acceptance
of restriction:

> Une esclave aux longs yeux chargés de molles chaînes
> Change l'eau de mes fleurs, plonge aux glaces prochaines.

In *Le Rameur* the difficulty and laboriousness of the row-
ing is conveyed by 'M'arrachent' and the extension of its
sounds throughout the first two lines; because of the various
points of articulation, the combination of sounds cannot be
said quickly or easily. In this context the word 'Penché'

demands effort and strength of pronunciation to overcome the plosive *p* just like the initial pull on an oar:

> Penché contre un grand fleuve, infiniment mes rames
> M'arrachent à regret aux riants environs.

The distinction between the three different techniques will not always necessarily be clear-cut, for it will depend upon the reader's interpretation of the meaning; the sound may be appropriate to one of the associations, and less obviously related to another. The example of the opening lines of *La Jeune Parque* showed an element of ambiguity, and it is this aspect which constitutes the third major technique employed by Valéry: while the pattern of sound is clear, the precise connection with the meaning may well be indefinable.

La puissance des vers tient à une harmonie *indéfinissable* entre ce qu'ils *disent* et ce qu'ils *sont*. 'Indéfinissable' entre dans la définition.
L'impossibilité – ou du moins la difficulté – de définir cette relation, combinée avec l'impossibilité de la nier, constitue l'essence du vers.[48]

The sound fulfils the rôle of assuring the unity and continuity of the lines, while the meaning shifts within this pattern, and thus the sound comes to be associated with varying effects. This is evident, for example, in stanza 7 of *Le Cimetière marin* where the poem moves from a concentration upon light and sun, to shade and death; a mirror reflecting the light of the sun will cast a shadow behind, in the same way as the poet's awareness of being separate from the scene he is contemplating leads to an awareness of his own mortality.

> L'âme exposée aux torches du solstice
> Je te soutiens, admirable justice
> De la lumière aux armes sans pitié!
> Je te rends pure à ta place première:
> Regarde-toi! . . . Mais rendre la lumière
> Suppose d'ombre une morne moitié.

The transition in ideas occurs within a tightly-knit stanza unified by the similarities of timbres, especially in the rhyme and with the ever-present *m* sounds. This sound occurs in 'âme', 'admirable', 'armes' and 'lumière' but also in 'ombre' and 'morne' in the last line; while there is a different range of certain sounds at the beginning and the end, expressing the contrast of elevation and light with the shade behind, the continuity of *m* and *r* and the richness of the rhymes with *i* common to all is less obviously expressive, except of unity itself. Later in the poem there are similar effects stressing the interconnection of light and dark; they are complementary rather than contradictory and the symmetry of the lines emphasises this sensual, aesthetic and philosophic union:

> Où tant de marbre est tremblant sur tant d'ombres;
>
> Le blanc troupeau de mes tranquilles tombes

The indissolubility of sound and sense is based not upon the coming together of definable qualities, one in the sound and one in the meaning, but precisely in provoking the impression of certain qualities in the context of the poem: their indefinability – as separate values – guarantees their indissolubility. The pattern of sounds need not always be expressive of something specific in order to be effectively part of the structure of the poem. A further example of 'harmonie indéfinissable' arises in the final stanza of *Aurore*.

> Elle sent sous l'onde unie
> La profondeur infinie
> Et frémit depuis l'orteil.[49]

The first seven lines of the last stanza have established the goddess 'Espérance' swimming through the water, a swan perhaps, stirring up a wave by the movement of the neck in the water. The whole poem has traced the gradual upward movement away from the depths of the self and sleep.

The lines present a pattern of sound around the rhyme *ni* and the nasal *ond*, and an opposition of meaning within this scheme: 'onde unie' refers to the surface and 'profondeur infinie' to the depths. There is no movement towards the depths in this stanza but an awareness of their presence far below; 'onde' becomes involved in this impression not because it is a 'voyelle sombre' but because of the dominating seman-tic influence of 'sous' and 'profondeur'; but since this then diverts the sound from the meaning of 'onde' this effect cannot be too specific. The whole effect becomes even more complex with the presence in the final line of two further *i* sounds. 'Frémit' dominates and creates an impression of tension associated with the extremity of 'infinie'; this reflects upon the *i* sounds, giving an effect of trembling excitement which at once echoes the 'confiance tendue' of stanza 8, and convinces the reader that the beautiful forms, the 'similitudes amies' which have reached clarity and definition in the form of a goddess Hope, have come to life as a living vibrant form.

The three techniques which emerge from the *Cahiers* clearly overlap to a certain degree; however distinct theoretically, the richness of meaning of Valéry's poetry assures a constant interrelation of expressive sound and 'harmonie indéfinissable'. It is not a question of putting different lines into different categories, but of establishing that the same lines offer varying prospects: there is no contradiction in supposing different possibilities in the same line, which may be emphasised at different readings or present simultaneously.[50]

In certain cases, then, expressive effects arise from the dominance of key words, extending their sounds over several contiguous words, but they in turn form part of a wider pattern of sound that establishes a continuity throughout the whole stanza. Valéry's poetry shows a systematic exploitation of ambiguity in the use of sounds, an ambiguity that is conveyed by the complex fusion of sound and sense, and which is eminently musical:

L'ambiguïté est le (domaine) propre de la poésie. Tout vers est équivoque, plurivoque - comme sa structure, sound + sense - l'indique.[51]

Le symbolisme n'est que la théorie rhétorique de l'*ambiguïté*. L'ambiguïté en tant que système. Ce mode équivoque est le plus grand rapprochement possible de la poésie avec la musique en tant qu'effet.[52]

10

RECITATIVE

Orfeo.
Le vers – comme le beau récitatif – ne doit être que la parole mûrie avec toutes ses inflexions et articles soulignés d'or – ses temps bien marqués, sa modulation bien déduite.

VI, 1917, p. 502.

In previous chapters the details of Valéry's compositional techniques have been studied, and in each case it has been seen that he was concerned to establish a parallel between poetry and the features of musical style. But it is necessary to consider, too, the overall impression of the poetry, and ask, in more general terms, to what kind of music this poetry can be compared most aptly. There is in his poems a characteristic tone, or range of tones, which may best be called the quality of recitative. While Verlaine's poetry evokes the 'chanson' and Mallarmé produced the great orchestrated works, Valéry's distinctive musical genre is recitative:

La grande différence entre Mallarmé et moi en ce qui touche la musique du vers est la suivante: c'est que Mallarmé recherche toujours l'effet d'orchestre, comme effet orchestral *L'Après-midi d'un Faune* me paraît un chef d'œuvre qu'on ne surpassera pas. Pour moi, au contraire, l'unité musicale dans le vers, c'est le son, la voix, le récitatif de Gluck, de Wagner parfois, mais par-dessus tout de Gluck.[1]

With *La Jeune Parque* Valéry created his own poetic voice and found a way of freeing himself from the overpowering example of Mallarmé, which is underlined by his use of the phrase 'pour moi, au contraire'.

The quality of recitative arises from the conjunction of the dramatic tone of address and the continually modulating pattern of sound. The poems are dramatic in the sense that the words on the page are spoken words; the poet or his 'characters' are speaking aloud, not writing or thinking silently. The sounds are striking not only in one line or another, but in the pattern that is woven through each stanza to form an integrated, modulating effect over the whole poem. The total impression is of a dramatically delivered, well-cadenced voice merging with a sensitive independent instrumental accompaniment. This chapter will examine the background to this idea, before analysing the dramatic tone of address in Valéry's poetry and taking a specific illustration from *La Jeune Parque*.

At the heart of this musical style of Valéry lies a personal sensitivity to the beauty of the human voice, an aspect which fascinated him as much in 1900:

Le chant d'Orphée - je découvre que la voix peut me faire un profond plaisir - c'est le contralto qui me pénètre de sa déclamation colossale.[2]

as in 1939:

Je suis très sensible au timbre de la voix que j'aime argenté - Dans le chant, le registre aimé est le contralto.[3]

The most notable reference was made in 1911; though written before he was approached by Gide to republish his early poems, before he even considered writing an 'adieu à ces jeux d'adolescence',[4] it portrays exactly the clear and ringing tone he was to achieve in *La Jeune Parque*.

A un certain âge tendre, j'ai peut-être entendu une voix, un contralto profondément émouvant . . .
Ce chant me dut mettre dans un état dont nul objet ne m'avait donné l'idée. Il a imprimé en moi la tension, l'attitude suprême qu'il demandait, sans donner un objet, une idée, une cause, (comme fait la musique). Et je l'ai pris sans le savoir pour mesure des états et j'ai tendu, toute ma vie, à faire, chercher, penser ce qui eût pu directement restituer en moi, nécessiter de moi . . . Une voix qui touche aux larmes, aux entrailles; qui tient lieu de catastrophes et de découvertes; qui va presser, sans obstacles, les mamelles sacrées / ignobles de l'émotion (bête); qui artificiellement et comme jamais le monde réel n'en a besoin, éveille des extrêmes, insiste, remue, noue, résume trop, épuise les moyens de la sensibilité, . . . et rabaisse les choses observables. On l'oublie et il n'en reste que le sentiment d'un degré dont la vie ne peut jamais approcher.[5]

The dramatic use of the voice in recitative became a model for his poetry. Originally he saw *La Jeune Parque* as a short piece of thirty or forty lines: 'Je voyais quelque récitatif d'opéra à la Gluck, presque une seule phrase, longue et pour contralto.'[6] In 'Le Prince et la Jeune Parque' Valéry explained how his concern for certain abstract problems gradually merged with his poetic attempts and led to the creation of some fragments of lines and associated words. His plan, he said, was clear:

Mon dessein était de composer une sorte de discours dont la suite des vers fût développé ou déduite de telle sorte que l'ensemble de la pièce produisît une impression analogue à celle des *récitatifs* d'autrefois. Ceux qui se trouvent dans Gluck, et particulièrement l'Alceste m'avaient beaucoup donné à songer. J'enviais cette ligne.[7]

Gluck was certainly different from the nineteenth-century musicians usually evoked by the symbolist poets. Valéry found in Gluck a number of artistic preoccupations very similar to his own. Not least of these was an interest in the Orpheus theme. Gluck's opera had impressed Valéry at an early age and the heading 'Orfeo' is often used as a title for notes in the *Cahiers*. Both artists were much preoccupied by the relationship between music and poetry: they insisted that one art cannot truly be itself without elements of the other. Valéry emphasised this feature constantly:

La poésie séparée du chant est presque contradictoire.[8]

Vers. Locution désormais reconnaissable comme un air.[9]

En fait de vers, j'ai fini par ne plus aimer ou souhaiter que les *phrases versifiantes* qui sont très comparables à des mélodies. Un poète est défini par ce quasi-chant – et ne peut l'être que par lui.[10]

Some 150 years earlier in *Mercure de France* Gluck had stressed the importance of good poetic texts, acknowledging the rôle of his collaborator for most of the operas, the poet Calzabigi:

Quelque talent qu'ait le Compositeur, il ne fera jamais que de la musique médiocre si le Poète n'excite pas en lui cet enthousiasme sans lequel les productions de tous les Arts sont foibles et languissantes . . . Toujours simple et naturelle, autant qu'il m'est possible, ma musique ne tend qu'à la plus grande expression et au renforcement de la Poésie.[11]

The common purpose behind the desire for integration was an unbroken musical effect. This is clearly indicated in Gluck's approach to the traditional distinction between instrumental passages, recitative and aria. Before Gluck the aria had been a vehicle for singers to display their vocal talents, especially in the repeat when all kinds of improvised ornamentation were allowed. Recitative, on the other hand, had been largely restricted to a narrative rôle: the story would be delivered as speech or perhaps on a single pitch with a sparse accompaniment of single chords. This form, which was known as 'recitativo secco', gave way in Gluck's music almost entirely to 'recitativo accompagnato', where the whole orchestra becomes melodically and dramatically involved, establishing a continuous musical line to link together chorus, recitative and aria. He reduced the virtuoso quality of the aria and wrote much less ornamented melodic lines, and though there are many impressive arias, there are also as in the oracle scene in *Alceste* or the opening of *Iphigénie en Tauride*, some major scenes in recitative. Gluck was aiming, as he explained in his preface to *Alceste*, to achieve a unified experience in which the chorus and dance were introduced at dramatically relevant places.[12] There is a striking parallel between these ideas of Gluck and Valéry's efforts to achieve a 'musique réduite, limitée' throughout the poetic texture, so that within the unified structure different parts may perform different functions: 'des vers, les uns chantent, les autres jouent des instruments, les autres gesticulent'.[13]

An additional influence on Valéry's concept of recitative was the example of Racine. Valéry relates how the recitation of *Athalie* to his children made a profound impression and opened his eyes to further possibilities of poetic diction. The lines of Racine were 'des récitatifs à peine un peu moins chantants que ceux des compositions lyriques'.[14] The great actress of the Comédie Française, la Champmeslé, was taught her 'diction chantée' by Racine himself, and her performances were in turn studied by Lully who upheld them as perfect examples of song. Valéry found much to admire in Racine – the poetic skill, the condensed style and richness of meaning of the alexandrine, the control of diction, the emotional power and depth of the characters. But perhaps for *La Jeune Parque* two features were especially significant: the sustained example of poetic and dramatic texture woven together, and the anguished cry of the isolated central heroine, alone on the stage, transcending all the action that evolved around her.

The force of the Racinian example was brought home by an article, which Valéry discovered by chance, on the poetic delivery of the famous nineteenth-century actress Rachel. The article related that Prince Georg von Hohenzollern had made notes on her interpretations of classical dramas, and had written a kind of musical notation for her voice, expressing rhythm, accents, breath marks and cadences. The precise details of her phrasing, pitch and timing are however less important than the attitude and emotional resonance of her tone, combined with her classical style of acting. The article was published in 1913, just as Valéry was beginning his poem and it evokes a presence remarkably like that of the Parque herself:

La sobriété, l'énergie et la grâce du geste, la magie du regard, la pureté de la diction, le son grave et métallique d'une voix sans égale . . .
Sa voix de contralto . . .
Sa surexcitation nerveuse se communiquait aux spectateurs . . .
  Elle respirait à pleins poumons avant de parler, comme une personne qui se trouve au bord de la mer et qui se livre avec joie à la fraîcheur de l'élément.[15]

In the final section of the poem the Parque comes to the edge of the sea and reflects, out loud, in a superbly sustained passage that maintains its syntactic tension over 17 lines, of which these are the opening and closing lines:

> . . . Alors, n'ai-je formé, vains adieux si je vis,
> Que songes? . . . Si je viens, en vêtements ravis,
> Sur ce bord, sans horreur, humer la haute écume,
> Boire des yeux l'immense et riante amertume,
> L'être contre le vent, dans le plus vif de l'air,
> Recevant au visage un appel de la mer;
>
> Feu vers qui se soulève une vierge de sang
> Sous les espèces d'or d'un sein reconnaissant!
>
> lines 495–513

The Parque represents not just the crisis of identity of a twentieth-century adolescent girl, but a heroine of Racinian stature, supremely aware, dominant, lyrical and yet resigned to her fate, accepting her position in the universe with a cry that emerges from the depths of her being. The dramatic force of the recitative, set within a classical tradition of tragedy and music, is ultimately a celebration of the human voice and the spoken word as the most accomplished form of control over experience.

Thus, although the terms that Valéry uses may vary ('modulation', 'voix', 'musique'), there remains nevertheless a consistent attempt to achieve the quality of recitative: it represents a desire to combine the musical qualities of melody, harmonics, rhythm and sonority with a particular tone of voice into a fluid, modulating whole. Again and again he emphasised that this is the key to his poetry; in 1918:

La voix, clef de la poésie. N'est pas un pur instrument de musique, mais autant d'usages et de significations et de places qu'elle a, autant de conditions offertes mais imposées à l'art poëtique. Ce complexe de musique et de sens.
Le *ton* de la voix est la signification d'une attitude par le rythme et par les intensités et les mesures.[16]

and in 1944 (after discussing the compositional technique of 'placing' words to balance, contrast or create tone, and the use of a word such as 'bordel' to compensate for the abstract colour of the text in *La Soirée avec Monsieur Teste*):

Si je puis voir en ce mode de composer une influence de la peinture, je vois mieux encore dans diverses choses qui j'ai faites celle de la musique. L'idée vague (chez moi, ignorant cet art) et la magie du mot *Modulation* ont joué un rôle important dans mes poèmes. *La Jeune Parque* fut obsédée par le désir de ce *continuum* – doublement demandé. D'abord, dans la suite musicale des syllabes et des vers, – et puis dans le glissement et la substitution des idées – images – suivant elles-mêmes les états de la conscience et sensibilité de la *Personne-qui-parle*.[17]

The drama in Racine arises from the tensions and conflicts built up between the different characters; but a more intense kind of conflict is present within the characters as they are torn between irreconcilable demands. This internal conflict is not less dramatic than the former; on the contrary, it provides the main driving force for the tragedy: the dramatic situation of Pyrrhus, Hermione and Oreste is entirely dependent upon the internal struggle of Andromaque, forced to choose between the memory of Hector and the life of Astyanax. The fact that neither Hector nor Astyanax appear only heightens the dramatic conflict and emphasises its irreconcilable nature.

Most of Valéry's poems are, like *La Jeune Parque*, 'une seule phrase longue' spoken by a single character. Even in the four poems of *Charmes* which do have dialogue – *Aurore*, *Au Platane*, *Cantique* and *Poésie* – the amount is very limited, serving to present or conclude the situation. As in Racine the dramatic tension arises from the different voices that speak through the one character, each with a distinct tone of address and each with a conflicting perspective. At one moment the clashes of several time scales are present, each showing a different aspect of the self. The predicament of the Pythie is made all the more harrowing by the recollection of her past innocent happiness and her fear for the future. By far the most complex effect was *La Jeune Parque* which Valéry described as 'un chant prolongé, sans action, rien que l'incohérence interne aux confins du sommeil'.[18] Developing this idea in the *Cahiers*, he wrote:

La plus belle poésie a toujours la forme d'un monologue. J'ai essayé de faire venir au monologue (dans la J.P.) ce qui me semblait la substance de l'être vivant, et la vie physiologique dans la mesure où cette vie peut être perçue par soi, et exprimée *poétiquement*.
Tandis que l'élément *historique* d'un MOI joue en général le rôle principal, j'ai – ici comme ailleurs – préféré son sentiment d'actuel éternel.[19]

The different 'participants' are most clearly indicated by the varying forms of address to herself:

Adieu, pensai-je, MOI, mortelle soeur, mensonge . . .

Harmonieuse MOI, différente d'un songe . . .

Mystérieuse MOI, pourtant, tu vis encore!
Tu vas te reconnaître au lever de l'aurore
Amèrement la même.[20]

Valéry referred to the section beginning 'Mystérieuse MOI' as a new Act; it echoes the opening of the whole poem and makes a striking contrast with the closing of the previous scene. She had been walking precariously towards the precipice ('L'insensible rocher, glissant d'algues, propice / A fuir') but now wakes from sleep almost surprised to find herself still alive. Her attitude is no longer agitated and distraught, but clear, accepting and even ironic ('Amèrement la même'). In the dawning light the mysteries of her own nature are less frightening, presenting 'sur la lèvre, un sourire d'hier' instead of anguished cries. Contrasting echoes of the opening of the poem are heard. While she first addressed herself impersonally ('Qui pleure là?' and 'Cette main glacée'), she now uses the second person. Earlier she had felt distant from herself as if seeing a separate hand raised against the light of the stars; she now recognises and accepts her identification with her own body:

> Regarde: un bras très pur est vu, qui se dénude.
> Je te revois, mon bras . . . Tu portes l'aube . . .   333–4

Where in Act I the stars are witness to her tears as she lies shivering and gleaming against the darkness:

> Que fais-tu hérissée, et cette main glacée,
> Et quel frémissement d'une feuille effacée
> Persiste parmi vous, îles de mon sein nu? . . .
> Je scintille, liée à ce ciel inconnu . . .
> L'immense grappe brille à ma soif de désastres.   13–17

now she is defined by the growing light of day and the fading of the stars marks the passing of the tears:

> . . . Et sur la lèvre, un sourire d'hier
> Qu'annonce avec ennui l'effacement des signes.   328–9

As a symbol of the quieting of her inner tensions, the violence of the sea has abated; the shelf of rocks, initially 'l'écueil mordu par la merveille' is now lapped with calm water

> . . . et seuil
> Si doux . . . si clair, que flatte, affleurement d'écueil,
> L'onde basse, et que lave une houle amortie!   335–7

The poem exploits the full range of the human voice, passing from the murmuring doubt of the opening, through her confusion of scorn and longing for the Serpent, to despair and torment, but also to the adoration of the islands, the fervent hymn to Spring and the joyous acceptance of light. The changes and tensions within the self are reflected in the complex arrangement of tenses and the subtle variations in the tones of address. She passes from exclamation to exhortation, questioning, imperatives, apostrophe and invocation. This dramatic force is present in all Valéry's poems in a variety of ways, as the poems reveal a perpetually changing dialogue with the self. Continually the reader is confronted with the poet's attempts to define himself in relation to his past, his present, his feelings or ideas, his body or the external world around.

A study of some of the changes made through composition reveals a continual movement towards direct address, from the third to the second person, from statement and description to exclamation and apostrophe. This is evident even in the later stages. For example the changes in *Fragments du Narcisse* between 1921 and 1922 are essentially a matter of additional material; but among the lines retained, the changes show a desire to make the poem more dramatically immediate and involving.

> Et que, repoussant l'ombre et l'épaisseur panique,
> Je vois, je tombe et viens de ce corps tyrannique

→ Alors, vainqueur de l'ombre, ô mon corps tyrannique,
  Repoussant aux forêts leur épaisseur panique,
  Tu regrettes bientôt leur éternelle nuit!   lines 66–8

Similarly:

> . . . Voici dans l'eau ma chair de lune et de rosée

→ Te voici, mon doux corps de lune et de rosée   line 115

> Voici mes bras d'argent dont les gestes sont purs!

→ Qu'ils sont beaux, de mes bras les dons vastes et vains!
                                                       line 117

Even the simple change of possessive adjective is significant; in line 121 'Mais que sa bouche est belle en ce muet blasphème!' 'sa bouche' is replaced by 'ta bouche'.

The vocative form is used frequently throughout the poem, ringing out like a cry of admiration, longing, and regret for a unity that cannot be:

> O douceur de survivre à la force du jour . . .

> O semblable! . . . Et pourtant plus parfait que moi-même . . .

Recitative

> O mon corps, mon cher corps, temple qui me sépares
> De ma divinité, je voudrais apaiser
> Votre bouche ...

But its dramatic force is employed throughout *Charmes* as well:

> Il faut, ô souple chair du bois
>   Te tordre, te détordre ...   *Au Platane*

> Douces colonnes, ô
> L'orchestre des fuseaux!
>   *Cantique des Colonnes*

> O ma mère Intelligence   *Poésie*

> O biche avec langueur longue auprès d'une grappe
>   *La Dormeuse*

> O Courbes, méandre   *L'Insinuant*

The vocative is only one of the forms of address used in *Charmes*: a wide variety of tones, of exclamations and questionings is to be found making it clear that the poems present the immense versatility of the spoken voice. These are a few examples:

interjections may be forcefully and rhythmically emphatic:

> Quoi! c'est vous, mal déridées!
> Que fîtes-vous, cette nuit,
> Maîtresses de l'âme, Idées?   *Aurore*

a direct anguished plea:

> Don cruel! Maître immonde, cesse
> Vite, vite, ô divin ferment,
> De feindre une vaine grossesse
> Dans ce pur ventre sans amant!   *La Pythie*

an insistent uncomprehending questioning:

> Qui me parle, à ma place même?
> Quel écho me répond: Tu mens!
> Qui m'illumine? ... Qui blasphème?   *La Pythie*

an anxious uncertain combination of expectation and disappointment:

> Des cieux même tu me sèvres,
> Par quel injuste retour?
> Que seras-tu sans mes lèvres?
> Que serai-je sans amour?   *Poésie*

219

Musical techniques in Valéry's poetry

a tone of comedy and satire:

> Holà! dit-il, nouveaux venus!
> Vous êtes des hommes tout nus,
> O bêtes blanches et béates!
>
> *Ebauche d'un Serpent*

a tone of grandeur and achievement:

> Fin suprême, étincellement
> Qui, par les monstres et les dieux
> Proclame universellement
> Les grands actes qui sont aux Cieux!
>
> *Ode secrète*

a lyrical tone of admiration and meditation:

> Quel pur travail de fins éclairs consume
> Maint diamant d'imperceptible écume,
> Et quelle paix semble se concevoir!
>
> *Le Cimetière marin*

In addition to these clear dramatic effects, Valéry achieves many subtle changes in the forms of address throughout the poems: the subjects are never allowed to languish for long in the impersonality of the third person. The poet and his subject enter into an intricate, developing relationship which involves changes of perspective in time and space, personification of material objects, divisions within the self, and movements of separation and identification.

The shifts in perspective are evident in *L'Abeille*, which eminently displays the qualities of a sonnet as 'une rotation du même corps autour d'un point ou d'un axe'.[21] The woman and the bee circle around each other, at first slowly, then suddenly fast, hesitant and then decisive, persistently casting a spell and inviting the sting that will awaken and satisfy her feelings and desires. Addressed directly at the beginning 'ta pointe, blonde abeille', the bee is commanded in the second stanza 'Pique . . . !' Her body, at first suggestively and seductively presented ('Je n'ai sur ma tendre corbeille, / Jeté qu'un songe de dentelle'), is emphasised in the second stanza along with her feelings of love: 'Pique du sein la gourde belle . . .', '. . . la chair ronde et rebelle'. In the first tercet the emphasis moves to the insistence, the call for quick action and an end to the prolonged suffering, while in the final tercet the command is addressed to the self finding pleasure and release, 'Soit donc mon sens illuminé'.

La Ceinture opens in the third person with a description of a sunset, 'le ciel couleur d'une joue'. The observer is also evoked, obliquely in the third person, in silent rapturous attention ('les yeux . . . le muet de plaisir'). This effect is prolonged over the first two stanzas with the observer passive and part of the scene, and the sunset a picture of movement and seductive charm. At the onset of the third quatrain the scene is made more immediate with the use of the demonstrative ('Cette ceinture'), while the common identity of the observer and the observed is stressed at the end of the stanza ('le suprême bien / De mon silence avec ce monde'), as though the poet can only find his own identity through the image. And yet he is conscious of this identity: as the light fades his awareness prepares his separation, the dramatic isolation emphasised by the use of the first person possessive adjective. In the final distich the duality is complete as the poet fully discovers his separate being alone in the darkening light ('Je suis bien seul, / Et sombre, ô suave linceul').

The poems of *Charmes* along with *La Jeune Parque* reveal a considerable variety of tone, giving the impression of a constant dramatic dialogue among the 'participants'. This living, spoken discourse is delivered against the modulating pattern of sounds, sometimes merging with them for expressive effects, sometimes pursuing separate though interrelated courses. As Scarfe has noted, recognising the importance of recitative in Valéry's poetry, the use of exclamations 'not only give dramatic life to his thoughts and feelings, but give his lyrical poetry, even at its most intellectual, the tone of a *cry*, a supplication, which acts powerfully on the reader'.[22] Indeed Valéry's comments on *La Jeune Parque* can be seen to have just as much relevance to his subsequent poetic achievement; the constant intention was to portray 'ce qu'il y a d'amour, de jalousie, de piété, de désir, de jouissance, de courage, d'amertume, d'avarice, de luxure, dans les choses de l'intelligence'.[23]

In the well-known letter to Mockel where Valéry explains his intentions in writing *La Jeune Parque*, the aspect of the musical monologue features prominently; he stresses that he was seeking the musical qualities of a song for a single voice: 'Faire un chant prolongé, sans action'. While incorporating as much 'intellectualité' as possible, he wished to 'sauver l'abstraction par la musique'. The composition, he said, took place in fragments, with only one of which he was completely satisfied:

De ces morceaux, il en est un qui, seul, représente pour moi le poème que j'aurais voulu faire. Ce sont les quelques vers qui commencent ainsi: 'O n'aurait-il fallu, folle,' etc.[24]

Again in the *Cahiers* Valéry singled out

O n'aurait-il fallu, folle, que j'accomplisse

and

A l'extrême de l'être, et belle de faiblesse

as lines which seemed 'de se faire par la continuité musicale et de la reproduire en retour'.[25] In discussion with Francis de Miomandre he stressed yet again the musical intention:

O n'aurait-il fallu, folle, que j'accomplisse . . .
Il faut faire sentir ici, mon cher Miomandre, quelque chose comme un solo de violon . . . Toutes ces liquides! . . .[26]

Although the phrase 'quelque chose comme . . .' guards against a too specific parallel (for he does not say 'il faut faire sentir ici un solo de violon'), the general sense would seem to confirm the interpretation of 'la musique verbale' which was advanced in Chapter 9, and especially the third category where the sounds take on an independent line of their own. This passage, then, comes closest to achieving that quality of recitative – 'une seule phrase, longue et pour contralto' – which Valéry was seeking in the poem.

The drafts reveal that it was one of the early fragments to be composed and in fact a detailed study of the manuscripts shows that from these initial sketches whole new sections of the poem were to grow, like melody and counter-melody, theme and variations. In the early plan entitled *Hélène*, Valéry indicates the sections of the poem so far:

> mal
> animal
> larme
> Sommeil
> O n'aurait-il fallu folle[27]

And the 'ébauche du premier état' contains the lines 381–6 'O n'aurait-il fallu . . . – Que sur ce long regard de victime entr'ouverte' (JP I, 15). The analysis here will be primarily concerned with the stages that led up to this version of the opening lines; it is not intended to trace the genesis of the whole of section XIV, but to show how the recitative-like quality comes to be formed in the very early stages of composition, for with the exception of the final manuscript to be cited, all the fragments date from 1913: in fact the study of the composition of this passage lies close to the birth of the Parque herself.

The scene proposed is one of recollection and reassessment evident in the tenses and moods of the first sketch; the confrontation of 'selves' is manifest as she remembers her former self, the experience she has undergone as well as the suggestion in the perfect conditional of what she perhaps ought to have done:

> je me suis ressentie
> feux
> violer
> Je faisais défaillir
> Une profonde enfant que je fus
> O n'aurait-il fallu folle, que je ne fisse
> du soir ce voeux de parfait sacrifice
> Jaillir de moi   III f. 13

a tone which is expressed below in the laconic 'Mourir ayant souri'.

All the manuscripts of this period are remarkable for both the spontaneous creativity that is evident and the extreme care with which they are reworked. There is none of the confident surge of writing seen for example in the later work on *La Pythie* where entire stanzas are written almost at once.

Here the creative effort is taut and concentrated, and proceeds with extreme caution as each line and even word is tried in multiple combinations before being allowed into the corpus of the work: each manuscript will produce only a line or two, provisionally, until he is certain of the melodic, harmonic and rhythmic implications.

Thus at the bottom of III f. 13 while the theme of death suggests 'pente', 'perte' and 'pure', the rhyme 'fisse/sacrifice' suggests 'complice' and the manuscripts that follow lead temporarily in two directions which are developed separately until their subsequent reincorporation. Valéry's immediate concern is with 'la pente' which he explores in the next MS., III f. 14, a kind of 'mini-palette' as the harmonics are drawn out while 'la musique verbale' suggests other words with similar sound patterns. As he explores 'pente – perte – pure' for example 'perte' moved to the end of the line gives 'offerte' then 'entr'ouverte', a dangerous glimpse into the depths of the self:

```
                              ruine        offerte
                              pas
La pente était si pure à mon  désir  de perte
Plus dangereusement ta ténèbre entr'ouverte

Ni plus distinctement
        Ni si pure une perte
        la (vie) entr'ouverte
```

This insight is effected by the serpent whose presence is quite explicit in these drafts: 'œuvre / couleuvre' (f. 14), 'je me suis ressentie / feux / violer' (f. 13). These images come together in f. 16 where the glimpse becomes 'le regard', which is also 'l'œil doré du serpent son instinct' evoked now in her very movements: 'Ni de pente plus doux et qui rampe à ta perte . . . Parmi le sable bu une arrière pensée'. And 'entr'ouverte' takes on the added overtone of physical suffering as the Parque becomes a 'victime entr'ouverte'. While still using the same rhyme, f. 18 offers the illuminating alternative: 'O faut-il oublier que je me suis offerte'.

III f. 19 demonstrates how central this passage is to the entire poem: a 'palette-idées', the manuscript summarises the crucial themes and sketches some lines, moving from 3rd person to 1st person address and back again, identifying above all the important attitude of the self as a participant in its own drama that will determine her voice:

> perdu le mystère qui la faisait vivre
> Quand l'horrible trésor qui soufflait son orgueil
>   palpitait   sous son œil
>   rayon
>   quand elle se mélange à la mort
>   et blesse de regards   à sa propre ruine
>
> . . .
>
> avant de finir
> Elle voit Elle ouverte
> cercle – œil – entrailles – découvert

In these manuscripts the musical techniques are closely in evidence as Valéry sketches in a melody-theme, gradually building the corpus of his work by experimenting with the harmonics, the sounds and the rhythms, creating connections and contrasts between the fragments, developing the implications of one draft into a more sustained melodic movement. Each of the manuscripts presents an insight into one moment of the creative process, a move into fresh uncharted territory, his inspiration guided only by the hints of previous moments like the composer playing again and again part of a work in order to discover what ought to come next.[28]

Thus I f. 7vo reverts to another aspect of the original manuscript, III f. 13, developing the key words 'feux – enfant – sacrifice – mourir':

>   fisse
>   Mourir la transparence ou le finir, sacrifice
>   Aux seuls feux de mon sort
>   De ma jeunesse nue
>   De mon ventre
>   D'une enfant que je fus toujours, le sacrif

and he then finds the line:

>   Mourir? Trouveras-tu │jamais│ plus simple sacrifice
>   transparente   │fin│
>   mort
>   Que disparaître
>   Toi qui déjà glissais parmi les soins du sort
>   Que glissant   –   –   au sort

enclosing 'jamais' and 'fin' as words he wishes to retain, though in fact the choice is only provisional for the rhyme. III f. 21vo begins 'Trouverais-tu jamais plus transparente fin' and a process of modulation effects gradual changes upon the next line:

Toi qui te connaissais un caprice du sort

Ton dédain plus léger des [caprices] du sort
          plus   figures
          exactes
          achevé
          fini

          exquis
plus   - -   horreur

In III f. 26 Valéry now attempts for the first time to put the fragments together and write a sequence of lines, with the adoption of ' . . . sort' for line 4 causing him to change 'fin' to 'mort' in line 3. He writes first:

O n'aurait-il fallu folle que je me fisse
          sacrifice
Trouveras-tu jamais plus transparente mort
Plus lucide dédain des figures du sort

and then tries to incorporate into this the suggestions of 'fin' and 'glisser' from I f. 7vo. He 'fills in' line 2 with 'L'abandon sur sa fin / d'un si . . .' and adds over the top of line 4 'Que glisser au'; then underneath he sketches an alternative opening couplet where the same sound in the rhyme finds new words:

      que j'accomplisse
Ma [—] fin de glisser sans supplice[29]
    de me lisser complice
      m'effacer
  d'achever avec supplice

The assonance of 'accomplisse – glisser – supplice' was too pronounced, however, and he sought within the same rhythmic movement a more subtle, modulated pattern of sound.[30]

With this reworking Valéry now reincorporates the two strands of development from the first manuscript and produces a typed version of 8 lines:

O n'aurait-il fallu, folle, que j'accomplisse
Ma merveilleuse fin de choisir pour supplice

Ce lucide dédain des nuances du sort?
Trouverai-je jamais plus transparente mort
Ni de pente plus pure où je rampe à ma perte
Que ce long regard de mon âme déserte?
Par quel retour sur soi, reptile, as-tu repris
Tes parfums de caverne et tes tristes esprits?

(line 4 amended to 'tu', line 6 to 'victime entr'ouverte')

I f. 15

The deliberate creation of the recitative can be observed here in the changes of person; while in the early stages of composition other issues dominate the poet's attention and he moves freely from one person to another, now as the section becomes more complete these minor adjustments are immensely important: III f. 21vo gave 'Trouverais-tu', III f. 26 'Trouveras-tu', but in I f. 15 he first types 'Trouverai-je', presumably for consistency with 'que j'accomplisse' and then emends it by hand to 'Trouveras-tu'.[31] These eight lines will constitute the opening six and closing two of the section (lines 381–6 and 423–4) when the process of internal generation will have expanded them to forty-four.

The following manuscript, I f. 16, gives the lines 381–4, 421–2, two lines whose rhymes are used for 87–8 ('mal / animal'), then 386 and 385. It is not until the fourth version some two years later in 1915 that the opening is developed, written under the heading 'O' that he adopted for this section: the first six lines ('O n'aurait-il fallu . . . / . . . victime entr'ouverte') are typed as in I f. 15, the next three ('Pâle elle se résigne . . . / . . . cette pourpre la laisse') are added in pen, and the tentative workings for the next line added in pencil:

Le moment souverain sourit à sa faiblesse
Indifférente, calme et/si belle de faiblesse   I f. 38

'A l'extrême de l'être . . .' is still to be discovered, but the passage is sufficiently developed to show the techniques of composition and to identify the deliberate effort towards a quality that has been termed recitative: the search for melody, harmonics, rhythm, 'continuité musicale' along with the creation of a particular tone of human voice. His efforts towards this goal are both painstaking and inspired, slow, hesitant, and yet proceed with a surge of creative activity that can be seen in the proliferation of material from one manuscript to another. These drafts are in fact so highly charged that traces can be sensed not only of other moments of the poem, but even of 'l'œil fixé' and 'l'œil doré du serpent' and the 'trésors horribles' and 'mystère perdu' of *La Pythie*. But above all it is possible to feel in these early manuscripts the sense of creative tension as the Parque's voice begins to ring out, 'presque une seule phrase, longue, et pour contralto', indeed as Valéry discovers his own authentic poetic voice.[32] This quality, manifest already in the composition of the opening lines, is of considerable importance for an appreciation of Valéry's poetry. Before turning, in conclusion, to an analysis of the final version, the achievement may be identified in a unique passage where Valéry comments upon his own work; referring evidently to a more advanced stage of this section of the poem, the text moves imperceptibly from commentary to a prose evocation of precisely that attitude which resonates throughout.

O

Une phrase de cinquante vers, profondément *mesurée*, pas une qui n'ajoute son mot et ne paye sa présence; chef-d'œuvre de mouvement et d'inflexions, chaque vers dédié, ou le distique, à une puissance, et une orchestration savante, due à l'*entrée* toujours contrastée de sonorités. Rappels de l'âme végétative au final d'une pensée, ou attaques.

Comme dans une belle prière, après l'invocation ou évocation du Plus-Haut-Que-Soi, le soi revient à lui-même, s'abaisse et s'attendrit, puis se ferme, se serre et descend au profond.

O Toi –

O – Moi!

Echangeons-nous maintenant.[33]

> O n'aurait-il fallu, folle, que j'accomplisse   381
> Ma merveilleuse fin de choisir pour supplice
> Ce lucide dédain des nuances du sort?
>   Trouveras-tu jamais plus transparente mort
> Ni de pente plus pure où je rampe à ma perte   385
> Que ce long regard de victime entr'ouverte,
> Pâle, qui se résigne et saigne sans regret?
> Que lui fait tout le sang qui n'est plus son secret?

Dans quelle blanche paix cette pourpre la laisse,
A l'extrême de l'être, et belle de faiblesse!   390
Elle calme le temps qui la vient abolir,
Le moment souverain ne la peut plus pâlir,
Tant la chair vide baise une sombre fontaine! . . .
Elle se fait toujours plus seule et plus lointaine . . .
Et moi, d'un tel destin, le cœur toujours plus près,   395
Mon cortège, en esprit, se berçait de cyprès . . .

The passage has a clear audible ring that makes the reader
hear the well-formed voice projecting this song of doubt. The
Parque is thinking back to the moment earlier in the night
when she had almost killed herself and now considers that
perhaps she should after all have achieved her 'merveilleuse
fin'. For the death, portrayed in an atmosphere of sexual
images, is seen as a means to the absolute, a point of identification with the universal laws; the 'transparente mort' represents for her 'le moment souverain'. Through knowledge she
might have freed herself from the constraints and problems
of individual personality and attained 'Ce lucide dédain des
nuances du sort'. With a cry of anguish, doubt and regret, she
wonders whether she did the right thing. And yet, strangely,
the passage is not totally morbid; for it is the human, doubting self, the ego, that is speaking, calling herself 'folle' and
uttering the vibrant exclamations, implicit even in the
moment of despair. The Parque 'on stage' at the moment is
the Racinian heroine, full of tragic questioning emotion,
caught in a seemingly insoluble situation, portraying to the
reader in a pure almost disembodied form the intensity of
feeling, sparing the reader the ugliness of reality, yet describing vividly and beautifully a scene of horror and despair.

The Parque sees her death as a way of killing off the cor-
poreal, sexual side of her nature: her mind, having separated
from her body, would look down on the 'victime entr'ouverte', and would be 'A l'extrême de l'être et belle de faiblesse'. The blood, the wound, the sexual images are vivid and
yet remote. The examination of how this is achieved involves
a detailed study of the complex changes of person and tense.
It needs to be emphasised that she is evoking a previous situation; she is still alive, using the present tense which, though
implied, is not spoken until line 406: 'Non, non! . . . n'irrite

plus cette réminiscence!' The present tense of lines 385–93 is an imaginative recreation of the past.

The whole situation of the opening lines is dependent upon the initial conditional perfect tense, 'O n'aurait-il fallu'. In 384 she begins almost trying to persuade herself of what she should have done, and hence addresses her present ego in the second person, 'Will you ever find . . .?', as if reasoning with herself. By 385 she now envisages her present ego in just such a situation, and dramatically uses the first person present tense as she feels reluctantly convinced, forcing herself to die: 'je rampe à ma perte'. She has persuaded herself by argument and force of feeling, and has now lost the awareness of her self as a living, thinking, feeling, sexual human being. In 386 she is already imaginatively dying and has become separate and disembodied. 'Pâle' suggests the pallor of the bloodless complexion as well as the shock and the fear. The mind is free, a separate entity addressed in the third person:

> Que *lui* fait tout le sang qui n'est plus *son* secret
> Dans quelle blanche paix cette pourpre *la* laisse.

The divisions implied by one part of the self looking at the other are emphasised by the use of the demonstrative 'ce long regard' and 'cette pourpre'.

The personal pronouns are now deliberately confused, merging the image of death and the Parque herself:

> Elle [la mort] calme le temps qui la [la Parque] vient abolir

She is beyond fear and beyond life, and the mind is ascending to form a distant, soon unrecognisable part of the absolute.

A hypothetical situation is thus portrayed by the Parque; she evokes, in an imaginatively vivid present tense, what might have happened and what she feels perhaps still ought to happen. As if to emphasise the reality of her feelings, the Parque shifts back in 395–6 to the real past and the recollection of the seriousness of her intentions: the intellectuality is as much a part of her being as the sexuality:

> Et moi, d'un tel destin, le cœur toujours plus près
> Mon cortège, en esprit, se berçait de cyprès . . .

The reader is led along the path with her, as she recalls, this time using the first person in the imperfect tense, the force of lucidity seeking freedom and fulfilment, taken up and absorbed into divine consciousness:

> Vers un aromatique avenir de fumée,
> Je me sentais conduite, offerte et consumée,
> Toute, toute promise aux nuages heureux! 397-9

And then, after the past tense 'je m'apparus', she begins to use the present again, rejoining the imaginative present used up to line 394; she appreciates not just the freedom from the body but the spiritual achievement, the mystery of identification with the universal principles represented by the smoke of a burning tree or incense. She is reliving the conflicts that led originally to the situation and is approaching the same point, but arriving from a different perspective of the self, from a different tense. Her persuasion seems to have convinced her as she identifies with the divine and loses her sense of personal being.

> L'être immense me gagne, et de mon cœur divin
> L'encens qui brûle expire une forme sans fin . . .
> Tous les corps radieux tremblent dans mon essence! . . .
> 403-5

She becomes silence.

Now, after a moment's pause, the narrative present, the living self of the ego is asserted: the memory and doubts are rejected: 'Non, non! . . . N'irrite plus cette réminiscence!' The forces of light are at work and the reliving of the past conflicts is now seen as gloomy and morbid:

> Sombre lys! Ténébreuse allusion des cieux,
> Ta vigueur n'a pu rompre un vaisseau précieux . . .
> 407-8

After a moment's more doubt, like a glance over her shoulder ('Parmi tous les instants tu touchais au suprême'), she sees that the sun has risen, representing power and wisdom, and she feels a sense of destiny in living and reflecting this glory. Knowledge and understanding of all these mysterious conflicts must be reached through subtlety and deviousness. She must learn from the experience of her own inner thoughts and the divisions of her consciousness:

Sois subtile . . . cruelle . . . ou plus subtile! . . . Mens
Mais sache! . . . Enseigne-moi par quels enchantements,
Lâche que n'a su fuir sa tiède fumée,
Ni le souci d'un sein d'argile parfumée,
Par quel retour sur toi, reptile, as-tu repris
Tes parfums de caverne et tes tristes esprits? 419–24

The need to establish the dramatic situation has led a little further than the particular lines which Valéry indicated as an example of 'continuité musicale', but, such is the unity of this tightly constructed section, that the rhythm of the argument carries the reader relentlessly forward. The changes of tense and person are used to great dramatic effect, forming an arabesque around the one point of continuity – the Parque herself in the act of speaking. The rhythm of the lines parallels that of the argument. Opening with a long tremulous exclamation, the pleading, doubting, persuading cry moves in long breathless phrases to a point of sublimity. Only twice in the first fourteen lines are the long rhythmic phrases broken, by 'folle' and 'pâle', both of them effects of the intensity of emotion. The sounds modulate through an extraordinary richness of combinations, the lines full of internal assonance and alliteration, the 'continuité du beau son' unbroken. The predominance of dental and labial consonants, combined with the purity of the range of vowels è, i, u create a sustained tension throughout the passage. As Valéry noted in the unpublished manuscript, the 'orchestration savante' of these lines is created by 'l'entrée toujours contrastée de sonorités'. Each line seems to offer the attack of a different consonant: the continuous line of music is achieved paradoxically not by repetition – which is strictly controlled – but by a modulating series of changing sounds:

La musique des vers est en relation étroite (*par les consonnes* entr'autres choses) avec la motricité particulière de la phonation.[34]

J'entends par *structure* le système de consonnes successives d'un fonctionnement verbal. Il y a passage d'un acte-consonne à un autre – et combinaisons.[35]

Above all the lines ring with the resonant tones of the human voice, with a recitative which reaches almost to the level of song, with the sound of that voice which Valéry heard and describes as

> une voix qui touche aux larmes, aux entrailles . . . qui éveille des extrê-mes, insiste, remue, noue, résume trop, épuise les moyens de la sensi-bilité.[36]

His intention was to write a song based on his conception of 'le sentiment physiologique de la conscience':

> il y a eu dans le désir ou dessein de cette fabrication l'intention absurde (peut-être faut-il l'absurde dans les projets de certaines œuvres?) de faire chanter une *Idée* de l'être vivant-pensant.[37]

In the resonant purity of the Parque's voice, Valéry so clearly attains those remarkable qualities of voice which he admired in Racine and which characterise his ideal poetry: *La Jeune Parque* has that 'inflexion de la voix digne d'une grande can-tatrice' and admirably matches Valéry's own standard: 'La plus belle poésie a la voix d'une femme idéale, Mlle Ame.'[38]

11

LA DORMEUSE

Le vers est un schème d'actes . . . une *forme* qui s'en dégage ou
qui engendre.

XXI, 1938, p. 279.

Le plus facile en musique est le plus difficile en poésie. Mesure -
enchaînements, modulation et il est presque impossible d'y faire
un développement *réglé*. Il est impossible de faire que l'œil ne
vole pas sur les lignes, filant sur le sens - brûlant les petits mots -
comme si l'écrit était un chemin menant à un *but* et c'est là le
contraire de la poésie.

   L'attente est impossible à imposer, et sans elle . . .

XXII, 1939, p. 633.

It is in the orchestration of all musical techniques that the
poet attains his greatest achievement: the combination of
parts into a fluid, modulating whole remains a guiding principle of composition at every stage. Thus at any single moment
in the reading of a poem, many different developments are
underway which complement each other, which imply movements, patterns, forms, reaching both forward and backward
in their immediate context and in the context of the whole
work.

Il y a un usage des mots . . . comparable par les effets à ceux de la musique et, quoique ceci soit vrai de *mots isolés*, c'est surtout par les rap-
prochements et combinaisons que l'on rend cet effet très sensible et
puissant.[1]

It is, says Valéry, to the extent that the poet can focus attention on the changing patterns of meaning, sound and rhythm
that he can achieve the purity, the non-referential quality of
music:

si le poète pouvait arriver à construire . . . des poèmes où la continuité
musicale ne serait jamais interrompue, où les relations des significations
seraient elles-memes perpétuellement pareilles à des rapports harmoni-

ques, *où la transmutation des pensées les unes dans les autres paraîtrait plus importante que toute pensée*, où le jeu des figures contiendrait la réalité du sujet, – alors l'on pourrait parler de *poésie pure* comme d'une chose existante.[2]

Or, as he expressed it in 'Propos me concernant':

Il n'y a que deux choses qui comptent, qui sonnent l'or sur la table où l'esprit joue sa partie contre lui-même.

L'une, que je nomme *Analyse*, et qui a la 'pureté' pour objet; l'autre que je nomme *Musique*, et qui compose cette 'pureté', en fait quelque chose.[3]

The examination of early drafts of the poems provides ample evidence of Valéry's attempts to realise such ideas. The poet is seeking to achieve an organic growth of his material by developments, dispersal and fusion of what has been written already. At each 'moment de composition' the poet is constantly involved in exploring new relationships of language: 'il ne cherche et ne doit chercher que ce qui lui semble efficace et possible *poétiquement* à chaque instant'.[4]

But what are the implications of this for a reading of the completed text? When presented with the published poem, it is essential to realise that the various musical techniques are not separate static forms, but are related both to each other and to the unfolding development of the work. The structures of themes, rhythms and sounds are not perceived in retrospect as distinct, formal patterns, but they are interrelated and perceived dynamically as the reading of the poem progresses. To the 'instants de composition' correspond the 'instants de lecture'; though not identical, they may provoke a similar creative involvement:

La vraie critique consisterait à trouver que tel écrivain se sert de tel type de transformations. ou plutôt que tel type de transformations est le sien. De phrase en phrase, ou, si l'on veut, d'idée en idée, et d'impulsion en impulsion.[5]

C'est du reste l'*instant* qu'il faudrait considérer.[6]

Hence the importance of 'l'attente', the unfolding appreciation of a work, the perception at every moment of developing structures: 'Toute phrase, tout vers est une attente – un mouvement préparatoire: le sens total se décide à la fin.'[7] It is, as Gérard Genette has observed, an idea of literature, 'qui le rapproche non seulement du formalisme contemporain . . . mais aussi des recherches actuelles du structuralisme'.[8] Genette quotes from Valéry's 'Propos me concernant' in support: 'Je voyais ou voulais voir les figures de relations entre les choses, et non les choses . . . Je *savais* que l'essentiel était *figure*.'[9]

Valéry's reference above to an understanding of a text 'de phrase en phrase' is made more explicit in a note written in 1944; he emphasises two essential features: the analysis of the developing parts on the one hand, and the perception of the overall structure on the other.

> Un vers est *le plus court* poème possible. Si donc on analyse *un vers* (isolable) on y trouve les traits essentiels du poème quant à la durée.
> Or l'unité *Vers* a un maximum. Il est clair que c'est le *nombre* d'impressions auditives successives au-delà duquel la combinaison de ces éléments ne se fait plus, par évanouissement des premiers.[10]

He makes a comparison with the ability of the eye to retain visual impressions for a certain, limited time, as when the impression of light remains after turning away from its source and is momentarily transferred on to the new visual impression.

> Si on applique ceci au Poème, on trouve donc des conditions de *conservation* qui sont imposées par la physiologie de l'esprit - les lois de la sensibilité; ou si l'on veut de la *mémoire continue*.[11]

Valéry is not here talking of the isolated 'beau vers' which tends on the contrary to destroy the unity of the poem. He is suggesting that the line is the initial level of the perception of 'harmoniques', 'musique verbale', 'thème-mélodie', from which features the structural unity of the whole is perceived:

> Mais on peut étendre cette propriété essentielle et développer cette conservation de l'unité au moyen de répétitions. D'où le réglage des vers, l'identité des rythmes, les rimes, refrains, allitérations. Toute la technique poétique est une organisation de la *répétition* - utilisée, rendue consciente - volontaire, imposée, préétablie, en vue de l'unité.[12]

In an attempt to integrate the techniques which have been identified, this chapter will study a single poem, *La Dormeuse*. After an examination of some of the early drafts, the musical techniques will be analysed as they are presented in the published work. In order to convey the developing structure and the notion of 'attente', it would therefore seem appropriate to tackle the poem 'de phrase en phrase, de vers en vers', identifying 'mélodie', 'harmoniques', 'rythme', 'musique verbale' as the analysis proceeds.

The theme of the poem relates to a long-standing preoccupation of Valéry. The *Cahiers* present a detailed study of 'rêve – sommeil – veille', in which he analysed the stages of sleep and the changes implied in the relationship of 'Corps – Esprit – Monde'.[13] His interest was not purely analytical, for the image of the sleeping woman figures prominently in his poetry, both in *La Jeune Parque* and *Album de Vers Anciens*. In 1891 Valéry published *La Belle au Bois Dormant*:

> La Princesse, dans un palais de roses pures
> Sous les murmures et les feuilles, toujours dort.
> Elle dit en rêvant des paroles obscures
> Et les oiseaux perdus mordent ses bagues d'or.

The poem is largely descriptive, portraying the surface beauty and surroundings of the sleeping beauty. She is pure, an ideal figure, in a state far removed from life:

> Princess pâle dont les rêves sont jolis
> A l'éternel dormir sous les gestes des Roses!

La Fileuse too presents a sleeping figure, an angelic picture of mystery, the dreaming woman remote from the world. Here, though, the imagery is linked with the beauty of the garden and the artistic world of the creator: the beauty of the rose and the work of the spinning-wheel have combined in an image of purity created by 'la fileuse' as she, having completed the work, dies. Sleep represents the absence of the intellect, a state of calm and rest, giving access to a different world of 'songe' and 'beauté'.

In *Eté* the figure is asleep on the sand and the movement of her breathing is associated with that of the waves rising and falling, a sleep that brings calmness: 'Bercez l'enfant ravie en un poreux sommeil'. But above all she is physically present, evoked in full sensuous form as a real life figure:

> Mais les jambes (dont l'une est plus fraîche et se dénoue
> De la plus rose), les épaules, le sein dur,

> Le bras qui se mélange à l'écumeuse joue
> Brillent abandonnés autour du vase obscur.

To this extent she has more in common with *Anne* than the previous poems. An early variant of *Anne* underlines this difference: 'la dormeuse déserte' was originally 'la dormante putain'. The first part of the poem stresses her naked physical presence, her sleeping form languishing on the bed:

> Anne qui se mélange au drap pâle et délaisse
> Des cheveux endormis sur ses yeux mal ouverts
> Mire ses bras lointains tournés avec mollesse
> Sur la peau sans couleur du ventre découvert.

Images from the previous poems occur as the poet moves through an evocation of her qualities. In stanza 2 her body is seen in terms of the play of light and shade ('D'air sombre l'aube basse enfle sa gorge lente' [1893] becomes 'Elle vide, elle enfle d'ombre sa gorge lente,' [1920]), while the image of the sea in her form and in the regular movements and sounds of sleep is given in lines 7–8:

> Une bouche brisée et pleine d'eau brûlante
> Roule le goût immense et le reflet des mers.

In stanza 3 the floral image is presented but not as an evocation of her ideal beauty; she is a victim regaining in sleep a trace of her former beauty: 'Tette dans la ténèbre un vestige de fleur' (1893) becomes 'Tette dans la ténèbre un souffle amer de fleur.' (1920) In 1893 the poem comprised only 6 stanzas, in 1920 it had 9, and in 1926 13. Valéry added images of the violence of love, sleep as death, and the contrast of her physical presence and mental absence which revealed the sorrow of her experience:

> Masque d'âme au sommeil à jamais immolée
> Sur qui la paix soudaine a surpris la douleur!

A later poem 'Ma nuit, le tour dormant . . .' is in many ways closer still to *La Dormeuse*, with its tight sonnet construction, the progression of the poet's viewpoint, the movement of involvement and detachment.

> Et ce bras mollement à tes songes m'enchaîne
> Dont je sens m'effleurer le fluide dessin
> De fraîcheur descendue au velours d'une haleine

Jusqu'à la masse d'ambre et d'âme de ton sein
Où perdu que je suis comme dans une mère
Tu respires l'enfant de ma seule chimère.

As Lawler comments, 'The form thus mirrors exactly the
theme which turns on itself in a moment of self-revelation.
By the concentrated force of his attention the poet is transformed from the detached observer he was, fully confident in
his powers; he is enclosed in his thought just as he encloses
it.'[14]

The variety of treatment evident in these different poems
exemplifies Valéry's contention that the same theme could
be the basis of many poems, as different studies or variations,
each reflecting his changing ideas. The ability of the poet to
enrich his language lies in his power to build up the harmonic
references of his vocabulary using metaphor and imagery.

La richesse du vocabulaire n'est pas mesurée par le nombre des mots
employés mais bien plus par le nombre des fonctions de ce mot, par le
nombre des rôles que l'on sait faire jouer à un mot donné.[15]

Perhaps above all the poem appears to be a further prolonga-
tion of *La Jeune Parque*, a development of a different moment, from a different perspective, moving outside the first
person monologue of the Parque herself:

Il faut céder aux vœux des mortes couronnées
Et prendre pour visage un souffle . . .
                         Doucement,
Me voici: mon front touche à ce consentement . . .
   Ce corps, je lui pardonne, et je goûte à la cendre.
Je me remets entière au bonheur de descendre,
Ouverte aux noirs témoins, les bras suppliciés,
Entre des mots sans fin, sans moi, balbutiés . . .
Dors, ma sagesse, dors. Forme-toi cette absence;
Retourne dans le germe et la sombre innocence.
Abandonne-toi vive aux serpents, aux trésors . . .
Dors toujours! Descends, dors toujours! Descends, dors, dors!
                              11.450–60

The composition of *La Dormeuse* was a long and compli-
cated process: over twenty-five sides of manuscript not
including the versions written in the various Cahiers of
Charmes. The fourteen lines of the poem demanded an extraordinary labour in comparison to the speed with which

L'Intérieur or *La Fausse Morte* were written; where these celebrate the sheer inventiveness of the creative muse, *La Dormeuse* reveals the slow patient attempts to find the poetic form that seemed almost furtively to seek expresssion 'à l'insu du poète'. The overall development is not easy to discern because there is so much rewriting: most of the manuscripts are a reshaping of the previous one, to which notes and alternatives are added and then incorporated into the succeeding version.[16] The first set of manuscripts from ff. 71–77 lead to a nearly complete poem, though in the quatrains quite far from the final version. There follows a process of 'decomposition' as a whole set of new lines are drafted, and then fitted into the earlier poem (ff. 78–82) forming a new first quatrain. Then there are further attempts at the second quatrain (f. 82v°) and a number of different versions are developed, while all the time minor changes to the rest of the poem are being made, condensing the images, tightening the structure and introducing temporarily quite new directions.

In the early drafts it can be seen that Valéry's analysis of 'sommeil' based upon his own experience of the woman's sleeping and waking is the starting point for a series of developments which establish the main melodic theme of the poem.

> Assiste au réveil de l'autre. Confrontation de deux Mondes.
> A quoi pensais-tu? A quoi rêvais-tu? Pièges et parfums . . .
> Sommeil – recueil mystérieux des forces et de la faiblesse
>
> > Ce sourire perdu sur les bords d'un soupir
> > Et dont l'âme à jamais cherche . . .[17]

The very personal nature of the evocation of the sleeping woman is evident in the first draft, f. 71: there is a very real sense of her presence not only in the celebration of the physical attraction ('Chère selon la chair', 'belle colorée', 'tes beautés') but in the particularly lyrical movement of the lines. The emotions of the poet are more in evidence than usual for Valéry, as he addresses the woman directly using the 'tu' form abundantly and giving a rhythmic sweep to the lines ('Paresse que tu es, douceur des heures, fleur', 'Oui, belle colorée à la couche endormie', 'Ce corps tendre . . . Il dort tout penché d'une douce chaleur / Dans le rayonnement d'un amour accalmie'. 'Tandis qu'à tes beautés tu me voyais sensible.') It was no doubt this feeling that inspired the distinctly less than perfect 'Ce corps tendre de qui je mangerais la mie'! Not that the feeling is only one of adoration; but if there are reservations, they express the anxieties between the two lovers, the feelings of desire and suffering, of a pain that arises from the centre of his attraction: 'Chère selon la chair, suivant l'âme ennemie', '. . . fleur / Mais poison', 'dommage idéal et malheur'. The sensual attraction that tempts his 'âme raffermie' confronts the inevitable distance that separates them; her very beauty is like a poisonous potion which he cannot deny himself.

Already at the bottom of this first MS. Valéry develops further ideas, and what is so striking is the extent to which the germs of the final version are there, unformed, pell-mell, with none of the connections and distinctions carefully made, and yet in a broad sweep of random lines and words he establishes the melody and notes from which he will construct his poem. In this first MS. many of the rhymes are conceived, the contrast between 'rayonnement' and 'secrets' is made, the sleeping form is presented as 'une sagesse endormie' and the body a place of divine offerings, 'Autel mystérieux tout chargé de [vains] tels dons'. The altar suggests a sacrificial lamb, and the image of her body stretched out like an animal leads to the more flattering idea of 'Biche langueur morte / offerte auprès la grappe'.

This essentially is the poem he develops during the first stage of composition though as he seeks to make it less obviously personal and more abstract her attractiveness seems at first to wane rapidly: she becomes 'la mangeuse de mie' and a 'receptacle' for her inner thoughts and dreams 'Vase frais plein toujours de profonde chaleur / Recueil mystérieux vase de vices et de toutes vertus' (*Cahier Charmes* II f. 22v°).

There is a brief change of tone and form as Valéry develops the more lyrical passage 'Fleur' (*Cahiers Charmes* II f. 23), producing a section in contrasting rhythm:

Fleur qui tends à l'abeille à l'âme au clair visage
Un piège de parfum
Tu places dans un paysage
Comme l'arome de quelqu'un
Sans toi plus étrangère (inhumaine) est cette ample nature
Indifférente à notre sort
Qui ne fait de sa créature
Qu'un présent offert à la mort

(*Cahier Voilier*)

But this is left aside and the composition progresses through these early manuscripts to the typed version of f. 77, the first complete sonnet version, with some interesting as well as surprising developments on the way. In f. 73 'accalmie' is contrasted to 'tempête', introducing the image of the sea which will create such an important part of the atmosphere; for the moment the image is only too obvious:

Forme comme la mer faussement endormie / accalmie   (f. 73)

Et l'empire éternel d'une croupe accalmie
Que baigne dans sa nappe une belle endormie   ondoyant
(f. 74)

and even:

Et l'empire éternel de l'onde et de l'ampleur
Que ta croupe fait prendre à ta couche accalmie   (f. 75)

In these drafts Valéry establishes the pattern of 'rimes embrassées': 'ennemie / chaleur / fleur / unie / accalmie / pleur / ampleur / endormie' (f. 74). The tercets begin to take shape in ff. 75–6 starting as a celebration of 'la perfection d'une absence drapée' and 'tes beaux abandons'; then after the hesitations and awkwardness of 'Derrière un mur / roc / fronton orné / sculpté / ferme de ton bel abandon perdons d'espoir', comes the discovery that in its jotted note sums up all the 'harmoniques' of the final line to be:

forme
Ton charme veille
Ta forme
beauté   vigilance
défi
et suffit

F. 77 then brings together all the work so far and presents an accomplished sonnet, recognisably *La Dormeuse* yet different in tone. If the open lyricism of the first MS. has been gradually depersonalised, the sonnet itself does not yet embody that pure sense of wonder which is alluded to in the final tercet:

> Chère, suivant la chair; selon l'âme, ennemie,
> Dont la narine aspire une invisible fleur
> Et de qui je ressens par la douce chaleur
> Tout le rayonnement d'une femme endormie;
>
> Ce corps tendre, de qui je mangerais la mie
> Me dut-il en coûter l'amertume d'un pleur,
> A l'empire éternel de l'onde et de l'ampleur
> Que commande à sa couche une croupe accalmie.
>
> Ton repos redoutable et chargé de tels dons
> Offre un autel sculpté de tes beaux abandons,
> O biche avec langueur longue auprès d'une grappe;
>
> Si tu parais absente, occupée aux enfers,
> Cette perfection qui de lents plis se drape
> Veille; ta forme veille, et mes yeux sont ouverts.[18]

Having reached this provisionally complete stage, Valéry's inventiveness takes off again with a series of developments that seem to 'decompose' the poem. Ff. 78 and 78v° begin the reworking of line 2 as he attempts all kinds of combinations; the essentially musical nature of the process can be felt as he rearranges the words as if they were notes:

<pre>
            Sous le doux
            Et cher masque aspirant une invisible fleur
                Ombre
Etre   Tu dors sous le beau masque aspirant une fleur

            montres
Songes   Tu jettes
            laisses

            Dormeuse au masque pur aspirant une fleur
                                                (f. 78v°)

            Qui   ombre
            Tu dors: le masque pur aspirant une fleur
            Ton doux masque aspirant une invisible fleur
            Ombre, par le doux masque aspirant une fleur
            Ton masque pur aspire une invisible fleur
            Tu dors, par le doux masque
                    le masque pur
            Ombre au doux masque d'ambre aspirant une fleur
                Dont le masque si pur aspire une fleur
                                                (f. 80)
</pre>

243

Now the image of the 'masque', which first appeared as a hurried note in f. 76, begins to take on its essential rôle as a figuration of the surface features of the sleeping form. Furthermore as lines 9 and 10 are reversed, a new opening to the tercets is created:

> Amas mystérieux de tes beaux abandons   offres
> d'ombres et
>
> amas doré
> Autel   pur   noble amas de riches abandons
> vivant amas   (f. 79)

And in f. 80 Valéry indicates the main 'harmoniques' of stanza 1: now the implications of the very first draft begin to take on their full value as he develops the theme of the inner secrets burning inside the woman. It is particularly interesting to follow the use of the verb in line 1; Valéry first wrote 'Tu dors, tu brûles l'ombre . . . Tu brûles [cher] foyer tels secrets dans ton âme . . . Toi qui brûles . . .' and then when reformulated as a question puts the verb into the plural: 'Quels secrets pour l'oubli brûlent ma jeune amie'![19] This leads to a reformulation of stanza 1:

> sagement
> Quels secrets lentement brûle ma jeune amie
> Ame sous le beau masque aspirant une fleur
> Et de quels foyers - - de naïve chaleur
> Naît ce rayonnement de la femme endormie? (f. 80v°)

an indication for stanza 2: 'Dormeuse comme une courbe', and at the bottom of the manuscript a kind of improvisation around certain key words. The tercets increasingly take their final shape, the first well nigh complete, offering the variant 'Autel, amas doré d'ombres et d'abandon', while the second has the clear syntactic movement: 'Que . . . / La Souveraineté d'un beau corps qui se drape / Veille'. MS. f. 81, which follows, indicates a more clearly erotic alternative for the last line: 'Ta forme parle et dit quels jeux seraient les nôtres', referring allusively to the 'noirs appétits'.

The manuscripts which follow show a variety of approaches to stanza 2, including attempts to reincorporate the earlier 'Chère suivant la chair; selon l'âme ennemi / Ce corps tendre

de qui je mangerais la mie'. One version explores more directly
the effect upon the poet:

```
                 corps tout
         Oui, ce pain parfumé d'une tendresse en fleur
                         de la jeunesse
         De mes      -      -        forme la nourriture

         Sais tu qu'il me poursuit dans d'éternels royaumes
         Qu'il triomphe toujours de mes plus purs fantômes
         Qu'il peuple, qu'il pâlit de p.        lascifs
         Les miroirs ténébreux de mes regards pensifs        (f. 83v°)
```

There is a sequence of interesting movements where 'l'âme
absente' suggests Psyché: 'ô puissante pâleur / Respire sans
Psyché' (f. 82v°), 'Tes charmes sans Psyché' (f. 85), 'Respire
sans Psyché, mystérieuse ampleur' (f. 86) and 'Le terrible
Psycheé d'une chaste couleur / Gagne / La souveraineté d'une
immense accalmie' (f. 89). Indeed this image is retained fairly
consistently almost until the very end:

```
Je contemple  Toute à l'accabler d'une  —  accalmie
              La chair prend de Psyché la puissante pâleur
              Mais sur un sein sur qui l'onde grave et l'ampleur
              Conspire au désir d'une telle ennemie        (f. 91)
```

It is also interesting to note the development of line 13 as
Valéry once again tries all kinds of combinations, experimenting with sounds, seeking a rhythmic shape to the line
that matches her form, and an 'harmonie indéfinissable' that
gives the sounds both smoothness and variety of contour.
Beginning with

```
         Cette parfaite paix qui de lents plis se drape        (f. 83)
```

then

```
         Ta beauté sans regards qui de lents plis se drape      (f.85)
```

he improvises with pencil additions beneath this typed version:

```
                 qu'un plis si calme drape
                 tels bras blancs
                             purs
         ventre

         La belle au ventre pur qu'un bras d'albâtre drape

         Ta grâce au ventre pur qu'un bras fluide drape
                             d'ambre
```

and in f. 87:

> Ta forme au ventre pur qu'un bras d'albâtre drape

Although Valéry has now reached a satisfactory composition of the first quatrain and the tercets, apart from some very significant changes between second and third person, the second quatrain still presents a number of problems, evident in f. 90 by the number of pencilled notes added to the typed MS. The prolonged labour over stanza 2 is rewarded finally by a movement which substantially shifts the force of the lines. Lines 5-6 of f. 90 ('Quel temple de ma perte, invincible ennemie / Plus forte que jamais') are omitted, thus delaying until line 8 direct reference to the threat that she represents. And in f. 92 the composition ends, as it had begun, with a 'trouvaille', the adoration of the sleeping, gently breathing form 'Souffle, – silence invincible accalmie' adding quickly in the margin the superb 'Tu triomphes ô paix'.

Though the changes between the versions are often minute, they demonstrate certain compositional techniques, the extent of Valery's attention to detail and, by implication, the criteria involved: a fluidity of sound which does not make the assonance or alliteration too obvious; a rhythmic movement that tends to sweep across the whole line and links lines and stanzas together; a language which is highly charged with harmonic resonances; a tightness of structure and concision of language with each line bearing as few words as possible whose value is purely syntactic; a certain distancing and abstraction which makes the reference more universal, less specifically personal. What is also so striking is the amount of work around a limited range of 'notes' arising out of the initial melody. The manuscripts demonstrate most clearly that composition is concerned primarily with the way the words are put together; the process shows that it is not simply a matter of the logical development of a subject, but of an attempt to create formal structures as in music. Valéry, it must be felt, goes a considerable way to achieving that ideal which he identified as unattainable in *Fragments des mémoires d'un poème*; the composer's skill, he says, lies in his ability to concevoir et mener l'ensemble avec le détail de son entreprise, voler de l'un à l'autre, et observer leur dépendance réciproque.[20]

Thus through a continual process of rewriting and reinvention the opening themes are expanded and the poem takes shape, until the perfectly balanced structure eventually emerges, resulting in 'une sorte de corps verbal qui ait la solidité, mais l'ambiguïté, d'un objet'.[21]

The study of the composition has revealed the extent to which the musical techniques are interrelated: attention must now turn therefore to the combination of effects presented in the published work.

La Dormeuse

> Quels secrets dans son cœur brûle ma jeune amie,
> Ame par le doux masque aspirant une fleur?
> De quels vains aliments sa naïve chaleur
> Fait ce rayonnement d'une femme endormie?

Though the title indicates the presence of the sleeping woman, the initial remarks are addressed by the poet to himself not to the woman ('son' line 1, 'sa' line 3). Moving to identification with 'ma' he then reverts to the separation of the opening, as though inviting the reader to join him in contemplation and questioning. A sense of mystery pervades: a kind of 'composition en abîme' is implied – the exploration of these secrets is another poem hidden from the poet, and from the consciousness of the woman too. The singular subject of 'brûle' is striking for it is not the expected 'Quels secrets . . . brûlent', but an inversion of verb and 'ma jeune amie' thus making the subject active. In addition to the warmth of the woman, the image of burning flames is presented: the 'soul' of the woman is metaphorically consuming the secrets of the heart.[22] The symmetry of the rhythmic division 6:6 is reinforced by the pattern of sounds '*Qu*els *s*ecrets dans *s*on *c*œur', quite different in vowels and consonants from the second hemistich which replies with '*ma . . .am*ie'.

The second line presents, in contrast, the gentle appearance of the sleeping woman. Though aware of the depths of the inner self, the poet can only perceive the outward presence of the face in repose. 'Masque' implies concealment of the secrets and also the sculptural meaning (mascaron) as a form of visual portrait, for it is through the intermediary of one's physical being that the inner self must communicate with the world around. 'Ame' is a keyword in Valéry's poetry, used with a variety of associated meaning. A note in one of the early manuscripts for *La Jeune Parque* shows 'âme = air, vent',[23] associated through the Latin 'anima' with 'souffle'. Though 'âme' and 'masque' portray the inner/outer contrast they are complementary and are incorporated into the sound-pattern of the previous line with 'ma – amie – âme – masque' and the rhyme of the caesura of line 1 with the end of line 2 'cœur – fleur'. The picture of outer delicacy and purity is completed by the image of the breath of the soul as the sweetness of a flower. A kind of purification is operating, manifest in a visual portrait of youth and innocence.

Faced with her mysterious appeal the poet insistently questions again in lines 3 and 4, as though a reformulation of the question may help to reveal the answer. He remains separate ('sa . . . chaleur') and, though specific ('ce rayonnement'), he generalises ('une femme') to indicate that the person before him represents the female form, rather than one particular woman. 'Sa naïve chaleur' indicates several harmonics of meaning: it is an indirect description of her physical person, warm and yet innocent, and adds to the total impression of a girl who is 'jeune . . . doux . . . naïve . . . [comme] une fleur'. But 'chaleur' also echoes 'brûle', the realm of the inner secrets reinforced by an archaic meaning of 'naïf' as 'natif'. And the inner nourishment of the flames is paradoxically 'vain' – unreal, or immaterial, for the dreams and memories of sleep have no substance. The deliberate avoidance of any 'musique verbale', the awkward contrast of vowels, the rhythmic impetus given by the enjambement throw all the stress upon the word 'rayonnement', the only four syllable word in the quatrain. The splendour is transposed on to the word itself, a verbal expression in the rhythm and sound of language of the visual 'éclat'. While the questioning and secrets are matched by harsh, unformed patterns of sound, there is an overall formal unity in the regularity of rhythmic division. The first hemistich of line 1 is echoed in rhythm and rhyme by the second hemistich of line 2:

> Quels secrets dans son cœur . . .
> . . . aspirant une fleur?

And while the rhyme scheme is *abba*, the caesuras of lines 3 and 4 rhyme internally 'aliments – rayonnement'.

> Souffle, songes, silence, invincible accalmie,
> Tu triomphes, ô paix plus puissante qu'un pleur,
> Quand de ce plein sommeil l'onde grave et l'ampleur
> Conspirent sur le sein d'une telle enemie.

After the questioning and mystery of the first stanza, the second is essentially an evocation of the final part of line 4: 'une femme endormie'. The poet is contemplating the sleeping figure and though moved to admiration it is the abstract quality of sleep rather than the person that provokes the response. The second person pronoun 'tu' occurs for the first time, but standing for the noun 'paix'; and while the specific reference of '*ce* rayonnement' is maintained in '*ce* plein sommeil', the possessive adjectives are absent and the poet seems moved largely by the tranquillity of the scene.

The impact of the first line is immediately striking. The sibilants provide a unifying force, while the rhythm of the woman's breathing is conveyed by the succession of short words; the mute -e and comma after 'souffle, songes, silence' compel the reader to stop after each word giving the impression of the slow regular intake of breath. The woman is completely self-sufficient in that moment – her body occupied only in breathing, her mind active with dreams, the world outside, like her reflective consciousness, enveloped in silence: it is a miniature but richly evocative portrait of Valéry's theme of 'Corps – Esprit – Monde'. Her restfulness is complete but she has become still more of an abstraction in his eyes, referred to as 'invincible accalmie'. Her peacefulness is all-powerful because it is innocent, beyond the reach of the poet or of the secrets. The phrase 'invincible accalmie' is composed of two nearly symmetrical patterns, first the short 'invin . . .' then the longer '. . . ible accalmie', which effectively builds its own self-contained structure that indeed seems indestructible.

These suggestions are expanded and modified in the lines that follow, the passive nature of 'invincible accalmie' echoed in the active assertion of a peace that is triumphant. The rhythmic emphasis of line 5 is thrown forward on to 'Tu triomphes', reinforced by the change of sounds and the hiatus. The suspense arising from the delay of the subject is resolved with 'ô paix . . .' as the sounds modulate into a new pattern. *'Tu tri*omphes' – *'plus pui*ssante', and the rhythm of the breathing is replaced by the reaction of the poet unable to restrain his admiration in the single rhythmic group 'ô paix plus puissante qu'un pleur'. An example of Valéry's 'sensibilité intellectuelle', it presents the ability of a non-emotional state to engender aesthetic feeling, a celebration of the peace and calm characteristic of the classical 'Colonnes'. The dual perspective is maintained since 'puissante' implies both the power of the sleeping form to subdue the emotions of the woman, and to stir those of the poet. 'Pleur' takes on particular harmonic reference in the context of Valéry's other work, reminding one of the tear which opens *La Jeune Parque* and the sorrow revealed in the sleeping *Anne*

> Laisse au pâle rayon ta lèvre violée
> Mordre dans un sourire un long germe de pleur.

The lines that follow (7–8) are perhaps the most highly charged of the poem, essentially 'harmonic', resisting any simple analysis by their multiple references. They exemplify the technique of composition whereby links are built between apparently disparate images, using, in musical terms, the second or third harmonic rather than the fundamental note. The syntax reads 'Quand . . . l'onde . . . et l'ampleur conspirent sur le sein d'une . . . ennemie'. 'L'onde' makes specific the image of the sea suggested in 'accalmie', the regularity of breathing taking on the gentle rhythmic sound of waves on the shore, the rise and fall of the breast associated with the swell of the sea. It makes a striking contrast to the imagery of fire in stanza 1. Along with the first direct mention of her body, comes a surprising new reference to her which dramatically closes the quatrain. At the end of the first and last line of each quatrain and linked by the same 'rime riche' the descriptions chart his attitudes towards her: 'ma jeune amie' – 'une femme endormie' – 'invincible accalmie' – 'une telle ennemie'.

The movement of sleep has stolen over the woman, surreptitiously conquering the 'secrètes araignées / Dans les ténèbres de toi!' Though the physical repose has quelled the stirrings of the consciousness, the vigorous language conveys the power of the struggle between mind and body. And it shows too the force of the poet's reaction. She is to him a considerable threat, except precisely when sleep, triumphant over her 'self', enables him to celebrate its victory, the absence of her consciousness finding its form in the consciousness of the poet.

The sibilants predominate the stanza maintaining a musical accompaniment of rhythmic breathing through the 'mots générateurs d'harmonie': 'souffle', 'songes', 'sommeil'. But it is evident that the 'musique verbale' operates differently in the second part of this stanza, for apart from the long vowels of 'l'onde grave et l'ampleur', the pattern of sound and rhythmic stress serve to emphasise the dramatic struggle that is taking place: 'Conspírent sur le séin d'une télle ennemíe'.[24]

> Dormeuse, amas doré d'ombres et d'abandons,
> Ton repos redoutable est chargé de tels dons,
> O biche avec langueur longue auprès d'une grappe,

From the questioning and distance of the quatrains, the poet moves, in the tercets, to identify with the woman observed, presenting the full emotional impact of the sleeping form implied in line 6. She is addressed directly with a series of second person possessives or noun phrases in apposition: 'Dormeuse, amas doré . . . ton repos . . . O biche . . . ta forme . . .' With only passing reference to 'l'âme absente' the tercets constitute a song of adoration, the awareness of her physical presence developed from 'le masque' and 'le sein' to the whole being.

The priceless value of her various attributes is suggested by 'amas'; that the word is more usually employed for objects only reinforces the absence of consciousness. An early version gives 'autel' for 'amas' with the idea of love as a form of sacrifice: 'autel doré d'offres et d'abandons' and recalling *La Jeune Parque*:

> Les dieux m'ont-ils formé ce maternel contour
> Et ces bords sinueux, ces plis et ces calices,
> Pour que la vie embrasse un autel de délices?

While the religious implications are omitted from the published version it is her sensual form that is described as laden with gifts. 'Amas' also gives more 'continuité musicale' and is linked in sound both with 'âme' and 'masque' the two key themes of the poem. Its use recalls the epigraph from Corneille used for *La Jeune Parque*: 'Le Ciel a-t-il formé cet amas de merveilles / Pour la demeure d'un serpent?'

The physical description is presented in paradoxical form, the golden light perhaps coming from the early sunlight, picking up 'rayonnement' in line 4. It presents a formal unity encompassing light and dark, presence and absence, physical being and mental separation, through a sonorous pattern of considerable impact. The initial word 'Dormeuse' provides the key sounds, the voiced dental consonant giving a metric pulse around which the vowels form an insistent chant. The initial pattern is repeated with the vowel nasalising 'dor . . . dor . . . d'om . . . don . . .' picking up the secondary vowel *a* from 'amas', which is also repeated and nasalised: '*a*m*a*s . . . *a*ban*d*on'. The consonants on the other hand show a contrary movement from nasal *m* to *b*: 'D*o*rm*e*use, *a*m*a*s doré d'*om*bres et d'*ab*andons'. Even the *é*, while introducing a different vowel note, is itself internally rhymed either side of the hemistich: 'dor*é* d'ombres *et*'.

The nasal *on* is carried over to the next line rhyming 'abandons / Ton . . . dons', the consonants modulating from *d* to *t*. It introduces a greater diversity of sound as the poet conveys his admiration with intensity of expression, the long vowels and liquid consonants combining with more flexibility of rhythm to create a kind of rubato effect especially on 'redoutable' and 'chargé'. 'Redoutable' implies an abandon that is awesome in its splendour, inspiring reverential fear before perfection. But it also recalls the theme of 'invincible', 'ennemie', though now a threat which the poet is confident he can overcome.

The third line of the tercet raises the intensity further with the rhythmic emphasis upon the second syllable 'O biche', as though the feeling overwhelms him. It marks too a greater sensuality of expression from 'amas' to 'repos' to 'biche'. A term of affection, it gives the image of an idealised female form, like the doe stretching its long neck to reach the grapes. It makes visually clear the position and form of the features implied in 'aspirant une fleur' as also, though to a rather different effect in *Anne* 'et d'une lèvre sèche, / Tette dans la ténèbre un souffle amer de fleur'. An earlier version put a comma after 'langueur': 'O biche avec langueur, longue auprès d'une grappe'; its removal shows the care of composition extending to the smallest detail, for it not only allows greater fluidity of rhythm, running over the hemistich, but adds a second harmonic to the adjective free to qualify both 'biche' and 'langueur'.

> Que malgré l'âme absente, occupée aux enfers,
> Ta forme au ventre pur qu'un bras fluide drape,
> Veille; ta forme veille, et mes yeux sont ouverts.

The first line of the second tercet in Mallarméan fashion invokes the absence of 'l'âme', briefly recapitulating the first stanza. As Valéry notes in 1936:

> Poème   Un sommeil est une forme
>   du temps
>   Sommeil, forme du temps
>   Figure d'une absence.[25]

The image of the soul in its own underworld expresses the torment of the self and adds a further suggestion of the flames of hell to 'brûle' in line 1. It is the fate that awaits Narcisse at the end of the *Fragments*:

> Mon âme ainsi se perd dans sa propre forêt,
> Où la puissance échappe à ses formes suprêmes . . .
> L'âme, l'âme aux yeux noirs, touche aux ténèbres mêmes,
> Elle se fait immense et ne rencontre rien . . .
> Entre la mort et soi, quel regard est le sien!   lines 303–7

But this is now accepted by the poet without apparent concern in the concessional phrase 'malgré . . .', that is sonorously integrated sharing the same *a*, *m*, *l*, and *b* sounds as before.

Sonorously the change occurs in the following line with the proliferation of *t*, *f*, *v* sounds, conveying the fluidity of form, the gentle contour of the arm draped over the stomach as though in protection, the image of purity from stanza 1 transposed to 'ventre'. The rhythm of the line, with its two qualifying phrases and the tri-syllabic 'fluide' delaying the verb until the final syllable, exemplifies the rhythmic undulation of form.

The full force of the resolution falls on the word 'veille': the immediate context of the line with the occlusives followed by a mute -e 'flui*de* dra*pe*' deliberately slows down the delivery. But also within the context of the tercets it marks the resolution of an interrupted syntax of ever-mounting tension:

> Dormeuse . . .
> Ton repos . . . est chargé de tels dons
> . . .
>
> Que . . .
> Ta forme . . .
> Veille;

The word resonates with admiration, as if completing a melodic phrase; it is followed by a pause at the semi-colon, a breathless, awed silence. The basic structure is then repeated forming a triumphant recapitulation or coda in two simply constructed clauses that present a resolution to the conflicts and tensions preceding. For the first time the poet refers explicitly to himself: with the discovery of the active vigilance of form comes the exultation of the creator. It is a poetic expression of Valéry's comments in *L'Ame et la Danse* on the life of the body reflecting that of the mind's inner world:

Que si une Raison rêvait . . . le songe qu'elle ferait, ne serait-ce point . . . ce monde de formes exactes et d'illusions étudiées? – Rêve, rêve, mais rêve tout pénétré de symétries, tout ordre, tout actes et séquences![26]

The end asserts a mutual reconciliation: if his observation has endowed the sleeping form with meaning by creating a work of art, equally the process of observation has affected his attitude and impressions and he is made aware that the form has its own self-possessed meaning. The phrase '. . . mes yeux sont ouverts', a striking assertion of the lucid watchful mind, is used by the Parque too in her conflict with the Serpent:

> . . . Apaise alors, calme ces ondes,
> Rappelle ces remous, ces promesses immondes . . .
> Ma surprise s'abrège, et mes yeux sont ouverts.
>
> lines 61–3

The indivisible relationship of the figure and the poet is expressed in a note in the *Cahiers* written at the same time as the poem: 'Percevoir, produire semblent se confondre dans la notion de *conscience*.'[27]

In this analysis of the poem attention has been focused on the 'harmoniques' and 'musique verbale' to show the manner in which an elaborate pattern of cross reference is built into the associations of meaning, sometimes allied to, sometimes independent of, the general musical fluidity of sound and rhythm. And as a form of recitative it has been shown to present a monologue developing different tones of address with questioning, apostrophe, tension and resolution.

The main melodic themes have been identified, but it will be useful to examine their structure in the overall poem as they display all the qualities of a musical form with statement, development, recapitulation and resolution. The question posed in the first two lines presents the two main themes, the 'secrets dans son cœur' and 'ma jeune amie', which are immediately qualified as 'âme' and 'masque'. Each is given a different character by a structure of separation and identification on the part of the poet, 'l'âme' addressed indirectly, 'masque' directly. The question pattern is repeated in parallel form, so that the first quatrain constitutes an exposition. The interdependence of themes is implied by the linking words 'par' and 'fait', the emphasis finally put, in the rephrased question, on 'ce rayonnement d'une femme endormie'. Valéry establishes, then, a melody and counter-melody which are clearly related although each has a quite different tone:

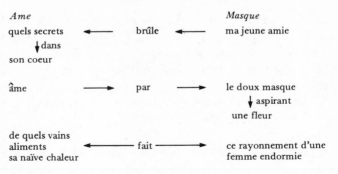

The tension between these two melodic themes and the changes in the poet's attitude of identification and separation will shape the remainder of the poem; the first stanza is balanced internally and is also balanced against the second quatrain: the questions and anticipation of the opening are now answered by an evocation of her sleeping presence and an elaboration of the poet's reactions. Furthermore both quatrains use the same *abba* rhymes and a similar absence of punctuation at the end of the third line. The second stanza develops the theme of 'masque' as 'femme *endormie*' as the poet identifies with an abstraction ('Tu' = 'paix'). The relationship is now far more complex as the main themes subdivide: the conquering power of sleep becomes a subject in its own right, a mediator in the struggle between 'âme' and 'masque'. The calm is invincible, the peace triumphant. But how permanent is the victory? Is it a triumph or a conspiracy? The 'songes' imply the 'secrets'; 'grave' suggests perhaps not only the undulating form but also the depths within. The 'invincible' subject acts therefore as a link between the two themes as the stanza proceeds by a series of alternations not unlike the development section of a sonata.

La Dormeuse

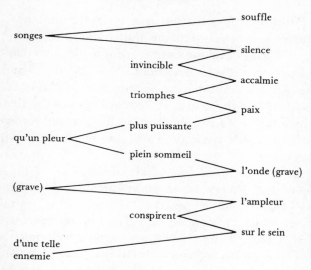

Anonymous still, 'Dormeuse' in line 9 nevertheless rings
with the private affection of 'ma jeune amie', after the impersonality of 'une femme endormie', the abstraction of 'invincible accalmie' and the threat of 'une telle ennemie'. Thus
the full stop at the end of the quatrains, the silence between
stanzas, the change of tone all contribute to give 'Dormeuse,
amas doré d'ombres et d'abandons' the force of opening a
new development, the beginning of the final movement of
the poem. The first tercet elaborates the theme of 'ce rayonnement' and the beauty of the physical being ('amas doré',
'chargé de tels dons', 'abandons', 'langueur'). But the struggle
between themes is becoming a fusion ('doré d'ombres'); the
languishing is yet quivering with eagerness ('langueur longue
auprès d'une grappe'); the threat is made explicit as 'ce plein
sommeil' becomes 'Ton repos redoutable' and the invincible
mask begins to assert its own animality, its own life. The
relationship between observer and observed moves to an ever
closer identification as 'Ton . . . Ta' now refer directly to the
woman. Through the complex syntactic structure the poem
moves to its climax in the second tercet; after a recapitulation of the theme of 'l'âme' ('malgré l'âme absente, occupée
aux enfers'), it leads to the discovery of 'ta forme [qui]

veille'. This new formulation is a synthesis that has arisen from the struggle between theme and counter-theme: between 'l'âme' and its development as 'enfer', as 'ennemie', as 'absence-présence de la conscience' on the one hand; and 'masque' and its development as 'sommeil', as 'innocence', as 'rayonnement' on the other. The restatement in the final line, like a coda, gives a stronger sense of finality and resolves the motif of the poet's separate-identifying relationship with the sleeping woman.

It is by the combination of all the aspects of his poetic technique that Valéry achieves his most distinctly musical effect. The unfolding patterns of melodies, harmonics, sounds, rhythms and tones give a dynamic movement to the formal structure of the sonnet, providing developments, tensions, anticipations and recapitulations that take language itself as close as possible to the quality of song. Arising from a contemplation of the relationship between the artist and his material, the poet and his subject, the poem is a hymn of adoration to the voluptuous secret of 'la forme sensible'. In a concise form, using a highly charged vocabulary and showing consummate skill in construction, Valéry has achieved in a miniature masterpiece the realisation of those musical procedures he so aptly discerned in Mallarmé's *L'Après-midi d'un Faune*:

Le poème est devenu une sorte de *fugue* littéraire où des thèmes s'entrecroisent avec un art prodigieux; toutes les ressources de la poétique s'emploient à soutenir un triple développement d'images et d'idées. Une extrême sensualité, une extrême intellectualité, une extrême musicalité se combinent, s'entrecroisent ou s'opposent dans cet ouvrage extraordinaire.[28]

CONCLUSION

Il chante, assis au bord du ciel splendide, Orphée!

Construire au son du lyre.

IX, 1923, p. 655.

Construction, wrote Valéry in an early note in the *Cahiers*, is simply a matter of applying one set of principles to another set of circumstances:

Construction. Mettre n choses dans l'ordre emprunté à une autre chose A.
Accommodation des choses n.[1]

The notion of taking one set of ideas and applying them elsewhere is one of the constants of Valéry's thought; it is to be found later the same year in a note on the functioning of the mind, and some twenty years later as the basis of a general theory of composition:

Toute construction est une certaine addition de fonctions. La composition des fonctions en est la clef.

Parmi ces fonctions il en est une remarquable, c'est justement celle qui donne aux autres leur formule de composition. Toute complexité est le nombre de fonctions ajoutés - ou nécessitées. Mais dans l'esprit même on ne distingue pas les organes des fonctions, on ne distingue que les fonctionnements . . .[2]

Composition générale
L'art suprême de la combinaison (presque jamais *évidente*) des objets apparents et des lois de ces objets introduites par eux ou avec les lois et les propriétés du 'champs de forces' - champ qui doit généralement être créé par ces objets mêmes, et qui consiste généralement en un *temps* pendant lequel ces objets *semblent* agir les uns sur les autres et se modifier réciproquement. (Mots, couleurs)
cf. symétries simples.
Maximum et minimum.
Celui qui compose dispose des choses d'un certain ordre, dans un autre ordre. Les définitions des divers 'ordres' et les relations entr'eux

259

que l'on se trouve, que l'on trouve, et celles que l'on donne, sont les 4 éléments de la composition.[3]

To a certain extent this procedure can be identified in much of Valéry's work, in the association of music and architecture for example, or in the attempt to understand the functioning of the mind in terms of mathematics.[4] The analogy between music and poetry is only one of the many analogies examined by Valéry, for his intention was to understand the principles underlying all forms of mental and creative activity in order to grasp 'l'attitude centrale à partir de laquelle les entreprises de la connaissance et les opérations de l'art sont également possibles'.[5] The principles of composition which he adduces from music, mathematics and architecture reveal the inner relationships and dynamic properties in a form that is necessarily non-specific, remaining essentially a theoretical absolute, a hypothetical universal method. The links between the different arts and sciences imply certain common factors, certain constant sets of procedures, but they can only be perceived and described in terms of each other. Does this mean then that any other analogy would have sufficed, that architecture or mathematics might have revealed as much in relation to poetry? In theory at any rate the answer must be affirmative, particularly in terms of the underlying principles of composition; for the musical analogy is not proposed to the exclusion of all others, and often in the *Cahiers* provides a point of departure for analyses that are pursued in many diverse directions, rather than a uniform point of arrival. But, on the other hand, not every analogy has the same status or is capable of generating equivalent results. At times it appears that the limitations of Valéry's knowledge of a particular field of activity restrict the value of the analogical approach; in linking so many different fields Valéry seems to establish a richly varied series of mental models rather than making any real advance in the direction of the abstraction of the mind itself.[6] But in one crucial way the analogy between music and poetry is of a different order to all others; for where Valéry was not an architect, a choreographer, a mathematician or a scientist, he was a poet and the analogy that is pursued most consistently in the *Cahiers* is not with architecture or dance or mathematics, but with music. What is above all striking both in the *Cahiers* and, it has been seen, in the poetry manuscripts themselves is the extent to which Valéry pursued not only the general notion of music as a defining quality of poetry, but also specific features of the art such as melody, harmonics, rhythm, all the while redefining them in poetic terms. The analogy can perhaps best be seen as throwing into relief certain common procedures and principles and, in so doing, focusing attention simultaneously upon those aspects that remain specifically and singularly part of the verbal art of poetry. Thus the formula may be rewritten so that n = 'langage' and A = 'Musique', as he clearly saw in 1910 even before he began the reworking of earlier poems for *L'Album de vers anciens*:

Ce pourrait être un art, une branche particulière de l'art que la traduction de la musique. De toute façon, c'est un exercice et qui l'entendrait bien, en tirerait de grandes finesses.[7]

Valéry was not a practising musician, but music did form an intimate part of his life: he was familiar with a wide range of past and contemporary music; he was in contact with a number of outstanding composers and performers; he enjoyed the busy musical life of his family as well as the many recitals, concerts and operas he attended; his understanding of the principles of musical composition was furthered by a series of friends and musical acquaintances; and above all, he was able to develop a coherent view of the application of musical principles to the composition of poetry. Music is the single most important factor in Valéry's poetry: it is both the goal by which the poetic ideal is defined and the means by which it is attained in composition. The central rôle of music in Valéry's work is underlined by a note referred to at the very beginning of this study and now given in full:

2 Nov. [1932] - lecture du W. [*Wagner: histoire d'un artiste*] de Pourtalès.
Excitation - la 'composition' qui est en moi en est tout excité
Mon âge . . sixty-one depuis samedi.
La musique m'aura manqué - et il me semble que j'aurais fait qq. chose

dans ce moyen – Mon 'système' trouvait là son moyen. Je me rappelle ma conversation avec Ravel en 1906 ou 7.

Il n'y a rien compris.

Il a fallu faire des acrobaties comme la Parque.

En poésie – surtout française – la composition est une impossibilité. Et il faut d'ailleurs perdre les 80% de son effort pour vaincre les résistances passives du langage, les associations *parasites* qu'il accroche à chaque mot – et dont certains ont fini par faire leur essentiel. Sans compter les habitudes du public et de soi-même. La composition est ce qui dans une œuvre porte l'homme – *base* et *mesure* de toutes choses. – ce qui demande une intuition ou présence de l'homme complet. Toutes les unités.[8]

Music is an expression of the complete man, as a language of the emotions, as a language of the mind and as a dynamic structure giving form to the aesthetic sensibility; it is the construction of all the human functions in one, a unity which Valéry expresses in *Chant de l'idée-maîtresse*:

> Viens à l'aide! Sois une chair et une charpente,
> Sois ma forme, mes yeux, ma langue, mes jarrets.
> Sois pour que je sois. Sois pour être!
> Obéis, que je sois le commandement que tu profères.
> Ma voix est la tienne et tu distingues
> Ma volonté. Mais tu veux . . . MOI! L'Idée!

Indeed, rather than to any purely instrumental expression, it is to the quality of song that poetry aspires:

Etat Chantant. A quoi répond le chant? Qu'est-ce qui veut qu'on chante? La réponse contiendrait la connaissance de la poésie. Cet état est un écart de l'état ordinaire.

Il exige émission – *aveu* – confession énergétique avec conservation. Modulation.

Le chant et les idées – *absorbe la parole interne.*

L'être s'écoute – trouve une surprenante *suite*, une continuation liée par un lieu mystérieux.

Et dans des *choses* proposées ou par la perception externe ou par l'interne, plus de liaisons que d'ordinaire. Elles semblent s'engendrer réciproquement.[9]

The titles of Valéry's works refer to various kinds of song more than any other musical form: *Charmes* (from the latin *carmen*: 'chant magique'), *Air de Sémiramis*, *Cantique des colonnes*, *Chanson à part*, *Chant de l'idée-maîtresse*, *Cantate du Narcisse*, and the *Psaumes* S, T, Y and Z. Other overt musical allusions in the titles are rare: there is an early sonnet

Conclusion

Ballet, a plan for *Narcisse, symphonie pastorale dans le style classique*, the prose passage 'Concerto pour un cerveau seul' (in 'Propos me concernant') and the short poem dedicated to Francis Poulenc *Colloque (pour deux flûtes)*. But as has been seen in the detailed study of the poetry, Valéry was not seeking to impose musical forms artificially upon different works; he does not propose one poem as a fugue, another as a sonata, one as a symphony, another as an opera. The relationship between music and poetry is deeper, more organic: Valéry was seeking the inherent characteristics of music, so that the voice of the Parque would take on the quality of recitative, the construction of *La Dormeuse* acquire the thematic complexity of a melodic development. The influence of music is intrinsic at every stage of writing and is to be felt not just in a title or a form, but in the particular care with which the various parts of the poem are woven together:

La grande affaire en poésie serait d'arriver à *composer*, ce à quoi personne ou bien peu sont parvenus.
Composer – Je m'entends! – aussi savamment qu'ils font un vers ou une strophe – ou un sonnet. Distribuer les *mots*, les mouvements, les types de vers. Bien séparer.[10]

Yet Valéry recognised that, in spite of his ambition, the process of composition is not an easily applied exercise. Though he may later have tended to emphasise the extent of conscious control, in 1919 at the height of his creative activity, fully involved in the writing of *Charmes*, he notes:

On a bien tort de dire: J'ai composé un poème . .
En vérité, il s'est fait comme il l'a pu. Quant à ceci: j'ai composé un poème, c'est là exprimer l'*idéal* du poète qui serait de bâtir avec tous ses moyens d'un côté sous ses yeux, de l'autre sous ses désirs. Ceci n'est pas. C'est impossible. Ni le but ne peut être infiniment net; ni les moyens entièrement dénombrés et possedés sur le moment; ni
    Que se passe-t-il donc?[11]

The subject is developed further in one of the poetry note-books: it is clear that however strongly Valéry might desire to focus attention upon an understanding of the process of composition, the writing reveals the strength of the creative surge within him and a recognition that too much cerebration will destroy the inspirational force of the poem:

> Analyse quant au langage et au vers
>
> Comprendre, être compris
>
> Le sujet vrai de ce poème est précisément son propre mode de formation.
> - Mais si j'y pense assez à fond pour trouver le 'principe' - je ne ferai pas le poème. Il sera tué du coup.
> - Je m'impose de faire comme si je devais aboutir.
> - Au lieu de parler du vers nommément, la définir - ainsi du langage ainsi du comprendre.
>
> Attendre. Entendre. Se souvenir - et de ce qui jamais n'a été. Comprendre c'est restituer l'expression au moyen du *sens* que l'expression même avait donné et abdiqué en nous. . . .
>
> Se souvenir de ce qui n'a jamais été? Mais alors il y aurait une sorte de forme du souvenir, qui n'est pas absolument liée au passé: du moins au *passé défini.* qui fait reconnaître sans avoir connu. De même que le passé peut nous revenir sans que nous ayons conscience de sa qualité de passé, de même le nouveau peut se donner comme ayant déjà été.[12]

Valéry is the poet-musician, creating form where none exists, fashioning works from the raw material of language. The poet seeks to attain the constructive powers of music in order to transform the transitory quality of everyday speech into the substantial and lasting form of poetry. Thus the myth of Orpheus as builder of a temple by the power of his song represents a major theme in Valéry's work and is to be found in many direct allusions to Orpheus himself as well as other related legends;[13] but above all it indicates an attitude, an aspiration, a hidden presence that animates the majority of the poems. In mythology Orpheus, son of Apollo and Calliope, was associated with taming animals, civilising man and founding cities, as well as with Euridice and the descent into Hades. Valéry's use of the myth in relation to the theme of love is an important feature which tends to become more prominent in his later work, but the central focus of his attention was explained to Debussy when they were planning to collaborate on a ballet:

J'avais songé incidemment au Mythe d'Orphée, c'est-à-dire l'animation de toute chose par un esprit, - la fable même de la mobilité et de l'arrangement.[14]

Conclusion

The theme was clearly expressed in the first version of the sonnet *Orphée* (1891) in which the demigod is able to control and organise the natural world, forming the blocks of stone into a temple through the supernatural power of his music:

Il chante, assis au bord du ciel splendide, Orphée!
Son œuvre se revêt d'un vespéral trophée
Et sa lyre divine enchante les porphyres,

Car le temple érigé par ce *musicien*
Unit la sûreté des rythmes anciens
A l'âme immense du grand hymne sur la lyre! ...

This image of the poet-musician delivering his song before the heavens, composing his music into a lasting edifice, will in fact provide a recurrent scene in Valéry's poetry; already certain key words or fundamental notes can be identified, around which he will later develop the harmonics

il chante	le ciel	les pierres
l'hymne	l'or	le temple
la lyre	l'azur	les porphyres
	le soir	

and there is the presence of 'Orphée' himself, as a metaphor for the voice that speaks in the poem, the poet himself.

The following year Valéry demonstrates in *Arion* that the command over nature may be attained not only by a demigod, but by a human who acquires divine power through his creative activity. Arion was a Greek poet-musician of the seventh century BC, a composer of dithyrambs in honour of Dionysus, in contrast to the Apollonian Orpheus. The epigraph to the poem '*Inter delphinas Arion*' recalls the legend according to which Arion was rescued from drowning by a dolphin which had been so charmed by his music that he carried Arion on his back to port: the gods placed the dolphin in the sky to commemorate the deed and formed the constellation Delphinus.[15] Though the dolphin is immortalised and Arion denied a place in the skies, the glory nevertheless belongs to the musician whose playing has saved him from the mortal waves.

Le luth luit sur le monstre élu pour un tel astre
Plus haut que le sourire adoré des oiseaux

Qu'amuse la beauté des larmes du désastre
A la figure sidérale du héros.

Dont la main d'or, dans la splendeur du soir, délivre
Par le luth où scintille un vol pur de sa chair
L'eau vagabonde, peau d'azur claire et nue, ivre
Au jeu de la mortelle écume de la mer.

Des papillons neufs naissent vers des fleurs futures,
Doux dans les boucles d'onde, ô fines chevelures
Qu'une profonde enfant démêle du cristal ...

Mais la lèvre du dieu par le silence insulte
Toute épaule limpide éparse au flot natal,
Vénus! ... et nul beau cri dans le ciel ne se sculpte!

Though in this early poem the debt to Mallarmé is very evident, the work also announces Valéry's *Ode secrète* written some twenty-five years later; but there it is the mortal who is elected to take his place in the constellations as a result of his labour, 'après la danse'. There are indeed some remarkably close parallels between the two poems, both in the setting and the expression. The scene is evening:

Dont le main d'or, dans la splendeur du soir   *Arion*

Mais touché par le Crépuscule   *Ode*

The light is glistening and there is an association between the twilight gleaming on the body of the hero and the stars sparkling in the sky:

Le luth luit ...
Par le luth où scintille un vol pur de sa chair   *Arion*

Jamais une telle lueur
Que ces étincelles d'été
Sur un front semé de sueur

Fin suprême, étincellement   *Ode*

While in *Arion* the tresses of hair in the spray are adorned with rather elaborate images of butterflies and flowers, in *Ode* there is the single striking image of the resting body bathed in the red light of dusk as with garlands of roses:

Ce grand corps ...
N'est plus qu'une masse de roses!

The context is mythological and universal as man creates his part in the universal scheme of monsters and gods: the constant struggle between the two sides of man's nature is projected into the sky which is an image of the mind:

> Le luth luit sur le monstre élu pour un tel astre
> Mais la lèvre du dieu par le silence insulte . . .   *Arion*

> Fin suprême, étincellement
> Qui, par les monstres et les dieux,
> Proclame universellement
> Les grands actes qui sont aux Cieux!   *Ode*

While *Arion* focuses upon the surface qualities, the superficial appearance of

> . . . la beauté des larmes du désastre
> A la figure sidérale du héros

Ode uses a similar image to evoke the projection of consciousness into a universal form, the struggle between Hydra and hero given an eternal, transcendent quality of infinite repose:

> Dormez, sous les pas sidéraux,
> Vainqueur lentement désuni,
> Car l'Hydre inhérente au héros
> S'est éployée à l'infini . . .

Though these comparisons serve in many respects to underline the differences of perspective between the two poems, they also add a particular significance to the poem and indeed to the entire collection of *Charmes*. Not only can *Ode secrète* be seen as a triumphal ode celebrating both the armistice of 1918 and Valéry's own triumph over words;[16] not only can it be read, as G. D. Martin convincingly argues, as a warning that 'as long as Man exists [the principle of antagonism] will exist within the human mind, and be reflected by that mind upon the external world',[17] it can also be seen as Valéry's own secret song, an intimate and deeply personal expression of his own lyrical power: the poem itself is his equivalent of the triumphal dance, of Arion's music, of Orpheus' song. Indeed 'ode' comes from the Greek 'ōidḗ', itself contracted from 'aeidō' (to sing), which was the word used for any poem that was intended for setting to music. Moreover this implication is supported by the epigraph to *Charmes*: 'deducere carmen', an invitation to the reader to seek out the magic spell, to look for the song, to recognise in Valéry the secret musician who has composed his songs with words.

When this image of the poet-musician is pursued through the poems of *Charmes* its presence may be identified within nearly all.[18] Different features emerge in each of the poems, for each one has its distinguishing song which adds to the resonances of the accompanying images; but a central image arises, implied rather than explicitly stated by the perpetual modulations about its focus: 'Il chante, assis au bord du ciel splendide, Orphée!' The song, originating in the depths of being, is projected towards the skies, forming a link between the human and the divine and as the musician plays the day through its course he acquires an artistic power over the natural world; ultimately the song may evoke an infinite calm, a transcendent repose, but above all the poems are a celebration of the different moments of the song, as an expression of that musical ideal of endless change and modulation which is put by Teste's interlocutor:

[la musique] me donne des *sensations abstraites*, des figures délicieuses de tout ce que j'aime, – du changement, du mouvement, du mélange, du flux, de la transformation.[19]

In *Aurore* the poet finds the source of his prophetic song within his own sensual being: 'Je . . . vais cherchant / Dans ma forêt sensuelle / Les oracles de mon chant.' In *Au Platane* the branches of the tree become harps resounding in the wind sending forth their song to creation, 'Afin que l'hymne monte aux oiseaux qui naîtront'. The silent song of the columns continues to reverberate up to the heavens in *Cantique des colonnes*, as though the temple had been constructed by Orpheus himself. With *Poésie* the song expresses transfiguration: the poet identifies so completely with the source of his inspiration that he transcends the human and glimpses the divine that is within, even if, like Arion, the escape from mortality into the infinity of the skies will ultimately elude him.[20] *Les Pas*, which has all the qualities of a tender song of adoration, suggests also a wider perspective: the title echoes both 'les pas sidéraux' of *Ode secrète* and the 'pas ineffables' of those other silent musicians, the columns, while the figure itself announces the divine gifts it will bestow. *La Ceinture* evokes vividly the fragile moment of dusk, rose-coloured yet about to give way to the silent, starry night; more clearly than ever one sees the poet-musician 'assis au bord du ciel splendide' recognising his mortality in the tenuous contact with the world. In *Fragments du Narcisse* the implied threat of this moment is still more explicit: the glow of evening light which reflects his image on the surface of the pool is, at the same time, that which threatens him most as it fades into the night. All the forces which moved in harmony to the divine song of Orpheus are now seen as a challenge to the tenuous image of self:

> Tout se mêle de moi, brutes divinités!
> Mes secrets dans les airs sonnent ébruités,
> Le roc rit; l'arbre pleure; . . .

The lyricism in this poem is personal and intimate; rather than proclaiming the unity of the forces of creation, Narcisse directs his hymn of praise towards his own body. He begs the gods to halt the movement of the heavens, for his only hope lies in the suspension, not the transcendence, of time. The only temple he can form is that of his own body, within which he is imprisoned; and transfiguration is explicitly inseparable from death: 'O mon corps, mon cher corps, temple qui me sépare / De ma divinité.'

La Pythie portrays the poet-musician overwhelmed by the power of a divine oracle; the struggle between 'les monstres et les dieux' – between the forces of the irrational and the constructive powers of the intellect which the music of Orpheus was able to unite – is enacted within the Pythie herself. The oracle resounds through her as if she were a divine harp, but the music that comes forth is sepulchral rather than celestial. The orphic unity does not appear until the end of the poem in the form of a divine voice transcending the struggle; the pure song of wisdom expressing the harmony of the universe is that of Orpheus, tamer of the natural world, or perhaps that of his father, the prophetic voice of the musician Apollo.

Conclusion

In *Ebauche d'un Serpent* there is no voice of universal harmony; instead the mocking, cajoling, seductive tones of the serpent convey the triumphs and the limitations of the intellect. The song of the tree of knowledge is an eternal round of aspiration and despair that must be for ever begun again as the goal retreats before each advance.

In *Le Cimetière marin* the poet-musician directs his song towards both the sea and the sky, in admiration, but also in emulation. If the sea represents the lucidity of Greek thought, the self is also its own temple commemorating time. The protagonist through his identification with the sea feels greater than human destiny and projects upwards from the sparkling surface his disdain for the gods. But the very movement towards ultimate lucidity, the contemplation of a timeless, immobile sun 'Tête complète et parfait diadème', surprises his awareness of his own transcience; the song will cease at death: 'Chanterez-vous quand serez vaporeuse?' The false consolation of immortality is rejected as consciousness and his living presence reassert their song in all the painful duality of existence: 'Le son m'enfante et la flèche me tue!'[21]

Yet another aspect of the relationship between the self and the world is embodied in *Le Rameur*; in quiet song he celebrates the seductive appearance of the natural world which he can see reflected in the water. But however enticing the 'charmes du jour', he defends himself against their spell; and, as he attempts in patient, eternal effort to row against the river and move towards the purity of non-being another note rings up to the skies, the slow insistent toll of the funeral bell, which is at once the rhythm of his oars and the announcement of his mortality.

The theme of the poet-musician is manifest in several contexts throughout *Charmes*, each with different implications. What emerges is not a single interpretation of the theme, but above all an attitude, a lyrical posture, for the song that rings out is the voice of the poem itself. The various implications seem drawn together in a stanza of *Palme* which is a restatement of the force of Valéry's own inner song resounding prophetically in the air:

> L'or léger qu'elle murmure
> Sonne au simple doigt de l'air,
> Et d'une soyeuse armure
> Charge l'âme du désert.
> Une voix impérissable
> Qu'elle rend au vent de sable
> Qui l'arrose de ses grains,
> A soi-même sert d'oracle,
> Et se flatte du miracle
> Que se chantent les chagrins.

This achievement places Valéry unmistakably among those writers 'qui ont tenté de faire . . . chanter ou danser le langage': the song embodies the qualities of perpetual change and movement which are in fact an expression of the self:

Le chant . . . meut et fait mimer, fait vouloir, fait frémir comme si sa variation et son étoffe étaient la loi et la matière de mon être.[22]

But aware as he was of the difficulties of application, Valéry recognises that the definition of poetry in terms of music can never be absolute.

La poésie est la recherche d'elle-même.
Elle est peut-être la possession et comme la science des causes qui ont la musique pour effets. (L'auditeur de musique secrète des causes pour les effets qu'il subit.)
Ce qui cause le mouvement de danse, l'élan, l'altitude, le recueillement, le désir –
Elle engendre aussi avec des objets divers juxtaposés un continuum. Ce que *tend* à former la Musique pour justifier ces mouvements, ces suspens, ces volontés pures, ces mimiques internes – cela est de la nature de la poésie.
Mais il n'y a que tendance.[23]

Or, as it is put most clearly in the equation cited above, when 'n' (language) is constructed according to the principles of 'A' (music), there must always be 'Accommodation des choses n'. While affirming the central rôle of music in Valéry's aesthetic theory and poetic practice, it is important to put this into perspective, for however productive the analogies that Valéry pursued, it is in the end the poetry that stands, self-sufficient and independent, as a unique expression of his artistic achievement. There will always be a tension between the aspiration towards music and the specifically verbal qualities of language: though music is an essential constituent of all the arts, it remains a part, never the whole; at the same time, the redefinition of terms that Valéry effects, demonstrates that the model offered by music proper enables language ultimately to surpass it, treating the referential quality of language as yet another variable to be incorporated into the unified texture of the whole poem. If these reservations must temper the rôle of music in relation to the verbal art of poetry, I am also aware that other aspects of the musical analogy have not been considered. The implications for the prose works open up, particularly when Valéry writes: 'Etre musical en prose est chose facile.'[24] Both the nature of the effects realised in the 'poèmes en prose' and the adequacy of the musical terminology are problems that remain outside the scope of the present work. Another important area that has been left untouched is the question of the works that were conceived from the outset for performance with music. Valéry became increasingly fascinated by the possibilities of achieving a 'division de ses moyens' by directing a changing emphasis upon dance, mime, music, song, decor and theme according to formal rules of order that would unite these disparate parts. In the light of the compromises forced upon Gide's text of *Perséphone* by Stravinsky's music – and of which Valéry approved – it would be interesting to examine Valéry's texts alongside the musical scores; but it has not been possible to consider here his approach to the composition of these works, the rôle he allowed for the musician or the relationship between the verbal music and the vocal or instrumental music.[25]

The questions which were identified at the outset of this study related to three principal areas of investigation: the nature of Valéry's knowledge of music and musicians; the possibility of establishing a connection between his knowledge of music and his poetics; and the extent to which musical techniques may be identified in the composition of the poems. It is clear that while Valéry's early interest in music arose from his association with Symbolism and with Mallarmé in particular, his conception of the relationship between music and poetry went far beyond the initial desire to 'reprendre à la musique son bien'. Valéry was to develop the concept of musical poetry to the point where music becomes an integral part of the poetry, as a defining quality and as a principle of composition. Through his musical environment he acquired a detailed knowledge of music which, though not of a technical nature, enabled him to understand aspects of the aesthetics and structural form of music as well as to distinguish between different compositional intentions. His attitude towards music remained ambiguous: the love and envy he felt for Wagner's music, the fascination with the power of music to affect the emotions and subjugate the mind, and his own often spirited reaction against domination; these ambiguities are inevitable for they reflect the extremes of Valéry himself, of that creative tension between Nous and Eros which provides such a deep motivation to his work. There emerges a personal response to music which encompasses the classicism of Bach, the formalism of Stravinsky and the clearly structured impressionism of Ravel. Furthermore this view of music, which lays emphasis upon compositional structures, upon unity, upon the unfolding of a complex web of internal relationships, can be seen to accord with Valéry's poetics and indeed to have provided much of the terminology in which his discussion of poetry is couched.

Above all, the evidence of the poetry manuscripts is decisive. For to confront music, poetics and composition is to impose a much more rigorous test on Valéry's musicality than is generally the case, but which is demanded by the logic of the argument and by the need to establish clear and consistent meanings for the terms of Valéry's musical vocabulary in accordance with his practice as a poet. It is not, of course, necessary to pursue a thorough analysis of the composition of every poem before hazarding an interpretation of the published text; indeed a danger becomes apparent in Valéry studies that selective quotation from the drafts, without the full evidence of the manuscripts or a coherent methodological approach, may be used to provide a spurious justification for a particular interpretation. The intention of the present study has therefore been to use a cross-section of complete

Conclusion

manuscripts in order to substantiate the link between music, poetics and poetry, and thereby identify and define the essential features of Valéry's music.

The duty of the critic, wrote Valéry, is to clarify the intentions of the writer and identify as far as possible the difficulties encountered:

Critiques.
On dit M. P.V. (d'après ses ouvrages) est ceci, cela etc. Mais il faudrait dire - M. P.V. dans telles intentions (que ns ignorons) et aux prises avec telles difficultés et conditions qu'il s'est données - (tel que ns ne connaissons pas entièrement) - a fait ceci et cela.[26]

There can be no doubt that the key to an understanding of Valéry's poetry lies in perceiving the relationship between the profoundly musical intention and the adaptation of language to this purpose. The identification of the techniques of composition in Valéry's poetry provides therefore a set of terms for the discussion of the distinctly musical achievement, and as such a new critical tool for an approach to the poems. For it is clear that any reading, however excellent, would be incomplete in Valéry's eyes if it did not discuss the unfolding musical development formed by the melodic structure, the harmonics of meaning, the rhythmic progression and implied delivery, as well as the patterns of sounds, their complex relationship to meaning and the overall tone of the voice as it aspires to the quality of song.

THE
COMPOSITION OF *LA PYTHIE*

The composition of *La Pythie* offers a particularly interesting example of the preparation and beginning of a poem, not least because of the importance that Valéry attributes to the principles of formal composition. This major poem is undoubtedly, after *Le Cimetère marin*, the most perfectly constructed of the longer poems of *Charmes*; and it presents in a way that no other poem does the penetration into the depths of the self, into 'la nuit obscure [de l'âme]': 'cette nuit, qui doit être l'absence de toute lumière naturelle, et le règne de ces ténèbres que peuvent seules dissiper des lumières toutes surnaturelles'.[1] In *La Pythie* the horrors of possession, the struggle against the serpent, the tormented efforts of the deep, impersonal self torn between being and knowing, purity and sensuality are portrayed 'dans le moment de la lecture', as an immediate simultaneous participation, where even in *La Jeune Parque* this struggle is a re-enactment as the Parque recalls what has already happened to herself.[2]

Some twenty years after the publication of *La Pythie* Valéry spoke of the composition in these terms:

La Pythie s'offrit d'abord par un vers de huit syllabes dont la sonorité se composa d'elle-même. Mais ce cers supposait une phrase, dont il était une partie, et cette phrase supposait, si elle avait existé, bien d'autres phrases. Un problème de ce genre admet une infinité de solutions. Mais en poésie, les conditions métriques et musicales restreignent beaucoup l'indétermination. Voici ce qui arriva: mon fragment se comporta comme un fragment vivant, puisque, plongé dans le milieu (sans doute nutritif) que lui offrait le désir et l'attente de ma pensée, il proliféra et engendra tout ce que lui manquait: quelques vers au-dessus de lui, et beaucoup de vers au-dessous.[3]

The passage presents many of the same ambiguities as Valéry's statement on the composition of *Le Cimetière marin*. Though

Appendix. The composition of *La Pythie*

a concise and striking account of the process of composition it does, on close analysis, contain a number of implications, stressing in particular the formal aspects at the expense of attention to the content of the work. The text is taken from the concluding part of Valéry's Zaharoff lecture at Oxford in which he seeks to illustrate by an example from his own poetry his theme that poetry forms a language within a language and may as often arise from a desire to develop a formal pattern as from the expression of a feeling:

tantôt, c'est une volonté d'expression qui commence la partie, un besoin de traduire ce que l'on sent; mais tantôt, c'est, au contraire, un élément de forme, une esquisse d'expression qui cherche sa cause, qui se cherche un sens dans l'espace de mon âme . . .[4]

Explaining the composition of *La Pythie*, there is the familiar emphasis upon the metric and sonorous pattern as an initial source and as a guide for further lines. He suggests that 'les conditions métriques et musicales' arose from the line and determined which of all the possible developments were acceptable: the formal properties took on a life of their own, and generated their own growth, helped only by the lucid mind of the composer. The content of the lines is clearly given cursory attention: any thematic or affective expression is seen merely as material for formal development. In studying the beginnings of the poem, it will be necessary to discover from other sources precisely what 'le désir et l'attente de sa pensée' consisted of.

From the somewhat ironic tone of a note in the *Journal*, it would appear that Valéry had put his position more forcefully still to Gide, revealing which was the line 'dont la sonorité se composa d'elle-même'.

Paul me raconte (ce dont je me doutais) que *La Pythie* est tout entière sortie d'un vers:

Pâle, profondément mordue.

Il a cherché la rime, les rimes. Elles ont dicté la forme de la strophe et tout le poème s'est développé, sans qu'il ait su d'abord ni comment il serait, ni ce qu'il allait y dire.[5]

But other factors must be added to this view presented by Valéry: his prior interest in the eight syllable line, the influence of his work on *La Jeune Parque*, and the clear state-ment of his intentions which emerges once the composition is underway.

It is known that, even before the first line was written, he had been thinking of using the octosyllable. While writing *La Jeune Parque* he used to consult Pierre Louÿs on stylistic points, and was urged by him to use the 8e more ambitiously.[6] Inspired by his friend and by the example of the breadth of tone and grandeur of Hugo's Odes, Valéry conceived the plan of a long poem with a fairly elaborate structure.[7] The rhyme scheme adopted in the very first stanza written is the same *ababccdeed* as in Hugo, and as Valéry subsequently used in *Aurore* and *Palme*, as well as nearly half the stanzas of *Ebauche d'un Serpent*.

La Pythie was begun at the same time as the *Serpent* and *Le Cimetière marin*, before he had completed work on *La Jeune Parque*. The poem is really a different approach to the struggle between innocence and sexuality, death and immor-tality, being and knowing which lies behind these other three poems. Considerable cross-fertilisation of ideas and similari-ties of vocabulary and metaphor show that essentially Valéry was using the same poetic language. The central theme is already outlined in the *Parque*:

> Je pense, sur le bord doré de l'univers,
> A ce goût de périr qui prend la Pythonisse
> En qui mugit l'espoir que le monde finisse   ll. 164–6
>
> Ce fut l'heure, peut-être où la devineresse
> Intérieure, s'use et se désintéresse   ll. 445–6

In similar expressive language both the Parque and the Pythie are described as 'pâle', meaning of course 'pale', but also sig-nifying in its Latin origin a religious fear.

> . . . Je sors pâle et prodigieuse   *J.P.* l. 90
>
> Pâle, profondément mordue   *Pythie* st. 1

Both are fashioned from the same vulnerable, sensual material, from the same clay of which God made human life: 'Ni le souci d'un sein d'argile parfumée' (*J.P.* 422); 'D'une argile en îles sensibles' (*Pythie* st. 9). And both, like hollow shells, have been taken over by some greater, more powerful force:

> Quelle conque a redit le nom que j'ai perdu   *J.P.* 446
>
> Mais une vierge consacrée,
> Une conque neuve et nacrée   *Pythie* st. 13

But above all both are obsessed by the presence within them of the Serpent as a force of knowledge and sexual awareness:

> J'y suivais un serpent qui venait de me mordre   *J.P.* 37

This common image leads back to the very beginnings of *La Jeune Parque* and in fact the early manuscripts of 1913 reveal a remarkable similarity of language to that found later in *La Pythie*. Valéry sketches the reaction of the Parque to her possession by the serpent which she explicitly calls 'rape': the loss of innocence is also the discovery of her mortality, as the very depths of her self are laid bare:

> je me suis ressentie
>   feux
>   violer
> Je faisais défaillir
>   *Cahiers Jeune Parque* III, f. 13 (1913)

> Plus dangereusement ta ténèbre entr'ouverte
> Ni plus distinctement
>   Ni si pure une perte
>   la (vie) entr'ouverte
>   III f. 14 (1913)

> . . . victime entr'ouverte   III f. 16

> perdu le mystère qui la faisait vivre
> Quand l'horrible trésor qui soufflait son orgueil
>   palpitait   sous son œil
>   rayon
>   quand elle se mélange à la mort
>   et blesse de regards   à sa propre ruine
>   mon œil
> Mélange à mes trésors horribles sa lumière
> . . .
> Elle voit Elle ouverte
> cercle - œil - entrailles - découvert   III f. 19

Appendix. The composition of *La Pythie*

And a few brief notes that are like a 'palette' for the poem:

> Mystère qui *meurt* avant
> Trésor horrible   palpitant   fume
> Visiblement
> flancs   rayons   mélancolique achevant d'[—]
>   Mélange   III f. 19v°

These images and indeed often the very words are to be found in *La Pythie*:

> ... l'âme
> Affreuse, et les flancs mugissants!   St. 1, 3–4
>
> Au point le plus haut de l'horreur
> Le regard qui manque à son masque
> S'arrache vivant à la vasque
> A la fumée, à la fureur!   St. 1, 7–10
>
> Hélas! Entr'ouverte aux esprits,
> J'ai perdu mon propre mystère!   St. 3, 7–8
>
> Don cruel! Maître immonde, cesse
> Vite, vite, ô divin ferment,
> De feindre une vaine grossesse
> Dans ce pur ventre sans amant!
> Fais finir cette horrible scène!   St. 4, 1–5

Moreover these stanzas are among the first of *La Pythie* that Valéry wrote. The comparison indicates convincingly the importance of the poem, at the very heart of the surge of creative activity that was to produce his major works. It demonstrates too the essential rôle of the poem in *Charmes*, not as the violent exception to an otherwise harmonious whole, not just as a poem about poetic inspiration, but as a central driving force, an uncovering of the depths of the self and of the conflicts and tensions that consciousness inevitably brings to existence.

Alongside the third version of the poem Valéry wrote a note which makes explicit 'le désir et l'attente de sa pensée:

Chaque strophe de cette *Pythie* aurait dû être une face de la chose – et chaque strophe une attitude psychique et physique.

And on another page:

Logique de la *Pythie*. Chemin de l'idée. Employer le corps à former les idées. Ce corps instrument de musique, de netteté.[8]

279

Appendix. The composition of *La Pythie*

These notes recall his attempt to show the physiology of consciousness and the changing states of the self, as he specifically comments in 1937:

Dans la *Parque* et la *Pythie*, seul poète qui, je crois, l'ait tenté, j'ai essayé de me tenir dans le souci de suivre le sentiment physiologique de la conscience; le fonctionnement du *corps* en tant qu'il est perçu par le Moi, servant de *basse continue* aux incidents ou idées. Car une idée n'est qu'un incident.[9]

And thus Valéry's discovery of the line 'Pâle, profondément mordue' has to be seen within its context: he was clearly attuned to certain aspects of theme, sonority and rhythm when the 'vers donné' emerged and these same three factors continued to influence the entire process of composition imposing a framework for the 'conditions métriques et musicales'.

The earliest MS., f. 95, presents a version of the first stanza which demonstrates the development around his initial line and makes clear the opening scene of the poem:

> La Pythie, auprès d'une flamme
> Noyée aux nuages d'encens   convulsivement belle
> Furieusement belle, l'âme
> Affreuse et les flancs mugissants
>   Hurle
> [Pâle] profondément mordue
> Et la prunelle suspendue
> Au point le plus haut de l'horreur
> Refuse la vie à son masque
> Qui veut s'arracher à la vasque
> A la fumée, à la fureur!

This ten line stanza has, from the handwriting, clearly been written all at once, and, unless a previously undiscovered draft comes to light, would suggest that the stanza had formulated in Valéry's mind, materialising as a supreme moment of inspiration, as precisely an instance of that possession which was to become the subject of his poem.

It is interesting to note, given the importance attributed to the line 'Pâle, profondément mordue' that in this first MS. he has deleted 'pâle' and written 'Hurle' over the top! (But he reverts to the original word and uses the idea to remodel line 3 in the next MS.) The draft adds alternatives for line 3 and then written quickly across the bottom of the piece of paper is a draft for the second stanza with two versions of lines 3 and 4: in a characteristic change Valéry moves from the simile 'comme un nageur' to the metaphor with a noun in apposition 'un fantôme nageur'.

The back of the MS. shows a rewriting of stanza 1, but most significant is the development of a third stanza, which is roughly drafted, then written again more neatly; continuing the portrait of the monstrous Pythie possessed and overcome by the god, it opens with the physical discomfort of the woman and introduces the images of the python encircling the tripod. In the fifth line the divine force has apparently overcome her power to resist and instead of the horror and torment there is now a divine calm; in place of the agonised cries ('hurle', 'hennir', 'les sanglots', 'les écumant enthousiasmes', 'vocifère') there emerges a limpid impersonal voice: 'cette voix nouvelle et blanche'.

> Où le martyr
> Cette femelle aux jambes froides
> Qu'entrave le python gluant
> Vocifère entre les ruades
> Du trépied sonore et puant
> Mais enfin le Ciel se déclare
> L'oreille du pontife hilare
>   vers
> S'aventure dans le futur
>   sainte
> Et [comme une] l'attente se penche
> Vers cette voix nouvelle et blanche
> Dont le corps cesse d'être impur
> D'un corps purgé
> Qui échappe d'un corps impur

These three stanzas all in descriptive register provide the shape to the poem; they demonstrate the movement from torment to calm and the production of the clear voice effected by the transition in line 5 'Mais enfin le Ciel se déclare'. The development around the initial line and the expansion of this theme have provided an exposition of the situation followed by a rapid conclusion, like an opening musical statement which establishes the melodic theme amidst an atmosphere resonant with suspense and a hurried resolution. The

tone of the piece is curiously like the second Act of Gluck's
Orfeo ed Euridice where the struggle with the Furies at the
entrance to Hades gives way to the light and joy of the Elysian
Fields. The implications of the third stanza are far-reaching
and the process is probably the most outstanding example of
the internal generation of a poem, for throughout the subsequent versions whole new sections will be created by an
exploration of the melodic and harmonic implications of this
opening theme: the entire development of the poem will be
inserted between lines 4 and 5 of this stanza so that in the
final version, while the first four lines are found in stanza 3,
the following six lines form stanza 22.

Thus the composition proceeds, through seven different
stages, in alternating moments of inspiration and careful calculation, each feeding the other and providing further new
material to incorporate into the poem.[10] The significance of
'les conditions métriques et musicales' is demonstrated in the
crucial rôle accorded to rhythm, sonority and modulation,
through which the poet constructs a density of structure and
forges a symbolic expression: descriptions are not left as
additional features attached to some person or object, they
are made an integral part of the image; the formal structure is
not built separately, but as part of the harmonics of meaning;
the inner logic of the form arises as the poem, almost organi-
cally, seems to grow from within itself. But this inner logic
is relative and, as Valéry says, only a necessity to the poet at
the moment of composition:

. . . ce cers supposait une phrase, dont il était une partie, et cette phrase
supposait, si elle avait existé, bien d'autres phrases. Un problème de ce
genre admet une infinité de solutions.[11]

When he sent a copy of the poem to his wife he wrote in the
accompanying letter: 'D'ailleurs, si c'était à recommencer, je
ferais toute autre chose. Mais l'ère de la production hâtive
est ouverte.'[12] And so the analysis must return to the main
themes and images of Valéry at the time of *La Jeune Parque*
and *Charmes*, to the poetic and intellectual preoccupations
which provided, as he says with ironic understatement, 'le
milieu (sans doute nutritif)' for the early fragment with its

ready-made sounds. Throughout the stages of composition it is evident that 'le désir et l'attente de [sa] pensée' become explicit in clear, thematic structures of melody and counter-melody, while harmony, rhythm, sound and tone all play a rôle both in inspiring new developments and shaping the material produced in the drafts. For there is a constant inter-action between the lucid mind of the composer and the sheer spontaneous creativity of the 'vers donnés': it is foreseen already in 1912:

Un coup de génie est l'œuvre des dieux. A eux seuls le *mérite*. Mais s'il y en a souvent, cette quantité indique que les dés sont pipés. Il y a une machine à les produire. Ce Génie de hasard est domestiqué. L'auteur est alors un homme intelligent qui a saisi les recettes de la pythie. Il a reconnu et appris à prendre l'attitude cachée, l'état de grâce dont chaque mouvement est *bon*.[13]

For:

La Pythie ne saurait dicter un poème. Mais un vers – c.à d. une unité – et puis une autre. Cette déesse du Continuum est incapable de con-tinuer. C'est le Discontinuum qui bouche les trous.[14]

NOTES

ACKNOWLEDGEMENTS

1 This notebook was offered for sale by auction in Paris at the Salle Drouot Rive Gauche 27–28 February 1979 and purchased by an anonymous collector from Geneva. The non-availability of the manuscript makes the evidence presented by Lawler all the more valuable.

2 Only two books have been wholly devoted to the subject of Valéry and music, E. Suhami, *Paul Valéry et la musique*, Dakar, 1966 and P. Roth-Mascagni, *Musique et géométrie de trois poèmes valéryens*, Brussels, 1979; the first is an MA thesis published by the University of Dakar and a useful introductory survey of what Valéry had to say about music; the second is a reading of *La Jeune Parque*, *Le Cimetière marin* and *Fragments du Narcisse* which analyses the 'musicality' and 'geometric patterns' as they arise in the poems. Among the articles cited in the Bibliography those by Fabre (1938), Honegger (1946), Austin (1970), Köhler (1976) and Renauld (1977) contain relevant comment, but the two most important articles are by J. Duchesne-Guillemin ('Paul Valéry et la musique', *Revue Musicale*, no. 210, January 1952, pp. 113–131) and H. Laurenti ('Musique et monologue: notes pour une approche valéryenne du poème', *Paul Valéry 1: Lecture de 'Charmes'*, *Revue des Lettres Modernes*, nos. 413–418, Paris, 1974, pp. 49–66). By far the greatest number of references to music is to be found within studies of Valéry's poetry, although I have found the works by F. Scarfe and Duchesne-Guillemin of particular help in this connection: Scarfe's work contains very useful sections on music as a technique in the poetry and on modulation of tone in *La Jeune Parque* while Duchesne-Guillemin's identification of 'Quatre formes de musicalité' and his analysis of *Charmes* 'Sous le signe de la Métrique' (in *Etude de 'Charmes' de Paul Valéry*) offers illuminating comment; Christine Crow's recently published *Paul Valéry and the Poetry of Voice* (Cambridge, 1982) clearly adds an important new perspective to this area of study. In approaching the manuscripts I have been guided by the immensely valuable studies of the composition of *La Jeune Parque* and *Le Cimetière marin* which are to be found in the works of L. J. Austin, G. W. Ireland, J. R. Lawler, F. de Lussy and O. Nadal.

284

INTRODUCTION

1 *Cahiers*, vol. XVI, 1932, Paris, C.N.R.S., 1957–62, p. 18; hereafter cited as XVI, 1932, p. 18.
2 Letter of 29 April 1891, in *Cahiers Paul Valéry I*, Paris, Gallimard, 1975, p. 44.
3 Letter to Pauline de Rin, in *Lettres à quelques-uns*, Paris, Gallimard, 1952, p. 53.
4 *Fragments des mémoires d'un poème, Œuvres*, tome I, Paris, Bibliothèque de la Pléiade, 1975, p. 1480; hereafter cited as *Œuvres*.
5 XXVII, 1943, p. 17.
6 *Lettres à quelques-uns*, p. 108.
7 II, 192, p. 840.
8 *Avant-propos à la Connaissance de la Déesse*, I, p. 1272. The quotation is undoubtedly from Mallarmé for a similar expression is to be found in a letter to René Ghil, 'Cet acte de juste restitution qui doit être le nôtre, de tout reprendre à la musique . . .' (7 March 1885 in *Propos sur la poésie*, ed. H. Mondor, Monaco, 1953, p. 139) and even more precisely in *Crise de Vers*: '. . . un art d'achever la transposition, au Livre, de la symphonie ou uniment de reprendre notre bien.' (*Œuvres complètes*, Paris, Pléiade, 1951, p. 367.)
9 The critical literature on this area is extensive but the following works are of particular interest: M. Beaufils, *Musique du son, musique du verbe*, Paris, 1954; C. S. Brown, *Music and Literature, a Comparison of the Arts*, Athens, Georgia, 1948; A. G. Lehmann, *The Symbolist Aesthetic in France*, London, 1950; P. Meylan, *Les écrivains et la musique*, Lausanne, 1952; G. Michaud, *Message poétique du symbolisme*, Paris, 1947; M. Naudin, *Evolution parallèle de la poésie et de la musique en France: rôle unificateur de la chanson*, Paris, 1968; E. Souriau, *La correspondance des arts*, Paris 1947. Two very important works which focus upon particular aspects are S. Bernard, *Mallarmé et la musique*, Paris, 1959, and L. Guichard *La Musique et les lettres en France au temps du Wagnérisme*, Paris, 1963.
10 For example, if Lamartine compares himself to 'le musicien qui a trouvé un motif, et qui se le chante tout bas avant de le confier à l'instrument' it is because poetry for him is a 'chant intérieur . . . triste comme la vie réelle . . . un gémissement ou un cri de l'âme'. ('Préface et commentaires des premières *Méditations*', *Méditations poétiques*, Paris, Garnier, 1968, pp. 326 and 308).
11 This interest is reflected in titles such as Hugo's *Odes et Ballades* as well as later in Banville's *Ballades joyeuses à la manière de Villon* and *Rondels à la manière de Charles d'Orléans*.
12 'Préface aux Nouvelles Histoires extraordinaires d'Edgar Poe'. Also in 'Théopile Gautier', *Œuvres complètes*, Paris, Pléiade, 1961, p. 686. See also comments on Baudelaire and Wagner p. 297 n. 35 below.
13 *Œuvres* I, pp. 611–12.

14 G. Michaud, *Message poétique du symbolisme*, Paris, 1947, p. 411.
15 Quoted in S. Bernard, *Mallarmé et la musique*, p. 14.
16 Letter to E. Gosse, in S. Bernard, p. 151.
17 *Crise de vers, Œuvres complètes*, p. 368.
18 *Le Livre, instrument spirituel, Œuvres complètes*, p. 381. As S. Bernard comments 'la conclusion de l'esthétique musicale mallarméenne, ce sera paradoxalement, une esthétique du Livre' (p. 35). For comments on Mallarmé and Wagner see pp. 78-9.
19 Valéry, lettre à Stéphane Mallarmé, [18] avril 1891, *Lettres à quelques-uns*, Paris, 1952, p. 47; and conversation quoted by Ch. du Bos, *Journal 1921-3*, Paris, Corrêa, 1946, p. 227.
20 See S. Bernard p. 123 and her remarks on 'Le Livre': 'Si le musicien pense avec des sons, le poète, lui, pense avec des mots, qui sont à la fois son et sens. A vouloir transgresser cette loi, Mallarmé ne pouvait parvenir qu'à l'Idée d'une œuvre pure: le chef d'œuvre absolu reste une page blanche' (p. 154). See also C. Crow, *Paul Valéry and the Poetry of Voice*, pp. 35-7.
21 L. Guichard, *La musique et les lettres* . . . , p. 243.
22 If the separation needs to be made here for the purposes of conceptual clarity, it will not always be possible to separate them quite so effectively, partly because the meanings are not in practice mutually exclusive and partly because the focus of Valéry's attention often shifts from one to another in the course of a single remark: indeed the interest of the notes may be found to lie precisely in this semantic shift as he tests the insights of one area of meaning upon another. Thus I have not sought to label them in any way after this preliminary discussion in the hope that the context makes clear which are implied.
23 III, 1904, p. 335.
24 IV, 1910, p. 477; see also V, 1914, p. 224.
25 VIII, 1922, p. 902; see also III, 1905-6, p. 826.
26 IV, 1906, p. 58.
27 XXIV, 1941, p. 469.
28 III, 1905-6, p. 807. This idea forms the basis of the phenomenological analysis of music pursued by Ernest Ansermet in *Les Fondements de la musique dans la conscience humaine* (Neuchâtel, La Baconnière, 1961): 'Il se trouve que les phénomènes de conscience mis en jeu devant la musique sont les mêmes que ceux qui sont à l'origine des déterminations fondamentales de l'homme dans sa relation au monde, à Dieu, à la société humaine; ils appartiennent à une zone de la conscience quasi inconnue . . . Impossible de se faire une idée claire de la musique sans se faire une idée de l'homme, sans voir se dessiner toute une philosophie et une métaphysique.' (p. 8).
29 XVII, 1934, p. 625; see also X, 1924, p. 375.
30 XIX, 1937, p. 863. Christine Crow emphasises 'the importance of [Valéry's] empirical discovery of the natural foundation of art in human experience' and quotes from Michael Black's *Poetic Drama*

as Mirror of the Will (London, Vision Press, 1977, p. 12): 'the "will" does not necessarily express itself immediately in either words or music: it is very often internal, silent, non-verbal. Both words and music are in areas immediately adjacent to that central silence, so that expression may then come, as words, or music (or both): but it may also come as bodily movement or dance or pictorial art or any other expressive form.' (In *Paul Valéry and the Poetry of Voice*, p. 6 and note 16 pp. 258–9).

31 IX, 1922, p. 136. But at other times he equates it with a lyricism and a vagueness that is alien to him: 'La poésie lyrique est celle qui cherche à produire les mêmes effets que la musique. . . . Elle [la poésie] représente des excitations – c.à d. des états vagues au moyen des mots qui sont précis. D'où l'incohérence caractéristique.' (IV, 1911, p. 592)

32 V, 1913, p. 148. This reaction was common to poets of the nineteenth century; see for example Lamartine: 'j'ai toujours pensé que la musique et la poésie se nuisaient en s'associant', Leconte de Lisle: 'Défense de déposer de la musique le long de cette poésie', and Mallarmé's alleged remark (on hearing that Debussy planned to set *L'Après-midi d'un faune* to music): 'Je croyais l'avoir fait moi-même.' (All cited in Marie Naudin, *Evolution parallèle de la poésie et de la musique en France*, Paris, 1968, pp. 221–3.)

33 VII. 1918, p. 69.

34 XIV, 1930, p. 268.

35 XXI, 1938, p. 456.

36 XXIX, 1945, p. 763. It is a quality that may equally be sought in prose: 'Si tu veux faire quelque discours, imagine-le en musique – et songe à tout ce que le musicien peut *noter*. Je suppose tes "idées" soient prêtes, et libres. Tiens-les imminentes et tout éveillées, et agi musicalement.' (IV, 1909–10, p. 381)

37 See Michael Black, *Poetic Drama as Mirror of the Will*: 'poetic language is . . . an attempt to bypass some of the process of conceptualization: to produce something more direct, like music. But that provokes an analogy, which remains only an analogy, however close . . . It is the *objective* that is identical: to put us in contact, as direct as can be, with the movement of other minds, other wills.' (p. 16)

38 VII, 1919–20, p. 425.

39 VII, 1921, p. 768; the differences between composer and performer and the importance of the virtuoso are discussed below.

40 'La poésie résulte d'une turgescence, d'une tonalisation de la voix articulée, dans toutes ses propriétés phoniques et psychiques et motrices' (X, 1925, p. 853). 'Mon "rêve de poète" eût été de composer un discours – une parole de modulations et de relations internes – dans laquelle le physique, le psychique et les conventions du langage puissent combiner leurs ressources . . . ce serait l'Etre *vivant* et *pensant* . . . poussant la conscience de soi à la capture de sa sensibilité . . . sur la *corde* de la *voix*' (XXII, 1939, pp. 435–6).

41 'Comme il y a beaucoup moins de convention dans la musique que dans le langage, il y a beaucoup plus de mérite à la poésie qu'à la musique' (XXV, 1941, p. 62). See also VII, 1918, p. 198.

42 XX, 1937, p. 323.

43 XXVIII, 1944, p. 414; see also XVII, 1935 p. 790 and XIX, 1937, p. 802.

44 XXV, 1941, p. 84.

45 XXVIII, 1944, p. 425.

46 'Esquisse d'un éloge de la virtuosité', *Vues*, Paris, 1948, p. 355.

47 VIII, 1922, p. 875. See also XIII, 1934, p. 508: 'La bonne diction des vers exige que le diseur se sente et se traite comme un instrument de musique dont on doit d'abord éprouver les sons, puis apprendre à jouer, puis étudier le morceau, puis les nuances. Mais la bonne "pensée" ne s'obtient pas autrement.'

48 'Esquisse d'un éloge . . .', p. 355.

49 Ibid. p. 356.

50 IX, 1924, p. 778; however when considering the French language in comparison to others he discusses the musicality of poetry solely in terms of the sound system of the language ('Images de la France', *Oeuvres* II, pp. 999–1000); in 'De la diction des vers' music incorporates sound, articulation and rhythm but specifically excludes at first words and meaning: 'Demeurez dans ce pur état musical jusqu'au moment que le sens survenu peu à peu ne pourra plus nuire à la forme de la musique.' (*Oeuvres* II, p. 1258); rhythm is sometimes included (X, 1924, p. 430), sometimes seen as a separate, related factor (VI, 1917, p. 433). I have chosen in most cases to use 'la musique verbale' because the reference to language is specific, although the emphasis upon modulation which is clearer in 'la continuité musicale' will sometimes be preferred.

51 'Introduction à la méthode de Léonard de Vinci', *Oeuvres* I, p. 1159.

52 XIX, 1936, p. 513; see also XIX, 1937, p. 759.

53 VIII, 1922, p. 586.

PART I. VALÉRY'S MUSICAL ENVIRONMENT

1 *Lettres à quelques-uns*, Paris, 1952, p. 36.

2 Letter O of *XV Lettres à Pierre Louÿs*, in *Oeuvres* II, p. 1575.

3 *Oeuvres* I, p. 16.

4 P. Féline, 'Souvenirs sur Paul Valéry', *Mercure de France*, no. 1089, Paris, July 1954, p. 405.

5 *Lettres à quelques-uns*, p. 15.

6 19 novembre 1890, *Lettres à quelques-uns*, p. 36.

7 Berlioz was performed at the Concerts Colonne which Valéry attended in the winter of the following year too, but since he thought he saw Mme de R . . . , the woman with whom he had fallen in love in Montpellier, he did not apparently hear a single note that was played. (O. Nadal, Introduction, *Valéry–Fourment Correspondance*, Paris, 1957, p. 28)

8 I, 1899, p. 571.
9 *Gide-Valéry Correspondance*, Paris, 1955, pp. 116 and 122. G. Jean-Aubry comments that Louÿs conveyed to Valéry more enthusiasm than actual discernment in his musical tastes. (Introduction, *Debussy-Louÿs Correspondance*, Paris, 1945, p. 22)
10 *Debussy-Louÿs Correspondance*, p. 165.
11 *Valéry-Fourment Correspondance*, p. 120.
12 *Gide-Valéry Correspondance*, p. 130.
13 *Gide-Valéry Correspondance*, p. 71.
14 pp. 73-4. He later mentions '[Le] *Crépuscule des Dieux* où l'admirable pullule. Mais *Siegfried* aussi, le chant de l'Oiseau! Une de mes révélations musicales' (p. 150).
15 *Gide-Valéry Correspondance*, p. 158.
16 *Gide-Valéry Correspondance*, pp. 171-2.
17 Geneviève Mallarmé, 'Mallarmé par sa fille', *Nouvelle Revue Française*, Paris, nov. 1926, p. 521.
18 *Œuvres* II, p. 1275.
19 *Ibid.* p. 1276.
20 A. Fontainas, 'Jeunesse de Valéry', *Paul Valéry Vivant*, Marseille, 1946, p. 67.
21 P. Meylan, *Les écrivains et la musique*, vol. II, Lausanne, 1951, p. 38.
22 Gide, *Si le grain ne meurt*, Paris, Livre de Poche, 1954, pp. 265-6.
23 *Œuvres* I, p. 24.
24 *Gide-Valéry Correspondance*, p. 170.
25 'Que voulez-vous que je dise . . .', in *Le Tombeau de Pierre Louÿs*, J.-E. Blanche et al. Paris: Editions du Monde Moderne, 1925; rpt. as 'Pierre Louÿs' in *Vues*, pp. 189-94.
26 *Debussy-Louÿs Correspondance*, Paris, 1945, p. 39.
27 *Ibid.* p. 32.
28 E. Lockspeiser, *Debussy: His Life and Mind*, vol. I, Cambridge, 1979, p. 241.
29 I, p. 88. Debussy later planned a work on the Tristan legend with Gabriel Mourey in 1907.
30 I, 1899, p. 660, and *Lettres à quelques-uns*, pp. 62-3.
31 *Debussy-Louÿs Correspondance*, p. 32.
32 Letter N dated 10 juin 1917, *XV Lettres* . . . , Paris, 1926.
33 *Gide-Valéry Correspondance*, p. 408.
34 'Paul Valéry vécu par les siens', *Entretiens* . . . , Paris, 1968, pp. 341-2. Ravel's *Sonatine* and *Alborada* were composed in 1905; Agathe was 7 years in 1913.
35 *Œuvres* I, p. 28.
36 'Paul Valéry et la musique', *Revue Musicale*, Jan. 1952, p. 116.
37 II, p. 183.
38 XVI, 1932, p. 18.
39 *Œuvres* I, p. 33.
40 *Œuvres* I, p. 34.
41 *Œuvres* I, p. 35.
42 IX, p. 523.

43 D. Mitchell, *The Language of Modern Music*, London, 1966, p. 46.
44 Quoted in I. Stravinsky, *Expositions and Developments*, London, 1962, p. 143. Further details are to be found in E. W. White, *Stravinsky. The Composer and his Works*, London, 1966, pp. 176-7.
45 V, 1913, p. 18. Although the note is not more closely dated, it would seem to correspond with the première on 29 May 1913 as page 3 of *Cahier* V is dated 11 avril 1913 and page 36 dated 13/7/13.
46 I. Stravinsky and R. Craft, *Memories and Commentaries*, London, 1960, p. 74.
47 Quoted in M. Schneider, 'Stravinsky face à la société', in A. Boucourechlier, O. Merlin, etc. *Stravinsky*, Paris, 1968, p. 109. *Les Noces* was first performed in public 1923, *l'Histoire du soldat* 1918, *Concerto* 1924, *Sonate No. 2* 1924, *Oedipus* 1927.
48 Preface to L. Aguettant, *La Musique de piano des origines à Ravel*, Paris, 1954, containing a letter from Valéry to H. Rambaud dated 17 March 1931.
49 XII, 1927, p. 384.
50 XII, p. 177.
51 XII, 1928, p. 888.
52 XIII, 1929, p. 695.
53 XIII, p. 762.
54 XIII, p. 824.
55 XIII, p. 828.
56 21 July 1929, XIII, p. 854.
57 XIV, p. 815.
58 XIV, p. 866.
59 XV, p. 102.
60 XV, p. 319.
61 XV, p. 243.
62 XV, p. 165.
63 XV, 1931, p. 162.
64 XV, 1932, p. 695.
65 XV, p. 630.
66 XVI, p. 56.
67 XVI, p. 18.
68 XVI, 1933, p. 360.
69 XVI, 1933, p. 514. Lotte Lehmann was a celebrated soprano known especially for her major rôles in works by Wagner and Strauss. Friedrich Schorr was an Austrian bass-baritone, known primarily for his Wagnerian rôles. Sachs no doubt refers to Hans Sachs, the central character of Wagner's *Die Meistersinger* and one of Schorr's principal rôles.
70 XVI, 1934, p. 870.
71 Reprinted in I. Stravinsky and R. Craft, *Memories and Commentaries*, London, 1960, p. 76. The article referred to was in the Paris *Excelsior*: it ended with these words: 'a nose is not manufactured, a nose just *is*; thus, too, my art'.
72 XVI, p. 173.
73 XVII, pp. 6-7.

74 *Encyclopédie de la Musique*, Paris, Fasquelle, p. 434.
75 XVII, p. 60.
76 *R.I.M.*, I, no. IV, Paris, Oct–Nov 1938, pp. 607–8. Valéry was elected to the editorial board in 1940, although this was the last issue published before the Revue reappeared in 1950. Valéry's appointment provoked in the 1940 issue an article of little interest by Paul Ferien, 'Hommage à Paul Valéry'.
77 XVII, p. 75.
78 XVII, p. 409.
79 XVII, pp. 659, 661, 675.
80 XVII, p. 164.
81 XVII, p. 774.
82 XVII, p. 828.
83 In E. Suhami, *Paul Valéry et la Musique*, Dakar, 1966, p. 22.
84 31 March and 2 April 1935, XVIII, p. 4.
85 R. Brussel, 'Sur le chemin du souvenir', *Revue Musicale*, mai–juin 1936, pp. 33–4.
86 XIX, p. 842.
87 XX, p. 48.
88 XX, p. 645.
89 XX, p. 438.
90 See below Part II Chapter 4.
91 XXI, p. 376.
92 XXVII, p. 276.
93 XXVIII, p. 217.
94 *Memories and Commentaries*, London, 1960, p. 76.

PART II. MUSIC AND POETRY

1. MUSIC AS A LANGUAGE OF THE EMOTIONS

1 'Au Concert Lamoureux en 1893', *Œuvres* II, p. 1275.
2 III, 1904, p. 187.
3 VII, 1921, p. 728.
4 XXIII, 1940, p. 910.
5 XXI, 1938, p. 843.
6 XXVII, 1943, p. 456.
7 XXVIII, 1944, p. 217.
8 V, 1915, p. 570.
9 *Existence du symbolisme*, *Œuvres* I, p. 699.
10 See below, pp. 49–51.
11 III, 1905, p. 579.
12 VII, 1919, p. 275.
13 Letter N, in P. Valéry, *XV Lettres à Pierre Louÿs*, Paris, 1926.
14 Letter L, 6 June 1917, *ibid.*
15 Letter N.
16 Letter N.
17 IV, 1912, p. 842. He attributes to music a 'puissance directe' or 'force sensorielle brute' greater than any other art (greater even than architecture because, he argues, one can more easily close the

eyes than block the ears). Literature has no equivalent to this immediate expressive power apart from the 'système grossier du "Faire croire", "Faire quasi-vivre" '. (XXIV, 1941, pp. 564–5) In the vast emotional compass and the capacity for rapid shift of perspective the 'excitations des grandes musiques' suggest a comparison not with poetry but rather with 'le Pouvoir, l'énergie scientifique ou politique'. (I, 1897, p. 171)

18 Œuvres I, p. 1722. First published in Modes et Manières d'aujourd'hui, Paris, 1922; reprinted in 'Petits textes', Nouvelle Revue Française, No. 172, Paris, 1928, p. 61.

19 Au concert Lamoureux, Œuvres II, p. 1274.

20 There were certainly no accessible guides available such as Deryck Cooke's The Language of Music showing an attempt to analyse the patterns of reactions built up around the terms of musical language.

21 II, 1902, p. 683.

22 Cf. Valéry's distinction between 'harmonie imitative' and 'le mot générateur d'harmonie' in the alliance of sound and sense, Part III, Chapter 9.

23 IV, 1910, p. 469.

24 IV, 1907–8, p. 239.

25 Letter N, XV Lettres à P. Louÿs, Paris, 1926.

26 V, 1916, p. 896. Cf. IV, 1910, p. 486: 'on trouve bien toujours des idées vagues pour le justifer, ce son qui tire des larmes d'abord et directement'.

27 V, 1914, p. 224.

28 Ibid.

29 XX, 1937, p. 68.

30 XII, 1928, p. 657.

31 VII, 1918, p. 24.

32 X, 1924, p. 33.

33 'Conscience et Etat de chant. . Poésie. Peut-on conduire la préoccupation poétique à un haut degré de conscience et de précision sans perdre ce qu'il faut de confiance dans le vague et dans l'abandon au mouvement qui semblent nécessaires à l'état de chant' (XI, 1926, p. 502). This crucial paradox is confronted explicitly in Christine Crow's Paul Valéry and the Poetry of Voice, Cambridge, 1982, p. xvii and p. 15.

34 IV, 1912, p. 888. The note compares responses to 'l'attente' in music and literature: 'l'attente réelle contient mille fois sur mille et une, un élément significatif: on attend quelque chose et quelque chose precise. La musique supprime cette chose et garde l'attente. D'où on peut conclure que la quelque chose, le significatif est ce qui dans chaque cas particulier, donne un sens à nos tranformations d'attitude et de rythmes propres. Et si cette chose manque, nous la secrétons toujours, comme si la conscience devait être pleine . . . car on ne peut connaître des choses sans se connaître en quelque manière – percevoir quoi que ce soit sans percevoir quelque soi, ni réciproquement se percevoir sans percevoir quelque autre chose.'

35 I am indebted to Professor Norma Rinsler for her comments and assistance in the formulation of these ideas.
36 IV, 1907–8, p. 336.
37 *Chronicle of my Life*, trans. from the French, London, 1936, p. 92.
38 *A Composer's World*, Harvard U.P. Cambridge, Mass., 1952, p. 38.
39 XX, 1937, p. 69.
40 Ibid. See also XV, 1931, p. 97: 'Ce qui me prend et me tourmente d'envie dans la grande et belle musique – (et même en toute chose) – c'est l'impression d'une phrase bien combinée – parfaitement sûre et nécessaire dans son évolution, et accordée.
    Or, – n'est-ce pas là ce qu'on trouve dans l'allure de la mémoire suivie? N'est-ce pas qu'une telle musique nous communique, *de l'extérieure*, l'état de certitude dans les puissances et les changements successifs que la mémoire parfois produit.'
41 IV, 1912, p. 888.
42 D. Mitchell, *The Language of Modern Music*, London, 1966, p. 39.
43 IV, 1908, p. 206. Copy of a letter to P. Féline 17 Jan. 1908.
44 XII, 1928, p. 918.
45 XIV, 1930, p. 475.
46 XXV, 1941, p. 335.
47 VI, 1917, pp. 571–2. See also V, 1913, p. 80: 'La musique est devenue par les Allemands l'appareil de la jouissance métaphysique, l'agitateur et l'illusionniste, le grand moyen de déchaîner des tempêtes nulles et d'ouvrir les abimes vides. Le monde substitué, remplacé, multiplié, accéléré, creusé, illuminé – par un système de chatouilles sur un système nerveux – comme un courant électrique donne un goût à la bouche, une fausse chaleur etc.'
48 *Œuvres* II, p. 21.
49 *Tel Quel*, *Œuvres* II, p. 476.
50 II, 1900–1, p. 157.
51 XIV, 1931, p. 824.
52 VI, 1917, p. 574.
53 XIV, 1930, p. 312.
54 XVII, 1934, p. 546.
55 VI, 1916, p. 372.
56 Letter N to Pierre Louÿs, *XV Lettres . . .* , Paris, 1926.
57 IV, 1907–8, p. 354.
58 E. Sewell, *Paul Valéry: the Mind in the Mirror*, Cambridge, 1952, p. 38.
59 'Quelques pensées de Monsieur Teste', *Œuvres* II, p. 73.
60 E. Sewell, p. 38.
61 *Œuvres* I, p. 181.
62 H. Laurenti's work *Paul Valéry et le théâtre*, Paris, Nizet, 1974, contains an excellent analysis of the plans as well as *Amphion*, while Professor W. Stewart has written important articles on Valéry and the Orpheus myth (see Bibliography).
63 VIII, 1921, p. 460.
64 VIII, 1921, p. 41.

2. MUSIC AS A LANGUAGE OF THE MIND

1 Though Wagner may have glimpsed the power of 'des éléments psychologiques et physiques préparés à l'état pur' (IV, 1910, p. 477), he was, in Valéry's estimation, diverted from his 'meilleur pouvoir' by 'la folie de la gloire du Théâtre et la séduction inutile des grandeurs artificielles.' (IV, 1906, p. 58)

2 Quoted by F. Lefèvre, *Entretiens avec Paul Valéry*, Paris, 1926, p. 123.

3 *Quelques pensées de Monsieur Teste, Œuvres* II, p. 70.

4 XV, 1931, p. 165.

5 15 July 1931. J. L. Forain was best known as a cartoonist and was closely associated with the bohemian artistic circles of the 1880s and 1890s, including the journal of the *Chat Noir*.

6 XV, 1931, p. 187. The description of the theatrical elements of the occasion recalls the deliberately cardboard characters of Stravinsky's *Les Noces* and Valéry's own *Amphion* and *Sémiramis*.

7 XII, 1927, p. 384.

8 VII, 1920, p. 656; cf. XXII, 1939, p. 699: 'Musiciens n'aiment pas Wagner. W. inventeur – c'est autre chose que "de la Musique." . . .'

9 XVII, 1934, p. 60.

10 XIV, 1930, p. 751.

11 XIV, 1930, p. 375.

12 XVII, 1934, p. 60.

13 XVII, 1934, p. 60.

14 *Œuvres* I, p. 676.

15 XVI, 1932, p. 59.

16 E. Lockspeiser, *Debussy: his life and mind*, vol. I, Cambridge, 1979, p. 125.

17 XV, p. 483.

18 'Maurice Ravel ou l'esthétique de l'imposture', *Revue Musicale*, April 1925, p. 21.

19 Roland-Manuel, p. 19. The quotation from *Eupalinos* is in *Œuvres* II, p. 130.

20 III, 1905–6, p. 758.

21 Ernest Ansermet, in Roland-Manuel, p. 19.

22 Schoenberg for example used sonata form during his atonal period even though the sonata derives its formal pattern from a tonal concept of music.

23 II, 1902, p. 854.

24 *Tel Quel, Œuvres* II, p. 563.

25 X, 1924, p. 375.

26 VI, 1918, p. 884. He compares in this respect music to dreams: 'Il en est comme dans le rêve. Les causes ordinaires de nos mouvements deviennent les effets, tandis que les effects directement produits, deviennent causes. Cette méta-thèse est possible parce que la relation cause–effet dans le domaine psychologique n'est pas une *équation*. L'effet n'est pas homogène à la cause.'

27 IV, 1906, p. 58.
28 XIX, 1937, p. 893; see also XVIII, 1936, p. 881 where Valéry refers
to music as 'un partie opératoire pure'.
29 IV, 1910, p. 480.
30 XXVI, 1942, p. 10.
31 XXIX, 1945, p. 757.
32 XII, 1928, p. 915.
33 V, 1913, p. 80.
34 X, 1925, p. 756.
35 See J. Robinson, *L'analyse de l'esprit dans les Cahiers de Paul
Valéry*, Paris, 1963, p. 66 and pp. 70-2 and Valéry's remark in
Propos me concernant (*Œuvres* II, p. 1535): 'Je n'ai jamais pu
depuis 1891 considérer l'art de littérature qu'en lui comparant et
opposant un idéal, - un travail qui serait assez comparable à celui
du compositeur de musique (savante) ou du constructeur d'une
théorie physico-mathématique.' See also Valéry's remarks on the
relationship between geometry and music in for example VIII,
1921, p. 357 and X, 1925, p. 784.
36 XXVII, 1943, pp. 740-1.
37 XVII, 1934, p. 625.
38 II, 1900-1, p. 202; or as Jean Wahl said in a series of lectures on
Valéry at the Sorbonne, November 1967, 'la suite musicale est un
cas particulier des suites qui sont notre pensée'.
39 XIV, 1929, p. 115.
40 VIII, 1922, p. 694.
41 XI, 1926, p. 505.
42 V, 1915, p. 777.
43 X, 1924, p. 57. See also XIII, 1928, p. 71: 'La plupart, l'immense
plupart, de ceux qui écrivent, écrivent dans un système à la fois
très limité et non ordonné. D'ailleurs le langage commun est une
création du désordre. Quant à ceux qui ont le sentiment de cette
impureté et l'instinct du mode contraire, ils n'en ont point assez
conscience ou n'y mettent point assez de profondeur (même philosophes et surtout philosophes) pour tenter de pousser leur réflexions jusqu'à concevoir l'institution de sortes de *gammes* et de *tons*.
Les emplois de mots, les formes sont le vrai sujet d'attention de
l'artiste en philosophie.'
44 *Lettres à quelques-uns*, pp. 107-8.
45 'Fragments des mémoires d'un poème', *Œuvres* I, pp. 1472-3; The
importance of ornamentation is stressed by Christine Crow in *Paul
Valéry: Consciousness and nature*, Cambridge, 1972, pp. 158-9 and
in *Paul Valéry and the Poetry of Voice*, Cambridge, 1982, p. 261,
n. 2: 'The subject of ornamentation (Valéry had read Owen Jones'
Grammar of Ornament) also inspired his imagination as a means
of linking the abstract principles of mathematics and the natural
principles of plant growth, both models in poetic composition. 'Il
est remarquable que les mathématiques ont de commun avec la
poésie et la musique que chez elles - le fond devient l'acte de la
forme' (XV, 881).'

46 'Histoire d'Amphion', *Œuvres* II, pp. 1278-9.
47 I, 1894, p. 26; also true says Valéry for 'meubles, art militaire, finance' - but not for 'peinture, sculpture, littérature'.
48 I, 1894, p. 16. See also VII, 1920, p. 600 'Rapports de la musique dans l'espace' and his comments on the cathedral at Troyes: 'Portail gauche . . . décoration . . . faite d'arcs et piliers qui vont diminuendo, s'inscrivent dans leur subdivision formant 2 ou 3 *plans*. J'aurais volontiers pris des mesures car les modules des membres doivent former une hiérarchie. Effet très musical' (XII, 1928, p. 132).
49 *The Language of Music*, London, 1959, p. 31.
50 VII, 1918, p. 261. The links between music and architecture are well expressed by V. J. Daniel in her introduction to *Eupalinos and l'Ame et la danse*, London, 1967: 'the fundamental fascination of architecture for Valéry is that of a mind which constructs and composes. These two verbs, marking as they do the subjection of nature to the human mind and to human skill, the superiority of form over matter, account for Valéry's frequent association of architecture and music, both dependent on the exactness and perceptible relation of different parts to each other and to the whole.' (p. 32) But the limitations of the analogy are also expressed: 'As with architecture, Valéry is more concerned with dance as an idea than as a subject, for him it is not a figurative or expressive art, but a function.' (p. 42) See also the comments of J. Hytier in 'Réminiscences et rencontres valéryennes', *French Studies*, 34, No. 2 (April 1980), 174-5.
51 *Eupalinos ou l'Architecte*, *Œuvres* II, p. 113.
52 'La liberté de l'esprit', *Œuvres* II, p. 1084.
53 XXVI, 1942, p. 584. In XVII, 1934, p. 365 he attributes a 'sens formel' to both Bach and Wagner.
54 XII, 1927, p. 68.
55 V, 1913, p. 59.
56 XIV, 1930, p. 603. In *De la Diction des vers* he advises the speaker to 'bien poser la voix'. (*Œuvres* II, p. 1256)
57 XIX, 1937, p. 878; see also XXIV, 1941, p. 564: 'à côté de la Force [sensorielle brute] se trouve la possibilité de complication - la possibilité de faire percevoir par les sensations, des formations et relations abstraites. Perspectives, combinaisons de lignes ou surfaces, parties d'orchestre - suites complexes, fugues.'

3. THE THEORY OF COMPOSITION: WAGNER AND THE UNIVERSAL MIND

1 XXV, 1941, p. 191.
2 VI, 1917, p. 700.
3 XXVII, 1943, p. 221.
4 I, 1899, p. 800 and XVI, 1933, p. 749.
5 J. Duchesne-Guillemin, 'Paul Valéry et la Musique', *Revue Musicale*, no. 210, jan. 1952, p. 116.
6 *Servitude et grandeur littéraires*, Ollendorff, 1922, p. 222.

7 See S. Bernard, *Mallarmé et la musique*, Paris, 1959, pp. 65-70.
8 'Richard Wagner: rêverie d'un poète français', *Œuvres complètes*, pp. 542-3.
9 *Crise de vers*, pp. 367-8.
10 *Gide–Valéry Correspondence*, Paris, 1955, p. 74.
11 XXIV, 1941, p. 564.
12 XV, 1932, p. 505.
13 XVI, 1933, p. 197.
14 *Œuvres* I, p. 1160.
15 *Œuvres* I, p. 1201.
16 Sept. 1891, *Gide–Valéry Correspondance*, p. 126.
17 *Œuvres* I, pp. 1830-2.
18 Letter to G. Samazeuilh in Richard Wagner, *Vues sur la France*, Paris, 1943, p. 19.
19 See Valéry's account in the letter to Rauhut, Oct. 1929, *Œuvres* II, p. 1577.
20 XVI, 1933, p. 322.
21 VII, 1920, p. 596.
22 15 Sept. 1860 in *Quatre poèmes d'opéra*, Paris, Mercure de France, 1941, p. xlv.
23 'Les N dimensions de Paul Valéry', *Entretiens sur Paul Valéry*, ed. E. Noulet, Paris/La Haye, 1968, pp. 16-17.
24 *Œuvres* I, p. 1206.
25 *Avant-propos à la connaissance de la déesse, Œuvres* I, p. 1277.
26 *Œuvres* I, p. 1199.
27 'Choses tues', *Œuvres* II, p. 506.
28 'Dernière visite à Mallarmé, *Œuvres* I, p. 631.
29 V, 1914, p. 221.
30 XVIII, 1935, p. 115.
31 19 October 1899, *Gide–Valéry Correspondance*, p. 358.
32 II, 1902, p. 840.
33 *Œuvres* II, p. 92.
34 J. Gracq, *Préférences*, Paris, 1961, p. 182.
35 L. Guichard, *La musique et les lettres en France au temps du wagnérisme*, Paris, 1963. Baudelaire found in Wagner the same preoccupation with a 'complexe et indivisible totalité' and responded enthusiastically to Wagner's ideas on the fusion of the arts, on the importance of leitmotifs and the correspondance of the senses; the article 'Richard Wagner et *Tannhaüser* à Paris' published in 1861 marks an important stage in the development of Wagner's influence in France, and it is here that Baudelaire argues that the worlds of poetry and music together lead to a perception of the very essence of things 'les choses s'étant toujours exprimées par une analogie réciproque' (*Œuvres complètes*, p. 1213). There are many points of similarity between Baudelaire and Wagner: the conflict between voluptuousness and spirituality, the redeeming figure of the ideal woman, the aspiration towards a mystic, visionary purity, the 'parenté de climat' involving reader and spectator in 'une impression d'intensité et d'altitude à laquelle ils s'abandonnent comme

dans un voluptueux vertige' (L. Guichard, *La musique et les lettres en France au temps du wagnérisme*, Paris, 1963, pp. 75–6). But Guichard is right to stress that the first edition of *Les Fleurs du mal* was published in 1857 before Baudelaire had heard Wagner: 'Baudelaire a traduit *poétiquement*, comme Wagner l'a fait *musicalement*, mais *indépendamment de Wagner*, un état spirituel où l'être, affranchi des liens de la pesanteur, goûte l'indicible pureté des régions hautes.' (*Ibid.* p. 77)

36 A paper by H. Köhler presents some echoes of Wagner in Valéry's work ('Valéry et Wagner', *Colloque Paul Valéry. Amitiés de jeunesse*, Paris, 1978, pp. 147–70). But the recent article by Pierre Renauld ('L'Influence de Wagner sur le poétique de Valéry', *Revue de Littérature Comparée*, 51 (1977), 249–56) has come closer to the more cautionary interpretation taken here. Renauld concludes: 'Cette tentative wagnérienne, bien qu'autrement orientée, offrait assez d'analogie avec les rêves de Valéry pour lui permettre de se reconstruire un Wagner à son usage et de le proclamer son maître.' (p. 225)

4. VALÉRY AND STRAVINSKY

1 I. Stravinsky and R. Craft, *Memories and Commentaries*, London, 1960, p. 76.

2 *Memories and Commentaries*, p. 74.

3 'A Memoir by Igor Stravinsky' in P. Valéry, *Collected works*, ed. J. Mathews, vol. 3, London, 1960, p. xii. Also in *Memories and Commentaries*, p. 75. Further details of the collaboration are to be found in Patrick Pollard, *Proserpine; Perséphone. Edition critique*, Lyon, 1977, pp. 29–34. When Stravinsky first played the music to him Gide could only mutter 'C'est curieux, c'est très curieux.' And he commented to Maria van Rysselberghe 'C'est tout de même gênant de donner des vers à mettre en musique à un musicien russe . . . il prend les vers à rimes féminines pour des vers de treize pieds et a une tendance à mettre l'accent sur la muette. Ça s'est du reste fait souvent, et tant pis.' (Pollard, pp. 31–2) Consultation of the score shows this to have been a common procedure: Gide opens with an alexandrine and ten octosyllabic lines; set to music the syllables become 12/9/8/9/8/9/10/9/9/9/9; but although the mute -e of 'terre' and 'mystères' is voiced there is a musical symmetry in the phrases ending lines 2, 4 and 8, while a different shape to the phrase unites 'confi-es/chéri-e/prairi-es/ravi-e' in lines 6, 7, 9, 10. Later in lines 124–8 Gide's 8/12/8/8/8 becomes 10/13/8/8/10 with the voicing of the mute -e accompanied by a change from three-eight to four-eight time for a single bar at the end of the lines.

4 *Gide–Valéry Correspondance*, p. 517.

5 XXII, 1939, p. 562.

6 *op. cit.* p. 74.

7 *Correspondance*, p. 517.

8 *The Poetics of Music*, Bilingual edition, Cambridge, Mass., 1970, p. 4.
9 *Œuvres* I, p. 1342.
10 P. Collaer, *La Musique moderne 1905–55*, Paris, 1955, p. 84.
11 Or as Valéry said after the completion of *La Jeune Parque*: 'la *forme* de ce chant est une *auto-biographie*'. (VI, 1917, p. 508.)
12 *Poetics of Music*, pp. 62 and 64.
13 *Ibid.* pp. 64 and 66. Cf. Valéry's stress upon the 'caractère volontaire du vers classique.' (XII, 1927, p. 147.)
14 I. Stravinsky and R. Craft, *Expositions and developments*, London, 1962, pp. 147–8.
15 *Poetics of Music*, p. 64.
16 XXV, 1941, p. 317.
17 *Poetics of Music*, p. 104.
18 I. Stravinsky and R. Craft, *Conversations*, London, 1959, p. 19.
19 XXV, 1941, p. 283.
20 'La création artistique', *Bulletin de la société française de philosophie*, Paris, jan. 1928, p. 12.
21 *Poetics of Music*, p. 86; cf. p. 84: 'Plus l'art est contrôle, limité, travaillé et plus il est libre.'
22 *Poetics of Music*, p. 98.
23 *Œuvres* II, p. 1369.
24 Stravinsky, quoted by P. Collaer, *La Musique moderne*, Paris, 1955, p. 89. Cf. Ravel to Vaughan Williams: 'Comment sans piano pouvez-vous trouver des harmonies nouvelles?'
25 VII, 1921, p. 908. The point is taken up again in *Fontaines de mémoire* with reference to language, *Œuvres* II, p. 1371.
26 *Conversations* p. 21. See also Stravinsky's 'Avertissement': 'le classicisme lui-même ne se caractérisait pas du tout par ses procédés techniques, qui changeaient eux-mêmes autrefois comme maintenant à chaque époque, mais plutôt par ses valeurs constructives. La chose en elle-même (par exemple, en musique, un thème ou un rythme) n'est pas un matériel qui puisse suffire à l'artiste pour la création d'une œuvre. Il est évident que ce matériel doit encore trouver sa disposition réciproque, ce qui en musique, comme en tout art, porte le nom de la forme. Toutes les grandes œuvres d'art étaient marquées par cette qualité – qualité de rapport de choses, rapport du matériel à construction.' (Dec. 1927, in E. W. White, *Stravinsky: the composer and his works*, London, 1966, p. 531)
27 *La Musique moderne*, p. 98.
28 The extent to which the term 'harmony' may be used in reference to language will be more fully discussed in Part III, Chapter 7.
29 *The Poetics of Music*, p. 176.
30 X, 1925, p. 707.
31 *The Poetics of Music*, p. 178.
32 *La Musique moderne*, Paris, 1955, p. 85.
33 XXIII, 1940, p. 387.
34 *Memories and Commentaries*, p. 78.
35 III, 1905, p. 572.
36 August 1930, *Lettres à quelques-uns*, Paris, 1952, p. 191.

37 *Ibid.*
38 *Lettres à quelques-uns,* p. 190. Maurice Emmanuel, *Essai sur l'orchestique grecque: La Danse grecque antique d'après les monuments figurés,* Paris, Hachette, 1896, and in A. Lavignac, *Encylopédie de la musique et dictionnaire du Conservatoire,* part 1, Paris, 1913. E. J. Marey, *Le Mouvement,* Paris, Masson, 1894.
39 *Lettres à quelques-uns,* p. 190.
40 Stravinsky quoted in P. Collaer, *La Musique moderne,* p. 82.
41 *Œuvres* II, p. 151.
42 *Ibid.* p. 154.
43 *Ibid.* p. 155.
44 *Ibid.* p. 155.
45 *Ibid.* p. 158.
46 *Ibid.* p. 158-9.
47 *Ibid.* p. 173.
48 *Ibid.* p. 174.
49 *Ibid.* p. 174. See Norma Rinsler, 'The defence of the self: stillness and movement in Valéry's poetry': 'In the flame of the dancer, "la forme insaisissable de la plus noble destruction", one may reach the perfection of stillness, denying time and space, by means of a negation, by the rejection and destruction of everything which bars the way to that isolated state in which self-possession is possible. But few of us, it is implied, are capable of this.' (*Essays in French Literature,* No. 6, November 1969, p. 38)
50 *Ibid.* p. 174.
51 *Ibid.* p. 176.
52 *Ibid.* p. 167.
53 *Ibid.* p. 169.
54 *Ibid.* p. 170.
55 *Conversations with Igor Stravinsky,* London, 1959, p. 21.
56 M. Beaufils, *Musique du son, musique du verbe,* Paris, 1954, p. 202.
57 P. Collaer, *La Musique moderne,* Paris-Bruxelles, 1955, p. 58.
58 Quoted by Frédéric Robert in 'Valéry et ses musiciens', *Europe,* no. 507, July 1971, p. 108. Robert presents a full list of works set to music. In addition to those already cited, he gives:
Vincenzo Tommasini: *Trois mélodies* (*Les Pas, L'Insinuant, Le Vin perdu*), 1927-9, Editions Ricordi.
Marguerite D'Harcourt: *Deux Poèmes de Paul Valéry* (*Les Pas, La Ceinture*), 1930, Editions Sénart.
Pierre-Octave Ferroud: *Trois poèmes de Paul Valéry* (*Le Vin perdu, Les Pas, L'Abeille*), 1930, Edition Durand.
Mytho Sinadino: *Deux mélodies* (*Les Pas, La Ceinture*), 1933, Editions H. Maquaire.
Robert Bergmann: *Chants Lunaires* (No. 3 *Le Bois amical*), 1935, Editions Delrieu.
Arthur Hoérée: *Barcarolle, Performance, Salut,* 1938, Editions Choudens.
François de La Rochefoucauld: *Trois mélodies* (1er recueil *Les Pas, Le Sylphe, Au bois dormant*); *Trois mélodies* (2e recueil *Un feu distinct, Vue, Le Bois amical*), 1940, Editions Auber.

Robert Bernard: *Prélude au Cimetière marin*, poème symphonique pour orchestre, 1941, manuscript.

Henri Sauguet: *Le Bois amical*, 1945, manuscript.

Dom Clément Jacob: *Quatre poèmes tirés de 'Charmes'* (*La Dormeuse, L'Abeille, Les Pas, La Fausse morte*), 1948, manuscript; *Le Bois amical*, 1953, manuscript.

Daniel Lesur: *Cantique des Colonnes*, pour chœur d'enfants et deux harpes, 1954; nouvelle version pour chœur de femmes et orchestre, 1957, Editions Musicales Pathé-Marconi.

Noël Lee: *Paraboles*, 1964, manuscript.

(F. Robert, pp. 109–10)

59 *Œuvres* II, p. 154.

PART III. MUSICAL TECHNIQUES IN VALÉRY'S POETRY

5. COMPOSITION

1 J. Ballard, 'Celui que j'ai connu', *Paul Valéry Vivant*, p. 244.

2 M. Goudeket, *Près de Colette*, Paris, Flammarion, 1956, p. 109. Cf. Colette *Mes apprentissages, Œuvres complètes*, vol. 11, Paris, Flammarion, 1950, p. 119: 'Le dessin musical et la phrase naissent du même couple évasif et immortel: la note, le rythme. Ecrire, au lieu de composer, c'est connaître la même recherche, mais avec une transe moins illuminée, et une récompense plus petite. Si j'avais composé au lieu d'écrire, j'aurais pris en dédain ce que je fais depuis quarante ans. Car le mot est rebattu, et l'arabesque de musique éternellement vierge.'

3 A. Fontainas, 'Jeunesse de Valéry', *Paul Valéry Vivant*, pp. 70–1. But a publisher's deadline was not always so easily met, as a note written in December 1920 demonstrates; it indicates that a certain kind of rapidity of thought and intellectual excitement hinders rather than helps the writing of poetry: 'Ce matin, je devrais faire des vers, qui sont promis et attendus à midi. Mais j'ai une surexcitation intellectuelle qui ne peut que produire sans retour sur soi, et cela est contraire au chant, au retard qui fait les vers, à la maturation. Je ne suis bon qu'au "génie". *Je vais plus vite que les violons.*' (VII, p. 691)

4 XIX. 1936, p. 721.

5 *Œuvres* I, pp. 1207–8.

6 VI, 1918, p. 824.

7 XXIII, 1940, pp. 871–2.

8 IX, 1922, p. 8.

9 VIII, 1922, p. 523.

10 IX, 1923, p. 377.

11 XI, 1926, p. 464.

12 *Œuvres* II, p. 712.

13 W. N. Ince, *The Poetic Theory of Paul Valéry*, Leicester, 1961, pp. 96 and 117. The work of Ince in defining the relationship of 'inspiration' to 'technique' is of crucial importance. While Ince is

particularly concerned in his chapter on 'The Stages of Poetic Creation' to analyse the various stages in terms of Valéry's theoretical position, the interest in this study is more especially with the practical steps taken in the construction of the poetry.

14 *Discours sur Emile Verhaeren, Œuvres* I, p. 760.
15 VII, 1920, p. 660.
16 XVI, 1931, p. 301.
17 VI, 1917, p. 665.
18 VI, 1916, p. 112.
19 XXVIII, 1944, p. 675.
20 *Œuvres* I, pp. 1555–7.
21 XXIV, 1941, p. 449.
22 XXVIII, 1944, p. 675.
23 VII, 1920, p. 483. The example of the initial stage in the composition of *La Pythie*, which arose from the single line 'Pâle, profondément mordue' is discussed in the Appendix, pp. 275–83 below.
24 II, 1901–1, p. 132.
25 XXVI, 1942, p. 408.
26 IV, 1912, p. 886.
27 *Cahier Charmes* II, f. 6.
28 IV, 1912, p. 886.
29 XXVI, 1942, p. 669.
30 XII, 1927, p. 221.
31 XXI, 1938, p. 158.
32 VII, 1920, p. 499.
33 O. Nadal, *La Jeune Parque*, Paris, Club du Meilleur Livre, p. 186; Nadal's document II/13 shows a 'palette sons', II/16 a 'palette idée'. The MS. of *La Jeune Parque* III f. 22bis shows a 'palette rimes': a whole page of experiments with rhymes, sometimes just two or three words ('humée/fumée' 'suis-je/vertige', 'seuil/mon orgueil/écueil'), sometimes a longer list ('tempe/lampe/détrempe/trempe/rampe/hampe/campe'), while other words remain without rhyme ('nuque 'cap', 'ruine') etc.
34 II, 1900–1, p. 132.
35 VII, 1919–20, p. 388.
36 IX, 1923, p. 647.
37 *Paul Valéry Vivant*, pp. 289–90.
38 XXII, 1939, pp. 715–16.
39 XI, 1928, p. 607.
40 XXV, 1942, p. 651.
41 See, for example, palette VI, in Nadal, p. 194.
42 VI, 1916, p. 218.
43 XVII, 1934, p. 68: cf. XX, 1937, p. 427.
44 VI, 1916, p. 205.
45 XI, 1925, p. 168.
46 27 juin 1916, *Lettres à quelques-uns*, p. 116.
47 XII, 1927, p. 481.
48 XII, 1927, p. 350.
49 Letter to Maurice Denis, *Œuvres* I, p. 1624.

50 'Fragments des mémoires d'un poème', *Œuvres* I, p. 1473.
51 XXVI, 1943, p. 920.
52 *Rhumbs, Œuvres* II, p. 635.
53 Letter to A. Mockel, 1917, *Lettres à quelques-uns*, p. 124.
54 *Rhumbs, Œuvres* II, p. 636.
55 *Fontaines de mémoire, Œuvres* II, p. 1369; cf. 'Calepin d'un poète', *Œuvres* I, p. 1483.
56 Valéry spoke of the poem as 'une œuvre qui soit presque la contre-partie de *La Jeune Parque*, autrement simple dans sa forme et ne donnant lieu à presque aucune difficulté de compréhension, en portant surtout mon effort sur l'harmonie même de la langue'. ('Sur les *Narcisse*', *Paul Valéry Vivant*, p. 290)
57 *Œuvres* II, pp. 1369–70. Cf. the important article by L. J. Austin, 'Modulation and movement in Valéry's verse', *Yale French Studies*, 44 (1970): 'as poetry depends for its effect upon succession, the analogy with music is closer [than with architecture] . . . the specific music device which meant most to Valéry was precisely that of modulation' (pp. 21–2).
58 VI, 1917, p. 760.
59 XVI, 1933, p. 829.
60 XXIII, 1940, pp. 205–6.
61 VIII, 1921, p. 357. See also letter to A. Mockel: 'Le sonnet . . . peut se consacrer à faire percevoir toutes les faces d'un seul et même diamant. C'est une rotation du même corps autour d'un point ou un axe.' (*Lettres à quelques-uns*, p. 124) Or again: 'les quatre parties rempliront chacune une fonction différente de celle des autres, et cette progression de différences dans les strophes cependant bien justifiée par la *ligne* de tout le discours.' ('Calepin d'un poète', *Œuvres* I, p. 1454) His conception had changed considerably from the early idea of the sonnet composed 'en vue d'un effet final et foudroyant'. (*Sur la technique littéraire, Œuvres* I, p. 1831)
62 L. J. Austin, 'Paul Valéry compose *le Cimetière marin*', *Mercure de France*, April 1953, p. 593.
63 VII, 1921, p. 499: cf.: 'La suite réelle a été *abcdefg*. L'œuvre réelle finale sera *bedg* par exemple – qui en est déduite. *d* n'a pu naître que de *abc* mais cette genèse est supprimée.' (VI, 1917, p. 496)
64 *Cahier Charmes* I, f. 24.
65 Valéry initially agreed with Alain that the end required development and promised to reinstate the deleted stanzas in a future edition of *Charmes*; but in fact he did not, and Alain recognised that 'le poète avait raison. La vérité des passions et des émotions n'est pas ce que dicte la raison, mais plutôt c'est comme le soupir du corps dénoué' (Alain, in P. Valéry, *Charmes*, Paris, 1928, p. 144).
66 J. R. Lawler, *Lecture de Valéry*, p. 153.
67 VIII, 1922, p. 657.
68 VI, 1916, p. 387.
69 XV, 1932, p. 480.
70 X, 1925, p. 739.
71 XXIII, 1940, p. 371.

72 VI, 1916, p. 253.
73 O. Nadal, *La Jeune Parque*, Paris, 1957, p. 354.
74 Letter to H. Mondor, 16 février 1941, *Lettres à quelques-uns*, p. 231.
75 XIV, 1931, p. 808.

6. MELODY

1 For example this detailed and extensive analysis written in *Cahier* II (1900–1901, p. 269): 'Que fait le verbe dans la mélodie? Comment un sentiment ou une excitation sont-ils réfléchis sur la mélodie et c.à d. reconstruits. Un son musical frappe par sa *spécialité*. Comment s'unifie la diversité mélodique? La vue fait croire que l'unité coloriée se déclare et se forme hors de nous. Mais la successive oreille oblige le sons en nous.

La Musique exige une connaissance a priori d'un certain ordre des sons et par rapport à cet ordre une connaissance de la déviation que chaque mélodie ou couple de notes emporte. de plus chaque son est bref ou prolongé. Chaque son correspond à un état énergétique général et les sons classés ainsi donnent une progression plus rapide que celle de leurs hauteurs (prises en valeurs absolues).

Un couple de sons implique comme 2 nombres les valeurs intermédiaires. En tant que timbres, ils impliquent leurs harmoniques. La question est de mesurer d'abord le 'mouvement musical' ou la *distance* musicale, c.à d. le changement élémentaire produit par la substitution des sons.

Les idées élémentaires suggérées sont celle de mouvement – de substitution d'ascension ou chûte – de brusquerie et délicatesse d'à coups périodes etc. – d'atmosphère, espace pur – commotion, pénétration, poids et pas un mot de cet ordre qui ne puisse être *traduit* par un effet musical. Les thèmes sont des schèmes de variation de la connaissance, avec la caractéristique de se déterminer de plus en plus jusqu'à leur abolition – l'addition des impressions successives est bornée.
[. . .]
La mémoire reproduit rigoureusement très fréquemment le dessin musical. L'intelligibilité est ici comme toujours une formation de l'unité dans le temps.'
2 VIII, 1922, p. 827.
3 XXIX, 1944, p. 154.
4 IV, 1912, p. 806.
5 VI, 1916, p. 94.
6 IV, 1908, p. 270.
7 I, 1899, p. 851.
8 V, 1924, p. 375.
9 IV, 1906, p. 11.
10 XVI, 1933, pp. 878–9.
11 XVI, 1933, p. 279.
12 V, 1914, p. 95.

13 VI, 1916, p. 95.
14 III, 1905–6, p. 753.
15 In O. Nadal, *La Jeune Parque*, Paris, Club du Meilleur Livre, pp. 176–7.
16 VI, 1917, pp. 508–9.
17 XII, 1928, p. 705.
18 XXIV, 1941, p. 150.
19 VI, 1917, p. 533.
20 VI, 1917, p. 651.
21 Cf. IX, 1923, p. 306: 'Poésie etc. La génération des mots – idées – images par le mouvement. Le dit mouvement est engendré par une image – état. Les mots ou propositions sont comme les pas (d'une *marche*, ou bien ceux d'une *danse*) – car les pas réels sont mus par les perceptions des environs à chaque instant + la perception du but – objet.'
22 XXV, 1942, p. 609.
23 Transcriptions of documents II, 17, 19–20 in Nadal, *La Jeune Parque*, pp. 197, 199–201.
24 G. W. Ireland, 'Notes on the composition of *La Jeune Parque*', *Zeitschrift für französische Sprache und Literatur*, vol. 72, 1962, p. 24.
25 V, 1913, p. 25.

6. *LES HARMONIQUES*

1 VII, 1919–20, p. 419.
2 XXII, 1939, p. 604.
3 IV, 1907–8, p. 271.
4 Cf. E. Lockspeiser, *Debussy*, vol. II, Cambridge, 1979, p. 232.
5 Letter to Cazalis, oct. 1864 in *Propos sur la Poésie*, ed. H. Mondor, Monaco, 1953, p. 46.
6 Letter to François Coppée 5 déc. 1886, *Propos sur la poésie*, Monaco, 1953, p. 85.
7 *Crise de vers*, *Œuvres complètes*, Paris, Pléiade, 1945, p. 368.
8 Cf. C. S. Brown, *Music and Literature: a Comparison of the Arts*, Athens, Ga., p. 39.
9 'La création artistique', *Vues*, Paris, 1948, p. 303. This is the sense brought out by H. Laurenti: 'Le jeu complexe des "harmoniques", que Valéry avait lui-même tant de peine à définir, commande toutes les relations "poétiques": celles des éléments de même nature, mais aussi et surtout celles de la forme et du fond, du son et du sens, de "l'intus" et de "l'extra".' ('Musique et monologue . . .', *P. Valéry 1: Lectures de 'Charmes'*, 1974, p. 58) In fact Valéry talks of 'l'harmonie du son et du sens', 'un *rapport harmonique* entre le son et le sens' but not of 'les harmoniques du son et du sens'. See below Chapter 9.
10 *De la diction des vers*, *Œuvres* II, p. 1258.
11 II, 1902, p. 685.
12 XIX, 1936, p. 656.

13 XVI, 1933, p. 909. Cf. 'Les harmoniques sont les fonctions de la sensibilité' (XXV, 1941, p. 62); 'Harmoniques. Implexes de la sensibilité (XXIX, 1944, p. 305); '[Harmoniques:] propriétés de la sensibilité fonctionnelle pure – sans application à la connaissance "extérieure", mais conditions énergétiques, sans doute, du fonctionnement local' (XXVIII, 1944, p. 388). For a study of the notion of resonance in all its connections see W. N. Ince, 'Resonance in Valéry', *Essays in French Literature*, November 1968, pp. 38–57. Ince states that 'the domain, certainly the origin of resonance is alleged·to be human affectivity, all that is not intellectual awareness' (p. 39), and goes on to demonstrate that Valéry extends the notion to include all the arts: 'though they are all different through having various specific goals (which he rather despises), they all have in common the ordered exploitation of man's capacity for resonance' (p. 51) quoting IX, 1924, p. 802: 'Mais qu'est-ce que cette Poésie? C'est un état d'attente. Résonance. Chantant. Etat dans lequel les choses touchent directement les trésors de l'énergie centrale, et l'énergie éveille les choses.'

14 'Propos sur la poésie', *Œuvres* I, p. 1363.

15 'Propos sur la poésie', *Œuvres* I, p. 1363.

16 XXIV, 1941, p. 365. H. Laurenti discusses harmonics in *Paul Valéry et le théâtre*, Paris, 1973, pp. 125ff. Describing the 'état intrinsèque' as 'une valeur propre qui ne demande qu'à se renouveler' she shows that it evokes a feeling of 'l'improbable' in the reader or listener by means of a 'perception de sons successifs accomodée aux mouvements cachés', thus enabling the poem to achieve a symphonic-like effect. 'Ainsi la musique propose-t-elle au dramaturge le modèle d'un art fortement régi par des lois, mais susceptible d'unir l'humain et l'imaginaire, le significatif et le formel, de créer ainsi son espace propre, "harmonique" du monde sensible' (p. 129).

17 F. Lefèvre, *Entretiens avec P. Valéry*, Paris, 1926, p. 70.

18 XXVI, 1943, p. 918. See Judith Robinson, *Rimbaud, Valéry et 'l'incohérence harmonique'*, Paris, Archives des Lettres Modernes, 1979.

19 XXIII, 1940, p. 91.

20 II, 1900–1, p. 179.

21 *Au sujet du 'Cimetière marin'*, *Œuvres* I, p. 1503.

22 XXIX, 1944, p. 350.

23 XXIX, 1944, p. 351. Cf. 'Poésie. Harmoniques – psycho-physiques généralisées – sont la substance de la poésie. Par là est le *chantant*, le résonnant.' (XII, 1927, p. 435)

24 'Stéphane Mallarmé', *Œuvres* I, p. 676.

25 *Œuvres* I, p. 1463.

26 VI, 1917, p. 761.

27 'Le nombre des emplois possibles d'un mot par un individu est plus important que le nombre de mots dont il peut disposer. Cf. Racine, V. Hugo' (*Œuvres* I, p. 1180). See also P. Guiraud, *Langage et versification d'après l'œuvre de Paul Valéry*, Paris, 1953, p. 151 for statistical evidence of this.

28 VII, 1919, p. 270.
29 And to extend the range of overtones beyond Valéry, there are of
    course distinct echoes of Baudelaire here: while the hair and the
    light recall *La Chevelure*:

> O toison moutonnant jusque sur l'encolure! [. . .]
> Tu contiens, mer d'ébène, un éblouissant rêve[. . .]
> [Un port] Où les vaisseaux, glissant dans l'or et
>   dans la moire[. . .]
> Je plongerai ma tête amoureuse d'ivresse
> Dans ce noir océan où l'autre est enfermé;

the rest of Valéry's stanza recalls *Parfum exotique*, even to using
the same rhyme 'marine / narine':

> Guidé par ton odeur vers de charmants climats,
> Je vois un port rempli de voiles et de mâts
> Encore tout fatigués par la vague marine,
>
> Pendant que le parfum des verts tamatiniers,
> Qui circule dans l'air et m'enfle la narine,
> Se mêle dans mon âme au chant des mariniers.

30 VI, 1916, p. 247.
31 P. Guiraud, *Langage et versification* . . . , Paris, 1953, pp. 177–9.
32 A. Henry, *Langage et poésie dans l'œuvre de Paul Valéry*, Paris,
    1952. See also H. Köhler, *Poésie et profondeur sémantique dans
    "La Jeune Parque" de Paul Valéry*, Nancy, 1965.
33 P. Guiraud, *op cit.* p. 185.
34 *Œuvres* II, pp. 181–3.
35 Variants from the final version in the opening stanzas:

stanza 1	line 2	Chapeaux garnis de jour
	4	Chantant sur le contour
		Bougeant vivant
3	3	Au désir sans défaut
4	2	L'art de porter les cieux
6	1	O froides et dorés
		lines 2 and 4 reversed

36 Commenting on what he calls the 'polyphony' of the poem,
    Duchesne-Guillemin identifies three levels: 'idées', 'matière' and
    'femmes . . . leur féminité est indirecte, allusive; présente, mais
    cachée; comme à fleur de marbre. Elles sont des absences de
    femmes.' (*Etudes pour un Paul Valéry*, Neuchâtel, 1964, p. 98.)
37 The poem, now written in two columns on the page, consists of
    19 stanzas and two more arrowed in. (*Cahier Charmes* I, f. 32)
38 The exact order of stanzas in the 3rd version is 1, 2, 3, 4, 5, 6, 7,
    [8 added], 10, [11 added], 12, 13, 14, 18, 15, 16, 17, 9, and three
    stanzas subsequently deleted.
39 VI, 1917, p. 755.
40 XIV, 1930, p. 777.

8. RHYTHM

1 XVII, 1934, p. 434.
2 XVII, 1935, p. 820.

3 XVII, 1934, p. 199.
4 XXV, 1941, p. 103.
5 VI, 1916, p. 27.
6 VI, 1916, p. 101.
7 V, 1916, p. 898.
8 XXVI, 1942, p. 405. cf. VIII, 1921, p. 323.
9 VIII, 1921, p. 279.
10 XXVI, 1942, p. 405.
11 S. Mallarmé, 'Réponse à l'enquête de J. Huret', *Œuvres complètes*, Pléiade, p. 867.
12 IX, 1923, p. 514.
13 *Œuvres* II, pp. 156–7.
14 XXIV, 1941, p. 267.
15 *Œuvres* II, p. 160.
16 XXIV, 1941, p. 267.
17 VII, 1921, p. 738.
18 VII, 1918, p. 249.
19 XXVI, 1942, p. 452.
20 IV, 1913, p. 905.
21 XXII, 1939, p. 151. There is a difference between metre and rhythm, as Guiraud has explained: 'mètre et rythme sont distincts et entretiennent en même temps des rapports étroits.

Le mètre a pour fonction essentielle d'aider la mémoire en instaurant un ordre et un retour réguliers. Le rythme est libre et soumis aux exigences diverses de l'émotion. Il est régulier chaque fois qu'il a pour mission d'exprimer l'ordre, la douceur, l'apaisement, la monotonie, la tristesse. Il est brisé et désordonné chaque fois qu'il veut rendre un sentiment violent. Il épouse naturellement le mètre dans le premier cas, et essaie de s'en libérer dans le second.' *Langage et versification d'après l'œuvre de Paul Valéry*, Paris, 1953, p. 47.
22 XX, 1937, p. 414.
23 Letter to E. Gosse, *Revue de littérature comparée*, July–Sept. 1951, p. 358.
24 XV, 1931, p. 282.
25 *Œuvres* I, p. 1289.
26 F. Lefèvre, *Entretiens avec P. Valéry*, Paris, 1926, p. 62.
27 *Œuvres* I, p. 1503.
28 It has already been established that *La Pythie* was begun well before *La Jeune Parque* was completed, and the stanza 'Honneur des hommes . . .' is to be found already in the second stage of the poem.
29 *Le Cimetière marin* f. 261. I am indebted to Mme F. de Lussy for drawing this to my attention.
30 The next MS. shows a draft of the opening stanza and, written on top, the Zénon stanza. Has the image of the 'Idéale mer' combined with 'Chaleur tranquille' and 'C'est toi désir' to suggest the opening line of the new stanza: 'Le toit tranquille . . .'?
31 *Œuvres* I, p. 1503. Cf. a note written in 1913: 'Un écrivain "arti-

ficiel" comme moi dans mes vers, revient à soi cependant par un détour et malgré tout s'exprime car ne cherchant qu'une réussite objective, (ou l'effet rare à produire), toutefois il ne la trouve que dans un certain domaine où il incline selon son propre sens du plus apte et du réussi et qui est précisément celui de sa nature' (IV, p. 927).

32 *Œuvres* II, p. 636.
33 XIX, 1936, p. 154.
34 *Lettres à quelques-uns*, Paris, 1952, pp. 160–1.
35 II, 1900–1, p. 132.
36 Letter to P. Souday, *Lettres à quelques-uns*, p. 182.
37 *Catalogue de l'Exposition Paul Valéry à la Bibliothèque Nationale*, No. 275, p. 45.
38 Letter to Jacques Doucet, 1922, in Lawler, *Lecture de Valéry*, p. 21.
39 F. Porché, *Paul Valéry et la poésie pure*, Paris, 1926, pp. 60–62. The variety of effects arising from the use of different verse forms has been analysed with great perception by Duchesne-Guillemin in his chapter 'Sous le signe de la métrique', *Etudes pour un Paul Valéry*, Neuchâtel, 1964.
40 *Œuvres* II, p. 537.
41 XXI, 1938, p. 589.
42 P. Guiraud in his chapter 'Le Rythme', *Langage et versification d'après l'œuvre de Paul Valéry*, Paris, 1953 gives examples of these categories. Useful comments are to be found also in H. Morier, 'La Motivation des formes et des mètres chez Valéry, *Paul Valéry Contemporain*, Paris, 1974, pp. 325–52; he discusses in particular Valéry's use of the exclamation mark, the patterns of masculine-feminine rhymes, the 5-syllable line, the caesura, enjambement and the disjunction of syntax, sonnet structure and irregularities of metre.
43 *Œuvres* II, p. 1000.
44 *Cahier Charmes* II f. 22.
45 VI, 1917, p. 809.
46 VI, 1917, p. 729.
47 Alain, *Charmes*, Paris, 1928, p. 172.
48 'Ce en quoi les vers se distinguent les uns des autres a une *importance d'effet auditif au moins* égale à ce par quoi ils se ressemblent' (XXVI, 1942, p. 36).
49 XXVI, 1943, p. 807. See also X, 1924, p. 430: 'La partie musicale – rythme et melos donne les temps et l'énergie. Bonds, équilibres, tensions, cadences, retour au zéro.'

9. *LA MUSIQUE VERBALE*

1 'Commentaires de "Charmes" ', *Œuvres* I, p. 1510.
2 'Offrande', *Paul Valéry Vivant*, p. 83.
3 VI, 1917, p. 564.

4 *Poésie et pensée abstraite, Œuvres* I, p. 1327; cf. letter to A. Mockel, May 1918, *Lettres à quelques-uns*, p. 128.

5 VII, 1918, p. 163.

6 XX, 1924, p. 774.

7 XVIII, 1936, p. 786.

8 X, 1924, p. 254.

9 VI, 1917, p. 705.

10 *Œuvres* I, p. 1492.

11 *Ibid.*

12 XXVII, 1943, p. 444.

13 X, 1924, p. 31.

14 XXVII, 1943, p. 444.

15 VII, 1920, p. 538.

16 VII, 1918, p. 125.

17 VI, 1916, p. 170. 'Je reviens à moi qui parle fort vite (mais quand je fais des vers, je me les parle bas, et les écoute en moi très lentement).' 'Propos me concernant', *Œuvres* II, p. 1536. See also 'Esquisse d'un éloge de la virtuosité' where he compares the poet to a composer: 'Le créateur comptait ses mesures à loisir, et sa voix faible ou fausse lui suffisait à se dessiner, à l'état de murmure errant sur les confins du songe et de la forme, les mélodies les plus accidentés, sans souci des hauteurs ou des profondeurs des sons, ni de la difficulté des arabesques qu'il confiera à d'autres organes le soin et le souci de faire entendre et de fair valoir' (*Vues*, Paris, 1948, p. 356).

18 *Rhumbs, Œuvres* II, p. 635.

19 XXIII, 1940, p. 67.

20 Cf. the notes in the *Cahiers* containing experiments with different sound patterns, e.g. XVI, 1933, p. 546.

21 VIII, 1922, p. 584.

22 XXVI, 1942, p. 121.

23 VI, 1917, p. 732. On several occasions Valéry criticised Romanticism for diverting literature from its true concern with 'la parole' and 'le chant', leading either to artificially fabricated descriptions or 'balbutiements, rugissements, cris, jaculations': 'Dans les 2 cas la modulation s'est perdue et la divine continuité de la phrase, en même temps que l'équilibre des facteurs rhétoriques, le contrôle sur les images, sur la logique, sur l'object et les moyens du discours, se perdait.' (VI, 1917, p. 769)

24 *Questions de Poésie, Œuvres* I, p. 1285.

25 XV, 1931, p. 34.

26 XXIII, 1940, p. 197.

27 P. Guiraud, *Langage et versification d'après l'œuvre de Paul Valéry*, Paris, 1953, p. 74.

28 VI, 1917, p. 755.

29 Guiraud, *op. cit.* p. 74.

30 Guiraud, *op. cit.* p. 118. See also M. Gauthier's article 'L'Architecture phonique dans la poésie de Valéry', *Paul Valéry Contemporain*, Actes et Colloques no. 12, Paris, Klincksieck, 1974, pp. 377–

97, in which he studies '[la]' construction de l'aspect purement sonore des vers'. His method of identifying groups of consonants and vowels and their interplay offers a useful technique of analysis especially with regard to the formal symmetry of groups of sounds.

31 XXI, 1938, p. 822.

32 Jean de Latour, *Examen de Valéry*, Paris, 1935, p. 159. The drafts of this passage in *Cahier Charmes* III show how much reworking was involved in the composition as Valéry sought the perfect form of expression through nine successive versions. A major study of the manuscripts of *Narcisse* is presented in the recently published *Ecriture et génétique textuelle: Valéry à l'œuvre* / Ned Bastet et al.; textes réunis par Jean Levaillant. Lille: Presses universitaires de Lille, 1982.

33 'Au concert Lamoureux en 1893' *Œuvres* II, p. 1273.

34 XII, 1927, p. 213. See also XII, p. 771: 'Le fondement de la poésie comme *art* – c'est la non-relation régulière du son et du sens.'

35 'Richard Wagner et "Tannhäuser" à Paris', *Œuvres*, Paris, Pléiade, 1961, p. 1213.

36 *Œuvres*, Paris, Pléiade, 1951, p. 364.

37 *Œuvres*, p. 364.

38 'Poésie et pensée abstraite', *Œuvres* I, p. 1332.

39 VII, 1918, p. 151.

40 XX, 1937, p. 293.

41 IV, 1910, p. 489.

42 'Réflexions sur l'art', *Bulletin de la société française de philosophie*, Paris, 1935, p. 65.

43 in *Entretiens sur Paul Valéry*, éd. E. Noulet, Paris, 1968, p. 403.

44 *Tel Quel, Œuvres* II, p. 562.

45 XXIV, 1941, p. 150.

46 'Variation sur une pensée', *Œuvres* I, p. 458. My italics.

47 An early expression of this idea was by the critic Becq de Fourquières: 'On peut souvent constater que le mot générateur de l'idée . . . devient à son tour, au moyen de ses éléments phoniques, le générateur sonore du vers et soumet tous les mots secondaires qui l'accompagnent à une sorte de vassalité tonique', *Traité générale de versification française*, Paris, 1879, p. 220. A more recent example is G. Brereton's concept of the 'masterword' which he demonstrates with regard to Mallarmé's poem 'Le vierge, le vivace et le bel aujourd'hui', in *An Introduction to the French Poets*, London, 1956, p. 208.

48 VII, 1918, p. 151. Cf. VIII, 1921, p. 465.

49 A reading of this text by L. Bergeron seeks to make all the sounds expressive, independently of the meaning: '*è e en ou on u i.* Nous descendons graduellement vers les profondeurs sombres jusqu'à *ou* et *on*, pour remonter rapidement vers la surface et la lumière avec *u* et *i* . . . Dans le deuxième vers, nous avons le même effet de descente et de montée . . . C'est la parabole que décrit le plongeur.' (*Le son et le sens dans quelques poèmes de 'Charmes' de Paul Valéry*, Paris, 1963, p. 41.) Thus the *on* sound of 'onde' typifies

the depths, when semantically it is a surface wave and 'infinie' with its 'voyelle claire' is a return to the surface and the light, when in fact the 'profondeur' is infinite in a downward direction.

50 Cassagne's comments on Baudelaire could apply equally well to Valéry: 'Il ne conviendrait pas de chercher à donner aux assonances et aux allitérations de Baudelaire une signification trop précise. Quelquefois, et même souvent, elles n'expriment chez lui aucune idée ou aucun sentiment déterminé d'une façon particulièrement sensible. Dans ce cas l'effet produit est une impression plus ou moins forte de cohésion, de plénitude du vers, à laquelle d'autres causes peuvent d'ailleurs contribuer, mais qui est à coup sûr considérablement renforcé par ces échos discrets qui se répètent d'un bout à l'autre du vers et résonnent dans toutes ses parties. Ensuite, indépendamment de toute idée ou de tout sentiment suggéré, il y a certainement une caresse fort agréable pour l'oreille dans ces sonorités semblables qui se répondent au cours de la phrase poétique', A. Cassagne, *Versification et métrique de Baudelaire*, Paris, 1906, p. 71.

51 VI, 1916, p. 343.

52 VII, 1918, p. 69.

10. RECITATIVE

1 Valéry, reported by C. Du Bos, *Journal* 1921–3, Paris, 1946, p. 227.

2 II, 1900–1, p. 310.

3 XXII, 1939, p. 217. It is interesting to note that his preference for the contralto voice derives in part from the similarities in range with the spoken voice: 'Je déteste les notes très aiguës autant que les très basses. Ce sont celles qui s'éloignent du langage articulé.' *Ibid.* See also VI, 1917, p. 732: 'Les qualités que l'on peut énoncer d'une voix humaine sont les mêmes que l'on doit étudier et donner dans la poésie.'

4 Valéry in F. Lefèvre, *Entretiens avec Paul Valéry*, Paris, 1926, p. 56.

5 IV, 1911, p. 587.

6 Letter to A. Mockel, 1917, *Lettres à quelques-uns*, p. 123. Valéry wrote in the *Cahiers* about three months after publication of *La Jeune Parque*: 'Toujours poursuivi par l'Idée de cette phrase musicale – parlée-en-vers que je veux insatiablement faire . . . Seule phrase – un seul jet ou dessin, sans nulle *fatigue*. Comme je comprends *souvent* qu'un artiste puisse toute sa vie refaire, recommencer la même figure, chercher la même figure toujours plus approchée . . . *de quoi?*' (VI, 1917, p. 663).

7 *Œuvres* I, pp. 1492–3.

8 IX, 1923, p. 514.

9 VI, 1916, p. 139. 'Air: Morceau de musique écrite pour une seule voix, accompagnant des paroles' (*Dictionnaire Petit Robert*, Paris, 1967, p. 38).

10 XXIII, 1940, p. 162; he adds 'Mais Hugo? Déclame plus qu'il ne

chante.' The harshness of his judgement of Hugo is evident in VI, 1916, p. 170: 'Hugo a les mots – et il n'a pas la voix. L'acteur chez lui ou le déclamateur transpire, se rend indispensable – odieux. La voix chez Hugo est d'un orateur ridicule ou quand c'est très beau, non plus une voix mais la rumeur d'un orchestre.'

11 February 1773, quoted by W. H. Hadow, 'Music and Drama', *Collected Essays*, London, 1928, p. 175. See also Gluck's reply to La Harpe who had criticised the expression of violent passion in *Armide*: 'Je m'étois persuadé . . . que la voix, les instruments, tous les sons, les silences mêmes, devoient tendre à un seul but qui étoit l'expression, et que l'union devoit être si étroite entre les paroles et le chant, que le Poème ne semblât pas moins fait sur la Musique que la Musique sur le Poème' (in Hadow, *ibid.*, p. 176.).

12 The continuity of musical texture is apparent for example at the end of Act II of *Orfeo ed Euridice* with its intermingling of dance, ballet, chorus and aria; 'Che puro ciel' is termed '*quasi-récitatif*' and is placed between an aria which is taken up by the whole chorus ('E quest' asilo ameno e grato') and another chorus ('Vieni a' regni del riposo').

13 VI, 1916, p. 342. Cf. VI, 1916, p. 188: 'Un "opéra" en vers est possible. Il suffit de prendre un *sujet* de le découper en *ses* parties poétiques, de mettre des titres qui dispensent de trop d'explications – et de chanter chaque morceau avec variétés de nombres et de combinaisons. Ceci doit être chanté par La Fontaine, et cela *dit* par Racine et ceci mugi par Hugo et cela par la basse Baudelaire, convenablement costumés.' Or suggesting these poets as instruments: 'Il n'est pas impossible de conjuguer ces violons, ces cuivres et ces bois pour posséder un orchestre' (VI, p. 296). Later he suggests the same for the Dialogues: 'Les diverses voix dans le Dialogue ne seront que des instruments' (XIII, 1928, p. 323).

14 *Œuvres* II, p. 1257.

15 Article by A. Brisson in *Le Temps*, 1 décembre 1913, which Valéry quotes in 'Le Prince et la Jeune Parque', *Œuvres* I, pp. 1494–5.

16 VII, p. 164. See also XIX, 1937, p. 885: 'La Voix est l'instrument pathétique et dramatique par excellence. . . . Je ne sais comment me décrire cet effet de musique. Poésie du changement pur dans un *domaine* de la structure (de relations et de *compléments*) duquel ns avons le sentiment. Ce domaine est d'attentes implicites. Domaine de *phase*. Univers de la musique.'

17 XXIX, 1944, p. 93. Though many critics have picked up the references to recitative, especially in 'Le Prince et la Jeune Parque' and the letter to Mockel, the implications for an interpretation of the poetry have been until recently virtually neglected. Important exceptions were the work of Scarfe on dramatic monologue (in *The Art of Paul Valéry*, London, 1954) and the comments of Nadal on *La Jeune Parque* as 'un monologue à deux voix' using all the resources of the stage (*La Jeune Parque: étude critique*, Paris, 1957, p. 169), though both tend to focus upon the dramatic rather than the musical aspects. Critical interest has more recently focused

upon aspects of voice, with the brief but perceptive comments of Huguette Laurenti which bring out the connections between 'mono-dialogue', 'la voix' and 'musique' ('Valéry nous donne peut-être ainsi, en effet, une "clé" de sa poésie: chercher les séries de modulations, expression des mouvements, des heurts, des reprises propres au langage intérieur, peut conduire à saisir cette "voix" qui dévide son "charme" au long d'un récitatif toujours recommencé', 'Musique et monologue', *Paul Valéry I: Lectures de 'Charmes'*, Paris, 1974, p. 63), and Christine Crow's important work on *Paul Valéry and the Poetry of Voice*, Cambridge, 1982.

18 *Lettres à quelques-uns*, p. 124.

19 XVIII, 1935, p. 533. Cf. a near identical note which presents the following variation in the second part: 'Il s'agit de suivre le fonctionnement physiologique de la conscience, le fonctionnement du corps en tant que perçu par le Moi servant de basse continue aux incidents et aux idées' (XX, 1937, p. 250).

20 Though the first two are the same, from a different perspective: the 'Harmonieuse MOI' – the former self who before the dream was at one with the world and thought herself immortal – is now recognised as 'mortelle, mensonge'. This interpretation is supported by the excellent analysis of R. Fromilhague in ' "La Jeune Parque" et l'"autobiographie dans la forme" ', *P. Valéry, Contemporain*, Paris, 1974, pp. 226–8.

21 Letter to A. Mockel, 1917, *Lettres à quelques-uns*, p. 124.

22 F. Scarfe, *The Art of Paul Valéry*, London, 1954, p. 250.

23 XII, 1927, p. 68.

24 1917, *Lettres à quelques-uns*, Paris, 1952, p. 125.

25 XXI, 1938, p. 822.

26 F. de Miomandre, 'Souvenirs', *Paul Valéry Vivant*, p. 88.

27 Manuscript in Bibliothèque Nationale, JP I, 2.

28 'Poète – Pianiste.
L'exécution sur soi-même . . .
se placer tôt ou tard à l'état tel que ce qui vienne appelle ce qu'il faut comme céci était commandé par le premier, et que la suite ne soit que partie intégrante de ce qui est venu avant.' (VI, 1918, p. 824) Cf. J. M. Cocking, 'Working against chance', rev. of *The Poet as Analyst*, by J. R. Lawler, *Times Literary Supplement*, 18 July 1975, p. 809.

29 Illegible word, probably 'merveilleuse'. Note that 'complice' was used in the first MS. III f. 13.

30 Although this part of the poem (like 'A l'extrême de l'être . . .' later) is singled out by Valéry for its 'continuité musicale', it is interesting to note that neither line came complete as a ready-made 'trouvaille'. It is true that the words 'O n'aurait-il fallu folle' are written straight off at the very beginning, forming part of a clear thematic intention; nevertheless the remainder of the line and the following lines are only found after many experiments in the 'palettes' with the sounds and meanings of the initial idea.

31 See comments on this aspect of the final version, p. 230 below.

32 'Je suis convaincu que chaque poète prend une certaine intime voix, une allure vocale, un *chantant* virtuel *qui fait* son vers, et qui est intermédiaire *obligatoire*, entre 1° des états, 2° des fonctions. Déchiffrer un poète consisterait à trouver cette condition fonctionnelle – que je crois rigoureuse' (XXV, 1941, p. 265).

33 I am indebted to Madame Florence de Lussy, Conservateur du Fonds Valéry at the Bibliothèque Nationale, for this manuscript.

34 XVII, 1934, p. 376. The vibrant power of the voice and the quality he sought in poetry are well described in a note prompted by the Spanish music he heard when visiting Madrid: 'Ce chant me fait penser *Poésie*. Pour moi la *voix*. . . . La machine de la voix est comme le système musculaire de locomotion d'un animal en action. Serpent qui s'arc-boute pour bondir. Vol plané. La voix – évolution d'une énergie libre' (XVI, 1933, p. 360).

35 XVI, 1933, p. 392.

36 IV, 1911, p. 587.

37 XXV, 1942, p. 706.

38 VI, 1916, p. 170.

11. *LA DORMEUSE*

1 XXIX, 1945, p. 477.

2 'Calepin d'un poète', *Œuvres* I, p. 1463.

3 *Œuvres* II, p. 1524.

4 XXVIII, 1944, p. 428.

5 XXIX, 1945, p. 606.

6 XXVIII, 1944, p. 428.

7 V, 1914, p. 519.

8 'La Littérature comme telle', *Figures*, vol. I, Paris, 1966, p. 264.

9 *Œuvres* II, p. 1534.

10 XXVIII, p. 258.

11 *Ibid.*

12 XXVIII, 1944, p. 258.

13 See, for example, IV, 1911, pp. 491–585.

14 J. R. Lawler, *The Poet as analyst*, Berkley, Calif., 1974, p. 160.

15 VI, 1917, p. 774.

16 The dossier of manuscripts for *La Dormeuse* is numbered 71–92; the second draft is in *Cahiers Charmes* II f. 22vo; further fragments are in *Cahier Voilier*.

17 *Cahier Voilier*, quoted Lawler, *Lecture de Valéry*, p. 90. Cf. sketch of same line *Cahier Charmes* II f. 22vo.

18 For line 12, cf. a draft of *La Fausse Morte* where alongside 'Mais à peine abattu sur le sépulcre bas' Valéry added: 'd'où l'âme semble absente'. *Cahier Charmes* II f. 22.

19 See the discussion of this line p. 247 below. Valéry was still hesitating between 'brûle' and 'brûlent' in f. 86.

20 *Œuvres* I, p. 1483.

21 VI, 1916, p. 118.

22 Cf. M. Raymond, *P. Valéry et la tentation de l'esprit*, Neuchâtel,

1946, p. 14: 'Le premier vers serait étrangement racinien si *brûle* s'y écrivait *brûlent.* Valéry prend le verbe à la fois au sens propre, celui de la chimie (nous brûlons nos carbones comme le charbon dans un foyer) et au sens métaphorique (l'âme consume aussi, dans le rêve nocturne les "vains aliments" que lui fournissent la sensation et la mémoire). Il mêle en quelque sorte ces éléments chimiques et psychiques qui s'exhalent ensuite par le souffle et le songe.'

23 'La distinction de l'âme et du corps est impossible dans le détail. Dès que l'on précise il y a inextricable mélange' (III, 1905, p. 716).

24 Cf. the additions to the final version of *Anne* where instead of ending with the reposeful look of the young poet, love is presented as a battle: 'la vigueur et les gestes étranges / Que pour tuer l'amour inventait les amants'. Images of violence and shipwreck contrast with the physical surrender: 'L'amour t'aborde, armée des regards de la haine, / Pour combattre dans l'ombre une hydre de baisers!'

25 XVIII, 1936, p. 748.

26 *Œuvres* II, p. 154.

27 V, 1915, pp. 564–5.

28 'Stéphane Mallarmé', *Œuvres* I, p. 670.

CONCLUSION

1 II, 1902, p. 442.

2 II, 1902, p. 574.

3 IX, 1923, p. 448.

4 See for example XII, 1927, p. 304: 'Musique et Math. Archit. etc. il ne s'agit des rapports de sons – déterminations exactes de reconnaissance et de production. Produire une sensation identique à une donnée
ni des temps –
Mais à présent des combinaisons qui conservent qui se peuvent grouper et associer de sorte que *le tout dans chacune soit conséquence et partie* . . . et chaque combinaison ressentie comme extraite d'un nombre fini d'éléments.'

5 *Œuvres* I, p. 1201.

6 J. M. Cocking, questioning the scientific significance of 'the analogy-making propensities of [Valéry's] imagination' writes: 'Like many artists of his time, he does not so much discipline his thinking with disinterested observation as mould what he perceives to his own needs' ('Duchesne-Guillemin on Valéry', *Modern Language Review*, 62, No. 1 (Jan. 1967), 56.

7 IV, 1910, p. 471.

8 XVI, 1932, p. 18.

9 XVI, 1932, p. 75; cf. XV, 1931, p. 46: 'Pour qu'une œuvre – tableau, poésie – etc. *soit, existe comme par elle-même* = soit "Poésie", il faut qu'on ait trouvé et fixé le *Ton*. Alors la chose Chante.' The quality of 'le chant' lies thus in the nature of the relationships established between the constituent parts and the

ability to provoke a response to these structural relationships: 'Vers – le mouvement du vers, son enceinte, est une mise en présence de mots qui réagissent les uns sur les autres. C'est en quoi le vers "chante". Division du discours en durées permettant cette action réciproque.' (IX, 1923, p. 309) 'Le *chant* résulte de l'ordre. L'ordre de notre structure' (X, 1924, p. 300).

10 VII, 1919-20, p. 419; cf. XV, 1931, p. 148: 'Le génie littéraire *instantané* - celui de l'expression, des images est le plus répandu dans les temps modernes. Bien plus rare, le génie de composition – dont les productions sont d'ailleurs (et réciproquement) fort peu sensibles à la plupart.

Le moderne est à courte période. Variation du diapason. Jouissance à brève échéance.'

11 VII, 1919-20, p. 472.

12 *Cahier Charmes* II f. 2.

13 The Orpheus theme has been examined by Eva Kushner in *Le mythe d'Orphée dans la littérature française contemporaine*, Paris, Nizet, 1961; Valéry's treatment of the Orpheus legend is discussed by W. Stewart in 'Le thème d'Orphée chez Valéry', *Entretiens sur Paul Valéry*, ed. E. Noulet, Paris, Mouton, 1968, pp. 163-78.

14 1900, *Lettres à quelques-uns*, p. 63.

15 Though not apparently related in mythology, Delphinus is located below and to the left of the constellation Lyra, which includes Vega, one of the brightest stars in the northern sky.

16 J. R. Lawler, *Lecture de Valéry*, p. 230.

17 G. D. Martin, 'Valéry's *Ode secrète*: The enigma solved?', *French Studies*, vol. XXXI no. 4, October 1977, p. 432.

18 Many of the poems which show less direct evidence of the theme evoke a feminine presence and could be seen to relate to the other aspect of the Orpheus myth, Orpheus as the lover of Euridice; *La Fausse Morte*, for example, may be read as a variation on the story of Orpheus in the underworld. Much of course depends upon how broadly the theme of the poet-musician is interpreted. The references that follow are limited to fairly direct allusions to the 'core image' which has been identified above in relation to *Orphée* and *Arion*; but it has to be recognised that the absence of direct reference to song makes *La Dormeuse* no less a hymn of praise to 'la forme sensible', the poet composing the figure no less an Orphic presence.

19 *La Soirée avec Monsieur Teste, Œuvres* II, p. 22.

20 'On ne peut guère ne pas comparer *Poésie* à un "hymne" médiéval de supplication: les vers brefs et incisifs, le ton, l'attitude possèdent la simplicité fervente de tant de chants religieux écrits en latin' (J. R. Lawler, *Lecture de Valéry*, p. 24).

21 ' "Le son m'enfante et la flèche me tue" - c'est-à-dire la sensation me crée conscience (m'éveille), (la réflexion) (le sens) qui la suit me perce' (XVI, 1932, p. 47). ' . . . la strophe Zénon, - introduite pour *philosopher* le personnage virtuel - la *Personne-qui-chante*.' (XXIII, 1940, pp. 205-6).

22 'Calepin d'un poète', *Œuvres* I, p. 1449.
23 VI, 1918, p. 877.
24 XVII, 1934, p. 551; Valéry's disparagement is directed especially towards 'le dernier des genres . . . le descriptif. Là règne l'arbitraire et l'abondance des mots et beaux mots.'
25 Readers are referred to the articles by Ursula Franklin, Robert Pickering and Judith Robinson in *Bulletin des Etudes Valéryennes* on Valéry's prose works and to Huguette Laurenti's work on Valéry's theatre.
26 VIII, 1921, p. 321. See also XIII, 1928, p. 340 and XXV, 1942, p. 833.

APPENDIX: THE COMPOSITION OF *LA PYTHIE*

1 *Cantiques spirituels, Œuvres* I, p. 446. The poem has perhaps not always been accorded the critical attention it deserves. The only long study is by M. Maka de Schepper, *Le thème de la Pythie chez Paul Valéry*, Liège, 1969, which is concerned with the exposition of various aspects of the theme presented in the poem and in the rest of Valéry's work; but the study of the structure and the interaction of the themes as they develop in the poem is restricted to a short preface. M. Parent, *Cohérence et résonance . . .*, Paris, 1970, and J. R. Lawler, *Lecture de Valéry*, Paris, 1963 contain important studies of the poem, Lawler noting for instance that *La Pythie* is 'le point central de *Charmes*, une sorte de sommet qui résulte du mouvement le plus dramatique du recueil' (p. 264). More recently a stimulating analysis by C. Crow, recognising the connections between this poem and the rest of *Charmes*, has drawn attention to the poem's ambivalence towards impersonality of discourse, the 'Voix du Langage': 'However vainly, the Pythia struggles to *refuse* the universality represented by Langage which at the same time she knows is necessary to self-realisation.' (*Paul Valéry and the Poetry of Voice*, Cambridge, 1982, p. 175)
2 Cf. J. Levaillant, 'La Jeune Parque en question', *Paul Valéry Contemporain*, Paris, 1974, p. 150: 'L'événement perdu a eu lieu avant le premier mot du poème, il revient en *après-coup* tout au long . . . A mesure qu'il se développe, le pème cependant voudrait refaire, par les questions, le chemin *à l'envers.*'
3 'Poésie et pensée abstraite', *Œuvres* I, pp. 1338–9.
4 *Ibid.* p. 1338.
5 A. Gide, *Journal*, Paris, Pléiade, 1951, p. 751.
6 Recounted by F. Lefèvre, *Entretiens avec Paul Valéry*, Paris, 1926, p. 276.
7 Duchesne-Guillemin in *Etudes pour un Paul Valéry*, Neuchâtel, 1964, p. 115, refers to Hugo's Ode XLIII *Toute la Lyre* and a stanza from *Umbra* as possible sources of *La Pythie*.
8 From *Cahier Voilier*, quoted by Lawler, *Lecture de Valéry*, p. 134.
9 XX, 1937, p. 250.
10 It is not possible to develop here an extended analysis of the

manuscripts of the poem, which occupy 35 pages not including versions in the poetry notebooks. The dossier of manuscripts is numbered from 93 to 127: the plans for the order of stanzas ff. 93–4 and *Charmes* I f. 36VO; first stage of poem f. 95; second stage ff. 96–9; third stage *Cahier Voilier* ff. 1–5; fourth stage *Cahier Voilier* ff. 6–9, 11–14; fifth stage attached to a letter from Valéry to his wife, Valéryanum, bibliothèque Jacques Doucet VRY MS 1841; sixth stage *Charmes* I ff. 35–46; seventh stage ff. 100–8.

11 *Œuvres* I, pp. 1338–9.
12 July 1918, *Œuvres* I, p. 41.
13 IV, 1912, p. 887.
14 IV, 1912, p. 808.

BIBLIOGRAPHY

A: WORKS BY PAUL VALÉRY

'Piano et chant', in *Modes et manières d'aujourd'hui*. Paris, 1922; rpt. in 'Petits textes', *Nouvelle Revue Française*, No. 172, January 1928, p. 61; rpt. in *Œuvres* I, p. 1722.

'La Création artistique', *Bulletin de la Société française de philosophie*, séance du 28 janvier 1928. Rpt. in *Vues*, pp. 285-303 with extracts from the discussion pp. 304-9.

'Danse', in 'Petits Textes', *Nouvelles Revue Française*, No. 172, January 1928, p. 59; rpt. in *Œuvres* I, p. 1721.

'Réflexions sur l'art', *Bulletin de la Société française de philosophie*, séance du 2 mars 1935, 35, No. 2 (March-April 1935), 61-91.

'Hommage à Paul Dukas', *Revue Musicale*, No. 166 (May-June 1936), p. 323.

'Comment travaillent les écrivains', *Le Figaro*, 30 Oct. 1937; rpt. in *Vues*, pp. 315-21.

'Au lecteur', Introduction to 'Dialogue sur l'Art', by Pierre Féline, *Revue Musicale*, No. 184 (June 1938), pp. 330-2.

'Nadia Boulanger', *Revue Internationale de Musique*, 1, No. 4 (1938), 607-8.

'Esquisse d'un éloge de la virtuosité', with Louis Bonfiglio 'Paganini à Nice', in *Centenaire de Paganini*, Nice, 1940; rpt. in *Vues*, pp. 351-7.

Preface to *Serge Lifar à l'Opéra Défini par Paul Valéry Parlé par Jean Cocteau Vécu par Serge Lifar*, Paris, T. de Champrosay, 1943.

Preface to *Pensées sur la Danse*, by Serge Lifar, Paris, Bordas, 1946.

'Sur les Narcisse', in *Paul Valéry Vivant*, Marseille, Cahiers du Sud, 1946, pp. 283-90.

Vues, Paris, La Table Ronde, 1948.

Œuvres, Edition établie et annotée par Jean Hytier, 2 vols., Paris, Gallimard, Bibliothèque de la Pléiade, 1975, 1977.

Cahiers, 1894-1945, Vols. I-XXIX, Paris, Centre National de la Recherche Scientifique, 1957-61.

Cahiers, Ed. J. Robinson, 2 vols., Paris, Gallimard, Bibliothèque de la Pléiade, 1973, 1974.

'Note sur Lohengrin à l'Opéra', in *Colloque Paul Valéry: Amitiés de jeunesse*, Paris, Nizet, 1978, pp. 318-20.

Bibliography

B: CORRESPONDENCE

XV Lettres de Paul Valéry à Pierre Louÿs, 1915–17, Paris, 1926.
Réponses. 12 lettres écrites de 1915 à 1928, Paris, Au Pigeonnier, 1928.
'Lettre à Mathila Ghyka', in *Le Nombre d'or*, I, *Les Rythmes*, by Mathila C. Ghyka, Paris, NRF, 1931.
'Lettre à Robert Bernard', in *Paul Valéry Vivant*, pp. 294–5.
Berthelot, René, 'Lettres échangées avec Paul Valéry', *Etudes de Métaphysique et de Morale* (Jan. 1946), pp. 1–6.
Lettres à quelques-uns, Paris, Gallimard, 1952.
Correspondance André Gide–Paul Valéry, 1890–1942, Préface et notes par Robert Mallet, Paris, Gallimard, 1953.
'Lettre à Henri Rambaud', in *La musique de piano des origines à Ravel*, by L. Aguettant, Paris, Albin Michel, 1954.
Correspondance de Paul Valéry et Gustave Fourment, 1887–1930, introduction et notes par Octave Nadal, Paris, Gallimard, 1957.
Onze Lettres de Paul Valéry à Pierre Louÿs, 1891–92, in *Cahiers Paul Valéry*, 1, Paris, Gallimard, 1975, 19–56.

C: WORKS ON VALERY

1. Books

Alain, *Charmes*, Poèmes de Paul Valéry, commentés par Alain, 1928; rpt. Paris, Gallimard, 1952.
Arnold, A. James, *Paul Valéry and His Critics, a Bibliography: French Language Criticism 1890–1927*, New York, Haskell House, 1973.
'Paul Valéry, a Bibliography', in *A Critical Bibliography of French Literature*, gen. ed. R. A. Brooks, Vol. VI, The Twentieth Century, Part 2, New York, Syracuse University Press, 1980, 943–1023.
Austin, Lloyd James, *Paul Valéry: Le Cimetière marin*, Préface d'Henri Mondor, Grenoble, Roissard, 1954.
Ballard, Jean, 'Celui que j'ai connu', in *Paul Valéry Vivant*, pp. 237–46.
Bastet, Ned, *La Symbolique des images dans l'œuvre poétique de Valéry*, Annales de la Faculté des Lettres d'Aix-en-Provence, Travaux et mémoires, No. 24, Aix-en-Provence, 1962.
Bémol, Maurice, *La Méthode critique de Paul Valéry*, Clermont-Ferrand, G. de Bussac, 1950.
Paul Valéry, Paris, Les Belles Lettres, 1950.
La Parque et le serpent, Paris, Les Belles Lettres, 1955.
Bergeron, Léandre, *Le Son et le sens dans quelques poèmes de 'Charmes' de Paul Valéry*, Publications des Annales de la Faculté des Lettres d'Aix-en-Provence, No. 39, Aix-en-Provence, 1963.
Bourjea, Serge, 'L'Ombre-Majuscule - une exégèse de *La Ceinture*', in Laurenti, H., Ed., *Paul Valéry*, 1, *Lectures de 'Charmes'*, 121–45.

Bibliography

Cahiers Paul Valéry, Ed. Jean Levaillant, Vol. 1, *Poétique et poésie*, Paris, Gallimard, 1975.
Vol. 2, *Mes théâtres*, Paris, Gallimard, 1977.
Vol. 3, *Questions du rêve*, Paris, Gallimard, 1979.

Centenaire de Paul Valéry, Special issue of *Europe*, No. 507, Paris, Les Editeurs Français Réunis, 1971.

Cohen, Gustave, *Essai d'explication du 'Cimetière marin'*, Avant-propos de Paul Valéry au sujet du *Cimetière marin*, Paris, Gallimard, 1933.

Colloque Paul Valéry: Amitiés de jeunesse. Influences - Lectures, Université d'Edimbourg novembre 1976, texte établi par Carl P. Barbier, Paris, Nizet, 1978.

Les Critiques de notre temps et Valéry, présentation et notes de Jean Bellemin-Noël, Paris, Garnier, 1971.

Crow, Christine, *Paul Valéry: Consciousness and Nature*, Cambridge, Cambridge University Press, 1972.

Paul Valéry and the Poetry of Voice, Cambridge, Cambridge University Press, 1982.

Daniel, Vera, J., ed., *Eupalinos and L'Ame et la danse*, by Paul Valéry, London, O.U.P., 1967.

Dragonetti, Roger, 'Rythme et silence chez Paul Valéry', in *Aux frontières du langage poétique*, Ghent, Rijksuniversitat te Ghent, 1961, pp. 157–68.

Duchesne-Guillemin, Jacques, *Essai sur 'La Jeune Parque' de Paul Valéry*, Brussels, L'Ecran du Monde, 1947.

Etude de 'Charmes' de Paul Valéry, Brussels, L'Ecran du Monde, 1947.

Introduction à l'Ame et la Danse de Paul Valéry, Liège, Desoer, 1947.

Etudes pour un Paul Valéry, Neuchâtel, La Baconnière, 1964.

'Les "N" dimensions de Paul Valéry', in *Entretiens sur Paul Valéry* (1968), pp. 9–30.

Dufrenne, Mikel, 'L'Esthétique de Paul Valéry', in *En hommage à Paul Ricoeur*, Ed. G. B. Madison, Paris, Seuil, 1975, pp. 31–45.

Ecriture et génétique textuelle: Valéry à l'œuvre, Ned Bastet et al. Textes réunis par Jean Levaillant, Lille, Presses universitaires de Lille, 1982.

Elder, David E. M., 'Le finale fragmenté des *Narcisses* de Valéry', in *Cahiers Paul Valéry*, 1, 187–206.

Eliot, T. S., 'Leçon de Valéry, in *Paul Valéry Vivant*, pp. 74–81.

Entretiens sur Paul Valéry, Décades du Centre culturel international de Cérisy-la-Salle, 2-11 septembre 1965, sous la direction de Emilie Noulet-Carner, Paris La Haye, Mouton, 1968.

Entretiens sur Paul Valéry. Actes du colloque de Montpellier, octobre 1971, textes recueillis par Daniel Moutote, Paris, PUF, 1972.

Fabureau, Hubert, *Paul Valéry*, Paris, Editions de la Nouvelle Revue Critique, 1937.

Fehr, A. J. A., *Les Dialogues antiques de Paul Valéry. Essai d'analyse d'Eupalinos ou l'Architecte*, Diss., Leyden, 1960.

Bibliography

Féline, Pierre, 'A Montpellier, rue Urbain V', in *Paul Valéry Vivant*, pp. 42-8.

Fontainas, André, *De Stéphane Mallarmé à Paul Valéry: notes d'un témoin 1894-1922*, Paris, Edmond Bernard, 1928.

'Jeunesse de Valéry', in *Paul Valéry Vivant*, pp. 65-73.

Fromilhague, René, '*La Jeune Parque* et l'autobiographie dans la forme', in *Paul Valéry Contemporain*, pp. 209-35.

Gauthier, Michel, 'Les équations du langage poétique', Diss., Lille, 1973.

'L'Architecture phonique dans la poésie de Valéry', in *Paul Valéry Contemporain*, pp. 377-97.

Genette, Gérard, 'La littérature comme telle', in *Figures*, I, Paris, Seuil, 1966, 253-65.

Got, Maurice, *Sur une œuvre de Paul Valéry. Assomption de l'espace. A propos de 'L'Ame et la danse'*, 1957, rpt. Paris, SEDES, 1966.

Guiraud, Pierre, *Langage et versification d'après l'œuvre de Paul Valéry*, Paris, Klincksieck, 1953.

Index du vocabulaire du symbolisme, Vol. II, *Index des mots des poèsies de Paul Valéry*, Paris, Klincksieck, 1953.

Henry, Albert, *Langage et poésie dans l'œuvre de Paul Valéry*, Paris, Mercure de France, 1952.

Honegger, Arthur, 'En marge de *l'Histoire d'Amphion*', in *Paul Valéry Vivant*, pp. 116-18.

Hytier, Jean, *La Poétique de Valéry*, Paris, A. Colin, 1953.

Questions de littérature, Geneva, Droz, 1967.

Ince, Walter N., *The Poetic Theory of Paul Valéry: Inspiration and Technique*, Leicester, Leicester University Press, 1961.

Paul Valéry: Poetry and Abstract Thought, An Inaugural Lecture, University of Southampton, 1973.

'Valéry on "Bêtise et Poésie"; Background and Implications', in *Order and Adventure in Post-Romantic French Poetry: Essays presented to C. A. Hackett*, Ed. E. M. Beaumont, J. M. Cocking and J. Cruikshank, Oxford, Blackwell, 1973, pp. 136-48.

Ireland, G. W., 'Gide et Valéry, précurseurs de la nouvelle critique', in *Les Chemins actuels de la critique, Colloque de Cérisy-la-Salle, septembre 1966*, dirigé par Georges Poulet, Paris, 10/18, Union générale d'Editions, 1968, pp. 34-45, discussion pp. 46-57.

'*La Jeune Parque* - Genèse et exégèse', in *Entretiens sur Paul Valéry*, 1968, pp. 85-101.

Jallat, Jeannine, 'Valéry et les figures de rhétorique', in *Cahiers Paul Valéry*, 1, 149-85.

Karaïskakis, Georges and François Chapon, *Bibliographie des œuvres de Paul Valéry publiées de 1889 à 1965*, Paris, A. Blaizot, 1976.

Köhler, Hartmut, *Poésie et profondeur sémantique dans 'La Jeune Parque' de Paul Valéry*, Collection des mémoires, No. 13. Nancy, Université de Nancy, 1965.

'Valéry et Wagner', in *Colloque Paul Valéry: Amitiés de jeunesse*, pp. 147-70, discussion pp. 171-82.

Latour, Jean de, *Examen de Valéry*, Paris, Gallimard, 1935.

Bibliography

Laurenti, Huguette, 'Orphée et Wagner', in *Entretiens sur Paul Valéry*, 1971, pp. 79-85.

Paul Valéry et le théâtre, Paris, Gallimard, 1973.

'Musique et monologue: notes pour une approche valéryenne du poème', in *Paul Valéry*, 1, *Lectures de 'Charmes'*, pp. 49-66.

Laurette, Pierre, *Le thème de l'arbre chez Paul Valéry*, Paris, Bibliothèque française et romane, 1967.

Lawler, James R., *Form and Meaning in Valéry's 'Le Cimetière marin'*, Melbourne, Melbourne University Press, 1959.

Lecture de Valéry: une étude de 'Charmes', Paris, PUF, 1963.

The Poet as Analyst: Essays on Paul Valéry, Berkeley, Calif., University of California Press, 1974.

Lechantre, Michel, 'P(h)o(n)étique', in *Cahiers Paul Valéry*, 1, 91-122.

Lefèvre, Frédéric, *Entretiens avec Paul Valéry*, Paris, Le Livre, 1926.

Levaillant, Jean, 'La Jeune Parque en question', in *Paul Valéry Contemporain*, pp. 137-51.

Levinson, André, *Paul Valéry, philosophe de la danse*, Paris, La Tour d'Ivoire, 1926.

Lussy, Florence de, *La genèse de 'La Jeune Parque' de Paul Valéry: essai de chronologie littéraire*, Bibliothèque Paul Valéry No. 3, Paris, Minard, 1975.

Maka-de Schepper, Monique, *Le thème de la Pythie chez Paul Valéry*, Bibliothèque de la Faculté de philosophie et lettres de l'Université de Liège, fasc. 184, Liège, 1969.

Miomandre, Francis de, 'Souvenirs', in *Paul Valéry Vivant*, pp. 85-8.

Mondor, Henri, *Les Premiers temps d'une amitié: André Gide et Paul Valéry*, Monaco, Editions du Rocher, 1947.

L'Heureuse rencontre de Valéry et Mallarmé, Paris, Editions de Clairefontaine, 1948.

Précocité de Valéry, Paris, Gallimard, 1957.

Monestier, R., Ed., *Charmes*, by Paul Valéry, Paris, Nouveaux Classiques Larousse, 1958.

Morier, Henri, 'La Motivation des formes et des mètres chez Valéry', in *Paul Valéry Contemporain*, pp. 325-52.

Moutote, Daniel, 'Le Fonctionnement du langage poétique dans *La Jeune Parque*', in H. Laurenti, Ed., *Paul Valéry*, 2, *Recherches sur 'La Jeune Parque'*, 57-75.

Nadal, Octave, *Paul Valéry, la Jeune Parque: étude critique*, Paris, Le Club du Meilleur Livre, 1957.

'Les secrets du laboratoire,' in *Les Critiques de notre temps et Valéry*, pp. 168-74.

Noulet, Emilie, *Paul Valéry (études)*, Paris, 1938; rpt. Brussels, La Renaissance du Livre, 1951.

Suite valéryenne, Brussels, Editions des Artistes, 1959.

'Valéry', in *Le Ton poétique*, Paris, Corti, 1971, pp. 167-83.

'*Aurore* - essai d'exégèse', in H. Laurenti, Ed., *Paul Valéry*, 1, *Lectures de 'Charmes'*, 103-119.

Onimus, Jean, 'Lectures du *Rameur*', in *Paul Valéry*, 1, *Lectures de 'Charmes'*, 147-60.

Bibliography

Parent, Monique, *Cohérence et résonance dans le style de 'Charmes' de Paul Valéry*, Paris, Klincksieck, 1970.

'La "fonction poétique" du langage dans un passage de *La Jeune Parque* de Paul Valéry', in *Mélange de linguistique française et de la philologie et littérature médiévales offerts à M. Paul Imbs*, Paris, Klincksieck, 1973, pp. 471–80.

'La Fonction poétique du langage dans *Charmes*', in *Paul Valéry Contemporain*, pp. 61–73.

Parisier-Plottel, Jeanine, *Les Dialogues de Paul Valéry*, Paris, PUF, 1960.

Paul Valéry. Catalogue de l'exposition 31 janvier - 31 mars 1956 par Marcel Thomas et al. Préface de Julien Cain, Paris, Bibliothèque nationale, 1956.

Paul Valéry, special number of *Yale French Studies*, 44 (1970).

Paul Valéry. 1871–1971, Special number of *Australian Journal of French Studies*, 8, No. 2 (May–Aug. 1971).

Paul Valéry. Catalogue de l'exposition du centenaire 26 octobre 1971-16 janvier 1972. Par G. Willemetz, F. de Lussy et M. Barbin, avec la collaboration de C. Bouret. Préface par E. Dennery, N⁰ 275, Paris, Bibliothèque nationale, 1971.

Paul Valéry, special number of *Modern Language Notes*, 87, No. 4 (May 1972).

Paul Valéry, Ed. Huguette Laurenti, vol. 1, *Lectures de 'Charmes'*, *La Revue des Lettres Modernes*, Nos. 413–18, Paris, Minard, 1974.

Vol. 2, *Recherches sur 'La Jeune Parque'*, *La Revue des Lettres Modernes*, Nos. 498–503, Paris, Minard, 1977.

Vol. 3, *Approche du Système'*, *La Revue des Lettres Modernes*, Nos. 554–9, Paris, Minard, 1979.

Paul Valéry Contemporain, Colloques organisés en novembre 1971 par le C.N.R.S. et le Centre de philologie et de littératures romanes de l'Université des sciences humaines de Strasbourg, Part 1: *Paul Valéry et la pensée contemporaine*, Ed. Jean Levaillant, Part 2: *Présence de Valéry*, Ed. Monique Parent, Paris, Klincksieck, 1974.

Paul Valéry. Essais et témoignages inédits, Ed. Marc Eigeldinger, Neuchâtel, La Baconnière, 1945.

Paul Valéry Vivant, Marseille, Cahiers du Sud, 1946.

Pelmont, Raoul, *Paul Valéry et les Beaux-Arts*, Cambridge, Mass., Harvard University Press, 1949.

Pommier, Jean, *Paul Valéry et la création littéraire. Leçon d'ouverture prononcée au Collège de France, le 7 mai 1946*, Paris, Editions de l'Encyclopédie Française, 1946.

Porché, François, *Paul Valéry et la poésie pure*, Paris, Lesage, 1926.

Poulet, Georges, 'Valéry', in *Etudes sur le temps humain*, vol. 1, Edinburgh, 1949; rpt. Paris: Plon, 1972, pp. 386–99.

Pratt, Bruce, *Rompre le silence: les premiers états de 'La Jeune Parque'*, Paris, Corti, 1976.

Chant du Cygne: edition critique des premiers états de 'La Jeune Parque', Paris, Corti, 1978.

Priddin, Deirdre, ' "L'acte pur des métamorphoses" Paul Valéry and

Bibliography

Henri Bergson', in *The Art of the Dance in French Literature*, London, A. & C. Black, 1952, pp. 126–62.

Rauhut, Franz, *Paul Valéry, Geist und Mythos*, Munich, Max Hueber, 1930.

Raymond, Marcel, *Paul Valéry et la tentation de l'esprit*, Neuchâtel, La Baconnière, 1964.

Rey, Alain, 'Sens et discours poétique chez Valéry', in *Paul Valéry Contemporain*, pp. 39–48.

Robinson, Judith, *L'Analyse de l'esprit dans les Cahiers de Valéry*, Paris, Corti, 1963.

Rimbaud, Valéry et 'l'incohérence harmonique', Archives des Lettres Modernes, 184, Paris, Lettres Modernes, 1979.

Romain, Willy-Paul, *Paul Valéry. Le Poème. La Pensée*, Paris, Editions du Globe, 1951.

Roth-Mascagni, Pauline, *Petite prose pour 'Palme'*, Archives des Lettres Modernes, No. 170, Paris, Minard, 1977.

Musique et géométrie de trois poèmes valéryens, Collection 'Mains et chemins' No. 11, Brussels, A. de Rache, 1979.

Scarfe, Francis, *The Art of Paul Valéry: a study in dramatic monologue*, London, Heinemann, 1954.

Schmidt-Radefelt, Jürgen, *Paul Valéry linguiste dans les Cahiers*, Paris, Klincksieck, 1970.

Séchan, Louis, 'L'Ame et la Danse de Paul Valéry', in *La Danse grecque antique*, Paris, Ed. de Boccard, 1930, pp. 273–308.

Sewell, Elizabeth, *Paul Valéry: the mind in the mirror*, Cambridge, Bowes and Bowes, 1952.

Sørensen, Hans, *La Poésie de Paul Valéry: étude stylistique sur 'La Jeune Parque'*, Copenhagen, A. Busck, 1944.

Stewart, William H., 'Style, Form and Myth. The Orpheus sonnet of Paul Valéry', in *Stil und Formprobleme in der Literatur. 7th Congress of the International Federation of Modern Languages and Literature*, Heidelberg, Carl Winter, 1959, pp. 504-11.

'Le thème d'Orphée chez Valéry', in *Entretiens sur Paul Valéry*, 1968, pp. 163-78.

Suhami, Evelyne, *Paul Valéry et la musique*, Publications de la Faculté des lettres et sciences humaines, No. 15, Dakar, University of Dakar, 1966.

Todorov, Tzvetan, 'La "poétique" de Valéry', in *Cahiers Paul Valéry*, 1, 123-32.

Walzer, Pierre-Olivier, *La Poésie de Valéry*, Genève, Cailler, 1953.

Whiting, Charles G., *Valéry jeune poète*, Paris, PUF, 1960.

Ed., *Charmes ou Poèmes*, by Paul Valéry, London, Athlone Press, 1973.

2. Articles

Aguettant, Louis, 'Les Dialogues de Paul Valéry', *Revue critique des idées et des livres*, 35, No. 215 (Aug. 1923), 455-65.

Austin, Lloyd James, 'Paul Valéry compose *le Cimetière marin*', *Mercure de France*, (April and May 1953), pp. 577-608 and 47-72.

Bibliography

'La genèse du *Cimetière marin*', *Cahiers de l'Association Internationale des Etudes Françaises* (July 1953), pp. 253–69.

'Modulation and movement in Valéry's verse', *Yale French Studies*, 44 (1970), 19–38.

Bémol, Maurice, 'Genèse d'un poème. Fragment des Mémoires imaginaires d'un poète moderne', *Revue d'Esthétique*, 10, No. 4 (Oct.-Dec. 1957), 435–43.

Bidon, H., '*Amphion* de M. Paul Valéry', *Journal des Débats*, 10 juillet 1931, pp. 33–8.

Bilen, M., 'Introduction à la méthode de Paul Valéry', *Europe*, No. 507 (1971), pp. 22–37.

Brussel, R., 'Sur le chemin du souvenir', *Revue musicale*, (May–June 1936), pp. 33–4.

Bulletin des Etudes Valéryennes, Centre d'Etudes Valéryennes de l'Université Paul-Valéry, Montpellier, 1974 – [*B.E.V.*].

Centore, D., 'La Cantate du Narcisse et l'Après-midi d'un faune', *Cahiers de Sud* (Jan. 1942).

Chausserie-Laprée, Jean-Pierre, 'Deux figures de *la Jeune Parque*: une approche architecturale et musicale du texte poétique', *B.E.V.*, 4, No. 13 (May 1977), 19–31.

Chisholm, A. R., '*La Pythie* and its place in Valéry's work', *Modern Language Review*, 58, No. 1 (Jan. 1963), 21–8.

Cocking, John Martin, 'Duchesne-Guillemin on Valéry', *Modern Language Review*, 62, No. 1 (Jan. 1967), 55–60.

'Towards *Ebauche d'un Serpent*: Valéry and Ouroboros', in *Studies in honour of A. R. Chisholm*, Special number of *Australian Journal of French Studies*, 6, Nos. 2–3 (May–Dec. 1969), 187–215.

'Working against chance', review of *The Poet as Analyst* by James R. Lawler, *Times Literary Supplement*, 18 July 1975, p. 809.

Delbouille, P., 'Paul Valéry et le mythe des sonorités', *Zeitschrift für französische Sprache und Literatur*, (1960), pp. 129–38.

Derrida, Jacques, 'Les Sources de Valéry. Qual. Quelle', *Modern Language Notes*, 87, No. 4 (May 1972), 563–99.

Drucker, G. M., 'Paul Valéry et la Danse', *Arts*, 27 July 1945.

Duchesne-Guillemin, Jacques, 'Paul Valéry et la Musique', *Revue musicale*, (Jan. 1952), pp. 113–21.

'*L'Ame et la Danse* revisitées', *French Studies*, 23, No. 4 (Oct. 1969), 362–77.

'Valéry et Léonard', *Essays in French Literature*, 8 (1971), 57–71.

Dutton, K. R., 'Valéry's *La Jeune Parque*: towards a Critical Close Reading', *Australian Journal of French Studies*, 11, No. 1 (1974), 83–108.

Fabre, Antonin, 'Le rôle de la musique dans l'œuvre poétique de Valéry', *Mémoires de l'Académie de Vaucluse*, NS 3, 57 (1938), 35–47.

Fähnrich, Hermann, 'Music in the Letters of Paul Valéry', *Music and Letters*, 55 (1974), 48–60.

Féline, Pierre, 'Souvenirs sur Paul Valéry', *Mercure de France* (July 1954), pp. 402–33.

Bibliography

Gauthier, Michel, 'Du calembour à Paul Valéry: Linguistique et stylistique', *B.E.V.*, 7, No. 23 (March 1980), 31-40.

Genette, Gérard. 'Valéry et la poétique du langage', *Modern Language Notes*, 87, No. 4 (1972), 600-15.

George, André, 'Sémiramis', *Les Nouvelles littéraires*, 19 May 1934, p. 8.

Gheorge, Ion, 'Le mythe de la création par la musique chez Paul Valéry et Luciana Blaga', *Revue des Sciences humaines*, 134 (April-June 1969), 275-82.

Grubbs, Henry A., 'Two treatments of a subject: Proust's 'La regarder dormir' and Valéry's *La Dormeuse*', *PMLA*, 71, No. 5 (Dec. 1956), 900-9.

Honegger, Arthur, 'Valéry et la musique', *Style en France* (June 1946), pp. 46-7.

Hytier, Jean, 'Autour d'une analogie valéryenne', *Cahiers de l'Association Internationale des Etudes Françaises*, No. 17 (March 1965), pp. 171-89.

'Réminiscences et rencontres valéryennes', *French Studies*, 34, No. 2 (April 1980), 168-84.

Ince, Walter N., 'Paul Valéry - "poésie pure" or "poésie cuite"?', *French Studies*, 16, No. 4 (Oct. 1962), 348-58.

'Composition in Valéry's writings on Monsieur Teste', *L'Esprit créateur*, 4, No. 1 (Spring 1964), 19-27.

'La voix du maître, ou moi et style selon Valéry', *Revue des Sciences humaines*, 129 (1968), 29-39.

'Resonance in Valéry', *Essays in French Literature*, No. 5 (Nov. 1968), 38-57.

Ireland, G. W., 'Notes on the composition of *La Jeune Parque*', *Zeitschrift für französische Sprache und Literatur*, 72 (1962), 1-27.

Lalou, René, '*Amphion*, mélodrame de Paul Valéry', *L'Europe nouvelle*, 14 (1931), 917.

Lawler, James R., 'The technique of Valéry's *Orphée*', *Journal of the Australian Universities Modern Language Association*, No. 5 (Oct. 1956), pp. 54-63.

'Valéry's *Un feu distinct*', *French Studies*, 28, No. 2 (April 1974), 169-76.

Lechantre, Michel, 'L'hiéroglyphe intérieur', *Modern Language Notes*, 87, No. 4 (May 1972), 630-43.

Lhote, Marie-Josèphe, 'Le Faust wagnérien de Paul Valéry', *Revue de littérature comparée*, 46, No. 2 (April-June 1972), 272-84.

Loranquin, A., 'Paul Valéry et la musique', *Le Bulletin des Lettres*, 15 June 1964, pp. 241-5.

Malherbe, Michel, '*L'Abeille*: Poème euphonique? "Essai de recherche appliquée"', *B.E.V.*, 7, No. 24 (June 1980), 17-29.

Martin, Graham D., 'Valéry's *Ode secrète*: The enigma solved?', *French Studies*, 31, No. 4 (Oct. 1977), 425-36.

Peyre, Sully-André, 'Valéry *Amphion*', *Marsyas*, 142 (Oct. 1932), pp. 673-4.

Prunières, H., review of *Amphion* by Paul Valéry, *Revue musicale*, (Oct. 1931), pp. 239-41.

Bibliography

Renauld, Pierre, 'L'Influence de Wagner sur la poétique de Valéry', *Revue de Littérature comparée*, 51 (1977), 249–56.

Rinsler, Norma, 'The defence of the self: stillnes and movement in Valéry's poetry', *Essays in French Literature*, No. 6 (Nov. 1969), pp. 36–56.

'Valéry's variations on a theme', *Essays in French Literature*, No. 11 (Nov. 1974), pp. 47–68.

Robert, Frédéric, 'Valéry et ses musiciens', *Europe*, No. 507 (July 1971), pp. 101–10.

Robinson, Judith, 'Un nouveau visage de *La Jeune Parque*: le poème commenté par son auteur', *B.E.V.*, 7, No. 25 (Oct. 1980), 47–75.

Rosengarten, Yvonne, 'Paul Valéry et la Danse', *Archives internationales de la Danse*, 15 July 1934, pp. 93–6.

Schön, Nicole, 'Note sur *Un feu distinct* de Paul Valéry', *French Studies*, 26, No. 4 (Oct. 1972), 434–8.

Soulariol, Jean, 'Paul Valéry, ou la génération du poème', *Cahiers de la Nouvelle Journée*, No. 24 (1923).

Stewart, William H., 'Peut-on parler d'un "Orphisme" de Valéry?', *Cahiers de l'Association Internationale des Etudes Françaises*, No. 22 (1970), pp. 181–95.

Walzer, Pierre-Olivier, 'Valéry: deux essais sur l'amour; Béatrice et Stratonice', *Revue d'Histoire Littéraire de la France* (Jan.-Feb. 1968), pp. 66–86.

D: MUSIC AND MUSICIANS

Ansermet, Ernest, *Les Fondements de la musique dans la conscience humaine*, 2 vols. Neuchâtel, La Baconnière, 1961.

Les Ballets russes de Serge Diaghilev, Special number of *Revue musicale*, Aug. 1930.

Beaufils, M., *Musique du son, musique du verbe*, Paris, PUF, 1954.

Bernard, Guy, *L'Art de la Musique*, Paris, Seghers, 1961.

Bernard, Robert, *Histoire de la Musique*, Vol. 3, Paris, Nathan, 1962.

Berthelot, René, 'Défense de la poésie chantée', *Revue musicale* (Sept. 1938), pp. 89–94.

Boll, André, 'L'Art lyrique. Evolution du récitatif', *Revue musicale*, (Nov. 1952), pp. 19–32.

Boucourechlier, A. et al., *Stravinsky*, Paris, Hachette, 1968.

Bruyr, José, *Honegger et son œuvre*, Paris, Corrêa, 1947.

Buckle, Richard, *Nijinsky*, 1971; rpt. London, Penguin, 1975.

Cœuroy, André, *Musique et littérature*, Paris, Bloud et Gay, 1923.

Wagner et l'esprit romantique, Paris, Gallimard, 1965.

Collær, Paul, *La Musique moderne, 1905-55*, Paris Bruxelles, Elsevier, 1955.

Cooke, Deryck, *The Language of Music*, London, O.U.P., 1959.

Cooper, Martin, *French Music from the Death of Berlioz to the Death of Fauré*, London, O.U.P., 1951.

Cortot, Alfred Denis, *La Musique française de piano*, 3 vols, Paris, PUF, 1948.

Bibliography

Debussy, Claude Achille, *Correspondance de Claude Debussy et Pierre Louÿs, 1893-1904*, Ed. Henri Borgeaud, Introduction G. Jean-Aubry, Paris, Corti, 1945.

Dujardin, Edouard, 'Considérations sur l'art wagnérien', *Revue Wagnérienne*, Nos. 6-8 (July-Aug. 1887), pp. 153-88.

Dumesnil, René, *La Musique en France entre les deux guerres 1919-1939*, Genève, Editions du Milieu du monde, 1946.

Einstein, Alfred, *Gluck*, Trans. Eric Blom, London, Dent, 1936.

Feschotte, Jacques, *Arthur Honegger. L'homme et son œuvre*, Paris, Seghers, 1966.

Guichard, Léon, *La Musique et les lettres en France au temps du wagnérisme*, Paris, PUF, 1963.

Hadow, W. H., 'Music and Drama', in *Collected Essays*, London, O.U.P., 1928, pp. 162-90.

Harding, James, 'Les Six', *The Listener*, 86, No. 2230, 23 Dec. 1971, 880-1.

Hindemith, Paul, *A Composer's World*, Cambridge, Mass., Harvard University Press, 1952.

Honegger, Arthur, *Je suis compositeur*, Paris, Editions du Conquistador, 1951.

La Littérature française et la musique, Special number of *Revue musicale*, Jan. 1930.

Lockspeiser, Edward, *Debussy: His Life and Mind*, 2 vols, Cambridge, 1979.

Mendès, Catulle, 'Notes sur la théorie et l'œuvre wagnérienne', *Revue Wagnérienne*, No. 2 (March 1885), pp. 28-35.

Meylan, Pierre, *Les Ecrivains et la musique*, 2 vols, Lausanne, editions du Cervin, 1952.

Mitchell, Donald, *The Language of Modern Music*, London, Faber and Faber, 1966.

Myers, Rollo H., *Ravel: His Life and Works*, London, Duckworth, 1960.

Naudin, Marie, *Evolution parallèle de la poésie et de la musique en France: rôle unificateur de la chanson*, Paris, Nizet, 1968.

Poulenc, Francis, *Moi et mes amis, Confidences recueillies par Stéphane Audel*, Paris Genève, La Porlatine, 1963.

Correspondance 1915-1963, Réunie par Hélène de Wendel, Paris, Seuil, 1967.

Pourtalès, Guy de, *Wagner: histoire d'un artiste*, Paris, Gallimard, 1932.

Roland-Manuel, Alexis, 'Maurice Ravel ou l'esthétique de l'imposture', *Revue musicale* (April 1925), pp. 16-21.

Schloezer, Boris de, *Igor Stravinsky*, Paris, Claude Aveline, 1929.

'Les Spectacles d'Ida Rubinstein', *Nouvelle Revue Française*, No. 249 (Jan. 1934), pp. 1027-30.

Stravinsky, Igor, *Chronique de ma vie*, 2 vols, Paris, Denoël et Steel, 1935. Trans. *Chronicle of my Life*, London, Gollancz, 1936.

Poétique musicale sous forme de six leçons, The Charles Eliot Norton Lectures 1939-40, Cambridge, Mass., 1942; rpt. Paris, Editions le Bon Plaisir, 1952, Trans. A. Knodel and I. Dahl, *Poetics of Music*, Bilingual edition, Cambridge, Mass., Harvard Univ. Press, 1970.

Bibliography

Stravinsky, Igor and Robert Craft, *Conversations with Igor Stravinsky*, London, Faber and Faber, 1959.

Memories and Commentaries, London, Faber and Faber, 1960.

Expositions and Developments, London, Faber and Faber, 1962.

Igor Strawinsky, Special number of *Revue musicale* (Dec. 1923).

Igor Strawinsky, Special number of *Revue musicale* (May–June 1939).

Suarès, André, *Musique et poésie*, Vol. 5 of *La Musique moderne*, Paris, Claude Aveline, 1928.

Wagner, Richard, *Œuvres en Prose*, trad. française J. G. Prod'homme, Vol. 3 *L'Œuvre d'art de l'avenir*, Vols. 4–5 *Opéra et drame*, Vol. 9 *Le Drame musical*, Paris, Delagrave, 1907–24.

Ma Vie, 3 vols, trad. N. Valentin and A. Schenk, Paris, Plon-Nourrit et Cie., 1911–12.

Vues sur la France: suivis d'Hommages à Richard Wagner, Avant-propos et commentaires par Gustave Samazeuilh, Paris: Mercure de France, 1943.

Wagner et la France, Special number of *Revue musicale* (Oct. 1923).

White, Eric Walter, *Stravinsky's Sacrifice to Apollo*, London, The Hogarth Press, 1930.

Stravinsky. The Composer and his works, London, Faber and Faber, 1966; Berkeley, Calif., University of California Press, 1980.

Woolley, G., *Richard Wagner et les Symbolistes français*, Paris, PUF, 1931.

Wyzewa, Teodor de, 'Notes sur la littérature wagnérienne et les livres en 1885–1886', *Revue Wagnérienne*, No. 5 (June 1886), pp. 150–71.

La Littérature, Vol. 3 of *Nos maîtres: L'art wagnérien*, Paris, Perrin, 1895.

E: OTHER WORKS

Baudelaire, Charles, *Œuvres complètes, Texte établi et annoté par Y.-G. Le Dantec*, Paris, Gallimard, Bibliothèque de la Pléiade, 1954.

Becq de Fourquières, L., *Traité générale de versification française*, Paris, Charpentier, 1879.

Bernard, Suzanne, *Mallarmé et la musique*, Paris, Nizet, 1959.

Black, Michael, *Poetic Drama as Mirror of the Will*, London, Vision Press, 1977.

Blanche, J.-E. et al., *Le Tombeau de Pierre Louÿs*, Paris, Éditions du Monde Moderne, 1925.

Bonniot-Mallarmé, Geneviève, 'Mallarmé par sa fille', *Nouvelle Revue Française*, No. 158 (Nov. 1926), pp. 517–23.

Bremond, Henri, *La Poésie pure*, Paris, Grasset, 1926.

Brereton, Geoffrey, *An Introduction to the French Poets*, 1956; rpt. London, Methuen, University Paperbacks, 1960.

Brooks, Cleanth, *The Well Wrought Urn: Studies in the Structure of Poetry*, 1949; rpt. London, Methuen, 1968.

Brown, C. S., *Music and Literature. A Comparison of the Arts*, Athens, Georgia, University of Georgia Press, 1948.

Bibliography

Cassagne, Albert, *La Théorie de l'art pour l'art en France*, 1906; rpt. Geneva, Slatkine, 1979.

Versification et métrique de Baudelaire, Paris, Hachette, 1906.

Cocking, John Martin, 'Proust and Music', *Essays in French Literature*, No. 4 (Nov. 1967), pp. 13-29.

'Imagination as Order and as Adventure', in *Order and Adventure in Post-Romantic French Poetry: Essays presented to C. A. Hackett*, Ed. E. Beaumont, J. M. Cocking and J. Cruikshank, Oxford, Blackwell, 1973, pp. 257-69.

Colette, [Sidonie-Gabrielle], *Mes apprentissages*, in *Œuvres complètes*, Vol. 11, Paris, Flammarion, 1950.

Combarieu, J., *Les Rapports de la musique et de la poésie considérés au point de vue de l'expression*, Paris, Alcan, 1894.

Décaudin, Michel, *La Crise des valeurs symbolistes. Vingt ans de poésie française. 1895-1914*, Paris, Privat, 1960.

Delbouille, P., *Poésie et sonorités. La critique contemporaine devant le pouvoir suggestif des sons*, Paris, Les Belles Lettres, 1961.

Du Bos, Charles, *Journal*, Vol. 1 *1921-1923*, Paris, Corrêa, 1946.

Eliot, T. S., *The Music of Poetry*, The third W. P. Ker Memorial Lecture, 24 Feb. 1942, Glasgow, Jackson, 1942.

'From Poe to Valéry', A Lecture delivered at the Library of Congress, Washington, 19 Nov. 1948, in *To Criticize the Critics and other writings*, London, Faber and Faber, 1965, pp. 27-42.

Gauthier, Michel, *Système euphonique et rythmique du vers français*, Paris, Klincksieck, 1974.

Ghil, René, *Traité du verbe*, Paris, Giraud, 1886.

Gide, André, *Si le grain ne meurt*, 1926; rpt. Paris, Livre de Poche, 1954.

Journal. 1889-1949, 2 vols, Paris, Gallimard, Bibliothèque de la Pléiade, 1951, 1954.

Gombrich, E. H., *Meditations on a Hobby Horse*, London, Phaidon, 1963.

Goudeket, Maurice, *Près de Colette*, Paris, Flammarion, 1956.

Gracq, Julien, *Préférences*, Paris, Corti, 1961.

Grammont, Maurice, *Le Vers français. Ses moyens d'expression, son harmonie*, 1904; rpt. Paris, Delagrave, 1937.

Petit traité de versification française, 1908; rpt. Paris, Colin, Collection U, 1965.

Harding, Rosamund, *An Anatomy of Inspiration and an Essay on the Creative Mood*, Cambridge, Heffer and Sons, 1948.

Kushner, Eva, *Le mythe d'Orphée dans la littérature française contemporaine*, Paris, Nizet, 1961.

Lamartine, Alphonse de, *Méditations poétiques*, Paris, Garnier, 1968.

Lehmann, A. G., *The Symbolist Aesthetic in France. 1885-1895*, 1950; rpt. Oxford, Blackwell, 1968.

Mallarmé, Stéphane, *Propos sur la poésie*, Ed. H. Mondor, 1945; rpt. Monaco, Editions du Rocher, 1953.

Œuvres complètes, Texte établi et annoté par Henri Mondor et G. Jean-Aubry, Paris, Gallimard, Bibliothèque de la Pléiade, 1951.

Bibliography

Correspondance. 1862-71. Recueillie, classée et annotée par Henri Mondor avec la collaboration de J.-P. Richard, Paris, Gallimard, 1959.

Marouzeau, J., *Précis de stylistique française*, Paris, Masson, 1969.

Martino, Pierre, *Parnasse et Symbolisme*, Paris, Colin, 1967.

Mauclair, Camille, *Servitude et grandeur littéraires*, Paris, Ollendorff, 1922.

Mazaleyrat, J., *Pour une étude rythmique du vers français moderne*, Paris, Minard, 1963.

Michaud, Guy, *Message poétique du Symbolisme*, 3 vols, Paris, Nizet, 1947.

L'Œuvre et ses techniques, Paris, Nizet, 1957.

Mossop, D. J., *Pure Poetry. Studies in French Poetic Theory and Practice, 1746-1945*, London, O.U.P., 1971.

Pollard, Patrick, *Proserpine; Perséphone. Edition critique*, Collection Gide/Textes no. 1, Lyon, Centre d'Etudes Gidiennes, Université de Lyon II, 1977.

Raymond, Marcel, *De Baudelaire au surréalisme*, 1933; rpt. Paris, Corti, 1957.

Richards, I. A., *Principles of Literary Criticism*, 1924; rpt. London, Routledge and Kegan Paul, 1967.

Practical Criticism, 1929; rpt. London, Routledge and Kegan Paul, 1966.

Richard, Noël, *Profils symbolistes*, Paris, Nizet, 1978.

Smith, F. R., 'Georges Neveux and the Oral Element in Modern Poetry', *Australian Journal of French Studies*, 5, No. 1 (Jan.-April 1968), 84-103.

Souriau, E., *La Correspondance des arts*, Paris, Flammarion, 1947.

Spire, A., *Poésie et plaisir musculaire*, Paris, Corti, 1949.

Todorov, Tzvetan, *Poétique*, Vol. 2 of the multi-author series *Qu'est-ce que le structuralisme?*, Paris, Seuil, 1968.

Trannoy, A., *La Musique des vers*, Paris, Delagrave, 1925.

Verlaine, Paul, *Œuvres poétiques. Ed. Jacques Robichez*, Paris, Garnier, 1969.

INDEX

Index

Index

Index

Index

Index